The Septimal Moon Chapters

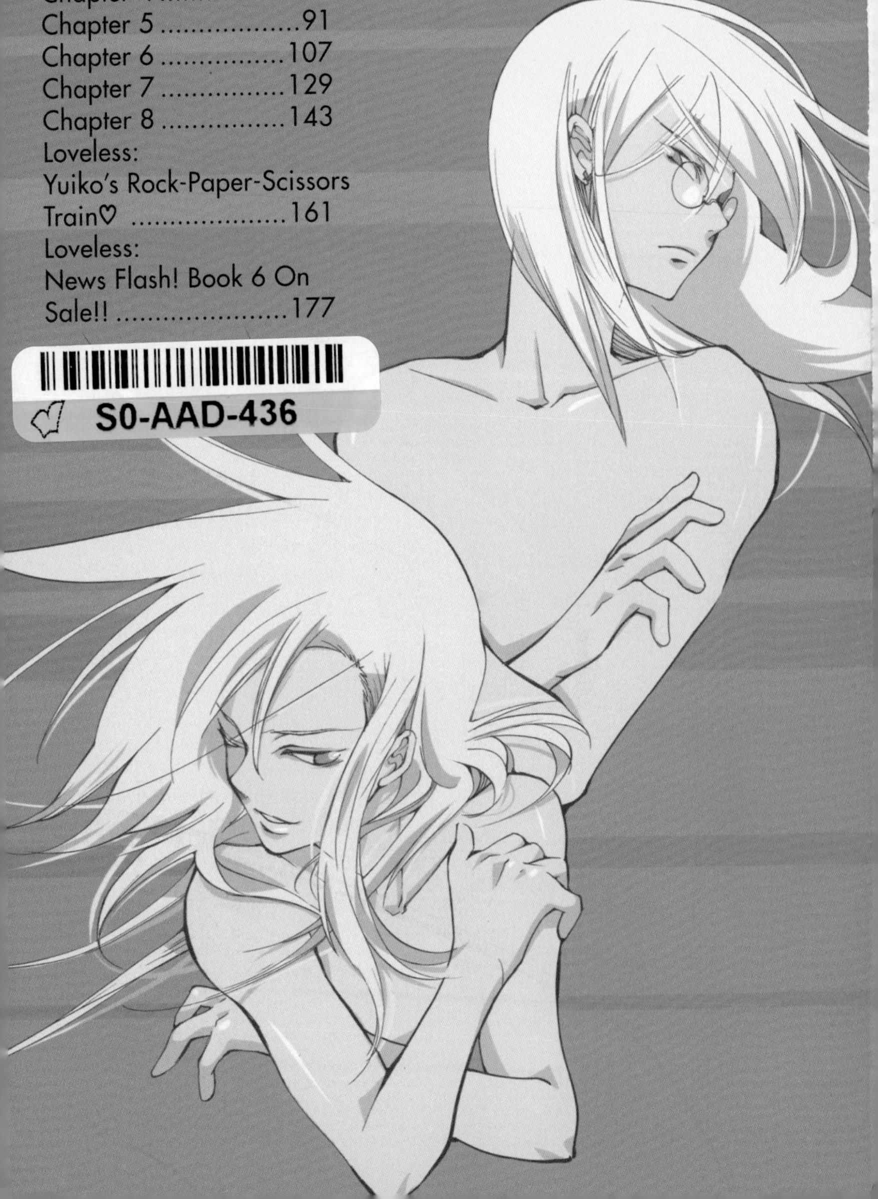

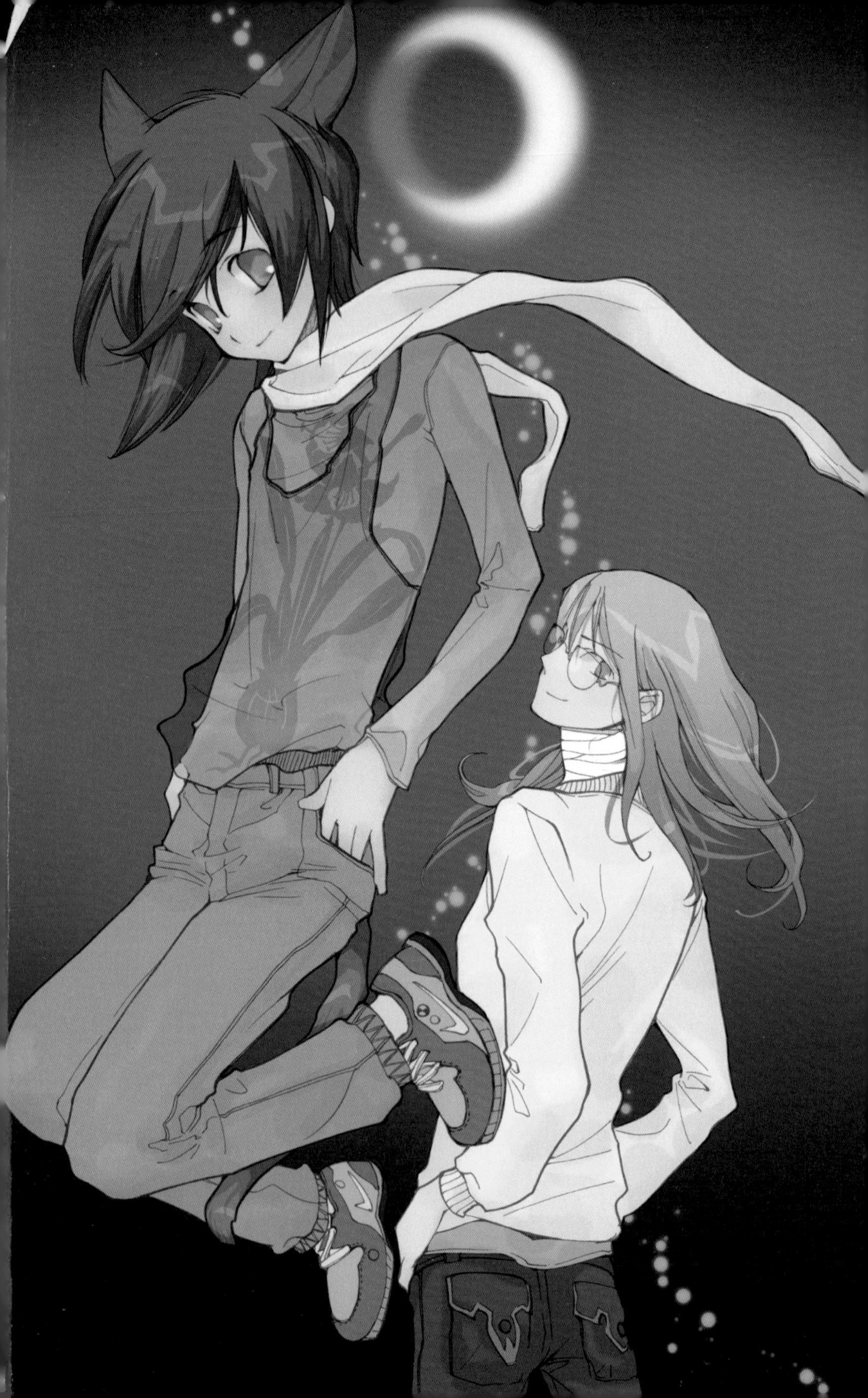

Volume 7

HAMBURG // LONDON // LOS ANGELES // TOKYO

Loveless Volume 7
Created by Yun Kouga

Translation - Ray Yoshimoto
English Adaptation - Christine Boylan
Retouch and Lettering - Star Print Brokers
Production Artist - Vicente Rivera, Jr./RUI KYO
Graphic Designer - Lindsay Seligman

Editor - Lillian Diaz-Przybyl
Digital Imaging Manager - Chris Buford
Pre-Production Supervisor - Erika Terriquez
Production Manager - Elisabeth Brizzi
Managing Editor - Vy Nguyen
Creative Director - Anne Marie Horne
Editor-in-Chief - Rob Tokar
Publisher - Mike Kiley
President and C.O.O. - John Parker
C.E.O. and Chief Creative Officer - Stuart Levy

A **TOKYOPOP** Manga

TOKYOPOP Inc.
5900 Wilshire Blvd. Suite 2000
Los Angeles, CA 90036

E-mail: info@TOKYOPOP.com
Come visit us online at www.TOKYOPOP.com

LOVELESS Volume 7 © 2006 by Yun Kouga. All rights reserved. First published in Japan in 2006 by ICHIJINSHA, Tokyo. English translation rights in the United States of America and Canada arranged with ICHIJINSHA through Tuttle-Mori Agency, Inc., Tokyo English text copyright © 2007 TOKYOPOP Inc.

ISBN: 978-1-4278-0457-0

First TOKYOPOP printing: November 2007
10 9 8 7 6 5 4 3 2 1
Printed in the USA

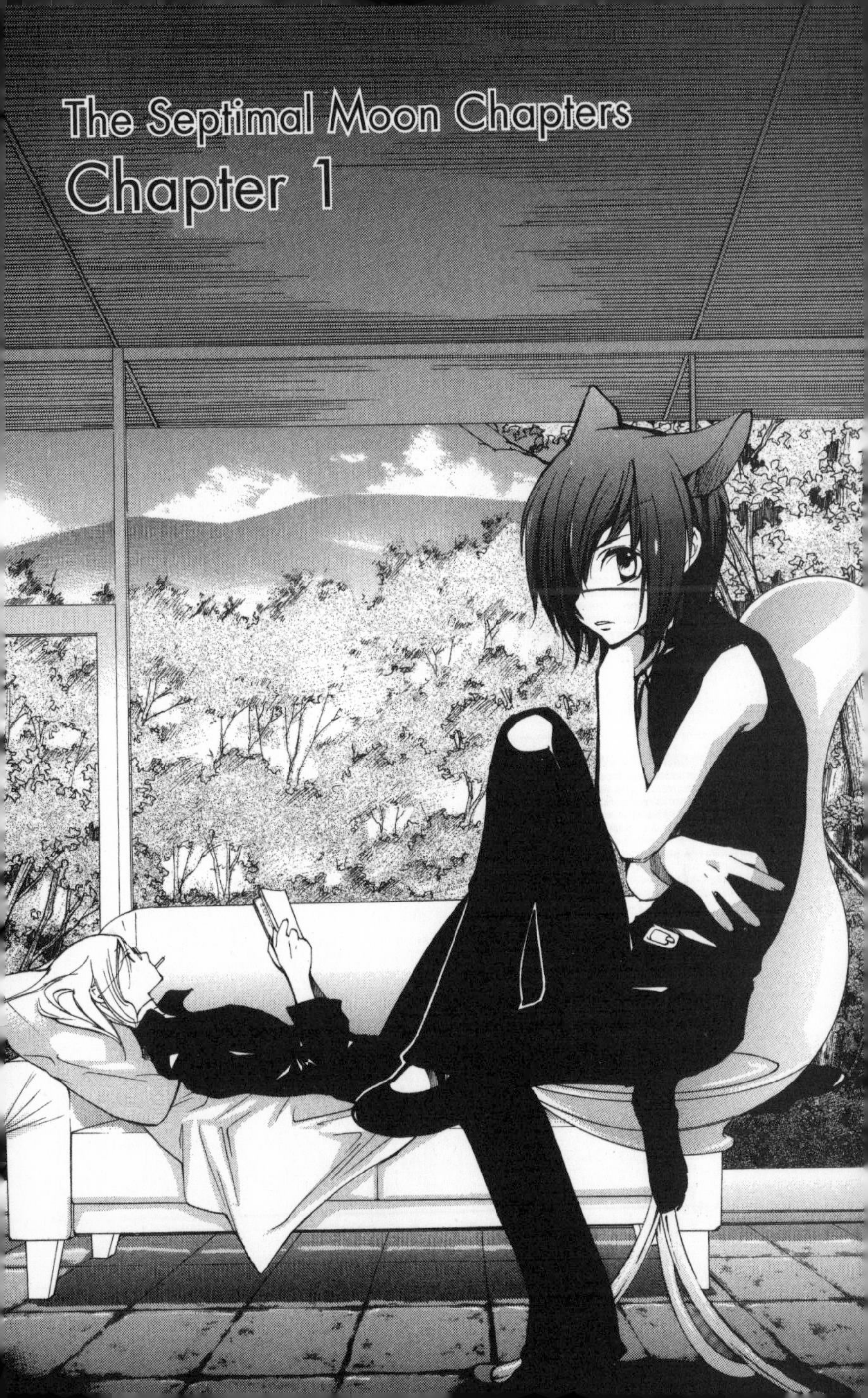
The Septimal Moon Chapters
Chapter 1

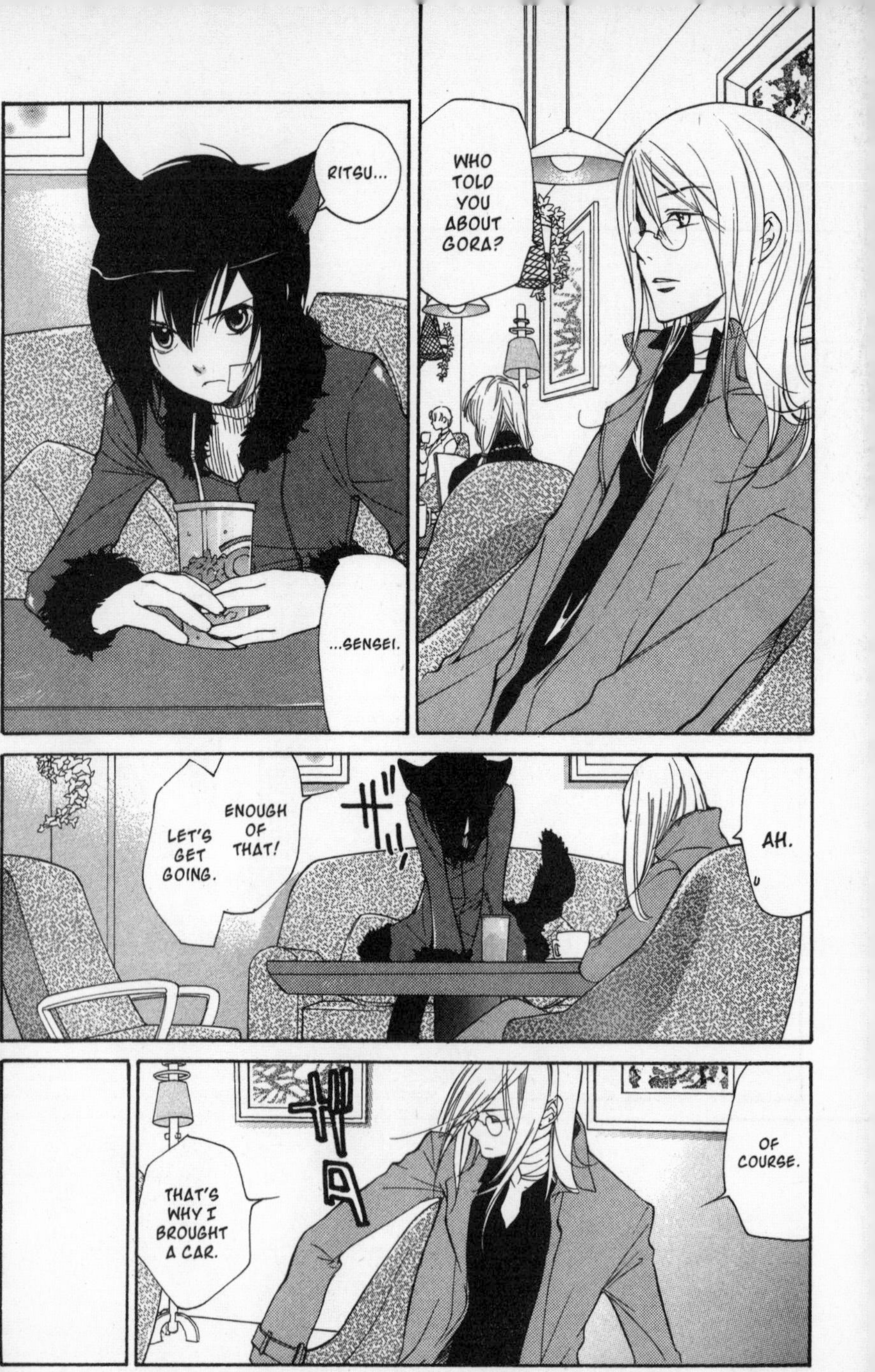
WHO TOLD YOU ABOUT GORA?
RITSU...
...SENSEI.
AH.
ENOUGH OF THAT!
LET'S GET GOING.
OF COURSE.
THAT'S WHY I BROUGHT A CAR.

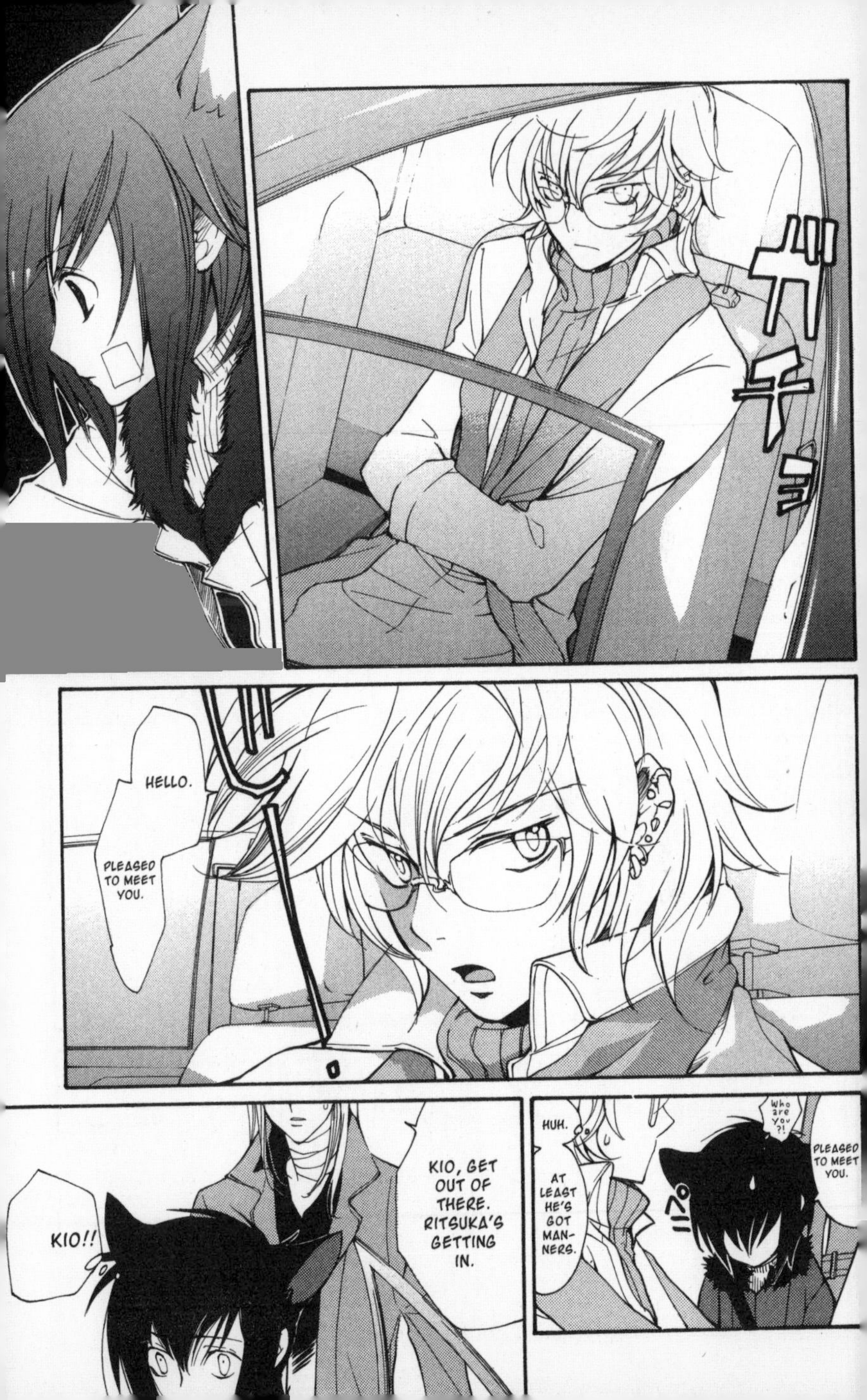
HELLO.
PLEASED TO MEET YOU.
Who are you?!
PLEASED TO MEET YOU.
HUH.
AT LEAST HE'S GOT MANNERS.
KIO, GET OUT OF THERE. RITSUKA'S GETTING IN.
KIO!!

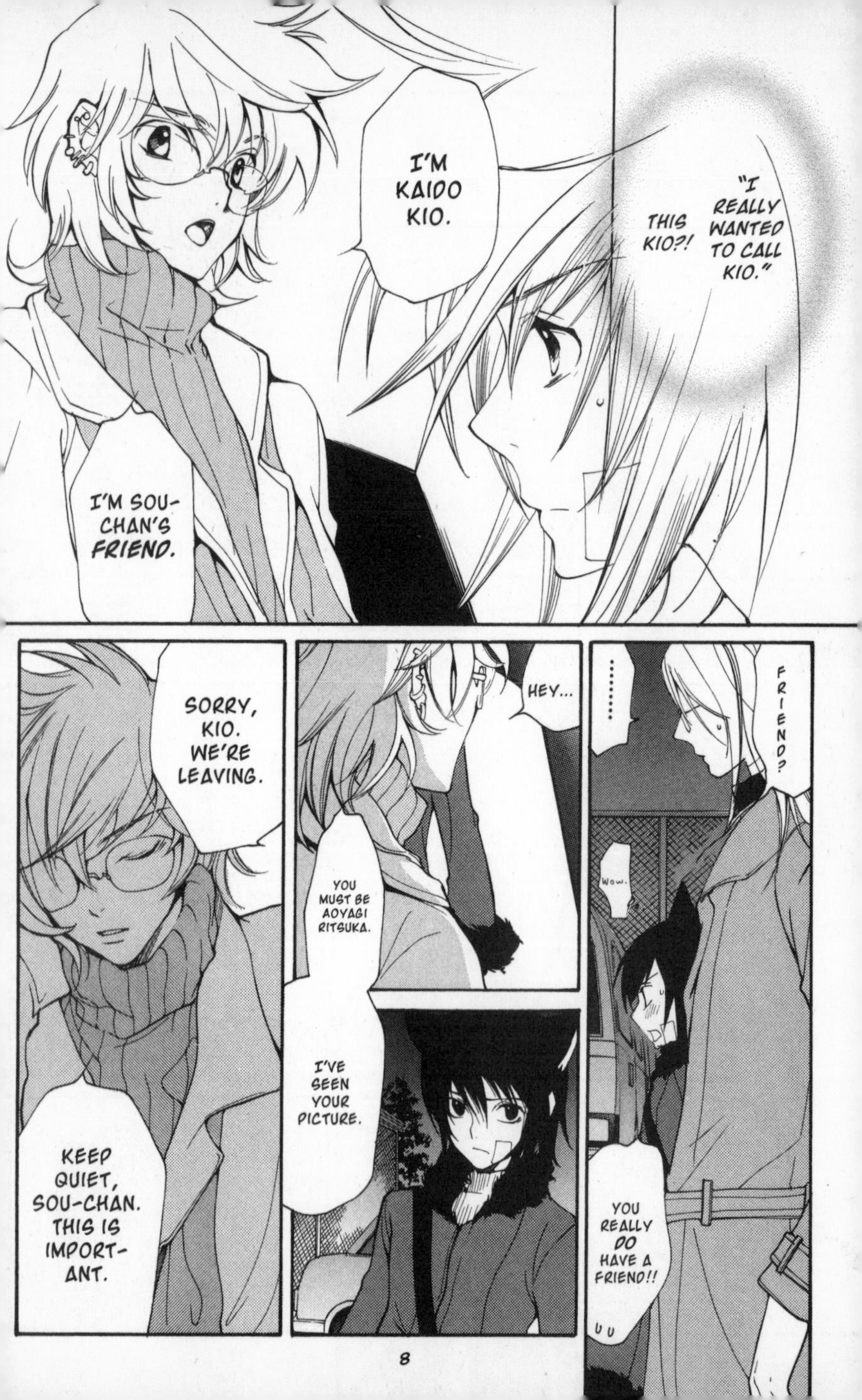
"I REALLY WANTED TO CALL KIO."
THIS KIO?!
I'M KAIDO KIO.
I'M SOU-CHAN'S FRIEND.
FRIEND?
......
WOW.
YOU REALLY DO HAVE A FRIEND!!
UU
HEY...
YOU MUST BE AOYAGI RITSUKA.
I'VE SEEN YOUR PICTURE.
SORRY, KIO. WE'RE LEAVING.
KEEP QUIET, SOU-CHAN. THIS IS IMPORT-ANT.

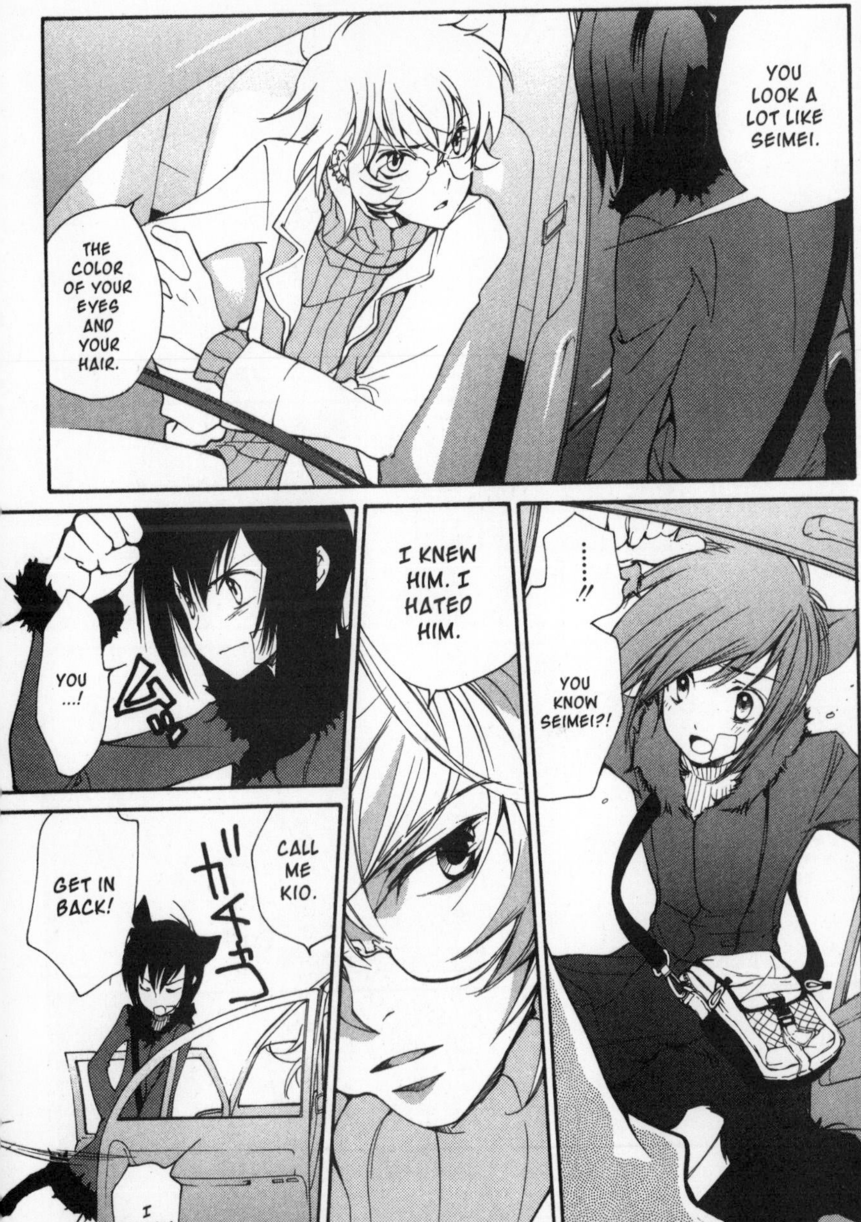
YOU LOOK A LOT LIKE SEIMEI.
THE COLOR OF YOUR EYES AND YOUR HAIR.
......!!
YOU KNOW SEIMEI?!
I KNEW HIM. I HATED HIM.
YOU ...!
CALL ME KIO.
GET IN BACK!
I WON'T!

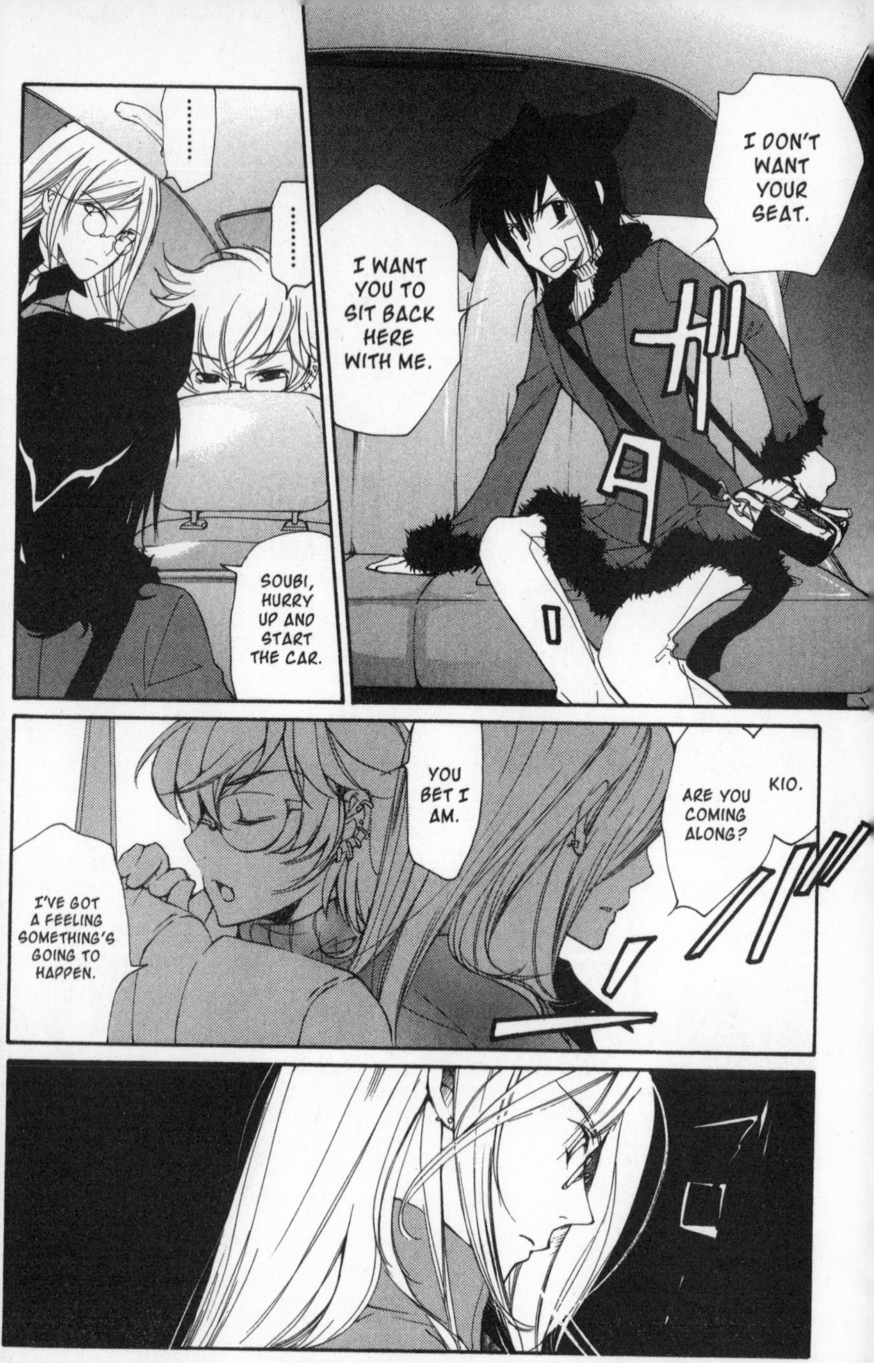
I DON'T WANT YOUR SEAT.
I WANT YOU TO SIT BACK HERE WITH ME.
....
....
SOUBI, HURRY UP AND START THE CAR.
KIO.
ARE YOU COMING ALONG?
YOU BET I AM.
I'VE GOT A FEELING SOMETHING'S GOING TO HAPPEN.

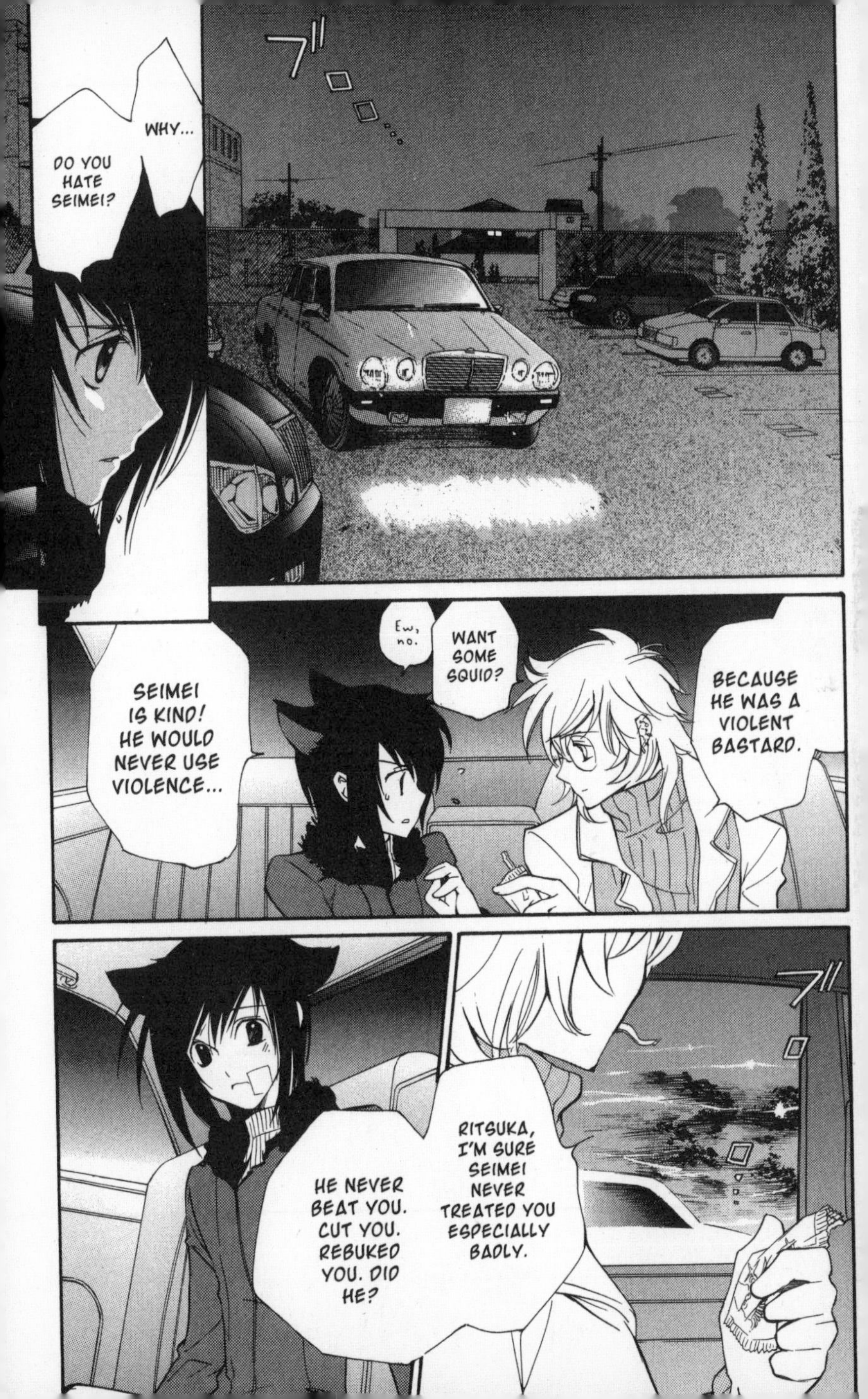
WHY...
DO YOU HATE SEIMEI?
BECAUSE HE WAS A VIOLENT BASTARD.
WANT SOME SQUID?
Ew, no.
SEIMEI IS KIND! HE WOULD NEVER USE VIOLENCE...
RITSUKA, I'M SURE SEIMEI NEVER TREATED YOU ESPECIALLY BADLY.
HE NEVER BEAT YOU. CUT YOU. REBUKED YOU. DID HE?

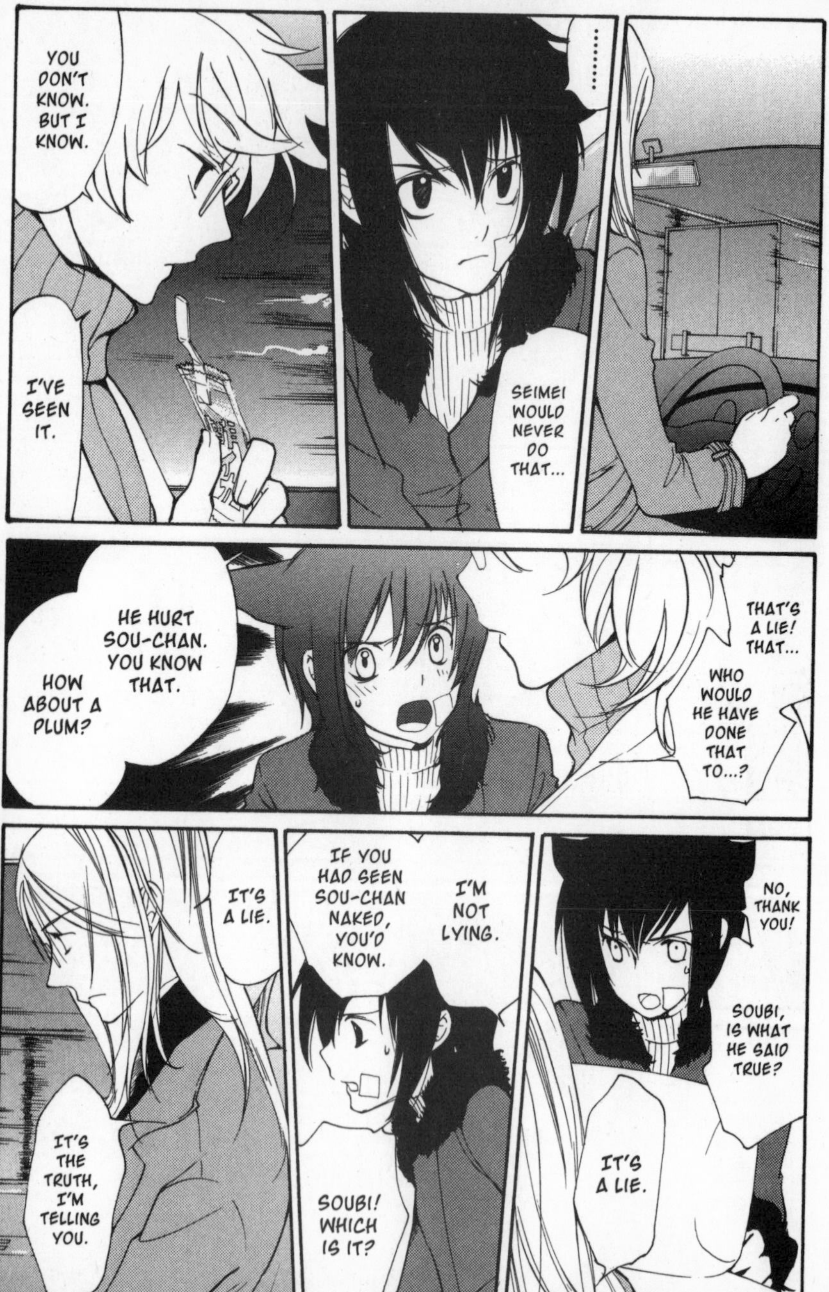
......
SEIMEI WOULD NEVER DO THAT...
YOU DON'T KNOW. BUT I KNOW.
I'VE SEEN IT.
THAT'S A LIE! THAT...
WHO WOULD HE HAVE DONE THAT TO...?
HE HURT SOU-CHAN. YOU KNOW THAT.
HOW ABOUT A PLUM?
NO, THANK YOU!
SOUBI, IS WHAT HE SAID TRUE?
IT'S A LIE.
I'M NOT LYING.
IF YOU HAD SEEN SOU-CHAN NAKED, YOU'D KNOW.
SOUBI! WHICH IS IT?
IT'S A LIE.
IT'S THE TRUTH, I'M TELLING YOU.

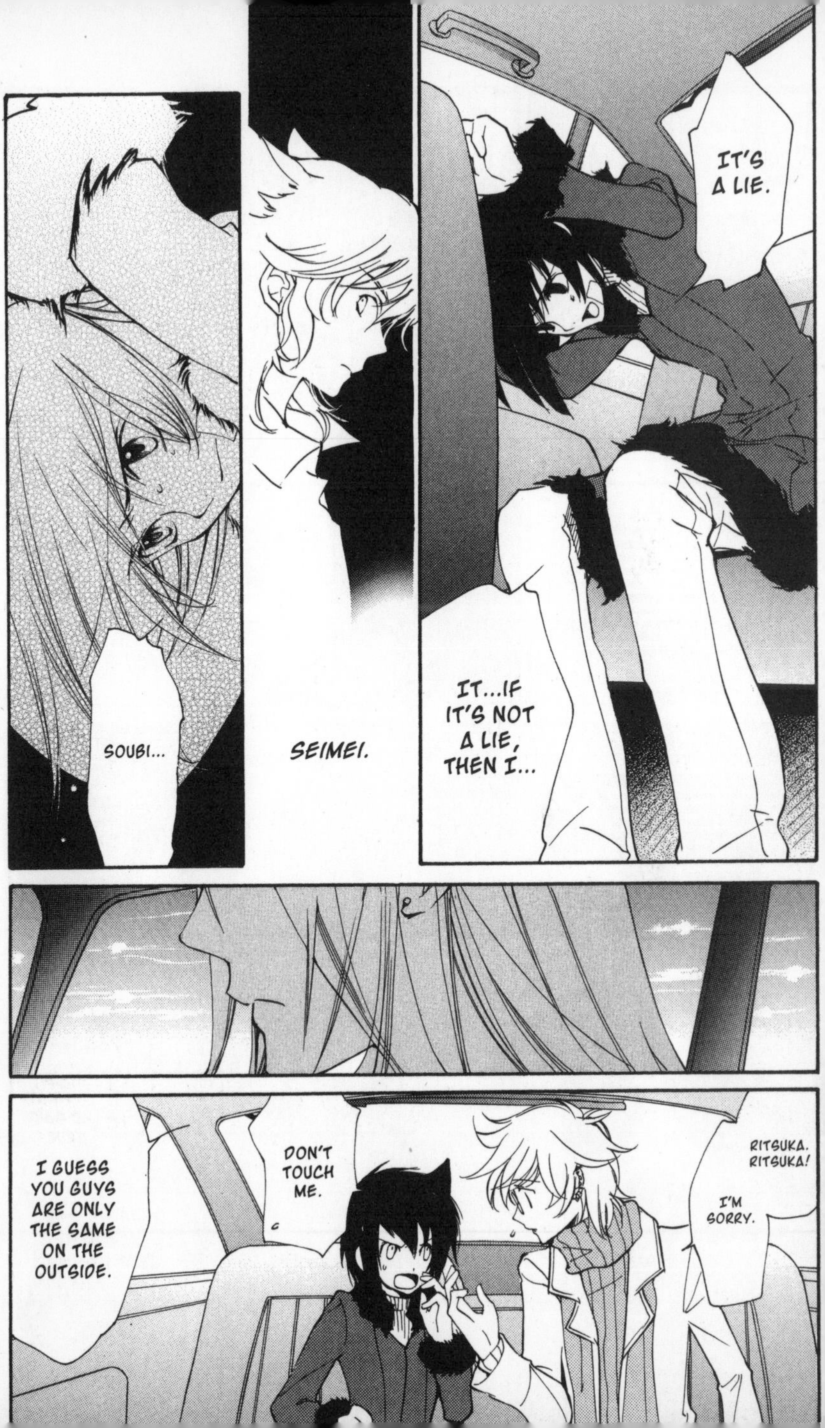
IT'S A LIE.
IT...IF IT'S NOT A LIE, THEN I...
SEIMEI.
SOUBI...
RITSUKA. RITSUKA!
I'M SORRY.
DON'T TOUCH ME.
I GUESS YOU GUYS ARE ONLY THE SAME ON THE OUTSIDE.

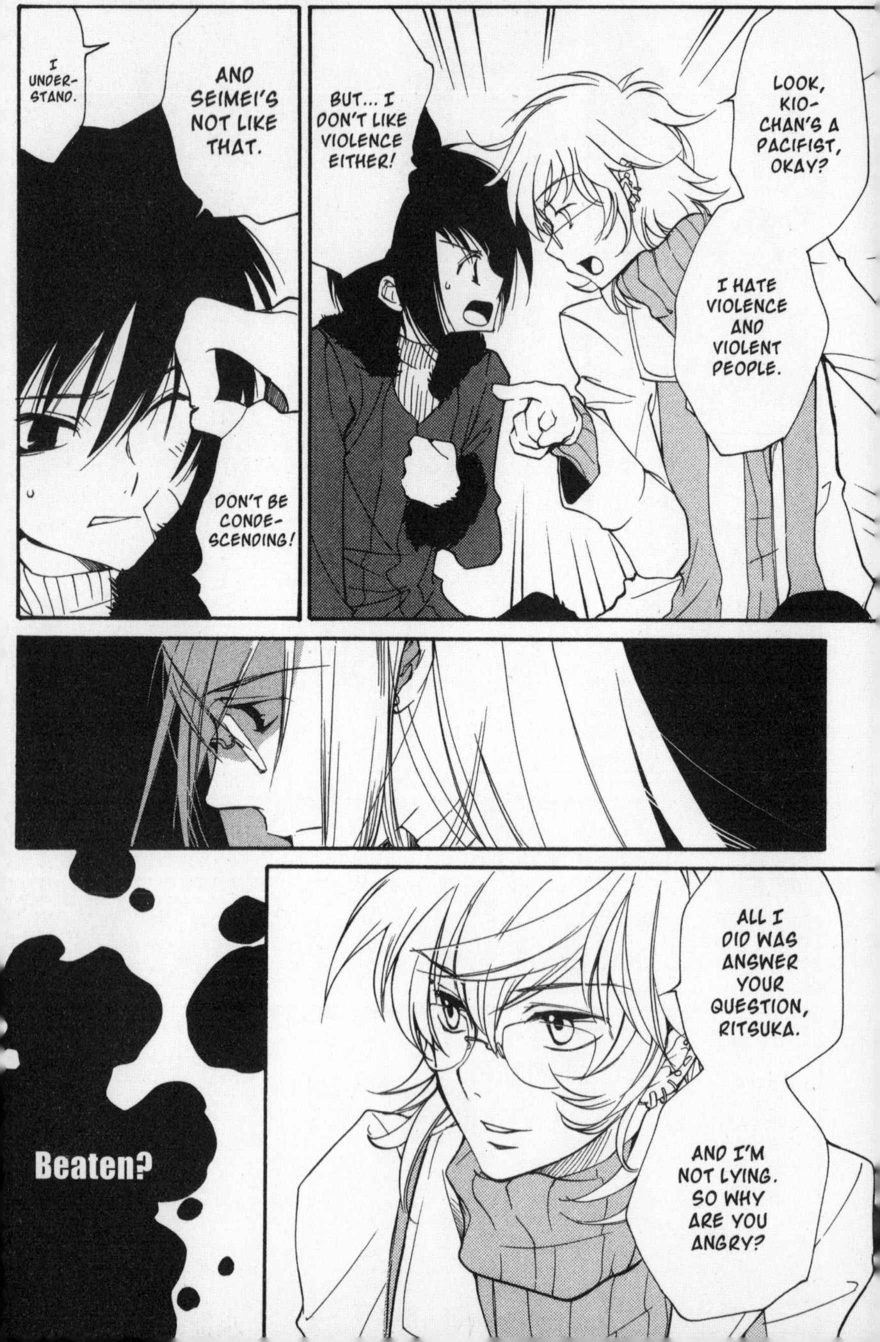
LOOK, KIO-CHAN'S A PACIFIST, OKAY?
I HATE VIOLENCE AND VIOLENT PEOPLE.
BUT... I DON'T LIKE VIOLENCE EITHER!
AND SEIMEI'S NOT LIKE THAT.
I UNDER-STAND.
DON'T BE CONDE-SCENDING!
ALL I DID WAS ANSWER YOUR QUESTION, RITSUKA.
AND I'M NOT LYING. SO WHY ARE YOU ANGRY?
Beaten?

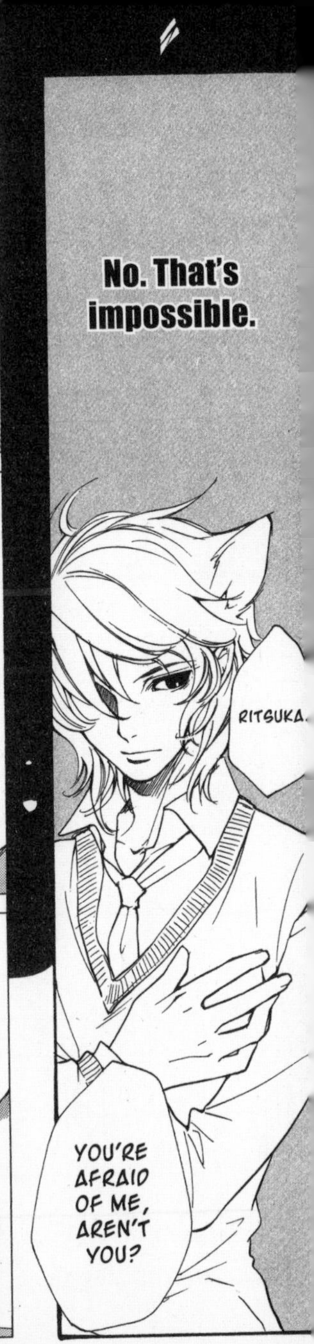
No. That's impossible.
RITSUKA.
YOU'RE AFRAID OF ME, AREN'T YOU?
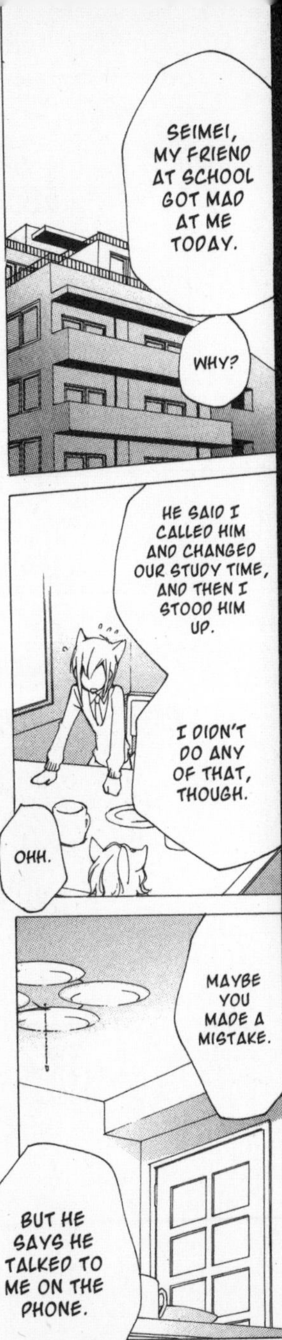
SEIMEI, MY FRIEND AT SCHOOL GOT MAD AT ME TODAY.
WHY?
HE SAID I CALLED HIM AND CHANGED OUR STUDY TIME, AND THEN I STOOD HIM UP.
I DIDN'T DO ANY OF THAT, THOUGH.
OHH.
MAYBE YOU MADE A MISTAKE.
BUT HE SAYS HE TALKED TO ME ON THE PHONE.

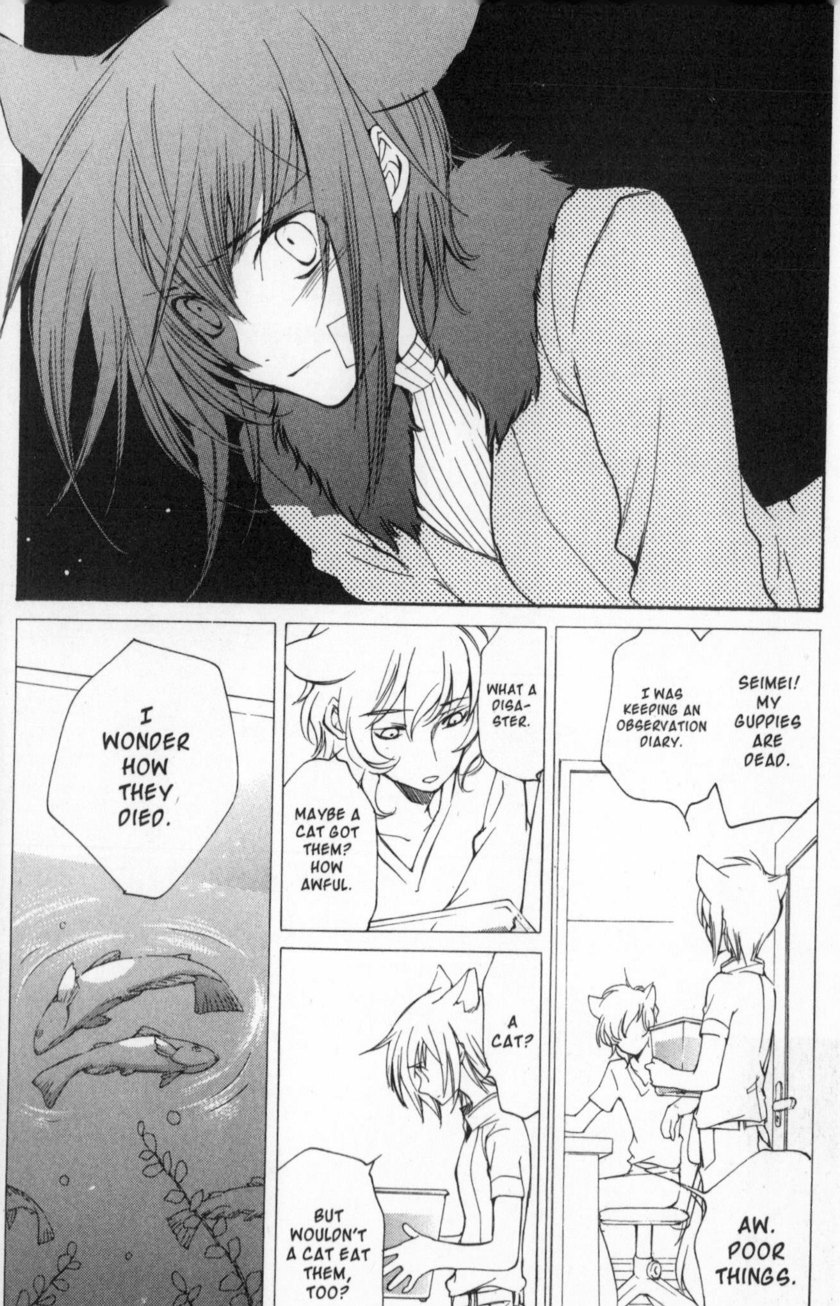
SEIMEI! MY GUPPIES ARE DEAD.
I WAS KEEPING AN OBSERVATION DIARY.
AW. POOR THINGS.
WHAT A DISA-STER.
MAYBE A CAT GOT THEM? HOW AWFUL.
A CAT?
BUT WOULDN'T A CAT EAT THEM, TOO?
I WONDER HOW THEY DIED.

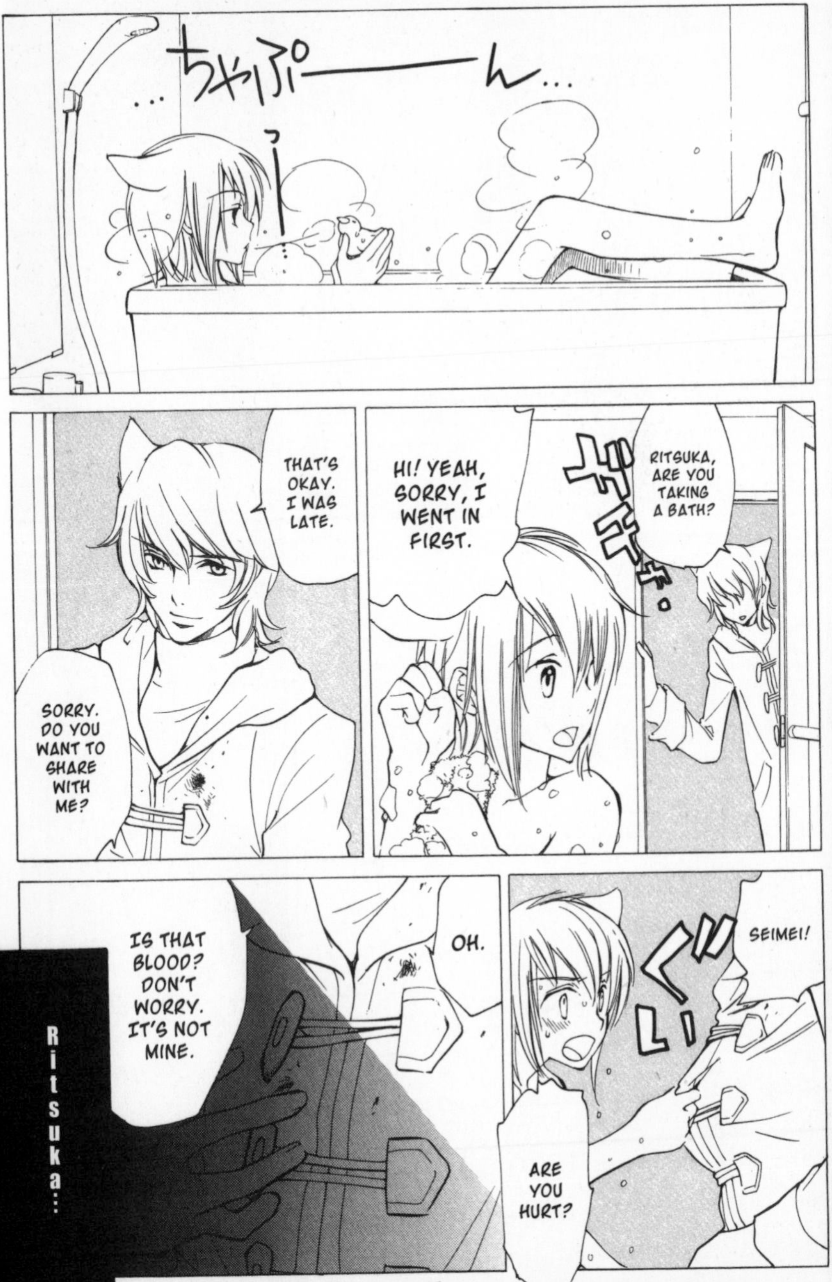
…ちゃぷーーーん…
RITSUKA, ARE YOU TAKING A BATH?
ガチャ。
HI! YEAH, SORRY, I WENT IN FIRST.
THAT'S OKAY. I WAS LATE.
SORRY. DO YOU WANT TO SHARE WITH ME?
ぐい
SEIMEI!
ARE YOU HURT?
OH.
IS THAT BLOOD? DON'T WORRY. IT'S NOT MINE.

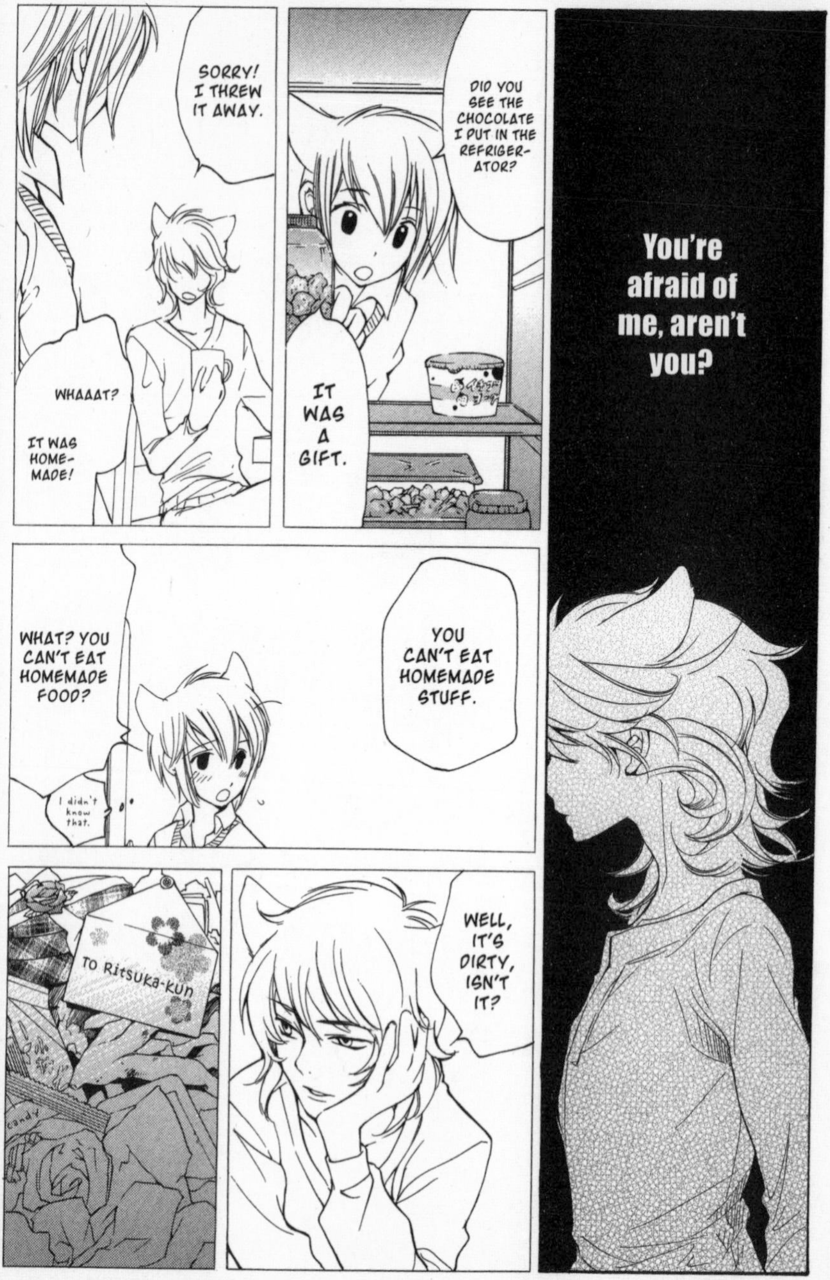

You're afraid of me, aren't you?
DID YOU SEE THE CHOCOLATE I PUT IN THE REFRIGERATOR?
IT WAS A GIFT.
SORRY! I THREW IT AWAY.
WHAAAT?
IT WAS HOMEMADE!
YOU CAN'T EAT HOMEMADE STUFF.
WHAT? YOU CAN'T EAT HOMEMADE FOOD?
I didn't know that.
WELL, IT'S DIRTY, ISN'T IT?
To Ritsuka-kun
candy

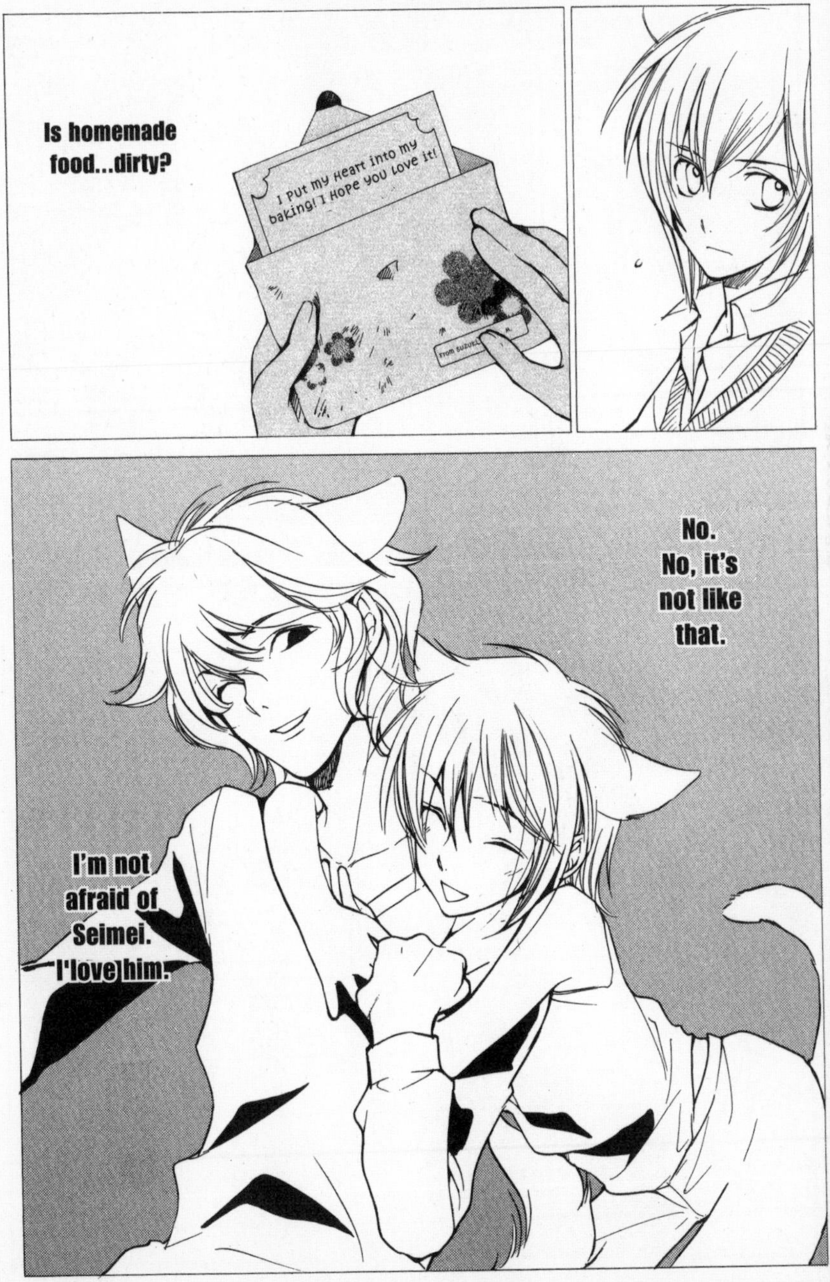
Is homemade food...dirty?
I Put my Heart into my baking! I Hope you love it!
From SUZUKI
No. No, it's not like that.
I'm not afraid of Seimei. I love him.

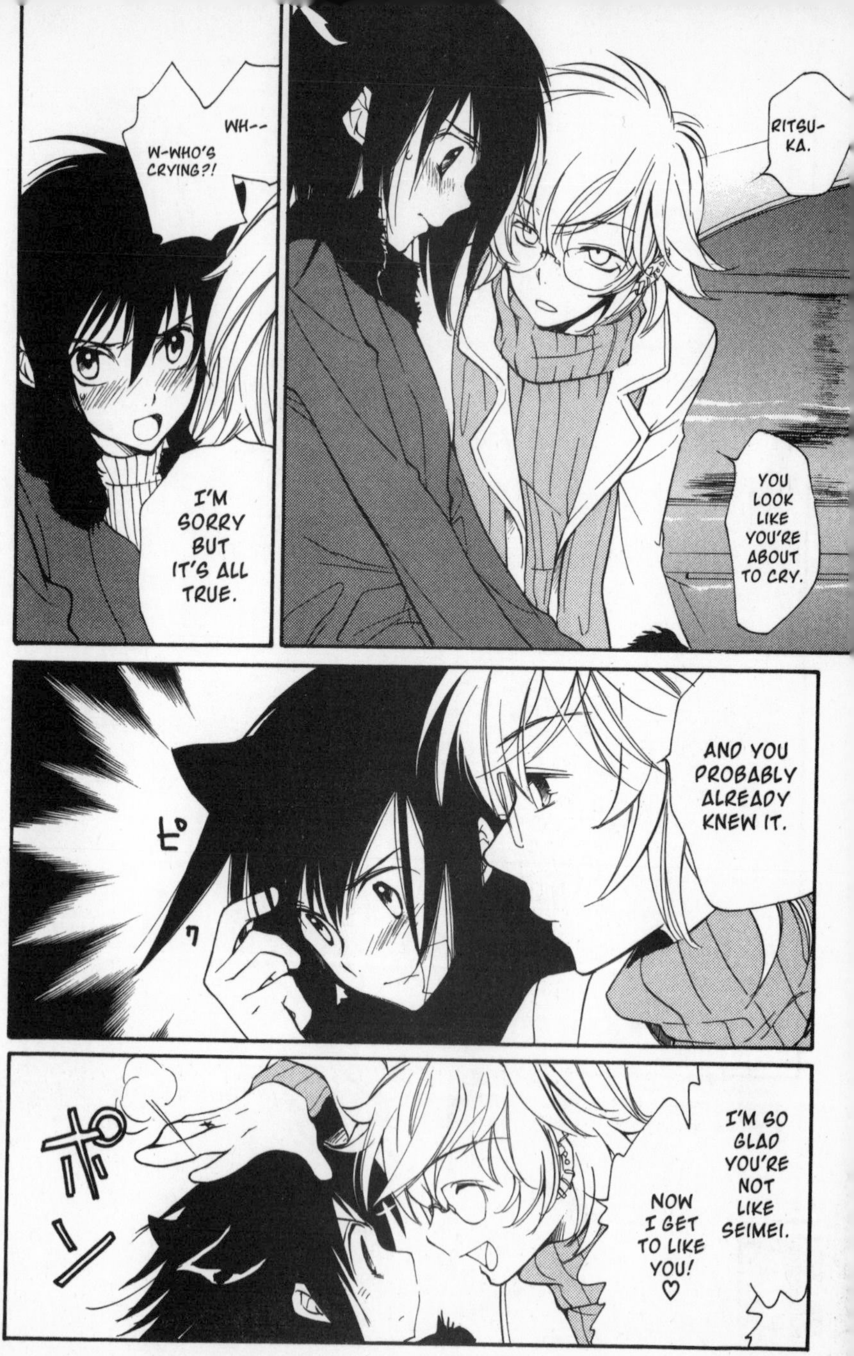
RITSU-KA.
YOU LOOK LIKE YOU'RE ABOUT TO CRY.
WH--
W-WHO'S CRYING?!
I'M SORRY BUT IT'S ALL TRUE.
AND YOU PROBABLY ALREADY KNEW IT.
ピク
I'M SO GLAD YOU'RE NOT LIKE SEIMEI.
NOW I GET TO LIKE YOU! ♡
ポン

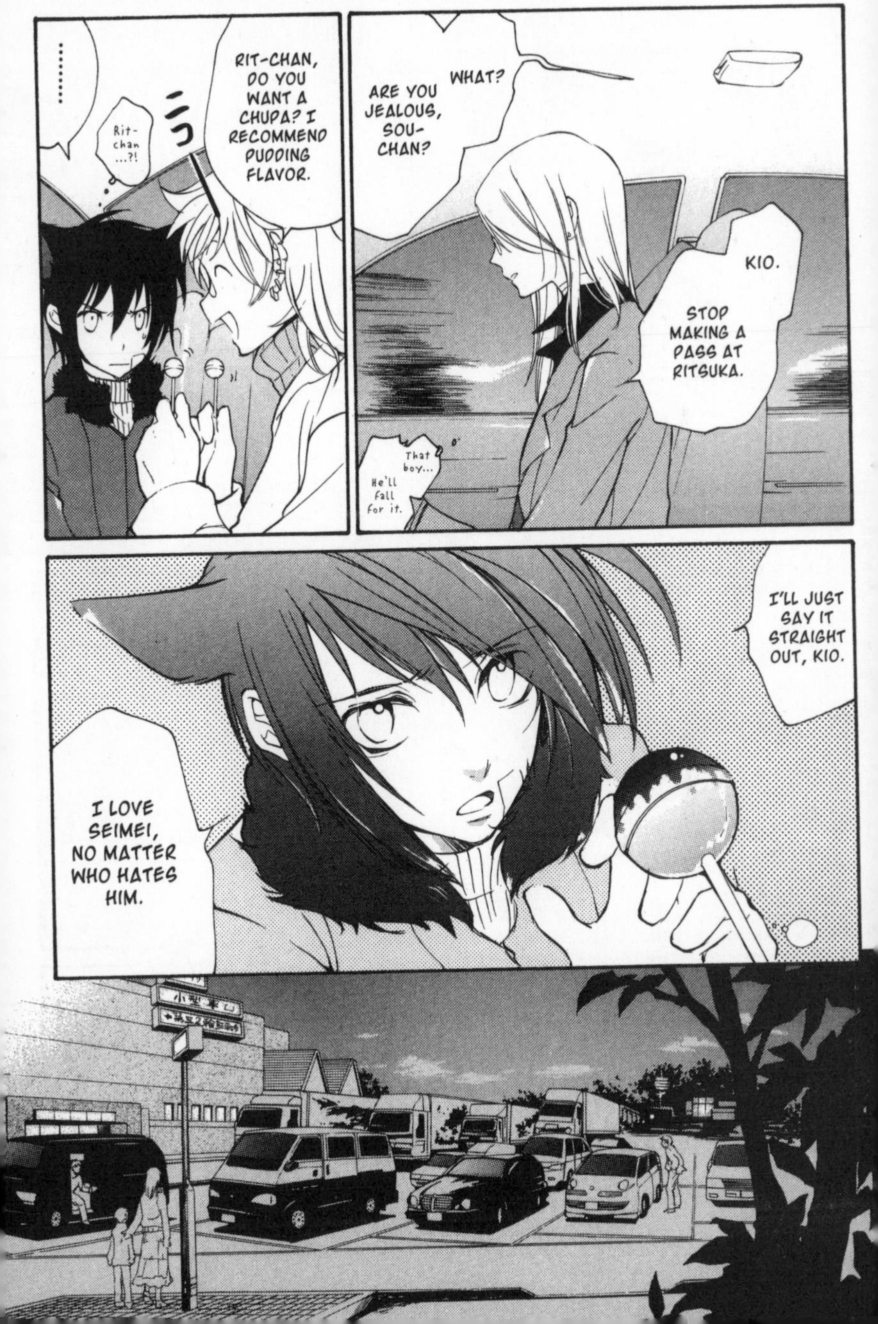
WHAT? ARE YOU JEALOUS, SOU-CHAN?
KIO.
STOP MAKING A PASS AT RITSUKA.
That boy... He'll fall for it.
RIT-CHAN, DO YOU WANT A CHUPA? I RECOMMEND PUDDING FLAVOR.
Rit-chan ...?!
......
I'LL JUST SAY IT STRAIGHT OUT, KIO.
I LOVE SEIMEI, NO MATTER WHO HATES HIM.

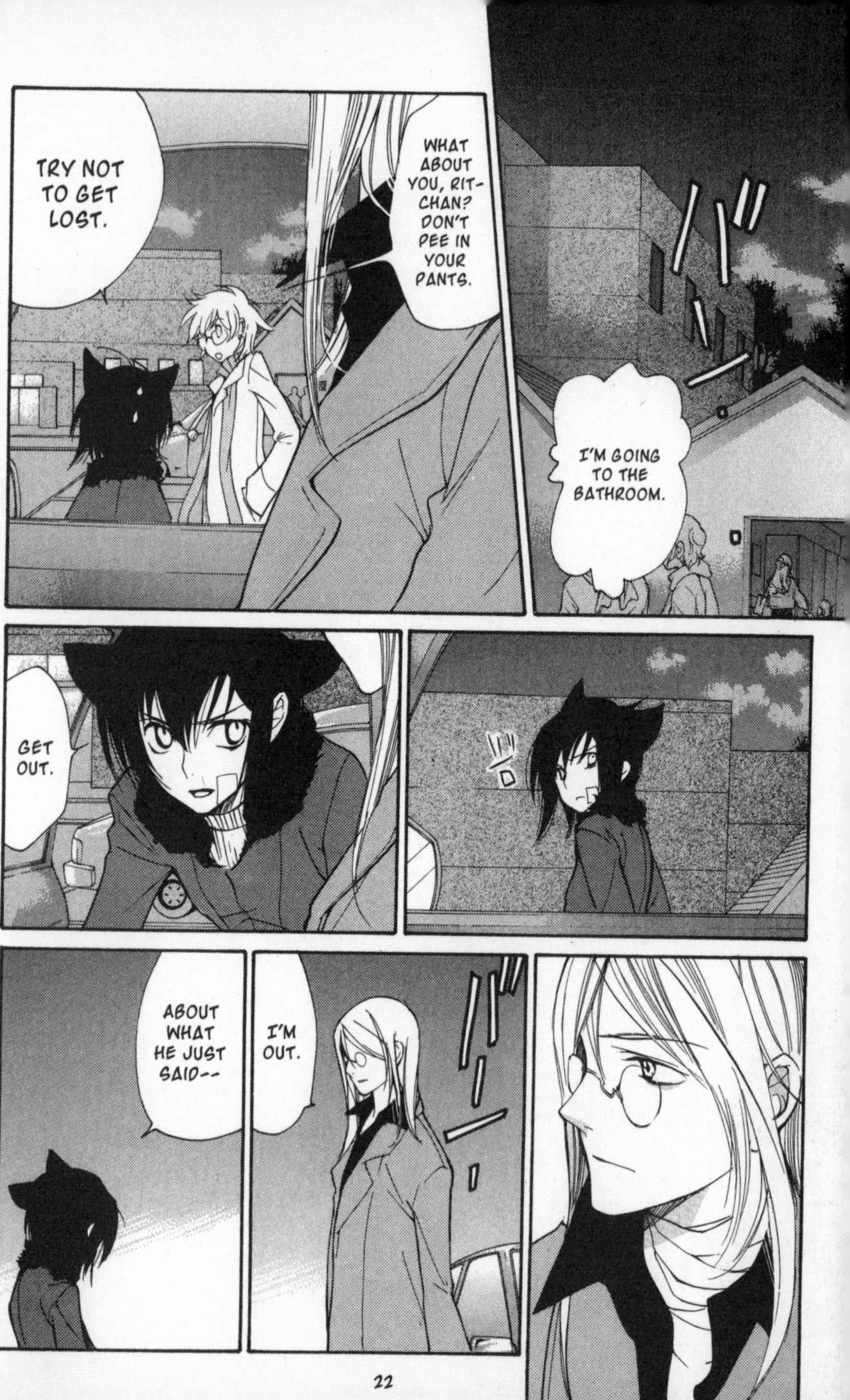
I'M GOING TO THE BATHROOM.
WHAT ABOUT YOU, RIT-CHAN? DON'T PEE IN YOUR PANTS.
TRY NOT TO GET LOST.
GET OUT.
I'M OUT.
ABOUT WHAT HE JUST SAID--

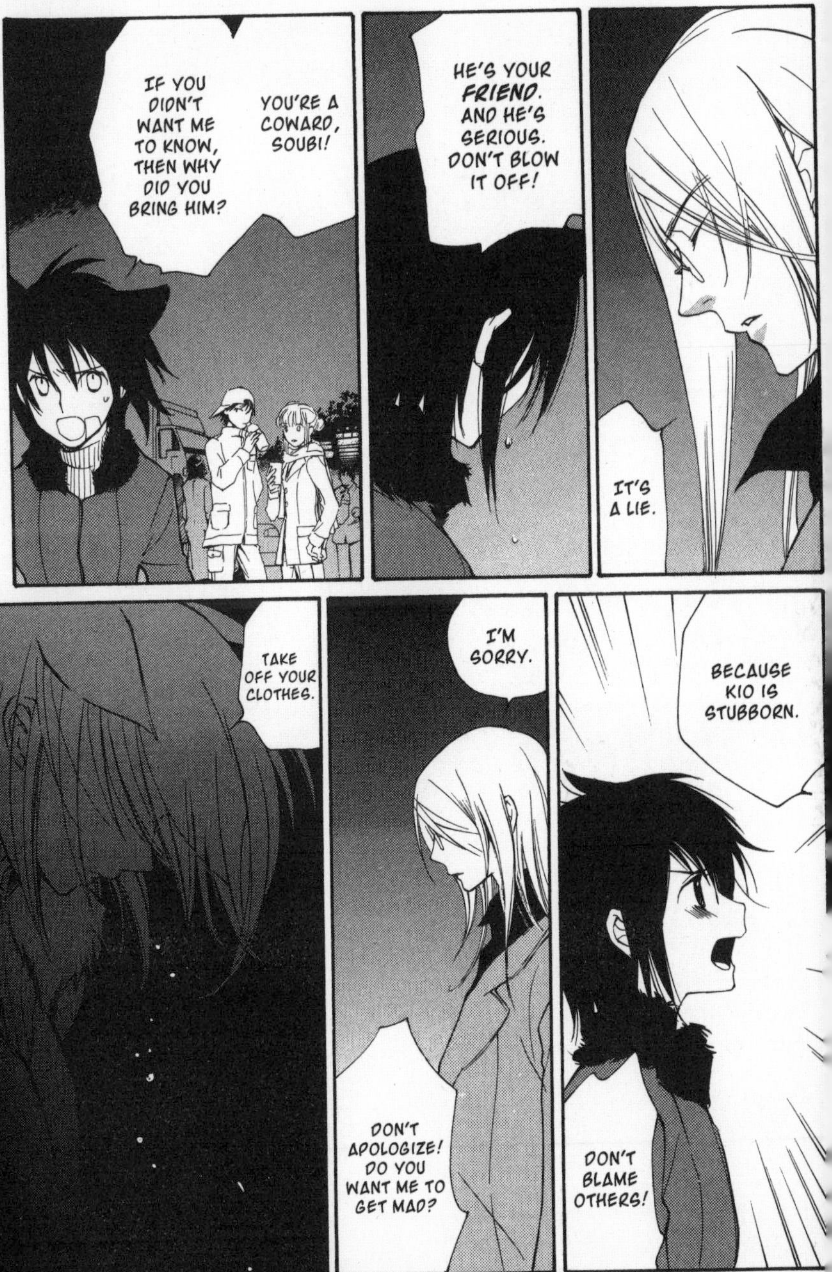
IT'S A LIE.
HE'S YOUR **FRIEND**. AND HE'S SERIOUS. DON'T BLOW IT OFF!
YOU'RE A COWARD, SOUBI!
IF YOU DIDN'T WANT ME TO KNOW, THEN WHY DID YOU BRING HIM?
BECAUSE KIO IS STUBBORN.
DON'T BLAME OTHERS!
I'M SORRY.
DON'T APOLOGIZE! DO YOU WANT ME TO GET MAD?
TAKE OFF YOUR CLOTHES.

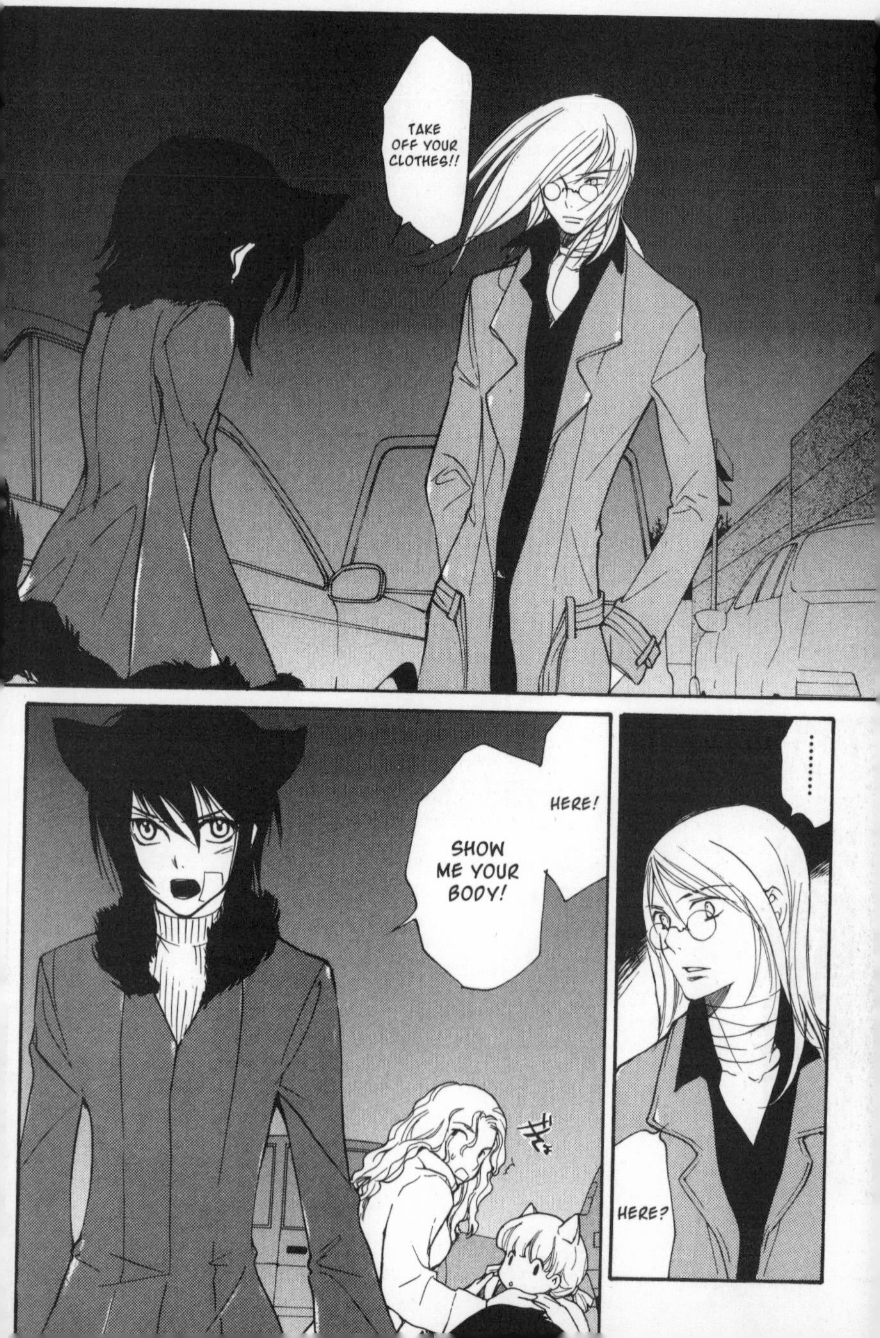
TAKE OFF YOUR CLOTHES!!
......
HERE?
HERE!
SHOW ME YOUR BODY!

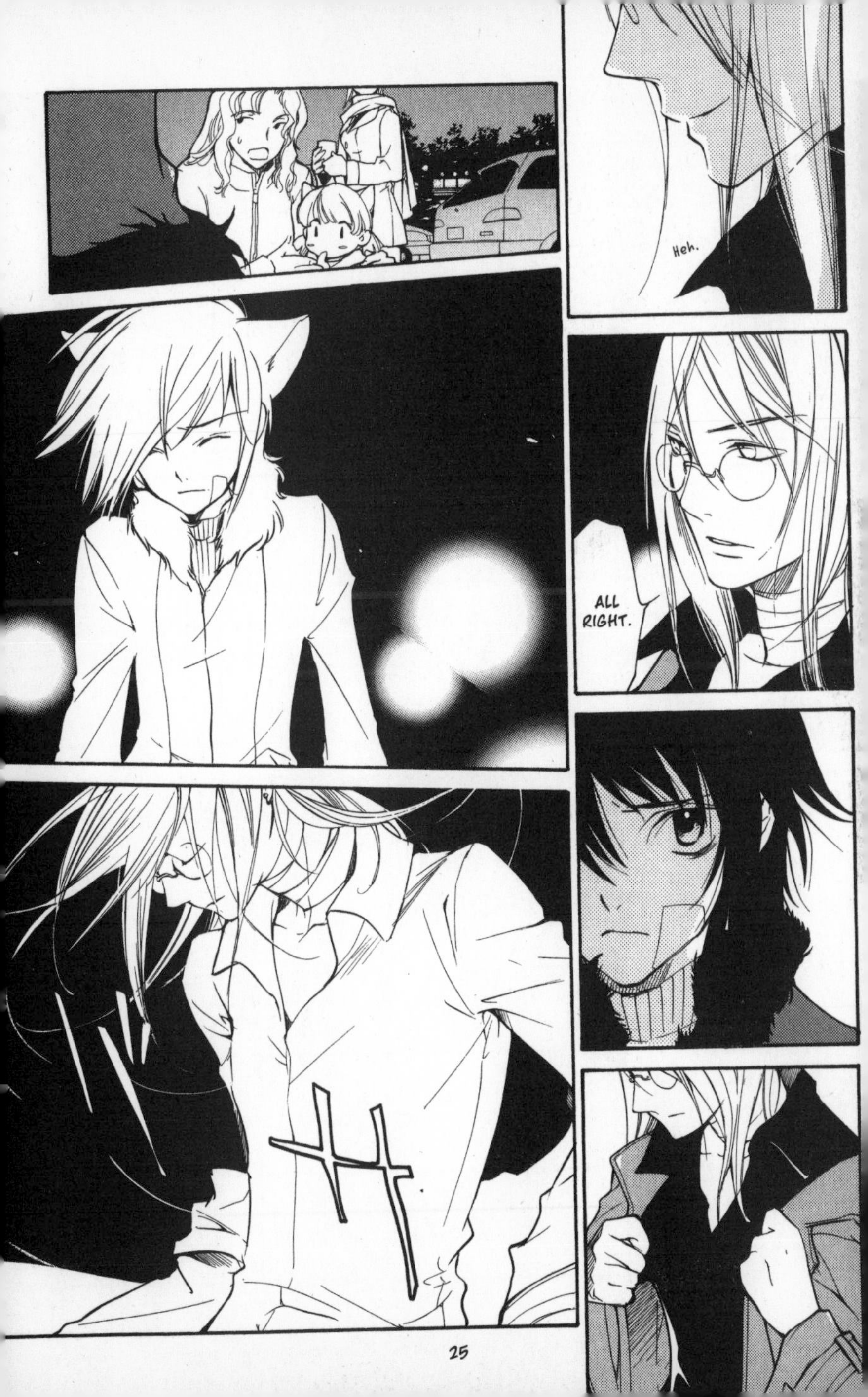
Heh.
ALL RIGHT.

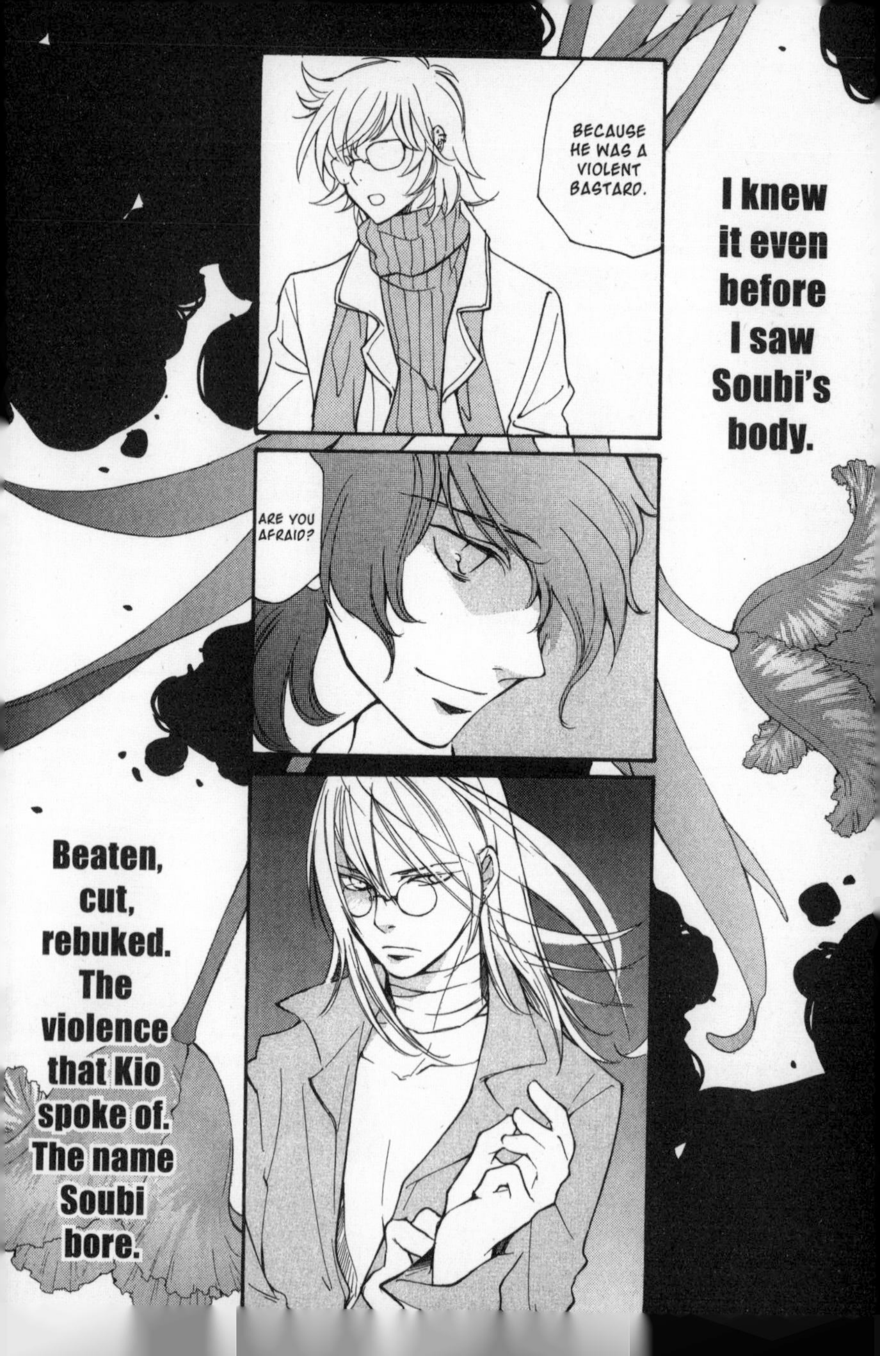
I knew it even before I saw Soubi's body.
BECAUSE HE WAS A VIOLENT BASTARD.
ARE YOU AFRAID?
Beaten, cut, rebuked. The violence that Kio spoke of. The name Soubi bore.

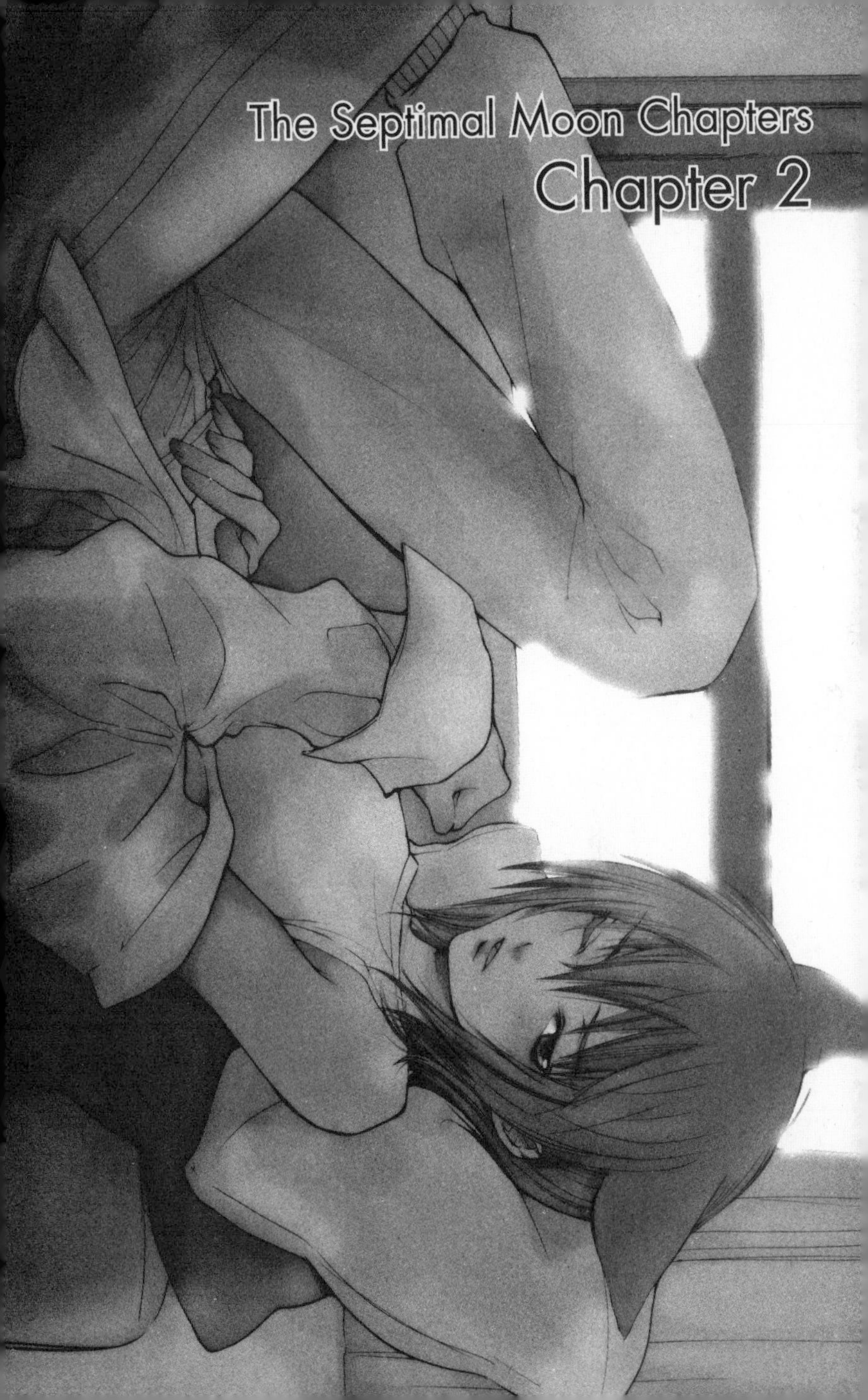
The Septimal Moon Chapters
Chapter 2

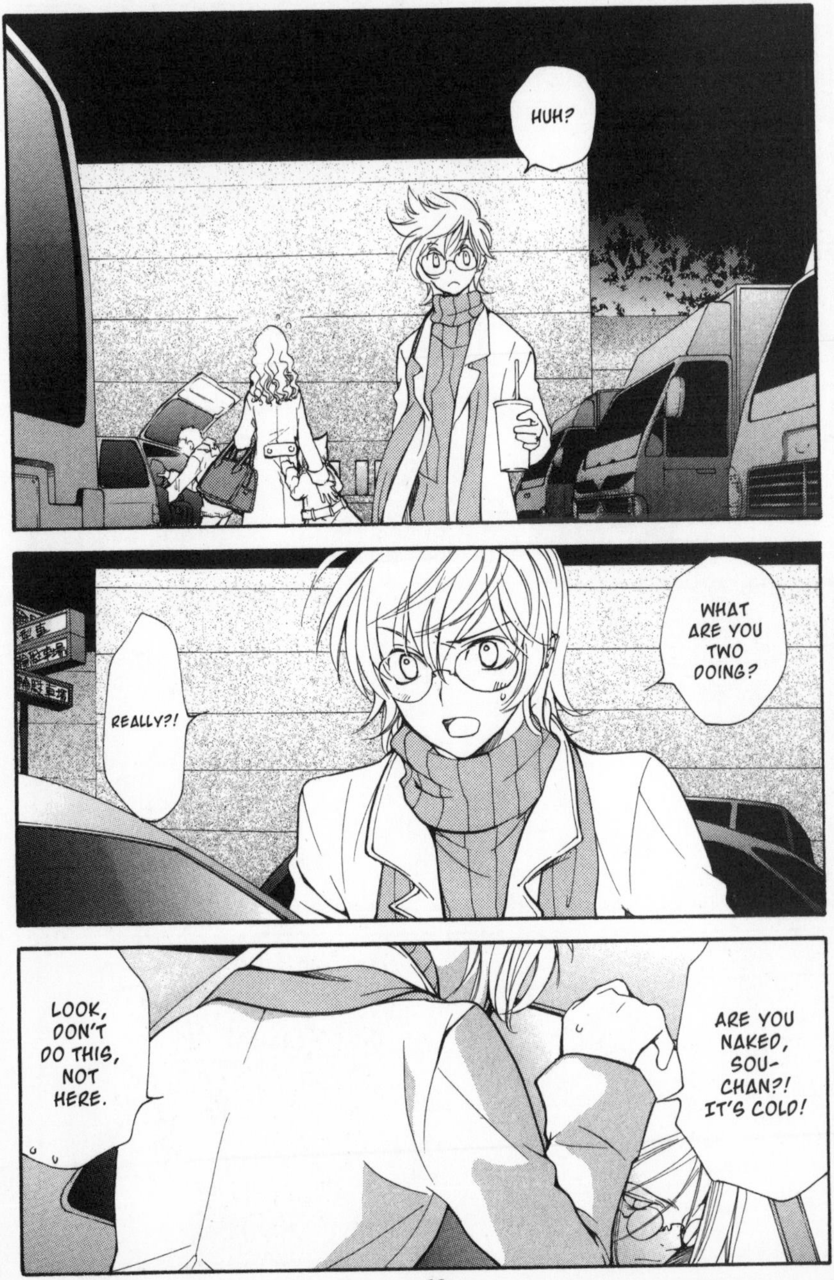
HUH?
WHAT ARE YOU TWO DOING?
REALLY?!
ARE YOU NAKED, SOU-CHAN?! IT'S COLD!
LOOK, DON'T DO THIS, NOT HERE.

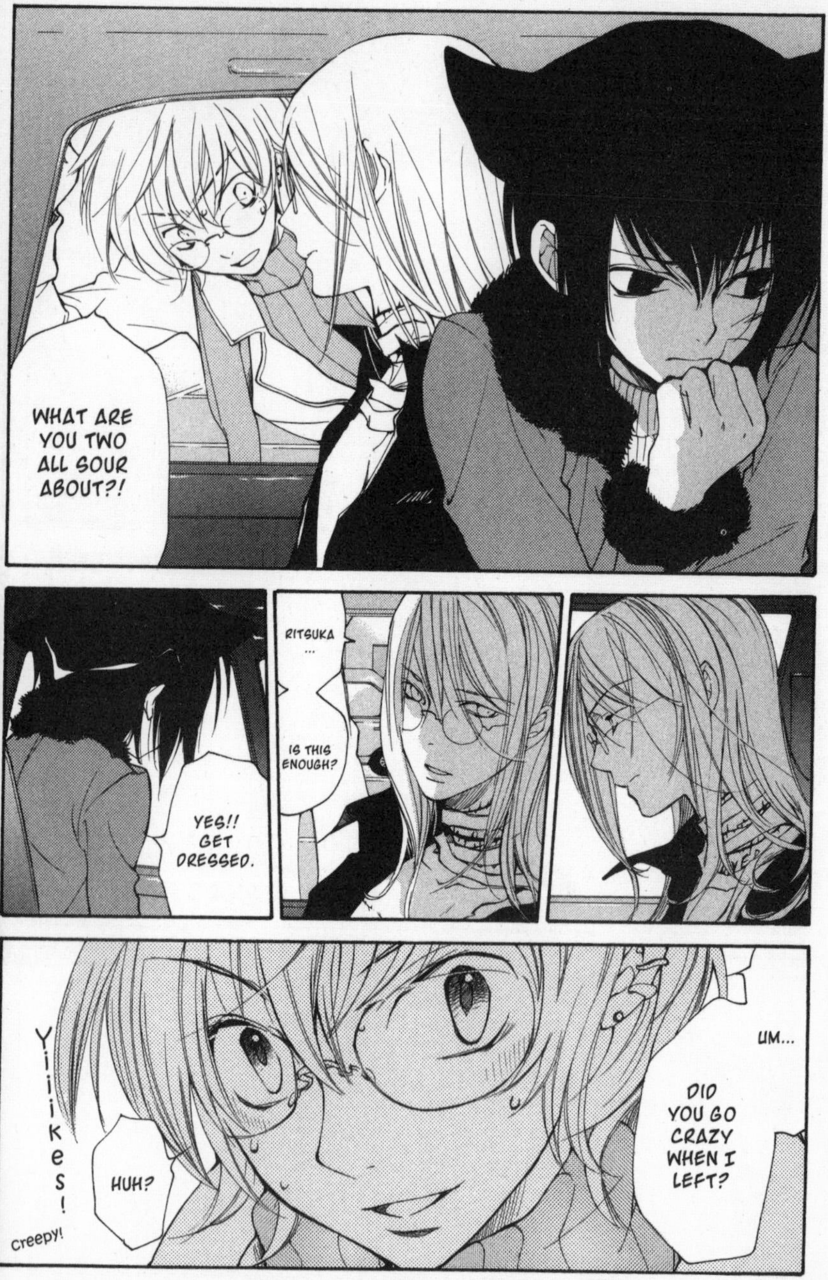
WHAT ARE YOU TWO ALL SOUR ABOUT?!
RITSUKA ...
IS THIS ENOUGH?
YES!! GET DRESSED.
UM...
DID YOU GO CRAZY WHEN I LEFT?
HUH?
Yiiikes!
Creepy!

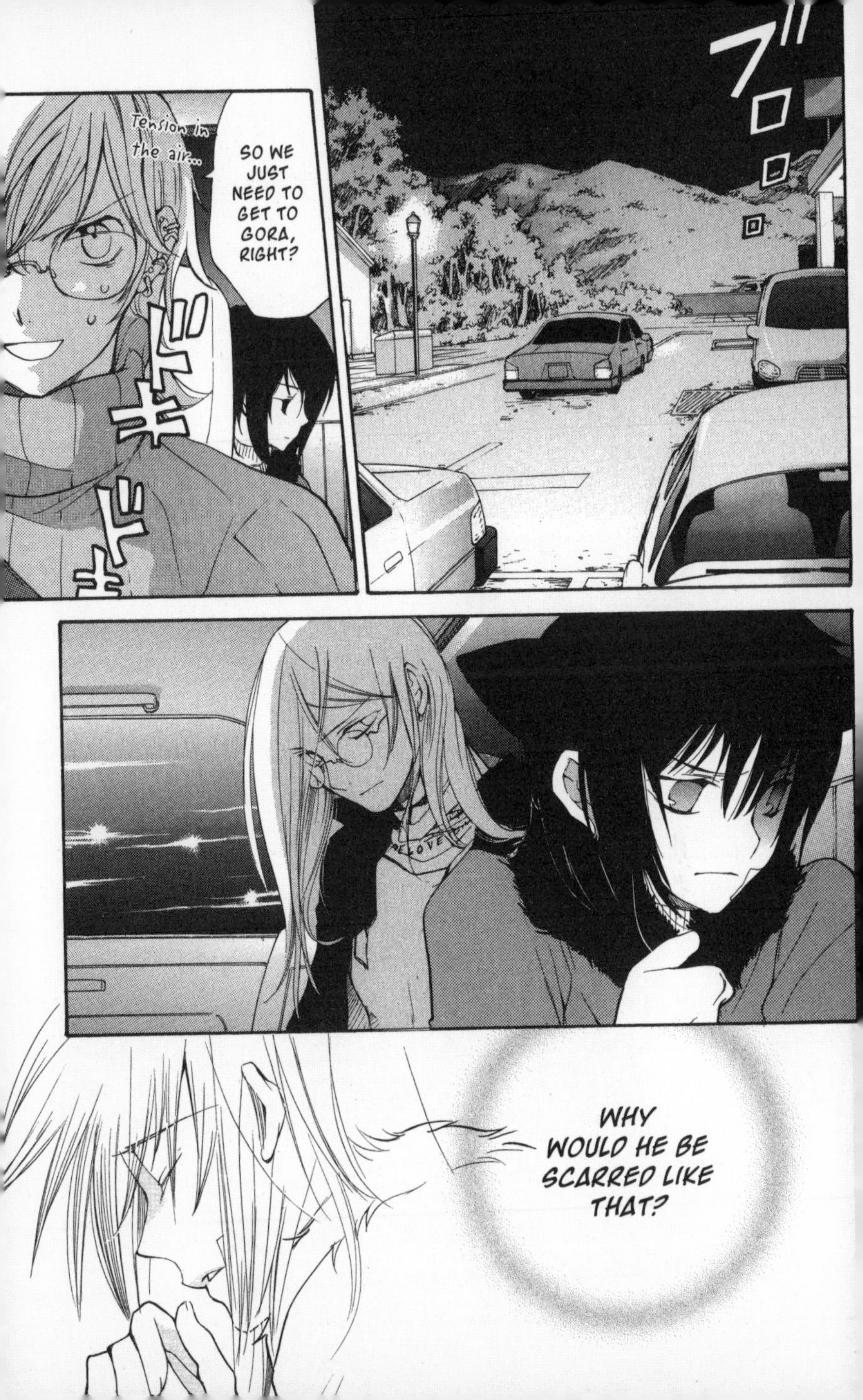
ブロロロ
Tension in the air...
SO WE JUST NEED TO GET TO GORA, RIGHT?
ドキドキ
WHY WOULD HE BE SCARRED LIKE THAT?

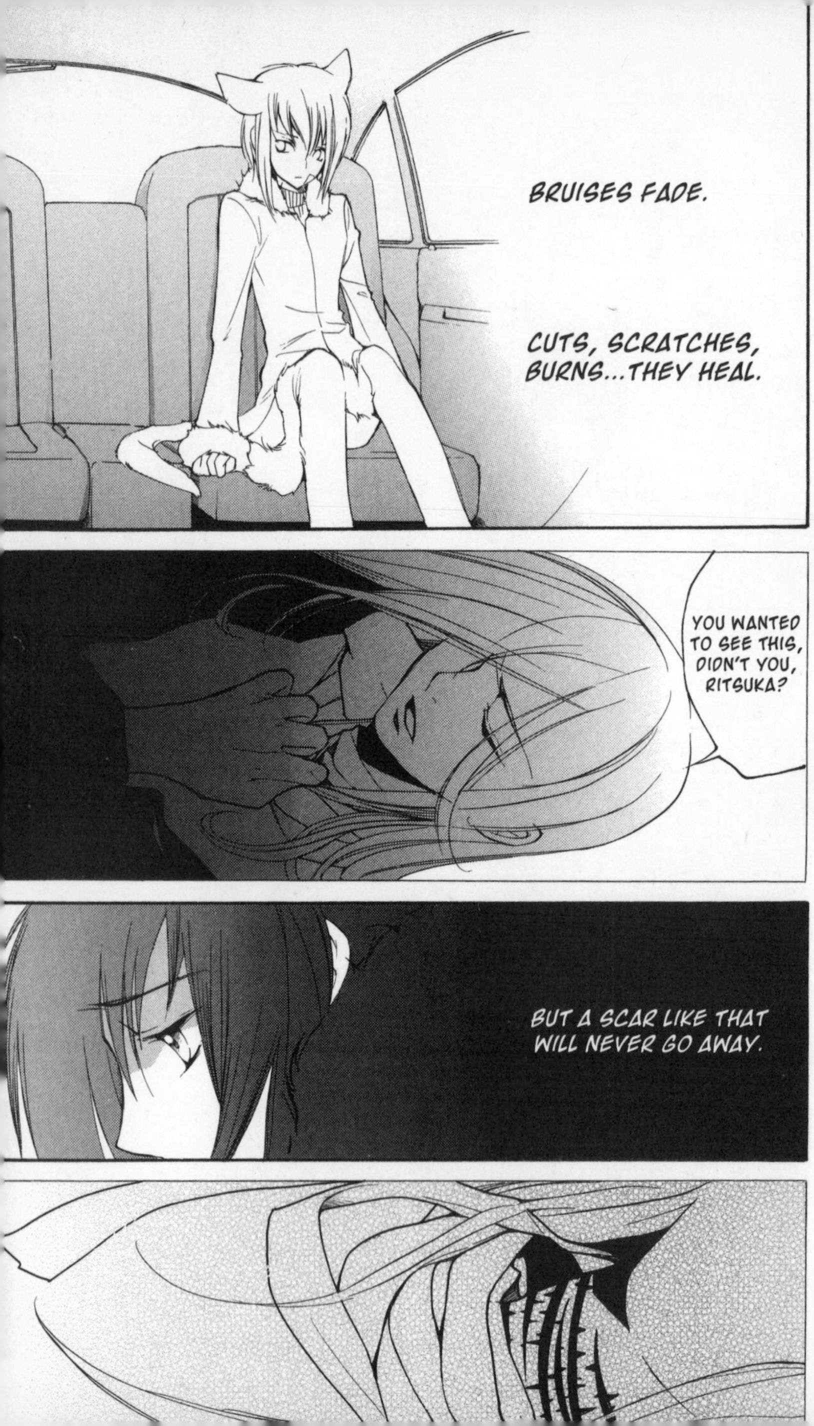
BRUISES FADE.
CUTS, SCRATCHES, BURNS...THEY HEAL.
YOU WANTED TO SEE THIS, DIDN'T YOU, RITSUKA?
BUT A SCAR LIKE THAT WILL NEVER GO AWAY.

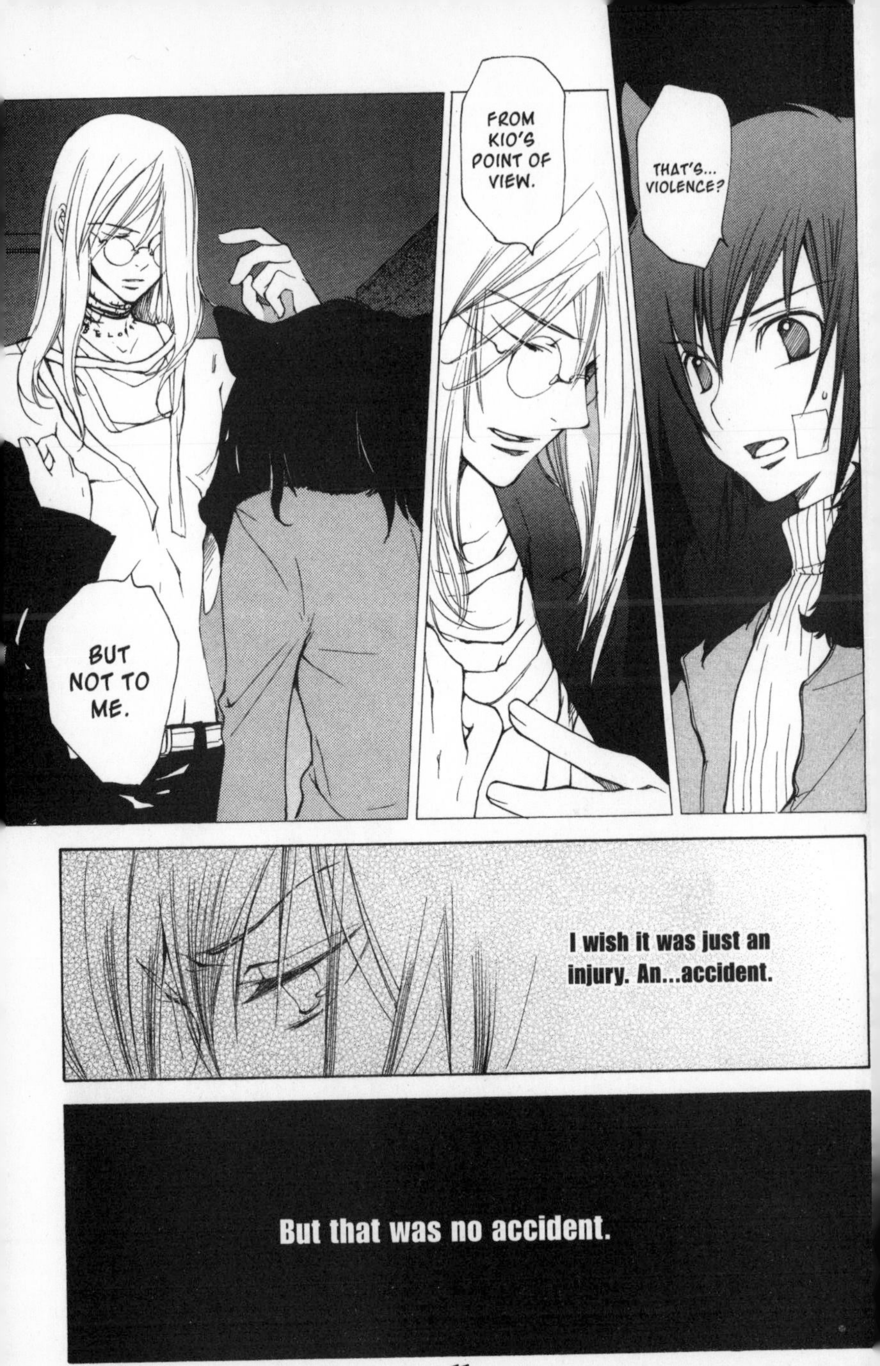
THAT'S... VIOLENCE?
FROM KIO'S POINT OF VIEW.
BUT NOT TO ME.
I wish it was just an injury. An...accident.
But that was no accident.

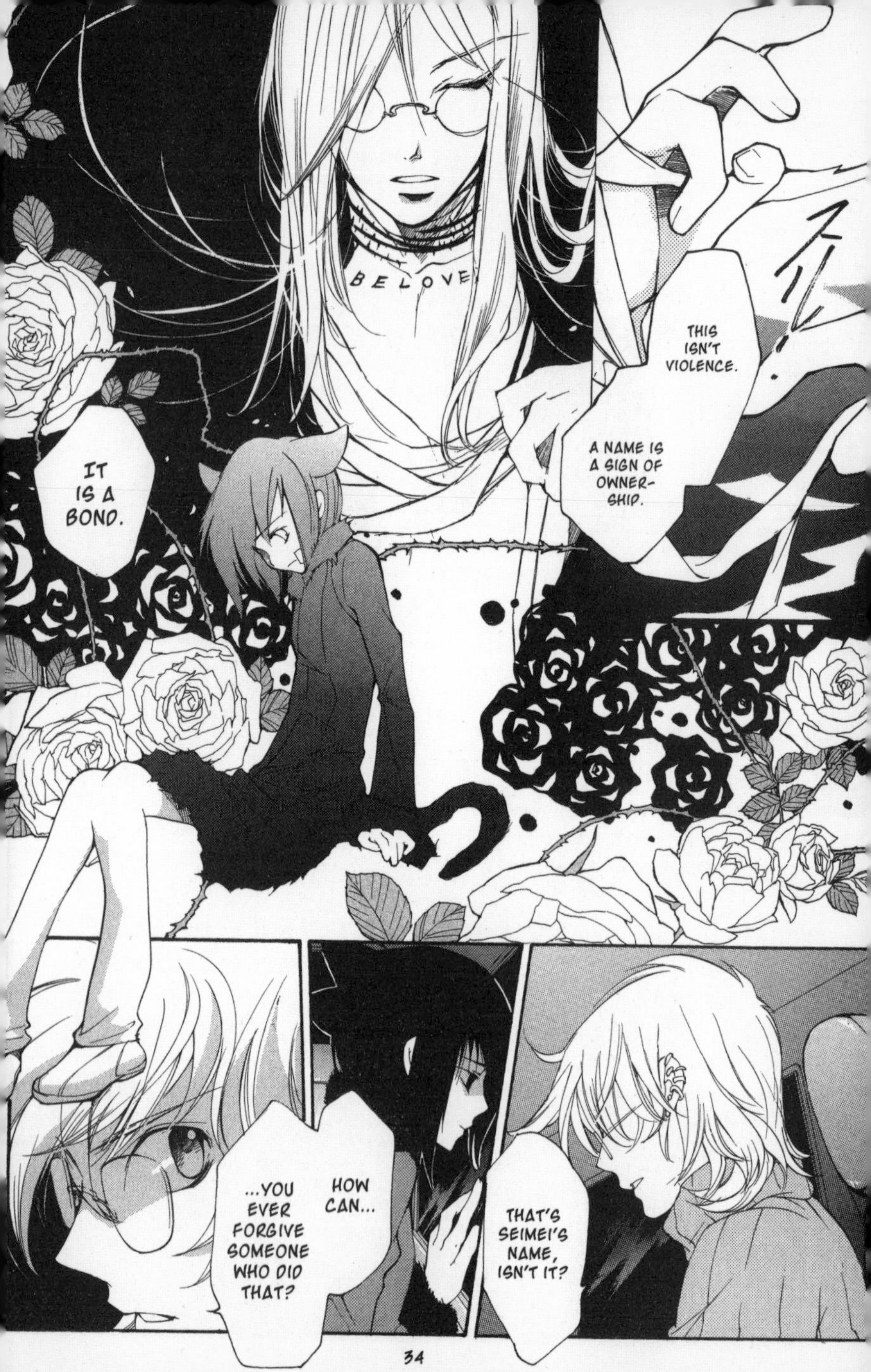
BELOVE
THIS ISN'T VIOLENCE.
A NAME IS A SIGN OF OWNER-SHIP.
IT IS A BOND.
THAT'S SEIMEI'S NAME, ISN'T IT?
HOW CAN...
...YOU EVER FORGIVE SOMEONE WHO DID THAT?

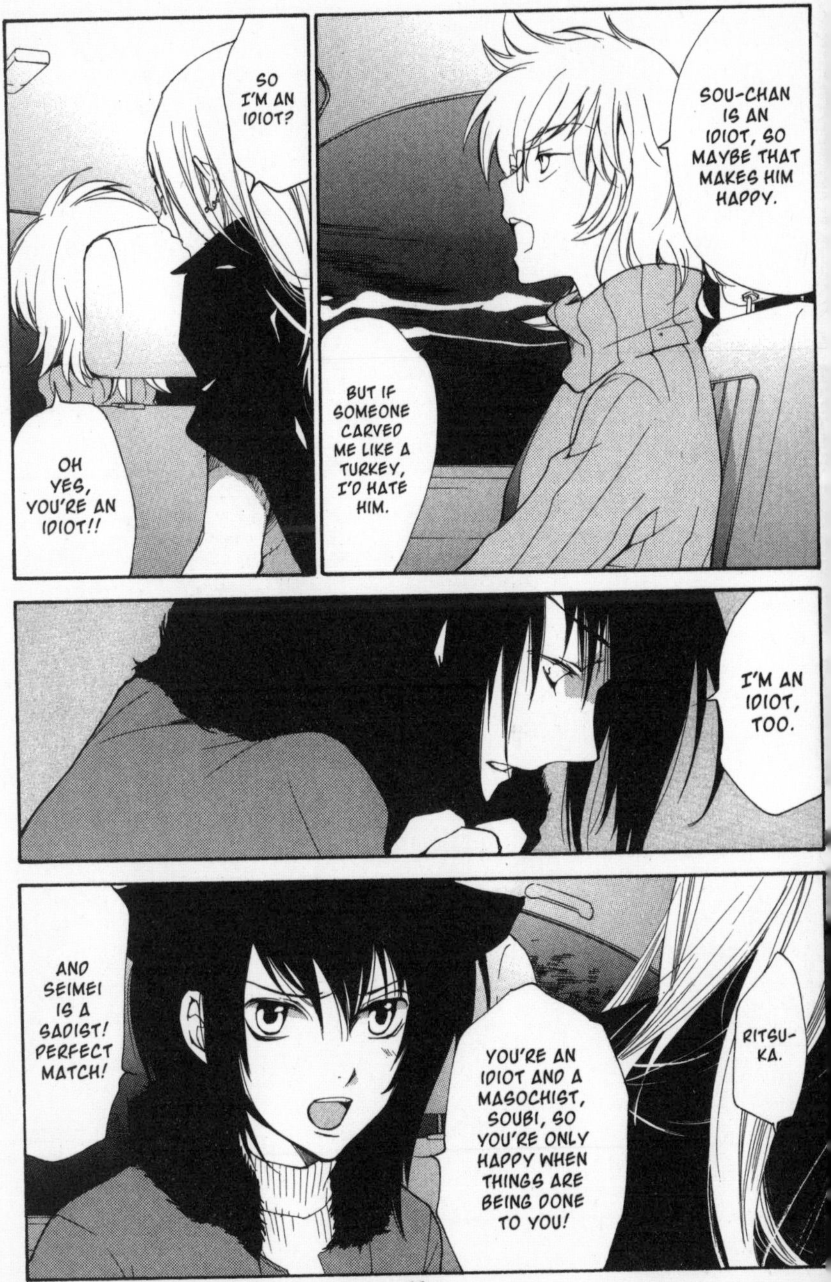
SOU-CHAN IS AN IDIOT, SO MAYBE THAT MAKES HIM HAPPY.
BUT IF SOMEONE CARVED ME LIKE A TURKEY, I'D HATE HIM.
SO I'M AN IDIOT?
OH YES, YOU'RE AN IDIOT!!
I'M AN IDIOT, TOO.
RITSU-KA.
YOU'RE AN IDIOT AND A MASOCHIST, SOUBI, SO YOU'RE ONLY HAPPY WHEN THINGS ARE BEING DONE TO YOU!
AND SEIMEI IS A SADIST! PERFECT MATCH!

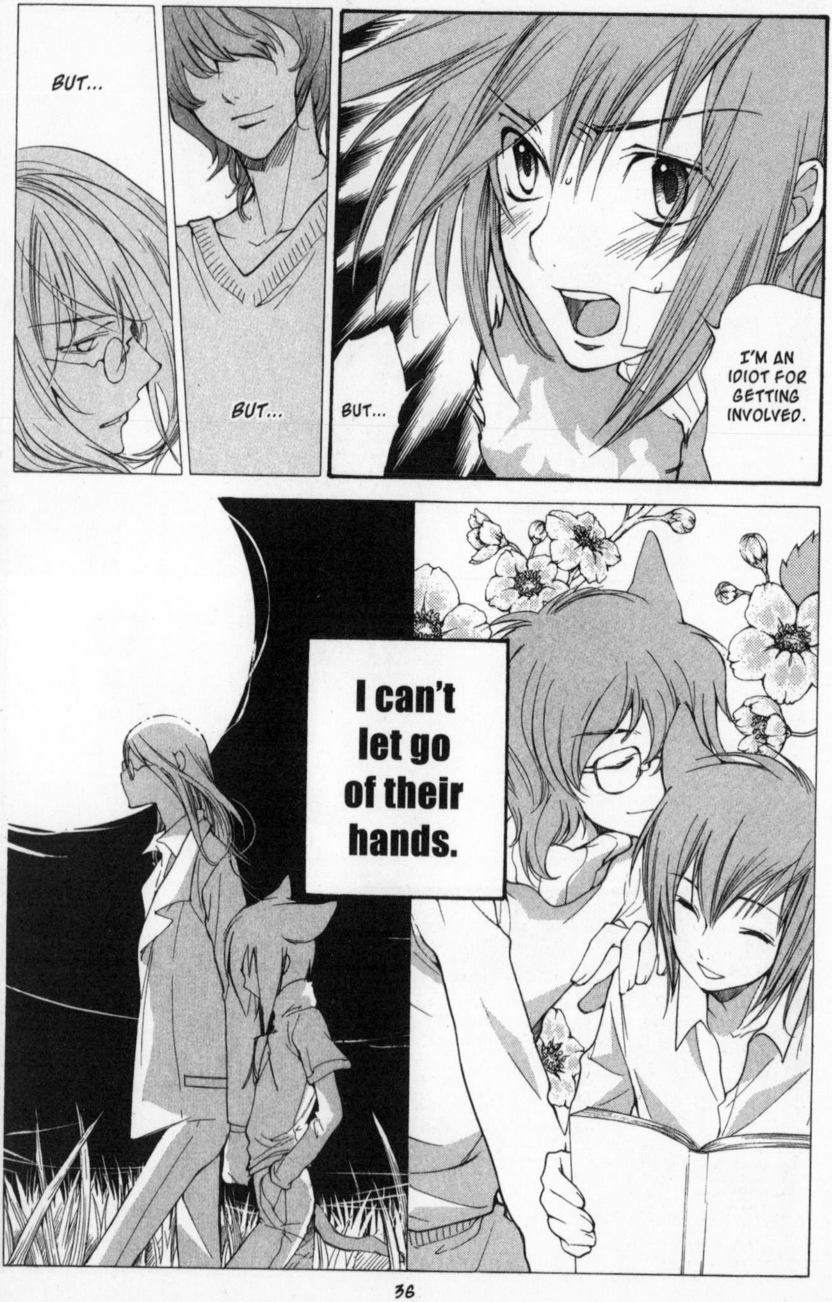
I'M AN IDIOT FOR GETTING INVOLVED.
BUT...
BUT...
BUT...
I can't let go of their hands.

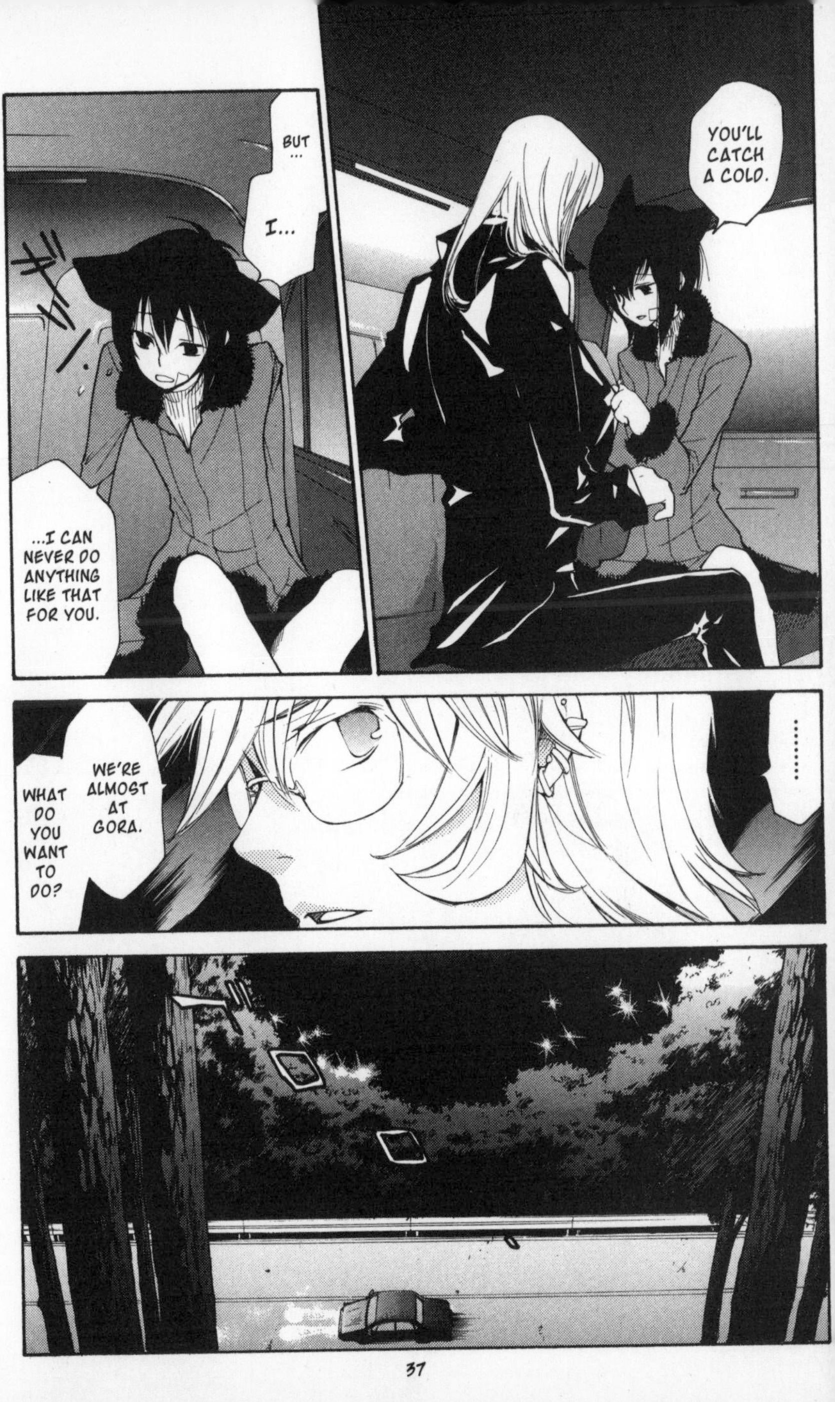
YOU'LL CATCH A COLD.
BUT ...
I...
...I CAN NEVER DO ANYTHING LIKE THAT FOR YOU.
......
WE'RE ALMOST AT GORA.
WHAT DO YOU WANT TO DO?

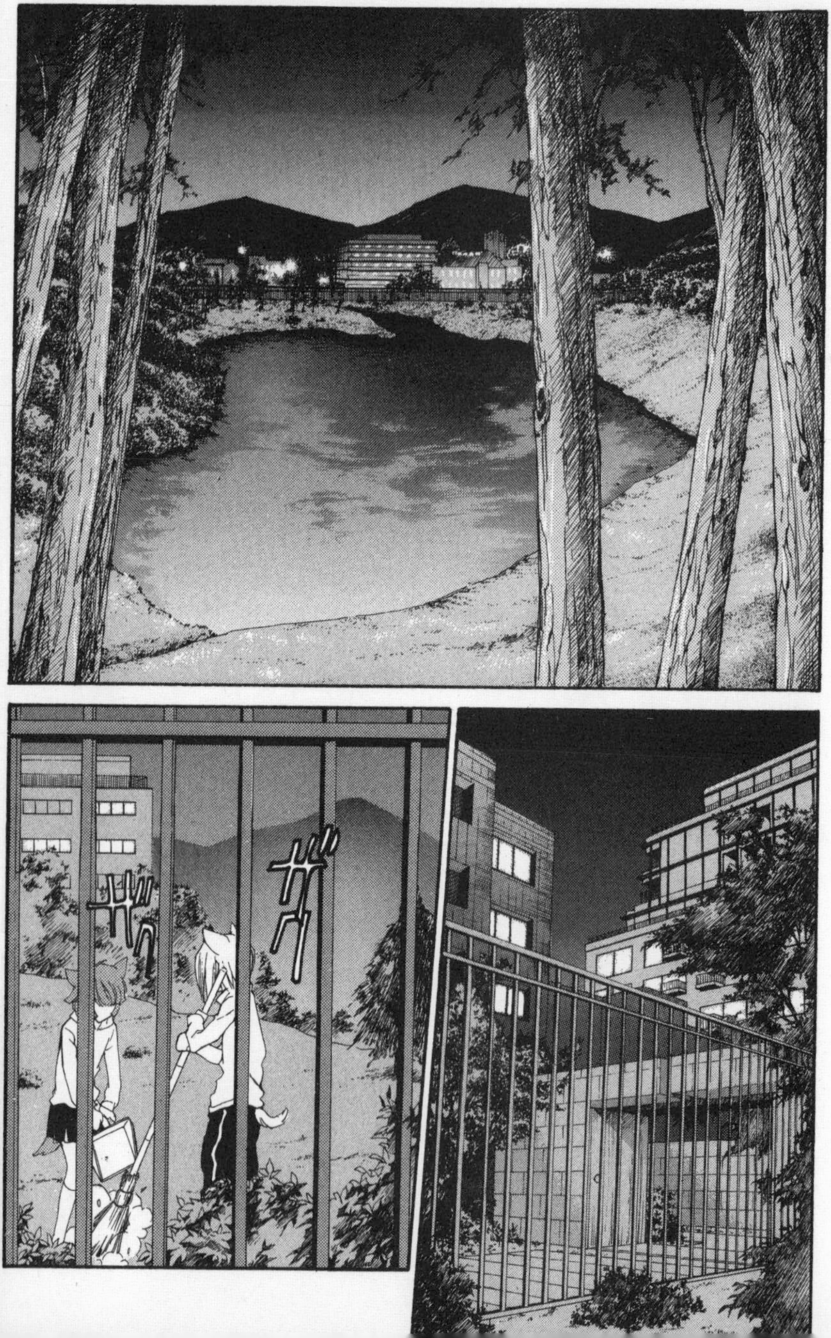
ザッ
ザッ

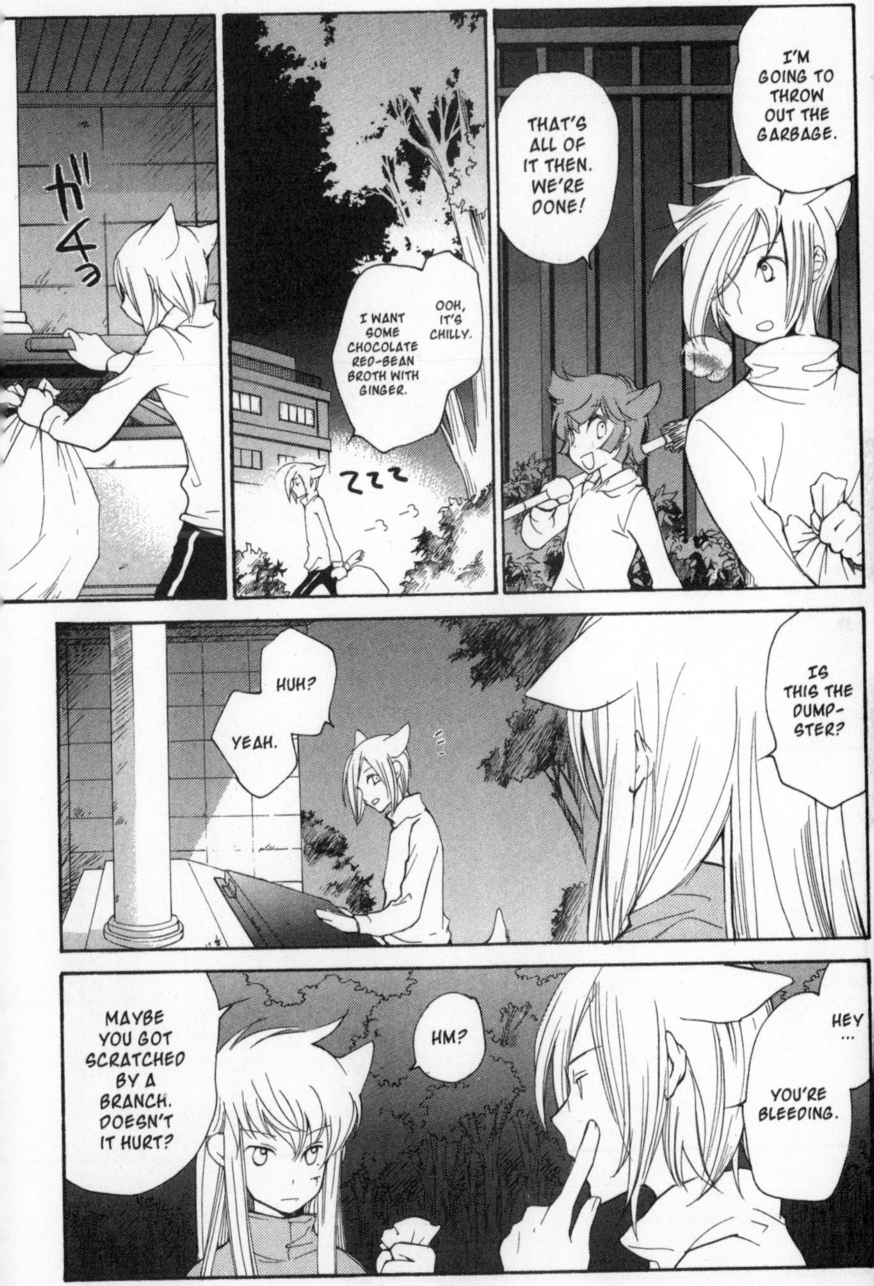
I'M GOING TO THROW OUT THE GARBAGE.
THAT'S ALL OF IT THEN. WE'RE DONE!
OOH, IT'S CHILLY.
I WANT SOME CHOCOLATE RED-BEAN BROTH WITH GINGER.
ガチョ
IS THIS THE DUMP-STER?
HUH?
YEAH.
HEY ...
YOU'RE BLEEDING.
HM?
MAYBE YOU GOT SCRATCHED BY A BRANCH. DOESN'T IT HURT?

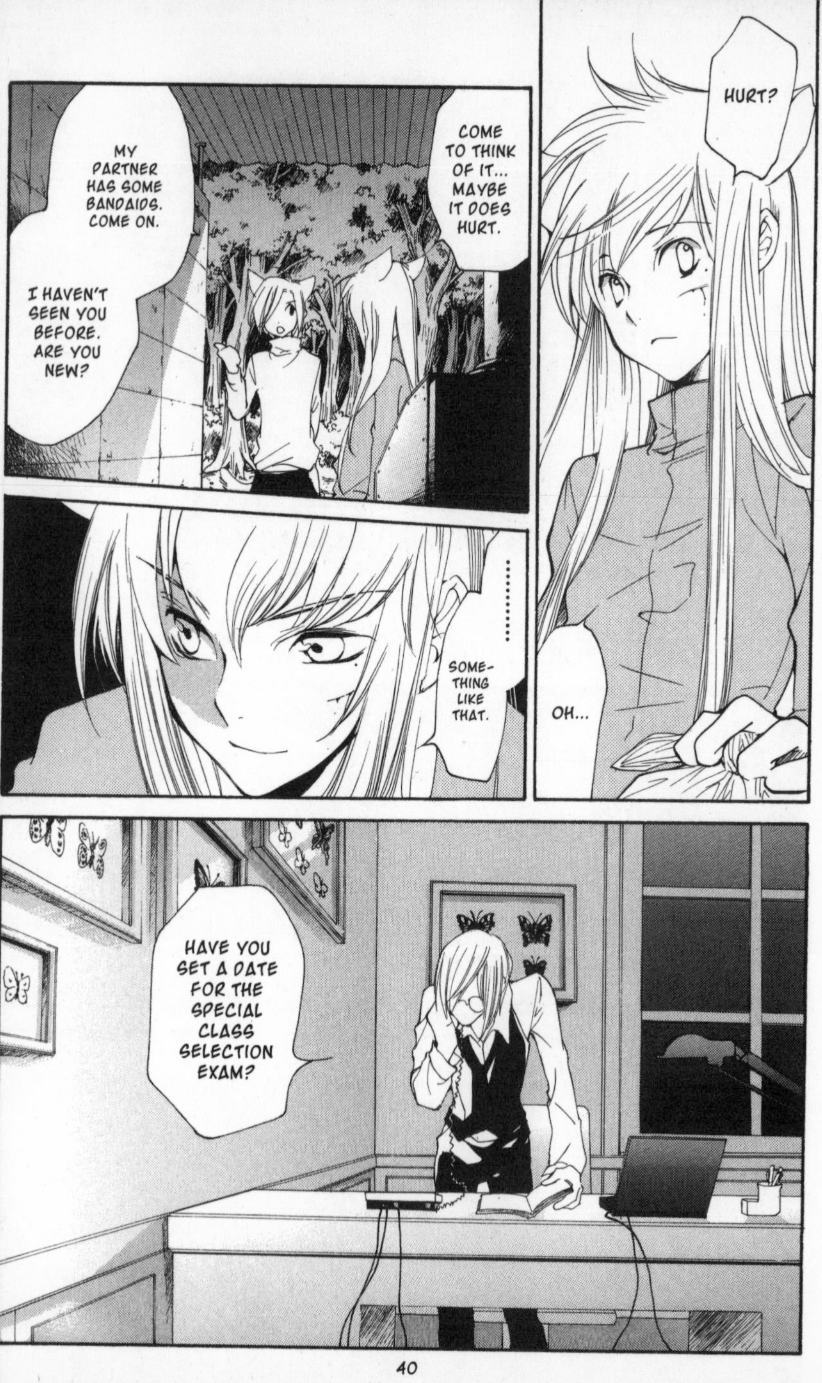
HURT?
OH...
COME TO THINK OF IT... MAYBE IT DOES HURT.
MY PARTNER HAS SOME BANDAIDS. COME ON.
I HAVEN'T SEEN YOU BEFORE. ARE YOU NEW?
....
SOME-THING LIKE THAT.
HAVE YOU SET A DATE FOR THE SPECIAL CLASS SELECTION EXAM?

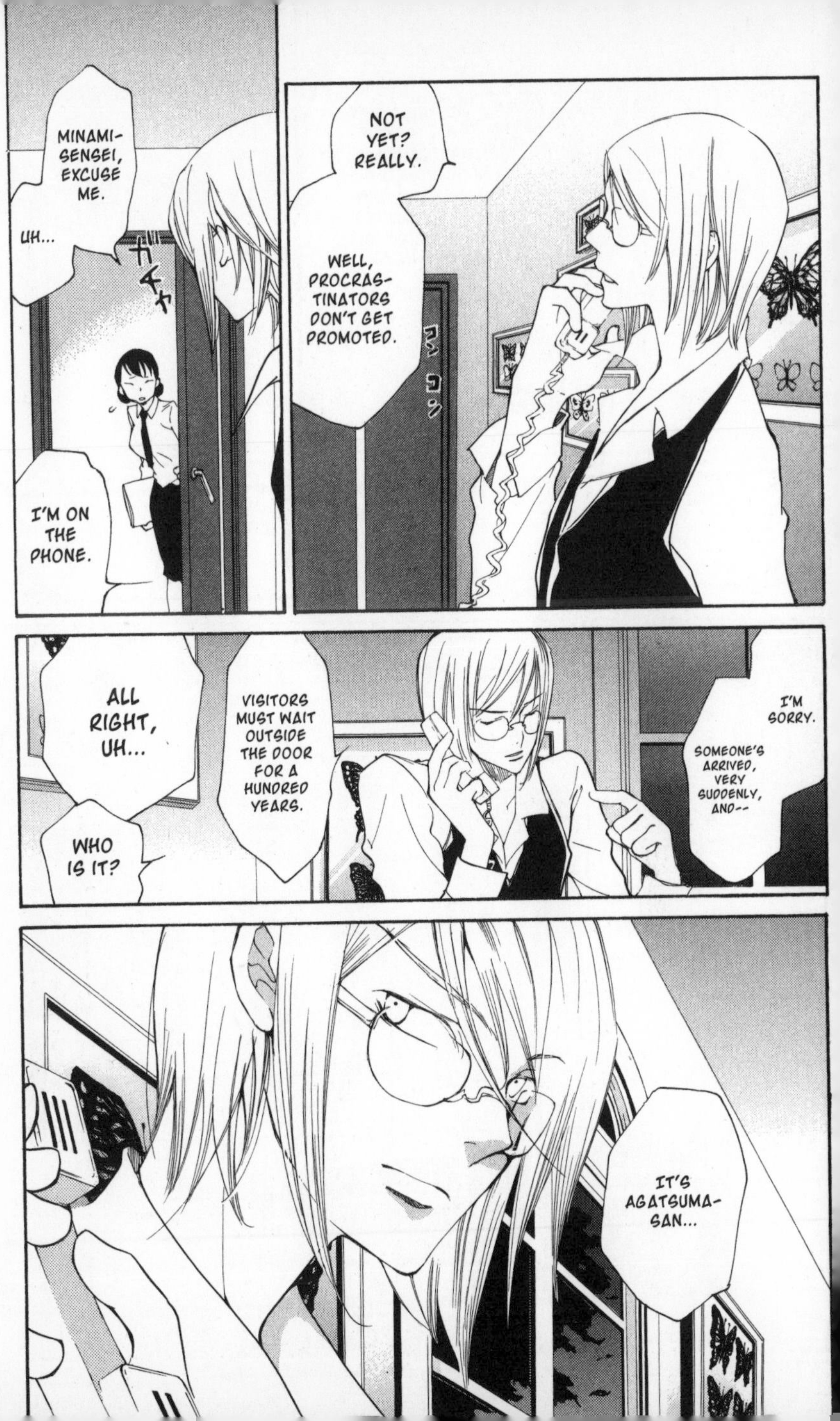
NOT YET? REALLY.
WELL, PROCRAS-TINATORS DON'T GET PROMOTED.
MINAMI-SENSEI, EXCUSE ME.
UH...
I'M ON THE PHONE.
I'M SORRY.
SOMEONE'S ARRIVED, VERY SUDDENLY, AND--
VISITORS MUST WAIT OUTSIDE THE DOOR FOR A HUNDRED YEARS.
ALL RIGHT, UH...
WHO IS IT?
IT'S AGATSUMA-SAN...

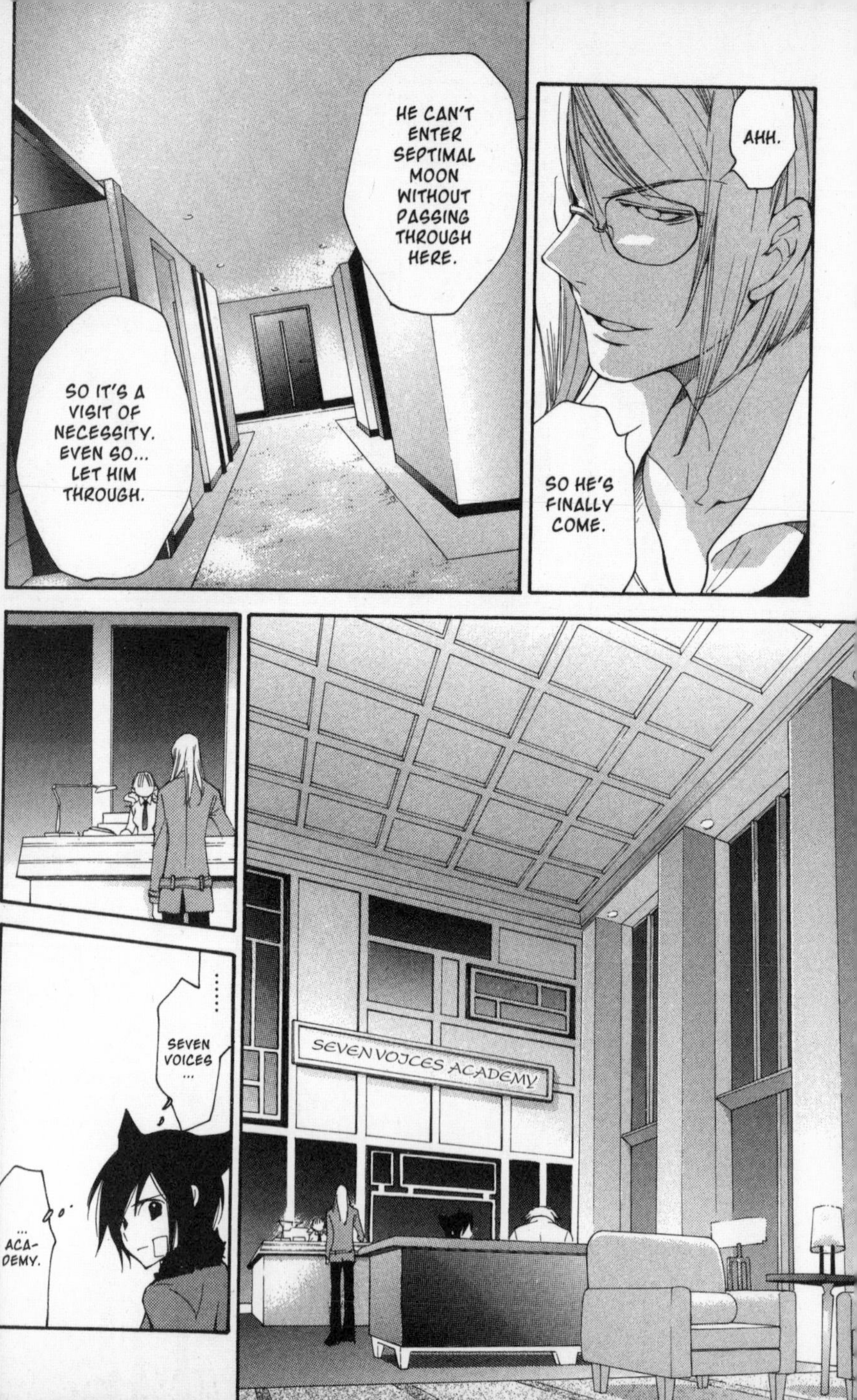
AHH.
SO HE'S FINALLY COME.
HE CAN'T ENTER SEPTIMAL MOON WITHOUT PASSING THROUGH HERE.
SO IT'S A VISIT OF NECESSITY. EVEN SO... LET HIM THROUGH.
SEVEN VOICES ACADEMY
......
SEVEN VOICES ...
... ACA-DEMY.

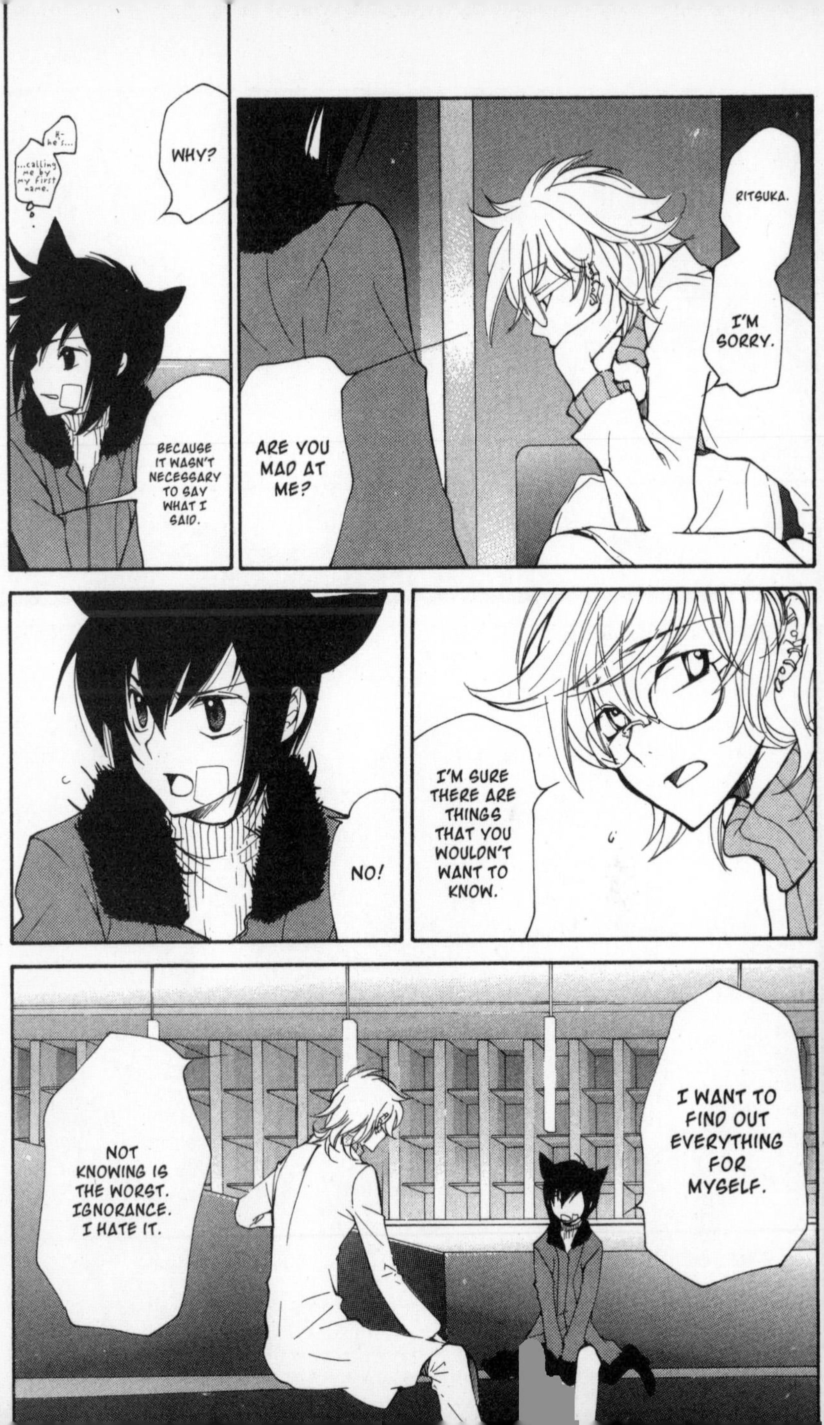
RITSUKA.
I'M SORRY.
WHY?
ARE YOU MAD AT ME?
H-he's...
...calling me by my first name.
BECAUSE IT WASN'T NECESSARY TO SAY WHAT I SAID.
I'M SURE THERE ARE THINGS THAT YOU WOULDN'T WANT TO KNOW.
NO!
I WANT TO FIND OUT EVERYTHING FOR MYSELF.
NOT KNOWING IS THE WORST. IGNORANCE. I HATE IT.

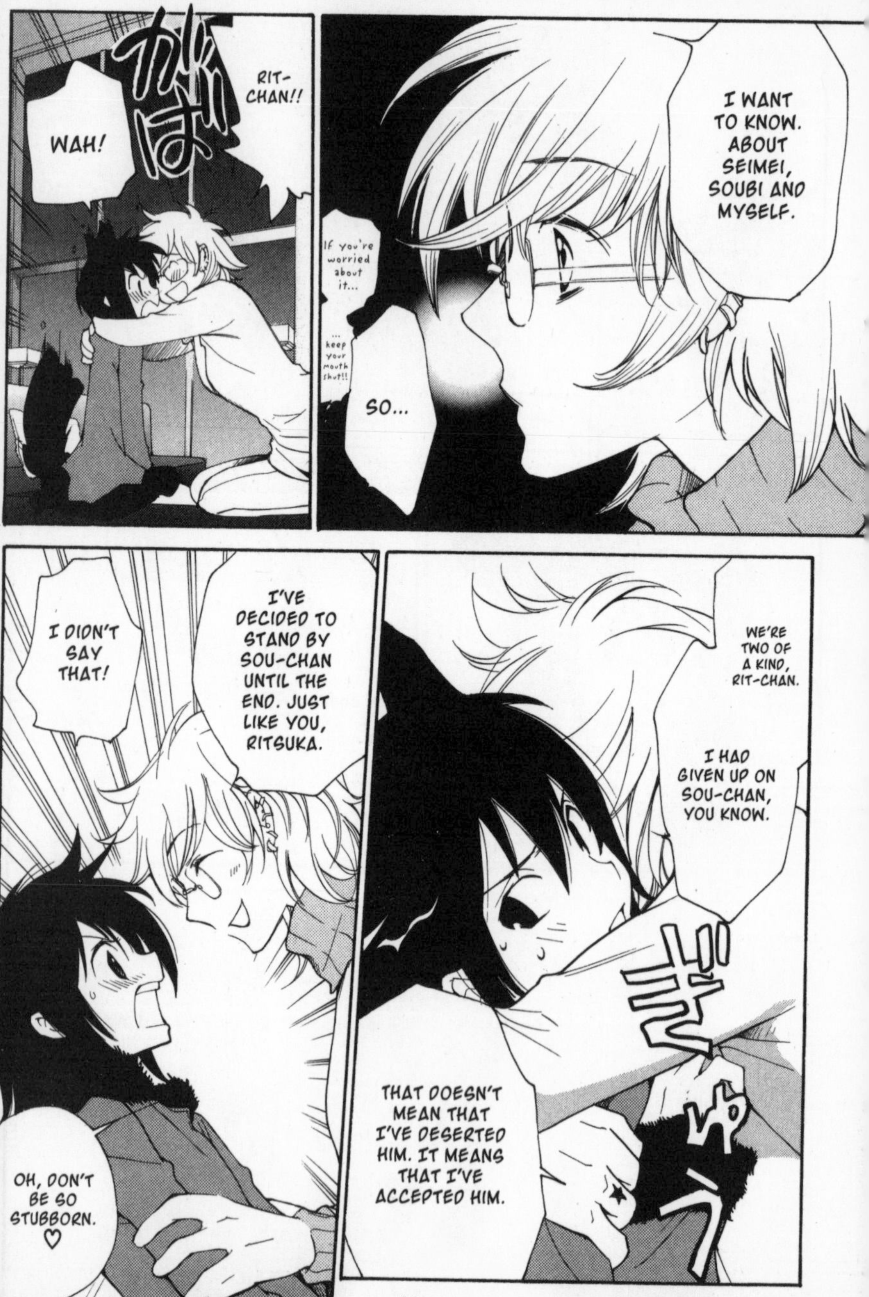

I WANT TO KNOW. ABOUT SEIMEI, SOUBI AND MYSELF.
If you're worried about it...
...keep your mouth shut!!
SO...
RIT-CHAN!!
かばっ
WAH!
WE'RE TWO OF A KIND, RIT-CHAN.
I HAD GIVEN UP ON SOU-CHAN, YOU KNOW.
ぎゅう
THAT DOESN'T MEAN THAT I'VE DESERTED HIM. IT MEANS THAT I'VE ACCEPTED HIM.
I'VE DECIDED TO STAND BY SOU-CHAN UNTIL THE END. JUST LIKE YOU, RITSUKA.
I DIDN'T SAY THAT!
OH, DON'T BE SO STUBBORN. ♡

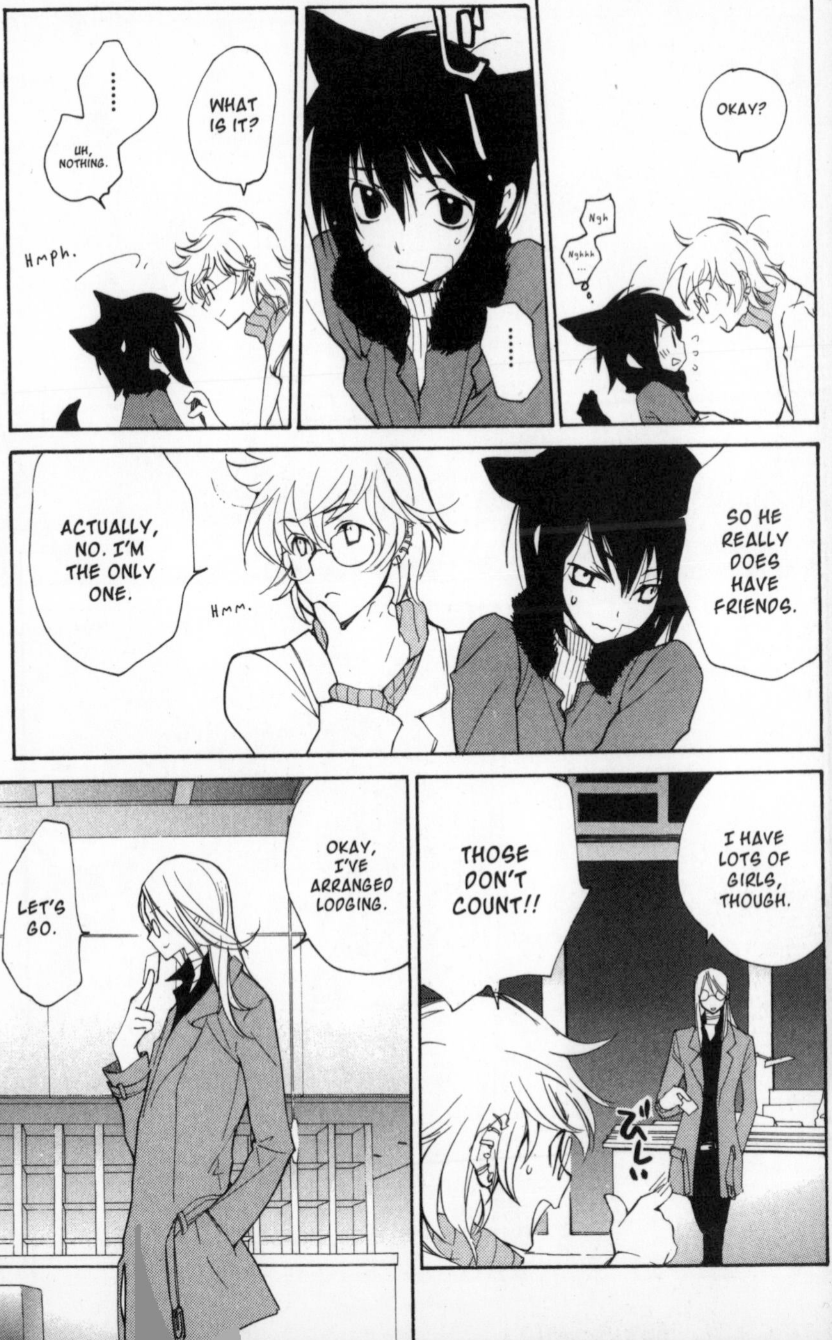
OKAY?
Ngh
Nghhh ...
......
WHAT IS IT?
......
UH, NOTHING.
Hmph.
SO HE REALLY DOES HAVE FRIENDS.
ACTUALLY, NO. I'M THE ONLY ONE.
Hmm.
I HAVE LOTS OF GIRLS, THOUGH.
THOSE DON'T COUNT!!
びしぃ
OKAY, I'VE ARRANGED LODGING.
LET'S GO.

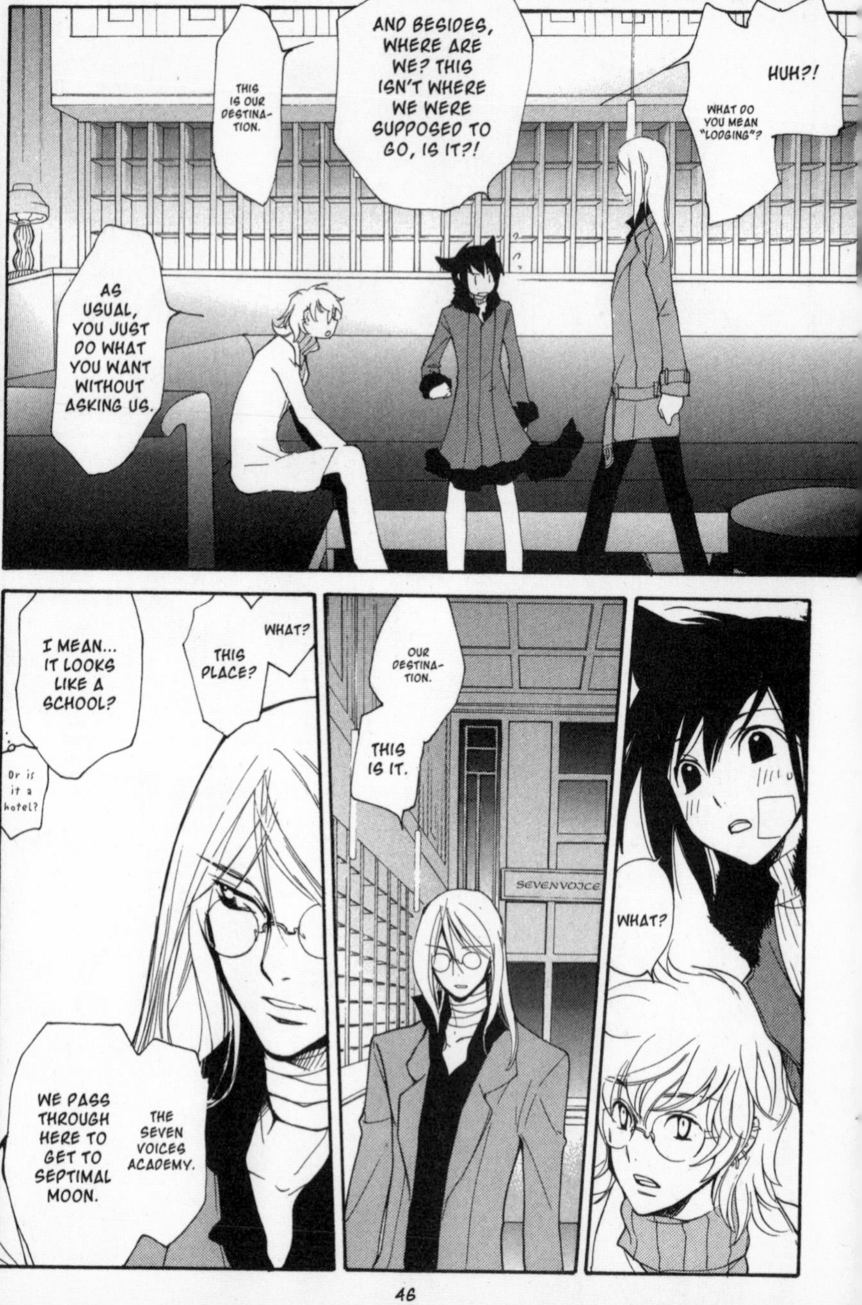
HUH?!
WHAT DO YOU MEAN "LODGING"?
AND BESIDES, WHERE ARE WE? THIS ISN'T WHERE WE WERE SUPPOSED TO GO, IS IT?!
THIS IS OUR DESTINATION.
AS USUAL, YOU JUST DO WHAT YOU WANT WITHOUT ASKING US.
WHAT?
OUR DESTINATION.
THIS IS IT.
SEVENVOICE
WHAT?
THIS PLACE?
I MEAN... IT LOOKS LIKE A SCHOOL?
Or is it a hotel?
THE SEVEN VOICES ACADEMY.
WE PASS THROUGH HERE TO GET TO SEPTIMAL MOON.

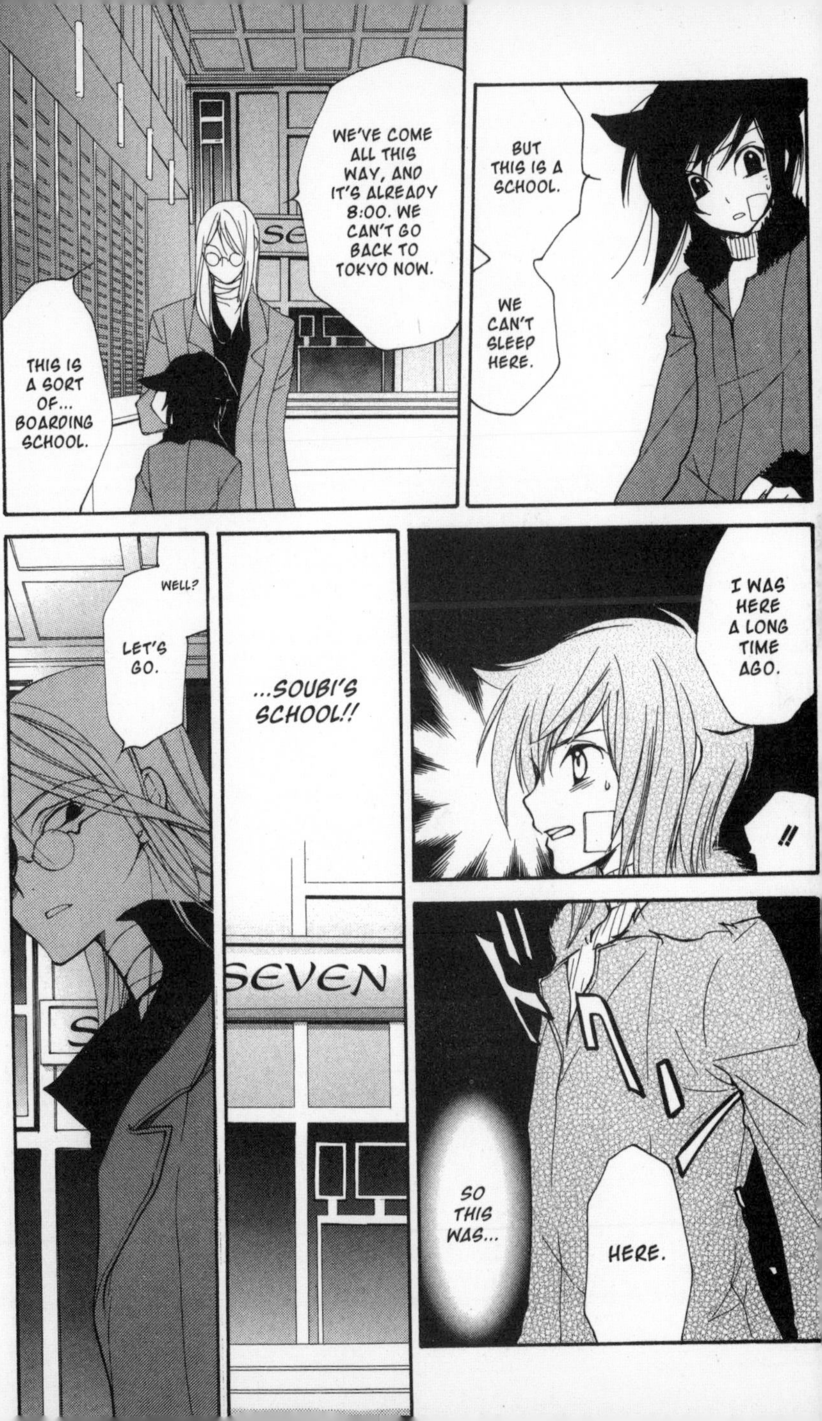
BUT THIS IS A SCHOOL.
WE CAN'T SLEEP HERE.
WE'VE COME ALL THIS WAY, AND IT'S ALREADY 8:00. WE CAN'T GO BACK TO TOKYO NOW.
THIS IS A SORT OF... BOARDING SCHOOL.
I WAS HERE A LONG TIME AGO.
!!
SO THIS WAS...
HERE.
...SOUBI'S SCHOOL!!
SEVEN
WELL?
LET'S GO.

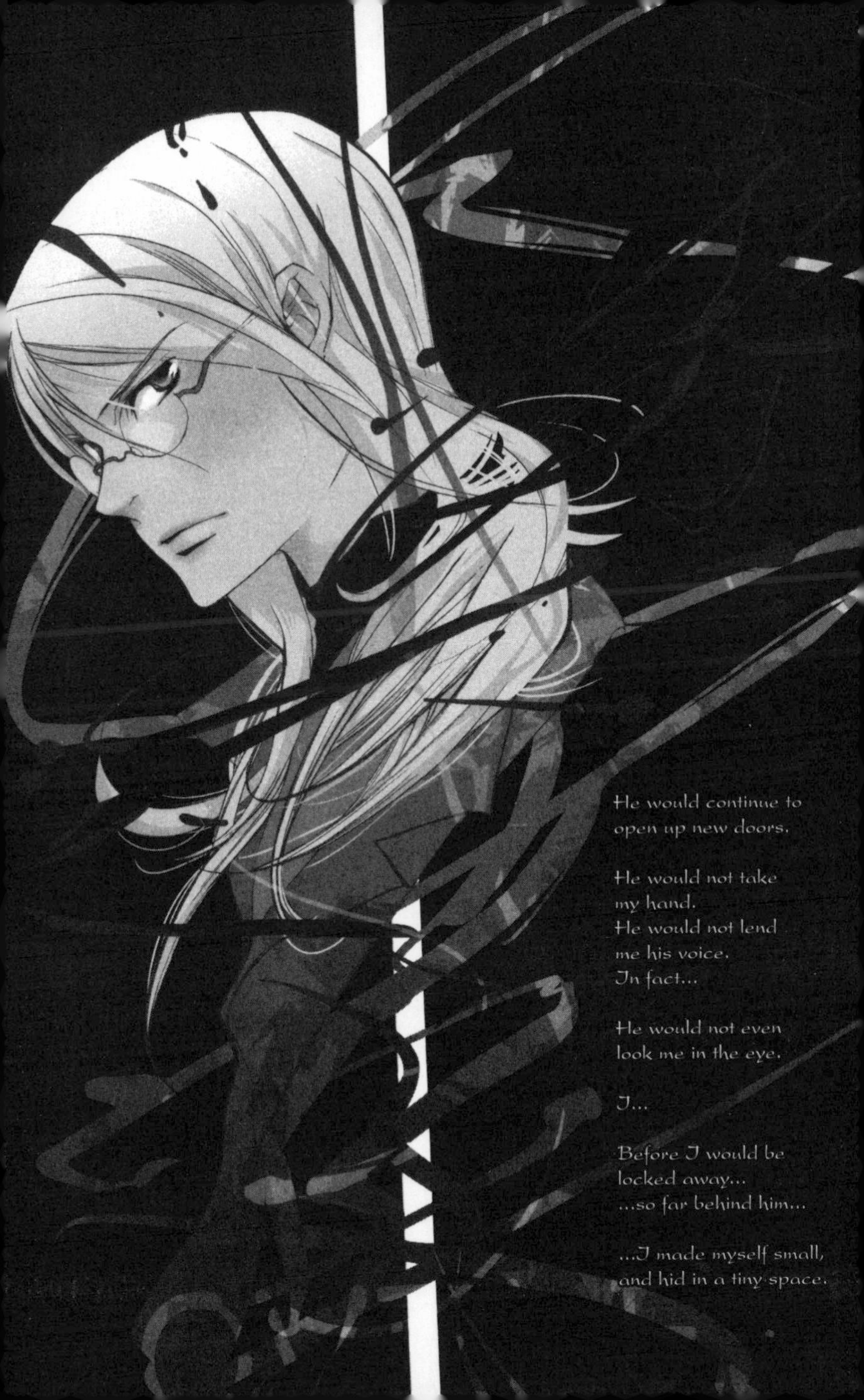
He would continue to open up new doors.
He would not take my hand.
He would not lend me his voice.
In fact...
He would not even look me in the eye.
I...
Before I would be locked away...
...so far behind him...
...I made myself small, and hid in a tiny space.

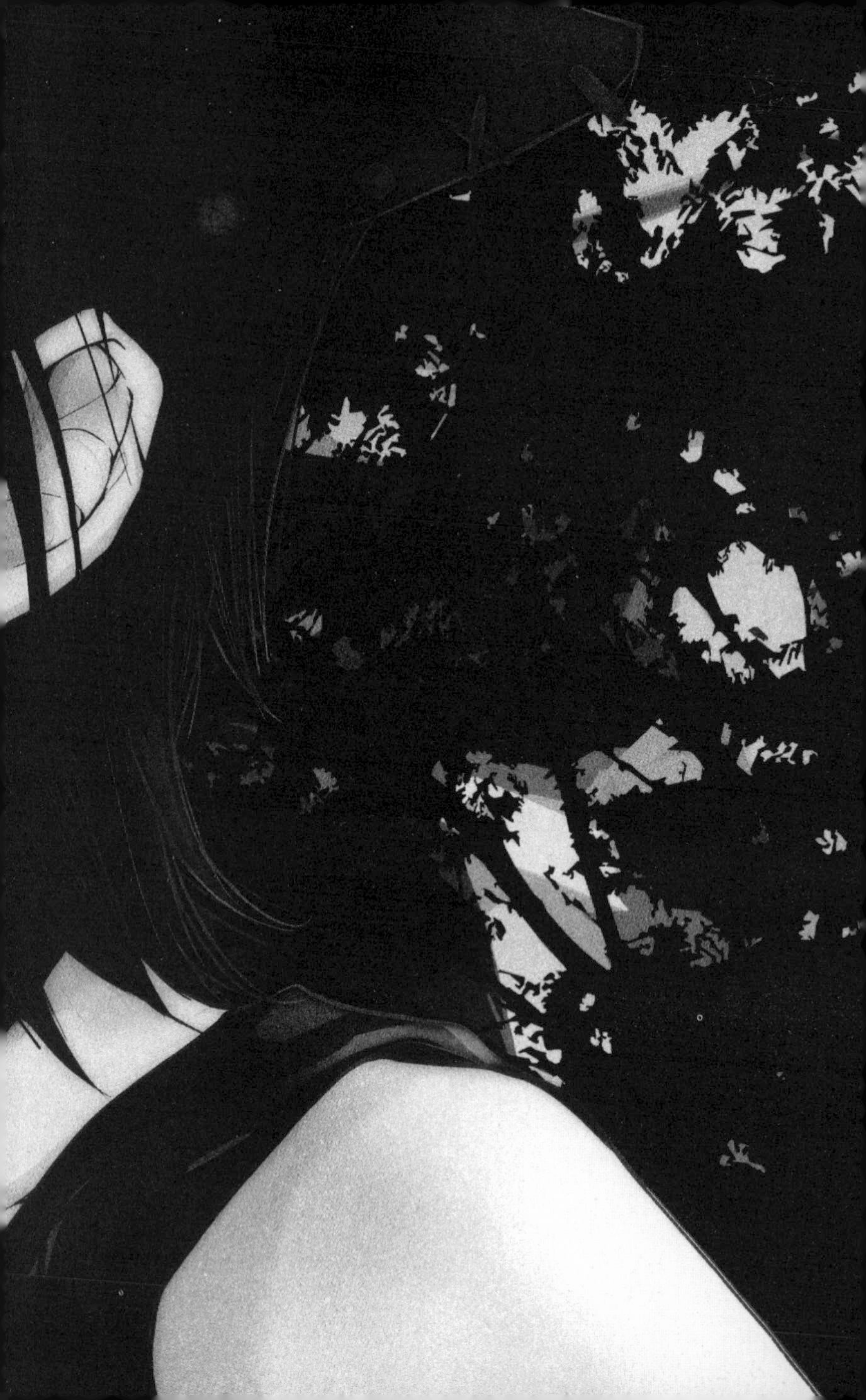

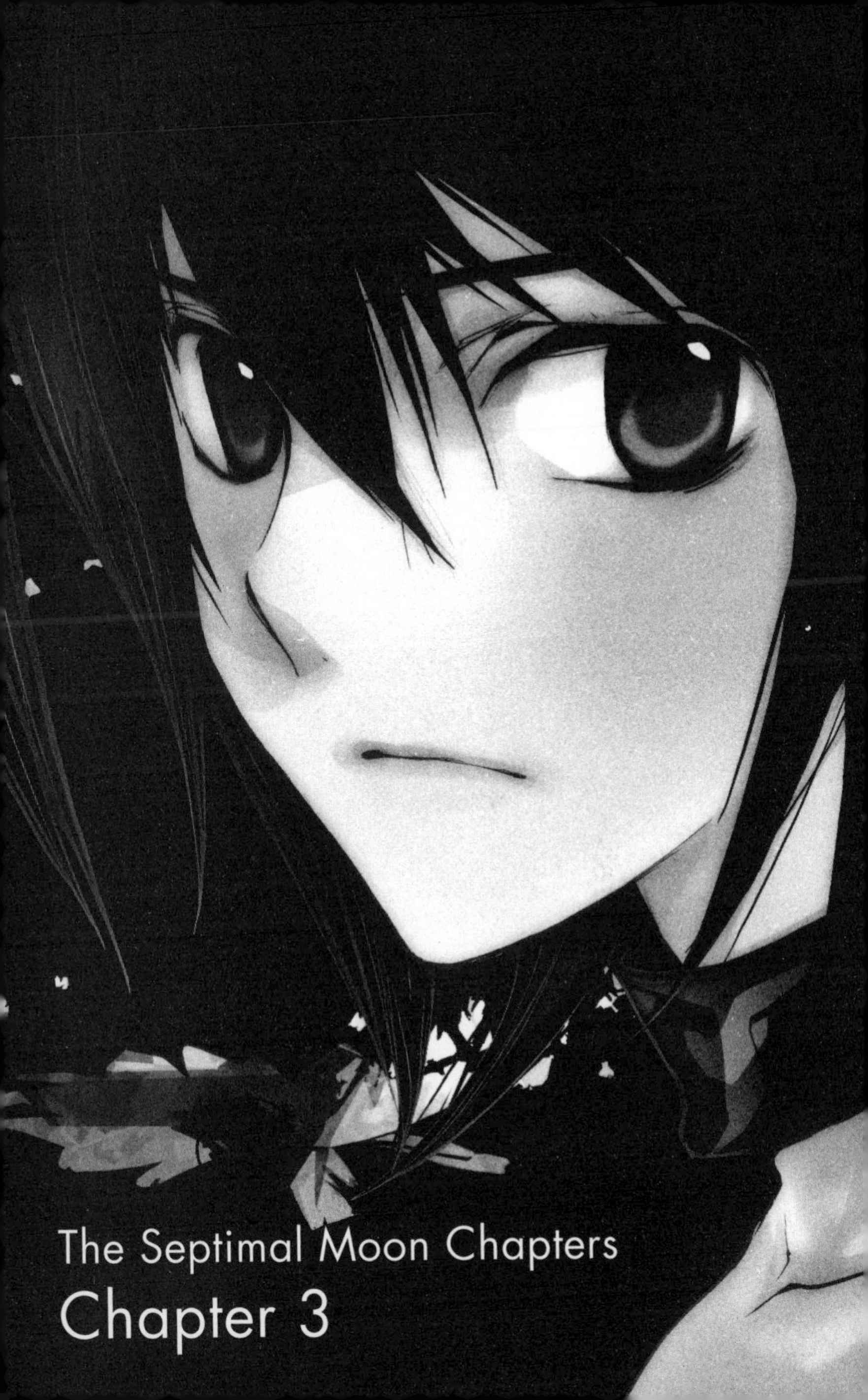

The Septimal Moon Chapters
Chapter 3

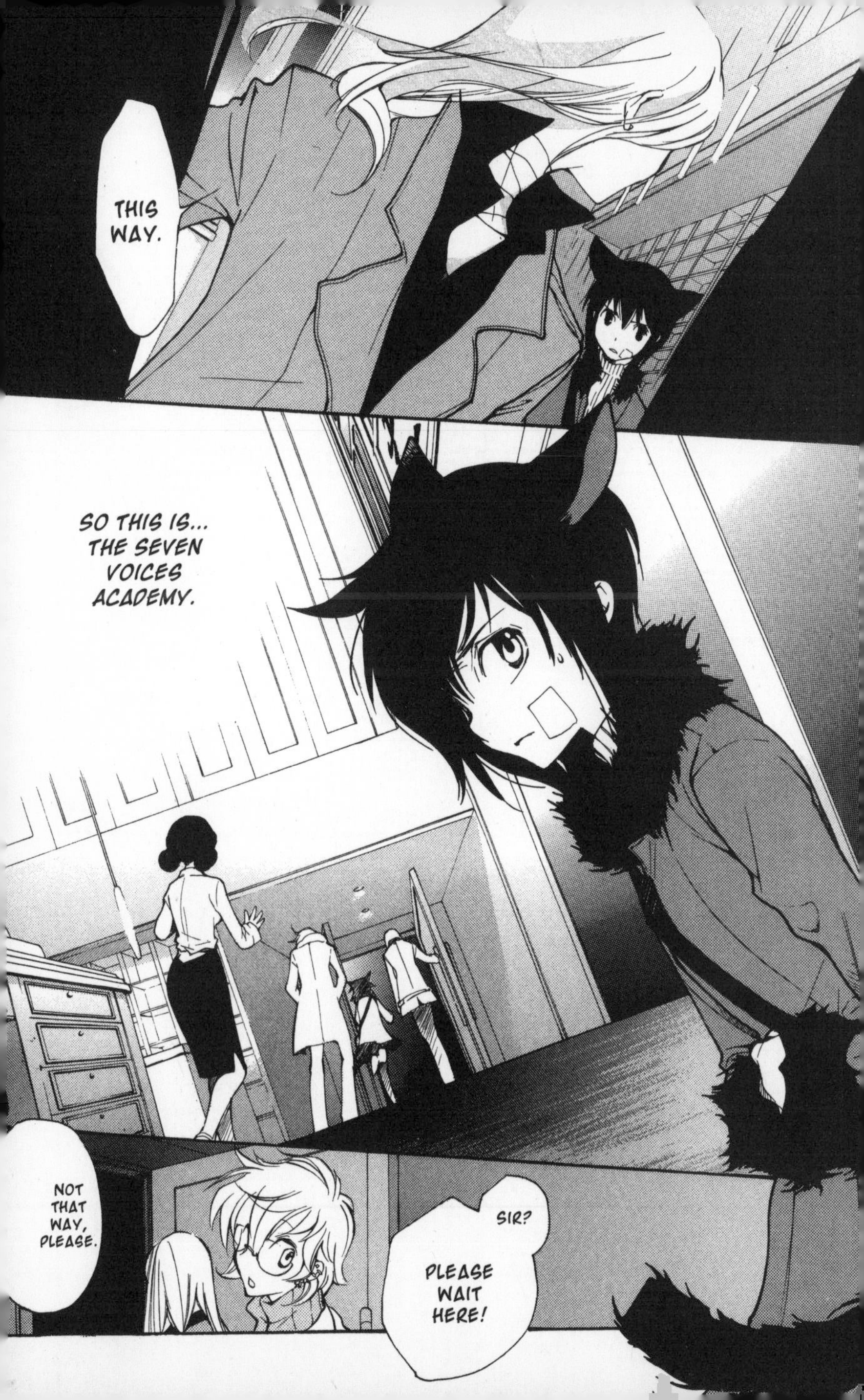

THIS WAY.
SO THIS IS... THE SEVEN VOICES ACADEMY.
SIR?
PLEASE WAIT HERE!
NOT THAT WAY, PLEASE.

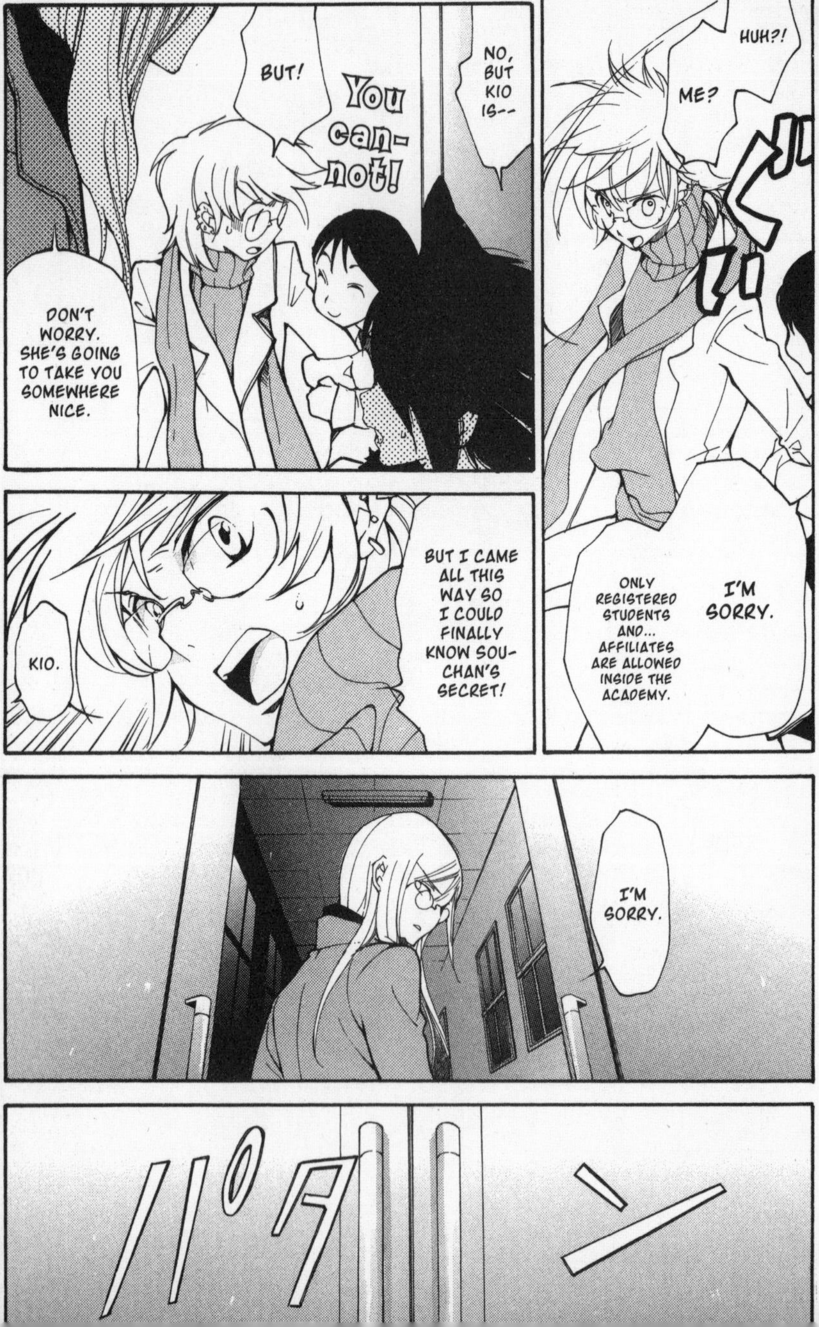
HUH?!
ME?
I'M SORRY.
ONLY REGISTERED STUDENTS AND... AFFILIATES ARE ALLOWED INSIDE THE ACADEMY.
NO, BUT KIO IS--
You cannot!
BUT!
DON'T WORRY. SHE'S GOING TO TAKE YOU SOMEWHERE NICE.
BUT I CAME ALL THIS WAY SO I COULD FINALLY KNOW SOU-CHAN'S SECRET!
KIO.
I'M SORRY.
パタン

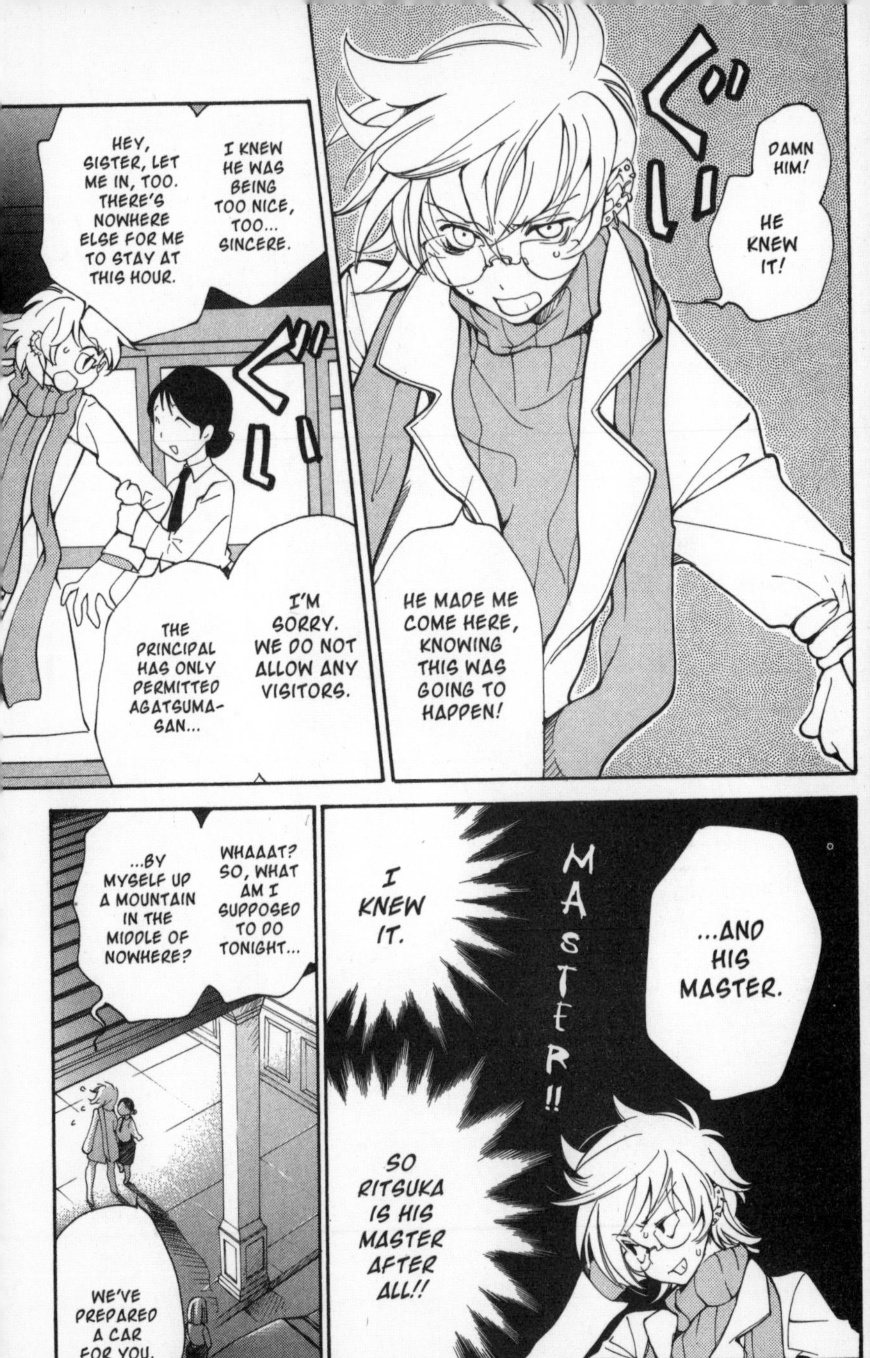
DAMN HIM!
HE KNEW IT!
HE MADE ME COME HERE, KNOWING THIS WAS GOING TO HAPPEN!
I KNEW HE WAS BEING TOO NICE, TOO... SINCERE.
HEY, SISTER, LET ME IN, TOO. THERE'S NOWHERE ELSE FOR ME TO STAY AT THIS HOUR.
I'M SORRY. WE DO NOT ALLOW ANY VISITORS.
THE PRINCIPAL HAS ONLY PERMITTED AGATSUMA-SAN...
...AND HIS MASTER.
MASTER!!
I KNEW IT.
SO RITSUKA IS HIS MASTER AFTER ALL!!
WHAAAT? SO, WHAT AM I SUPPOSED TO DO TONIGHT...
...BY MYSELF UP A MOUNTAIN IN THE MIDDLE OF NOWHERE?
WE'VE PREPARED A CAR FOR YOU.

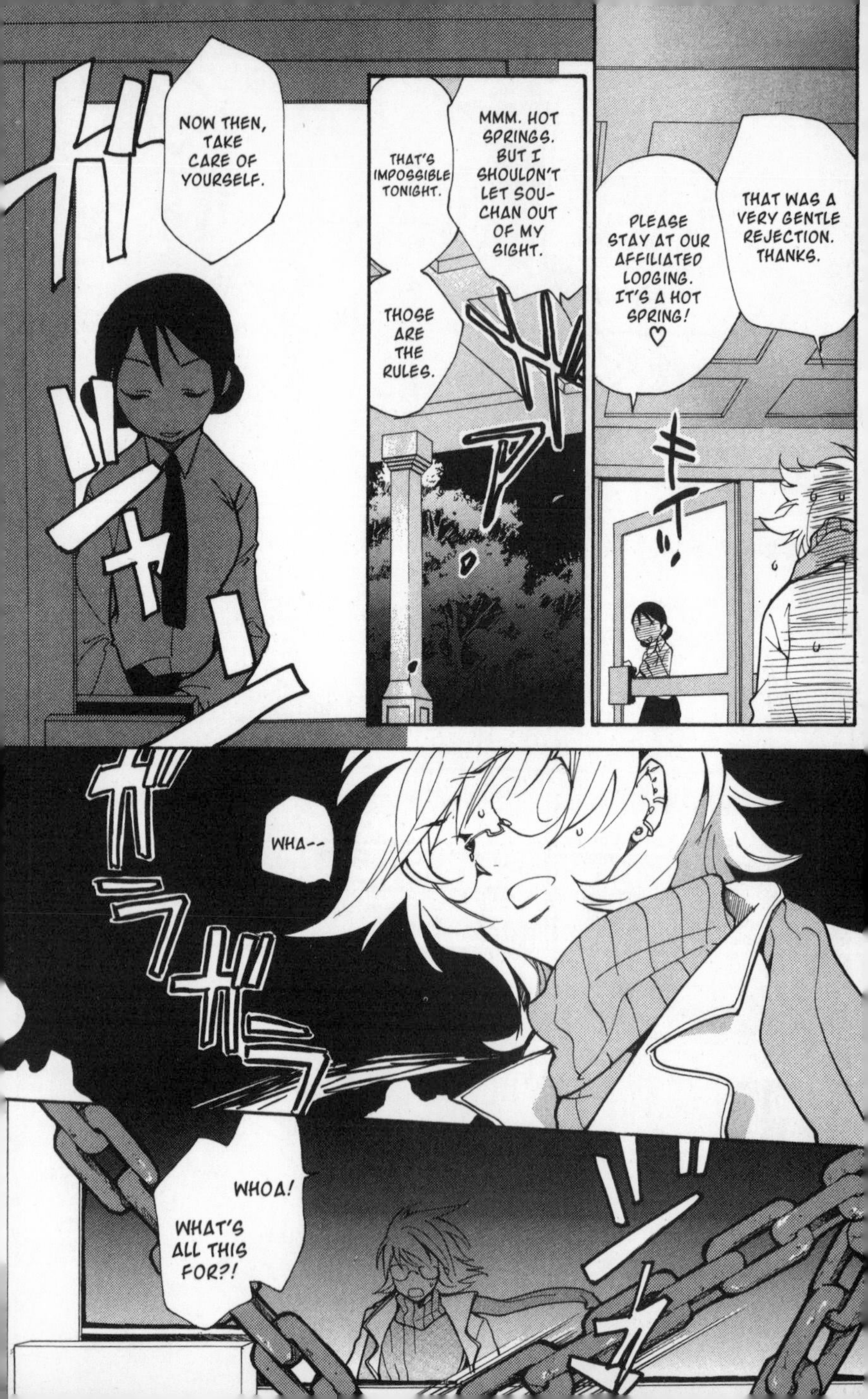
THAT WAS A VERY GENTLE REJECTION. THANKS.
PLEASE STAY AT OUR AFFILIATED LODGING. IT'S A HOT SPRING! ♡
MMM. HOT SPRINGS. BUT I SHOULDN'T LET SOU-CHAN OUT OF MY SIGHT.
THAT'S IMPOSSIBLE TONIGHT.
THOSE ARE THE RULES.
NOW THEN, TAKE CARE OF YOURSELF.
WHA--
WHOA!
WHAT'S ALL THIS FOR?!

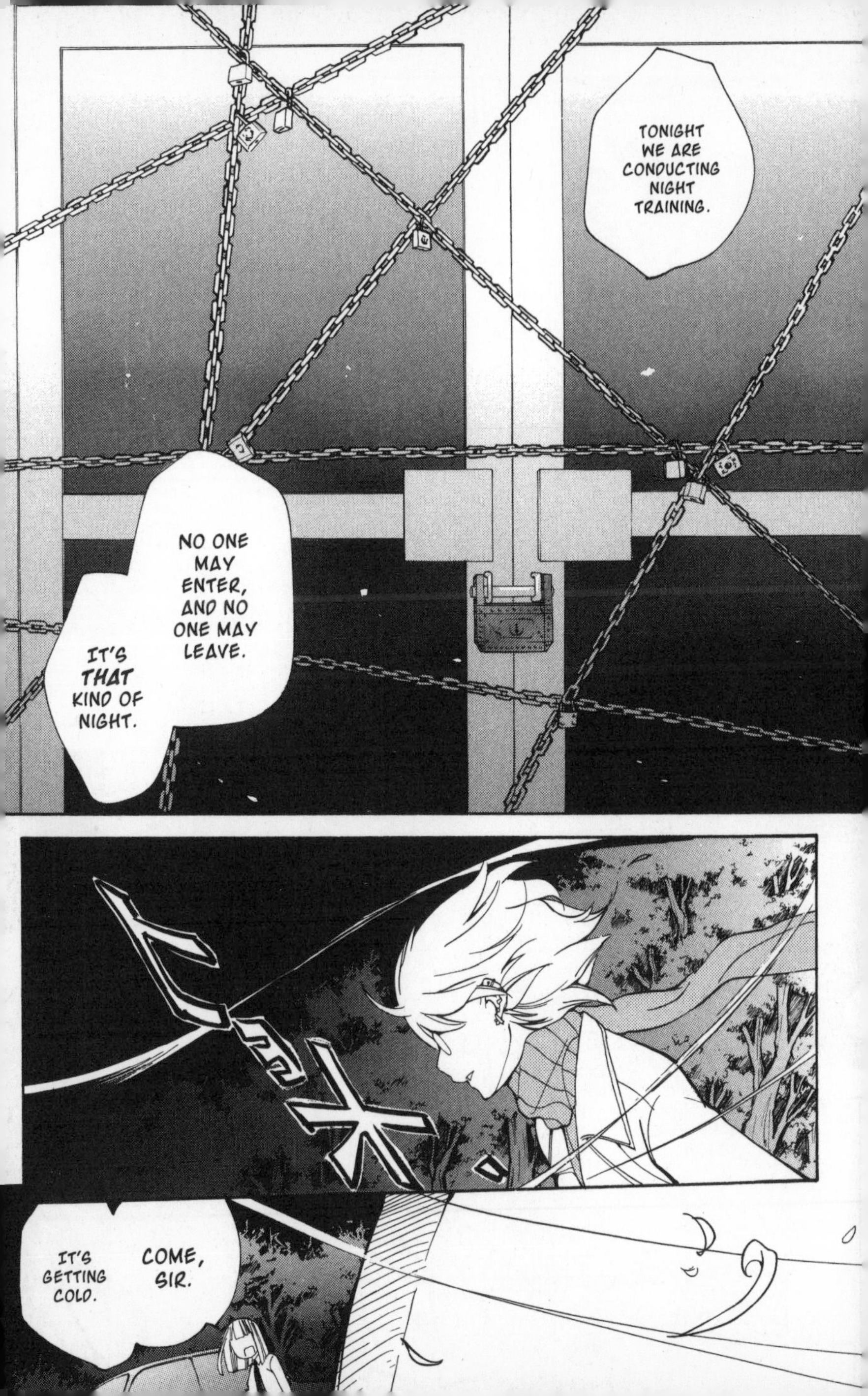
TONIGHT WE ARE CONDUCTING NIGHT TRAINING.
NO ONE MAY ENTER, AND NO ONE MAY LEAVE.
IT'S *THAT* KIND OF NIGHT.
COME, SIR.
IT'S GETTING COLD.

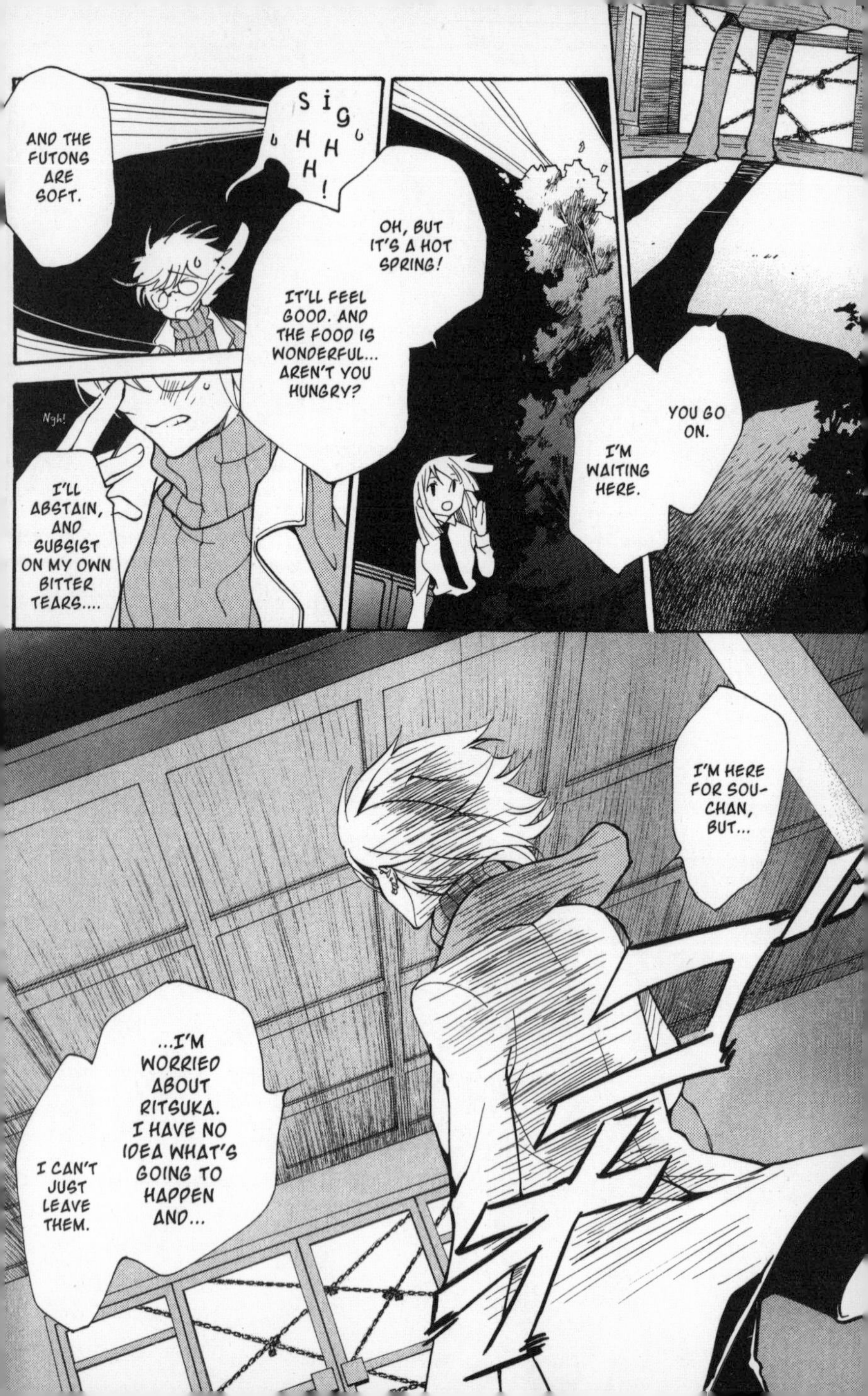
YOU GO ON.
I'M WAITING HERE.
OH, BUT IT'S A HOT SPRING!
IT'LL FEEL GOOD. AND THE FOOD IS WONDERFUL... AREN'T YOU HUNGRY?
SIGHHH!
AND THE FUTONS ARE SOFT.
Ngh!
I'LL ABSTAIN, AND SUBSIST ON MY OWN BITTER TEARS....
I'M HERE FOR SOU-CHAN, BUT...
...I'M WORRIED ABOUT RITSUKA. I HAVE NO IDEA WHAT'S GOING TO HAPPEN AND...
I CAN'T JUST LEAVE THEM.

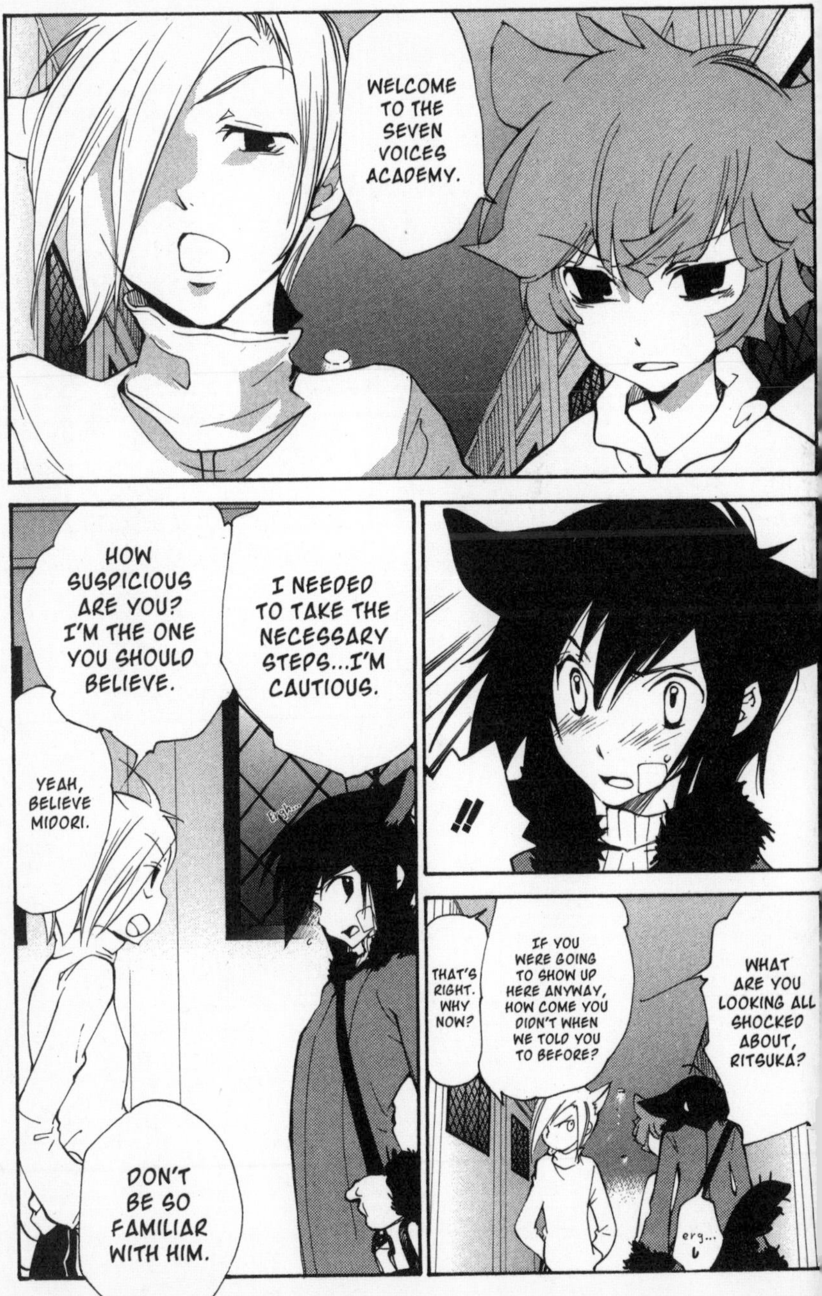
WELCOME TO THE SEVEN VOICES ACADEMY.
!!
WHAT ARE YOU LOOKING ALL SHOCKED ABOUT, RITSUKA?
IF YOU WERE GOING TO SHOW UP HERE ANYWAY, HOW COME YOU DIDN'T WHEN WE TOLD YOU TO BEFORE?
THAT'S RIGHT. WHY NOW?
erg...
I NEEDED TO TAKE THE NECESSARY STEPS...I'M CAUTIOUS.
HOW SUSPICIOUS ARE YOU? I'M THE ONE YOU SHOULD BELIEVE.
Ergh...
YEAH, BELIEVE MIDORI.
DON'T BE SO FAMILIAR WITH HIM.

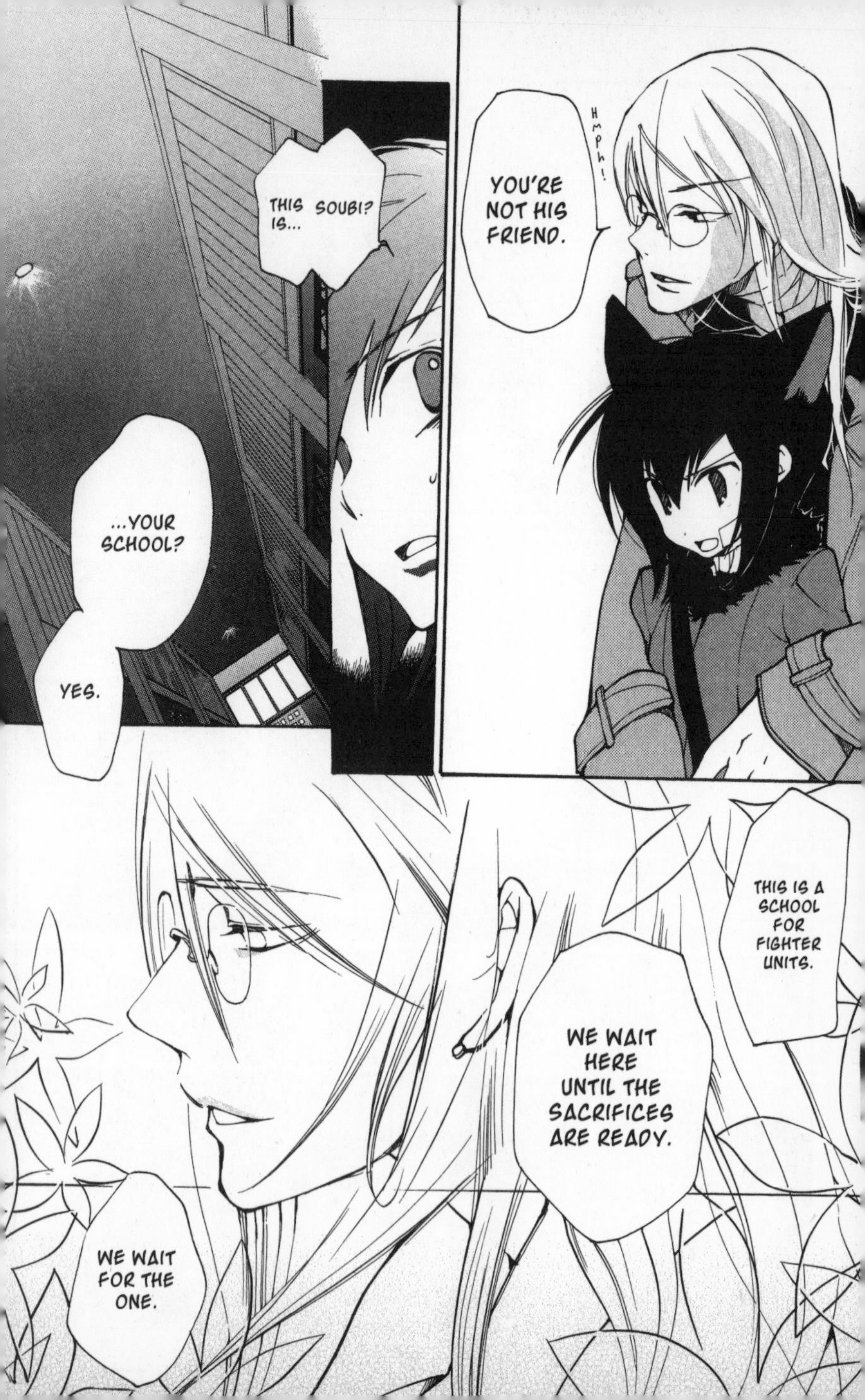

HMPH!
YOU'RE NOT HIS FRIEND.
SOUBI? THIS IS...
...YOUR SCHOOL?
YES.
THIS IS A SCHOOL FOR FIGHTER UNITS.
WE WAIT HERE UNTIL THE SACRIFICES ARE READY.
WE WAIT FOR THE ONE.

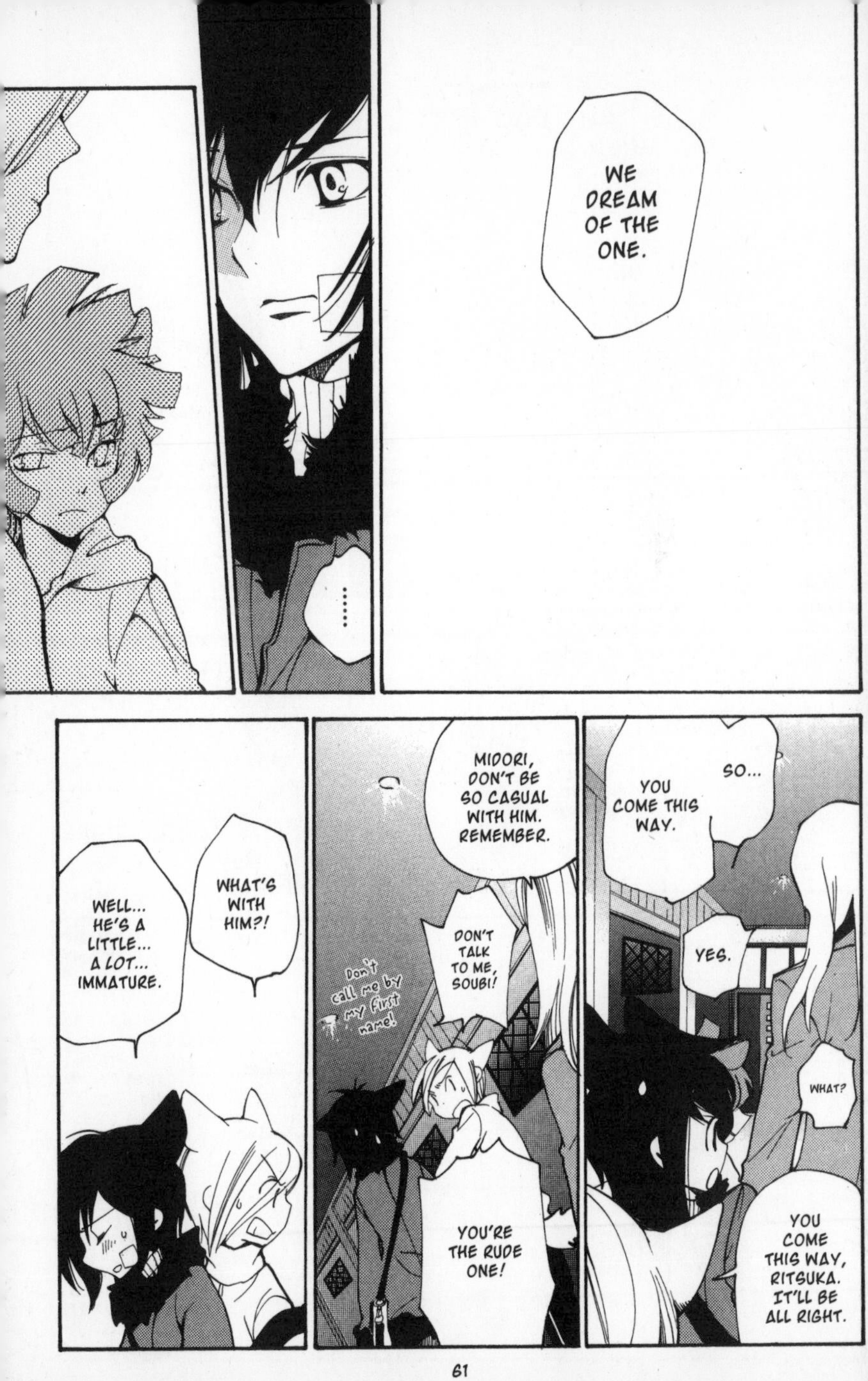

WE DREAM OF THE ONE.
......
SO...
YOU COME THIS WAY.
YES.
WHAT?
YOU COME THIS WAY, RITSUKA. IT'LL BE ALL RIGHT.
MIDORI, DON'T BE SO CASUAL WITH HIM. REMEMBER.
DON'T TALK TO ME, SOUBI!
Don't call me by my first name!
YOU'RE THE RUDE ONE!
WHAT'S WITH HIM?!
WELL... HE'S A LITTLE... A LOT... IMMATURE.

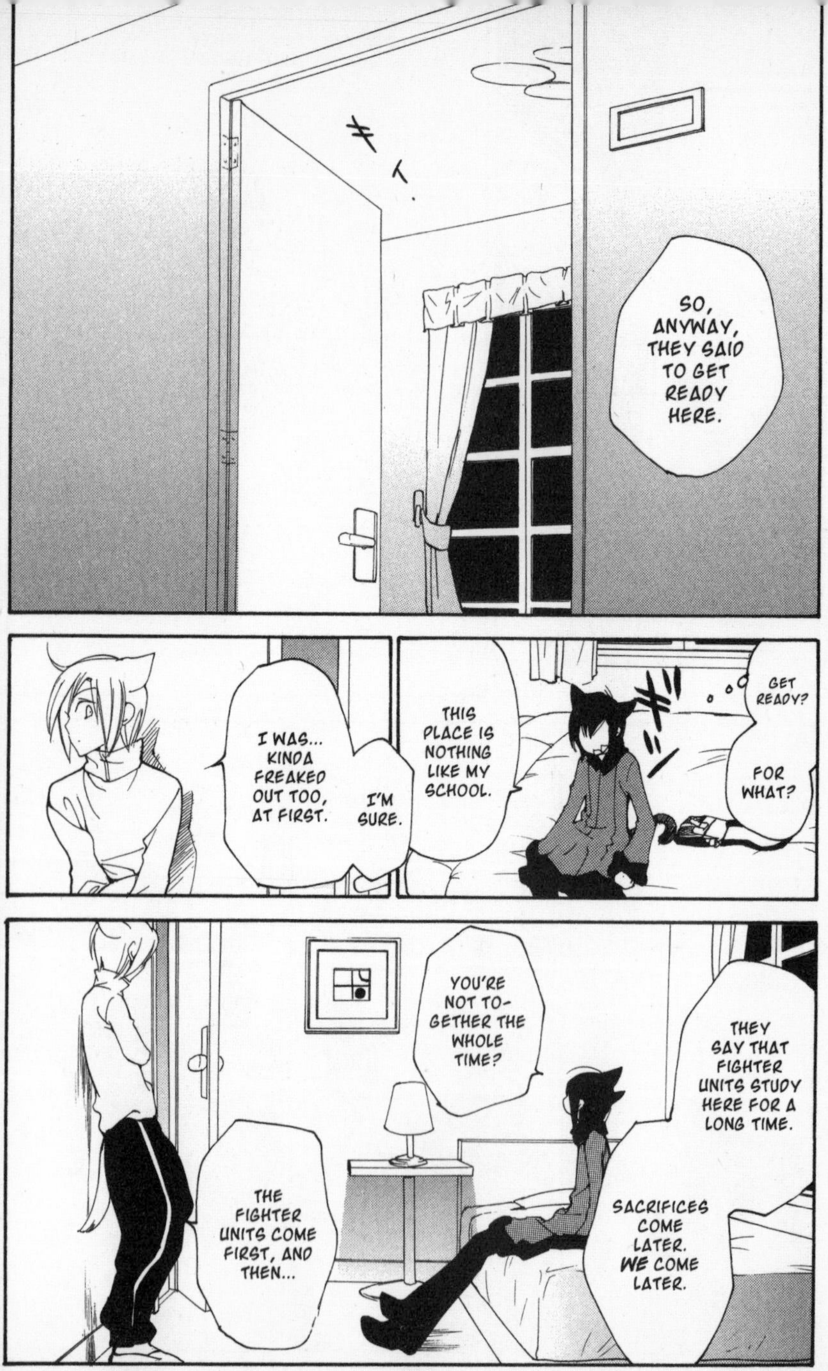
SO, ANYWAY, THEY SAID TO GET READY HERE.
GET READY?
FOR WHAT?
THIS PLACE IS NOTHING LIKE MY SCHOOL.
I'M SURE.
I WAS... KINDA FREAKED OUT TOO, AT FIRST.
THEY SAY THAT FIGHTER UNITS STUDY HERE FOR A LONG TIME.
YOU'RE NOT TO-GETHER THE WHOLE TIME?
SACRIFICES COME LATER. WE COME LATER.
THE FIGHTER UNITS COME FIRST, AND THEN...

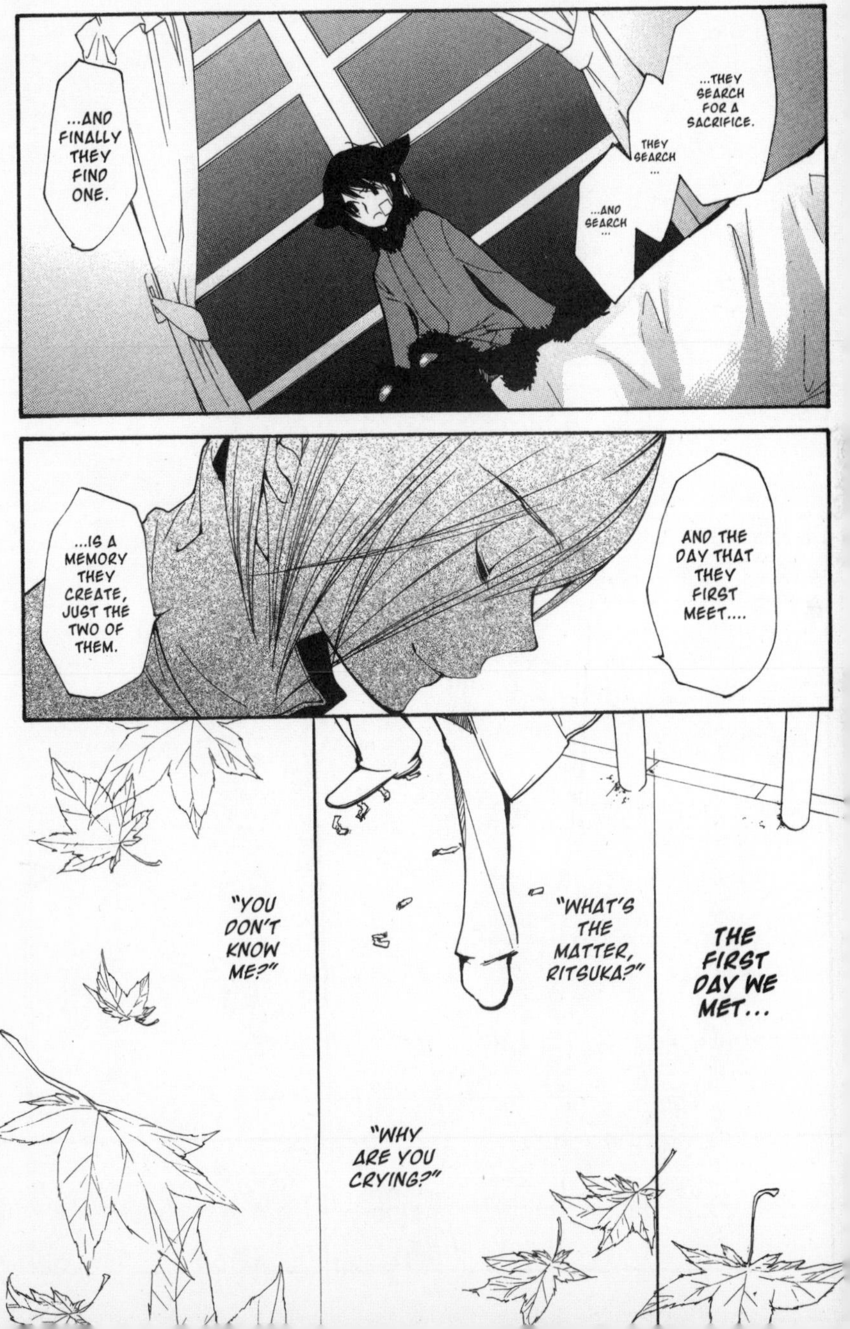
...THEY SEARCH FOR A SACRIFICE.
THEY SEARCH...
...AND SEARCH...
...AND FINALLY THEY FIND ONE.
AND THE DAY THAT THEY FIRST MEET....
...IS A MEMORY THEY CREATE, JUST THE TWO OF THEM.
THE FIRST DAY WE MET...
"WHAT'S THE MATTER, RITSUKA?"
"WHY ARE YOU CRYING?"
"YOU DON'T KNOW ME?"

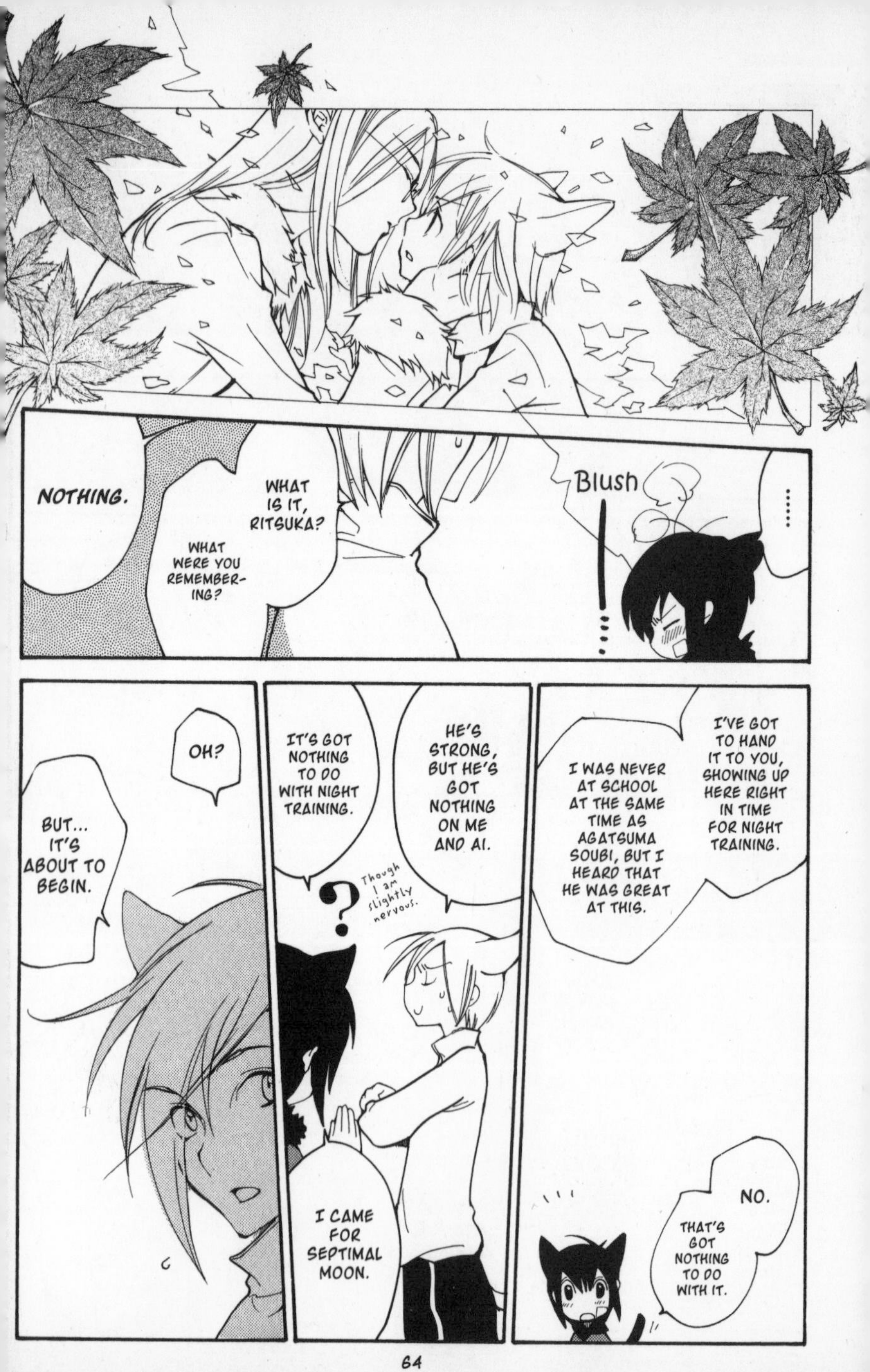
.....
Blush
WHAT IS IT, RITSUKA?
WHAT WERE YOU REMEMBERING?
NOTHING.
I'VE GOT TO HAND IT TO YOU, SHOWING UP HERE RIGHT IN TIME FOR NIGHT TRAINING.
I WAS NEVER AT SCHOOL AT THE SAME TIME AS AGATSUMA SOUBI, BUT I HEARD THAT HE WAS GREAT AT THIS.
NO.
THAT'S GOT NOTHING TO DO WITH IT.
HE'S STRONG, BUT HE'S GOT NOTHING ON ME AND AI.
IT'S GOT NOTHING TO DO WITH NIGHT TRAINING.
Though I am slightly nervous.
?
I CAME FOR SEPTIMAL MOON.
OH?
BUT... IT'S ABOUT TO BEGIN.

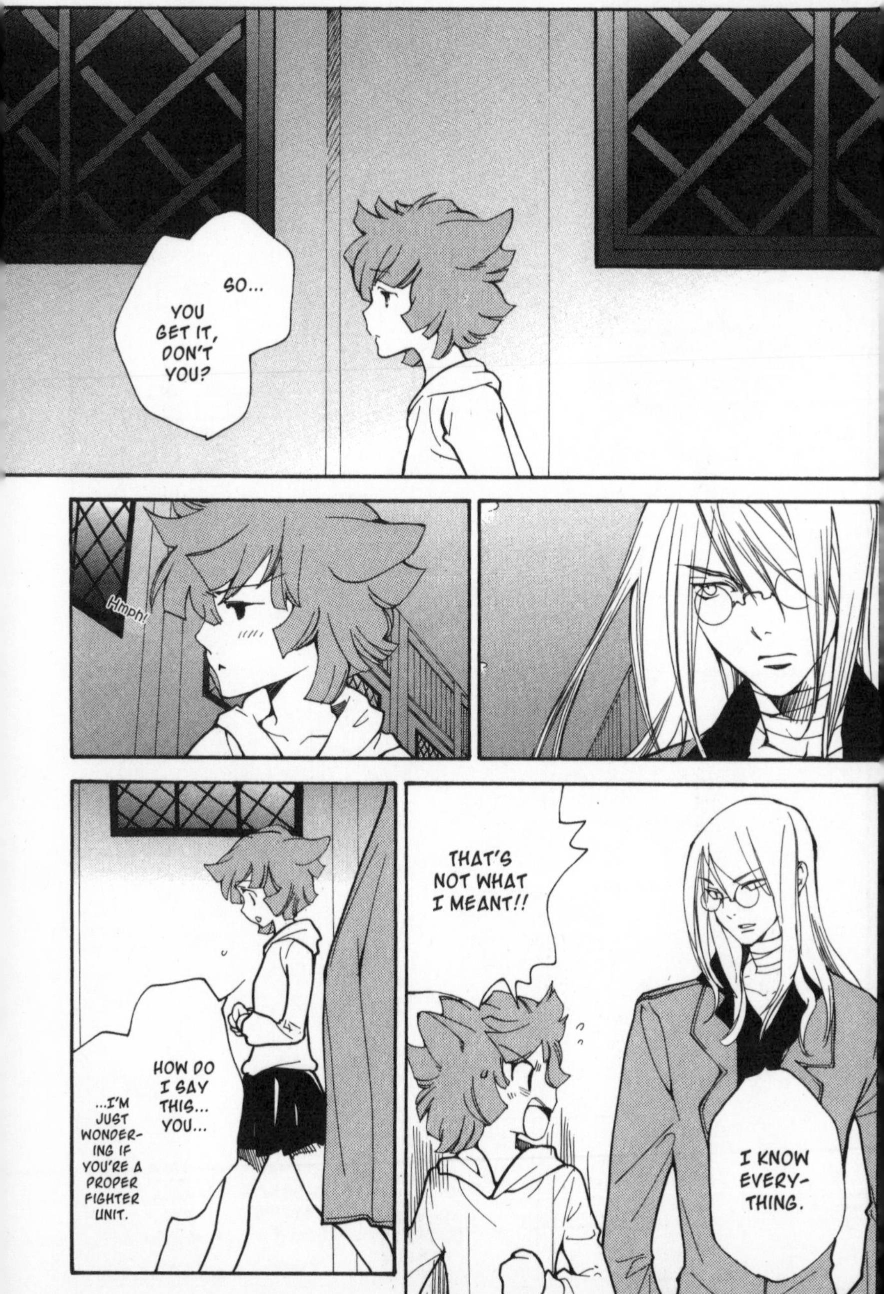
SO...
YOU GET IT, DON'T YOU?
Hmph!
I KNOW EVERYTHING.
THAT'S NOT WHAT I MEANT!!
HOW DO I SAY THIS... YOU...
...I'M JUST WONDERING IF YOU'RE A PROPER FIGHTER UNIT.

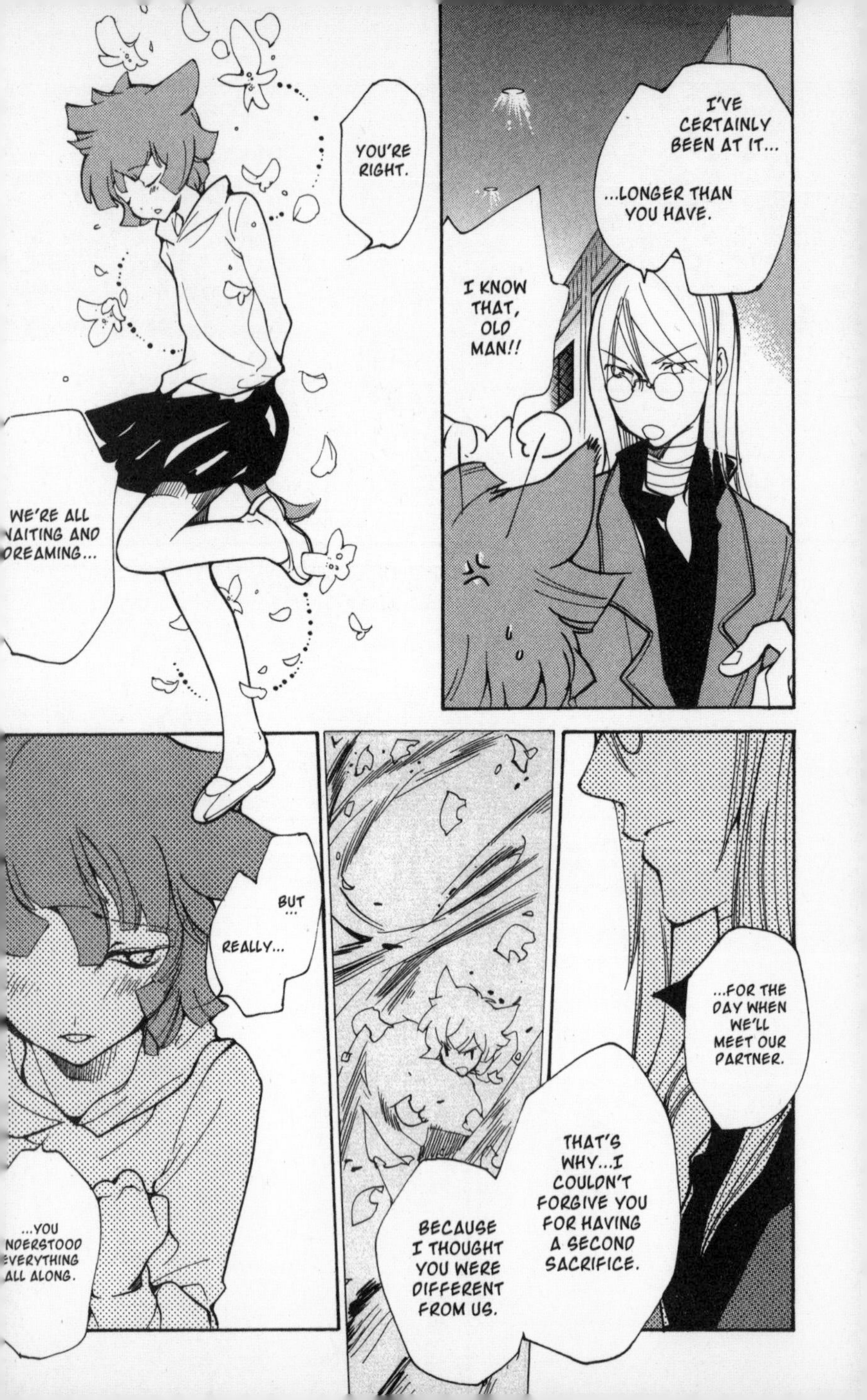
I'VE CERTAINLY BEEN AT IT...
...LONGER THAN YOU HAVE.
I KNOW THAT, OLD MAN!!
YOU'RE RIGHT.
WE'RE ALL AITING AND REAMING...
...FOR THE DAY WHEN WE'LL MEET OUR PARTNER.
THAT'S WHY...I COULDN'T FORGIVE YOU FOR HAVING A SECOND SACRIFICE.
BECAUSE I THOUGHT YOU WERE DIFFERENT FROM US.
BUT...
REALLY...
...YOU NDERSTOOD VERYTHING ALL ALONG.

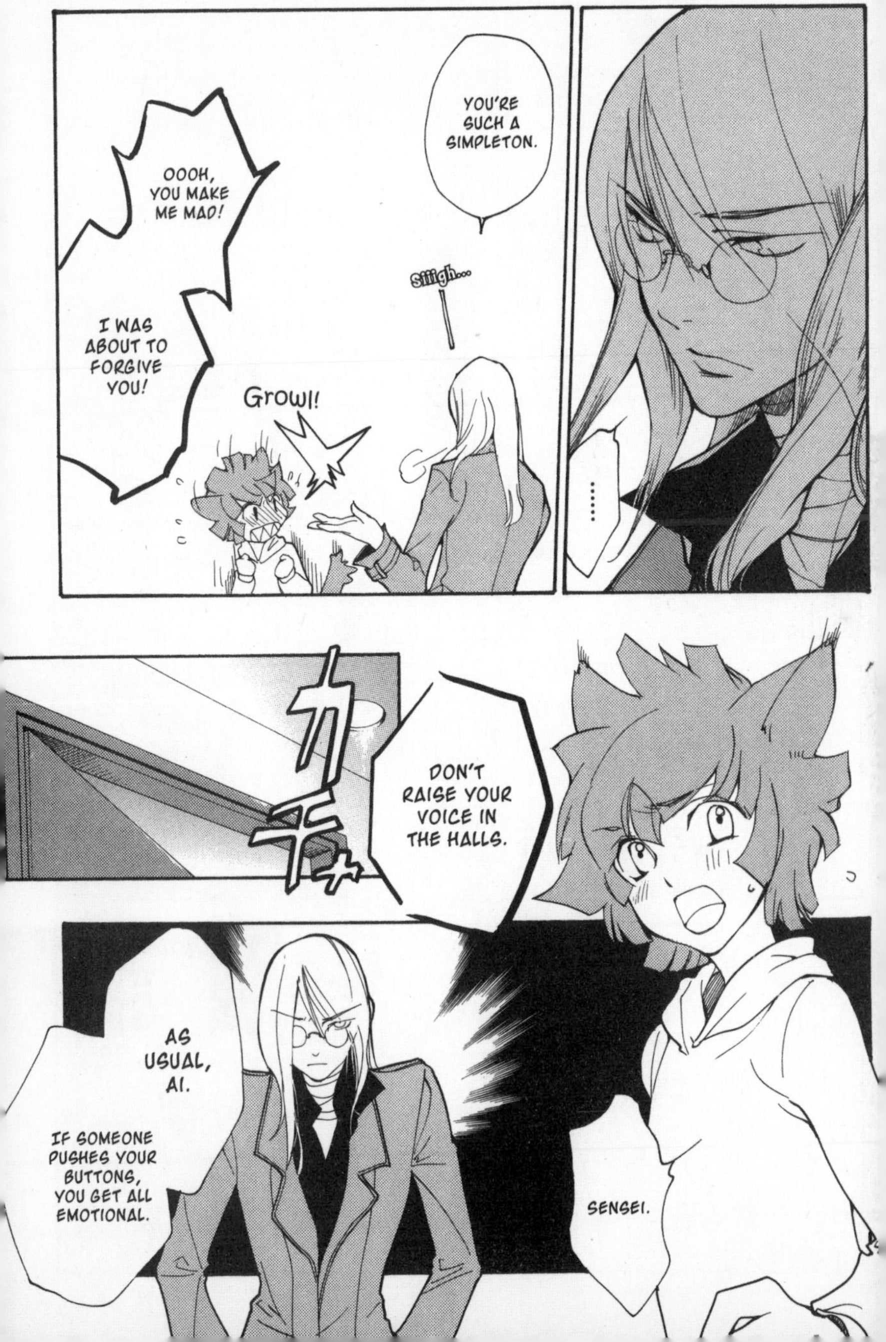
......
YOU'RE SUCH A SIMPLETON.
OOOH, YOU MAKE ME MAD!
siiigh...
I WAS ABOUT TO FORGIVE YOU!
Growl!
カチャ
DON'T RAISE YOUR VOICE IN THE HALLS.
SENSEI.
AS USUAL, AI.
IF SOMEONE PUSHES YOUR BUTTONS, YOU GET ALL EMOTIONAL.

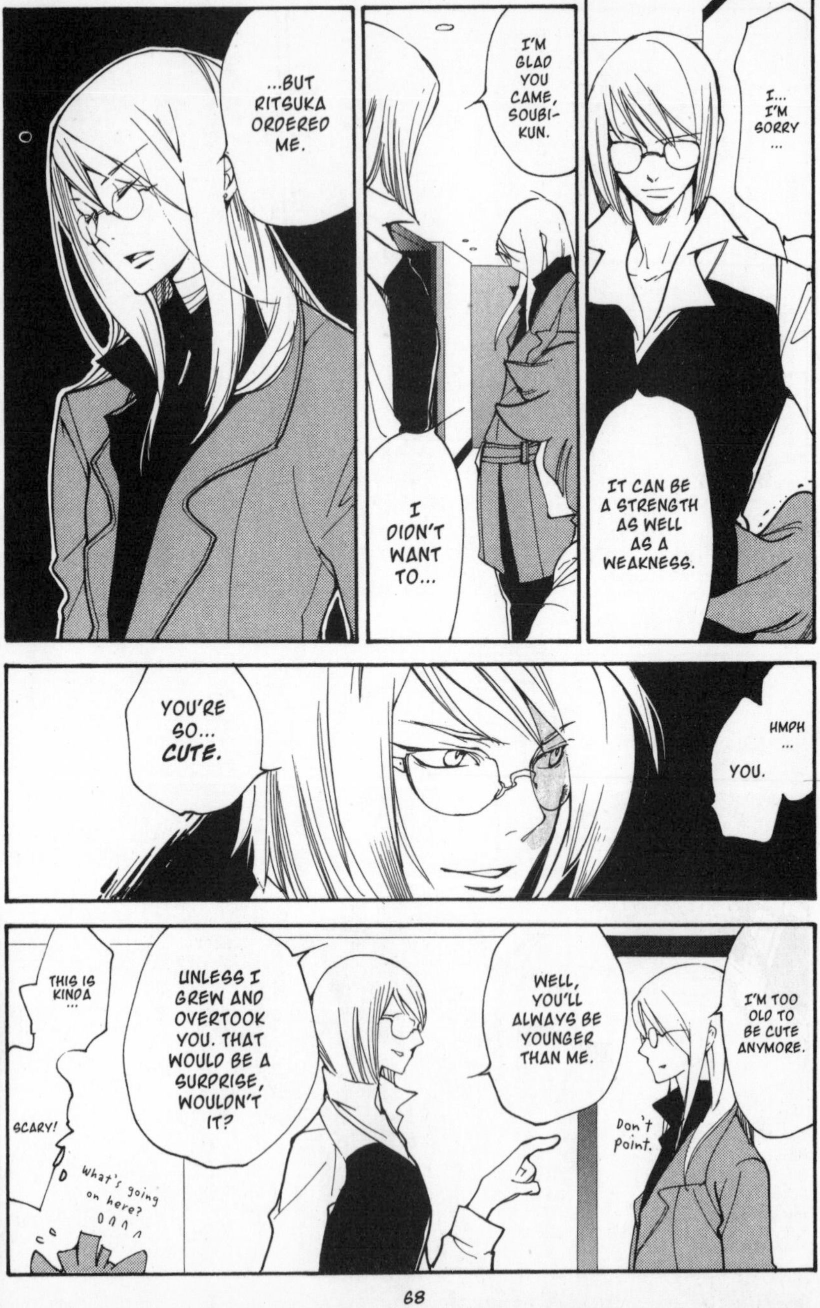
I... I'M SORRY ...
IT CAN BE A STRENGTH AS WELL AS A WEAKNESS.
I'M GLAD YOU CAME, SOUBI-KUN.
I DIDN'T WANT TO...
...BUT RITSUKA ORDERED ME.
HMPH ... YOU.
YOU'RE SO... CUTE.
I'M TOO OLD TO BE CUTE ANYMORE.
Don't point.
WELL, YOU'LL ALWAYS BE YOUNGER THAN ME.
UNLESS I GREW AND OVERTOOK YOU. THAT WOULD BE A SURPRISE, WOULDN'T IT?
THIS IS KINDA ...
SCARY!
What's going on here?

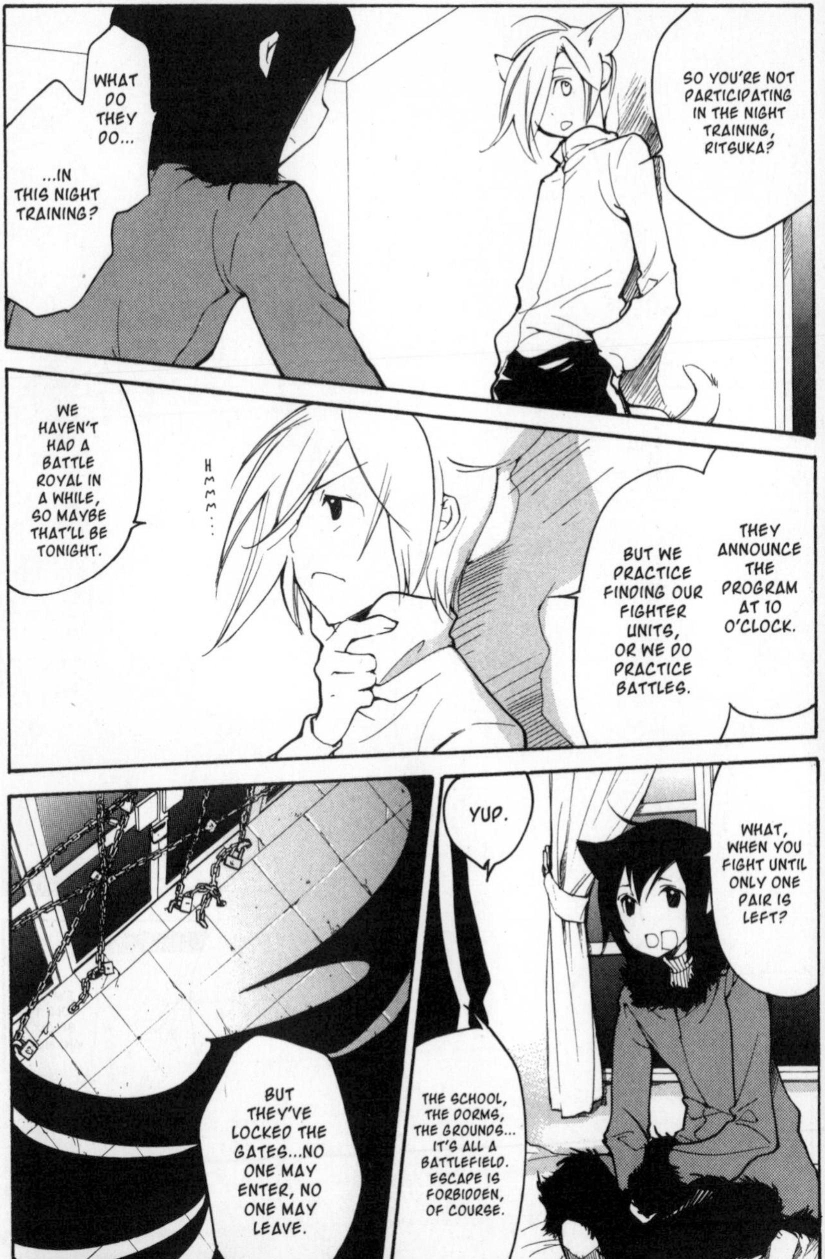
SO YOU'RE NOT PARTICIPATING IN THE NIGHT TRAINING, RITSUKA?
WHAT DO THEY DO...
...IN THIS NIGHT TRAINING?
THEY ANNOUNCE THE PROGRAM AT 10 O'CLOCK.
BUT WE PRACTICE FINDING OUR FIGHTER UNITS, OR WE DO PRACTICE BATTLES.
HMMM...
WE HAVEN'T HAD A BATTLE ROYAL IN A WHILE, SO MAYBE THAT'LL BE TONIGHT.
WHAT, WHEN YOU FIGHT UNTIL ONLY ONE PAIR IS LEFT?
YUP.
THE SCHOOL, THE DORMS, THE GROUNDS... IT'S ALL A BATTLEFIELD. ESCAPE IS FORBIDDEN, OF COURSE.
BUT THEY'VE LOCKED THE GATES...NO ONE MAY ENTER, NO ONE MAY LEAVE.

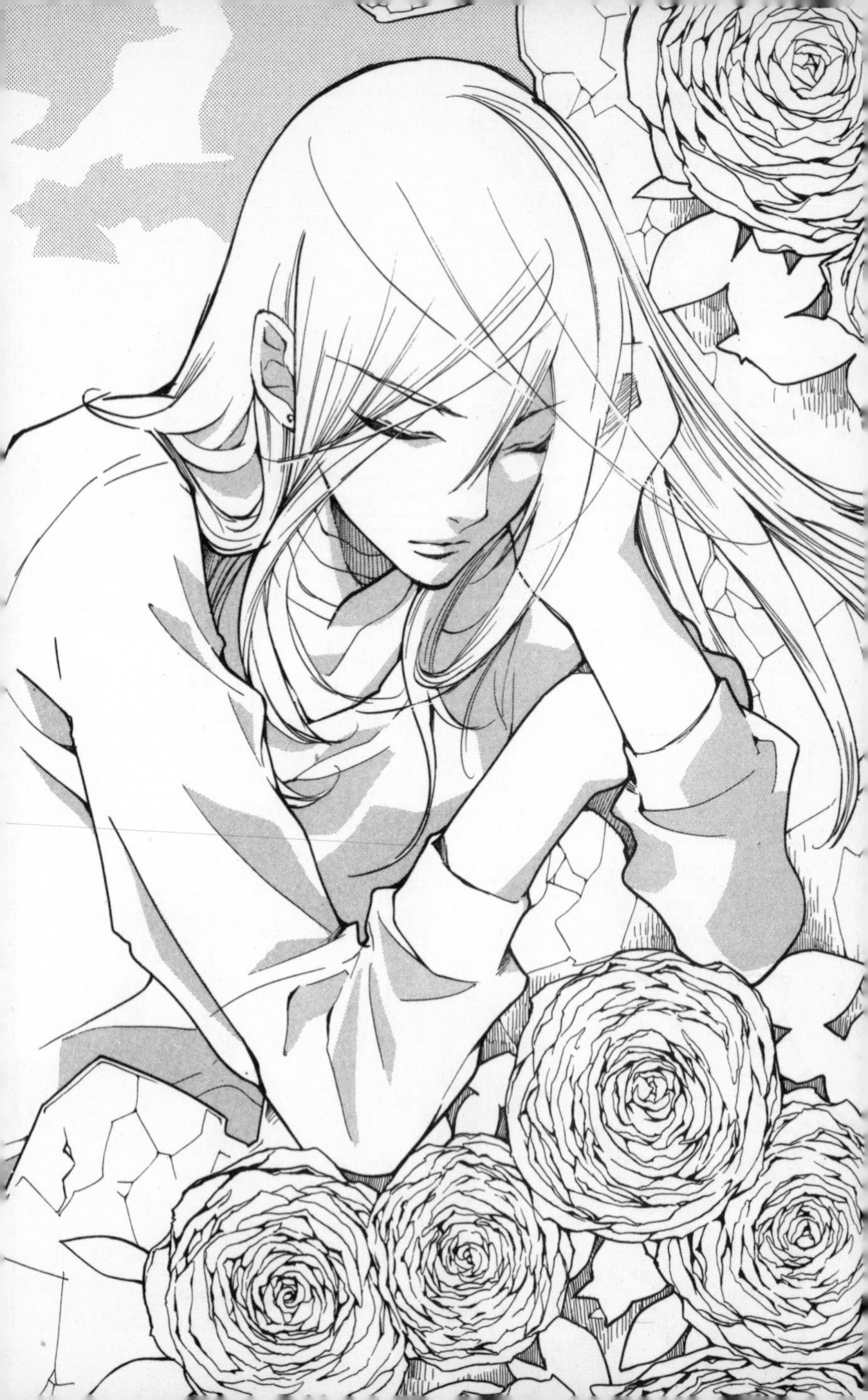

The Septimal Moon Chapters

Chapter 4

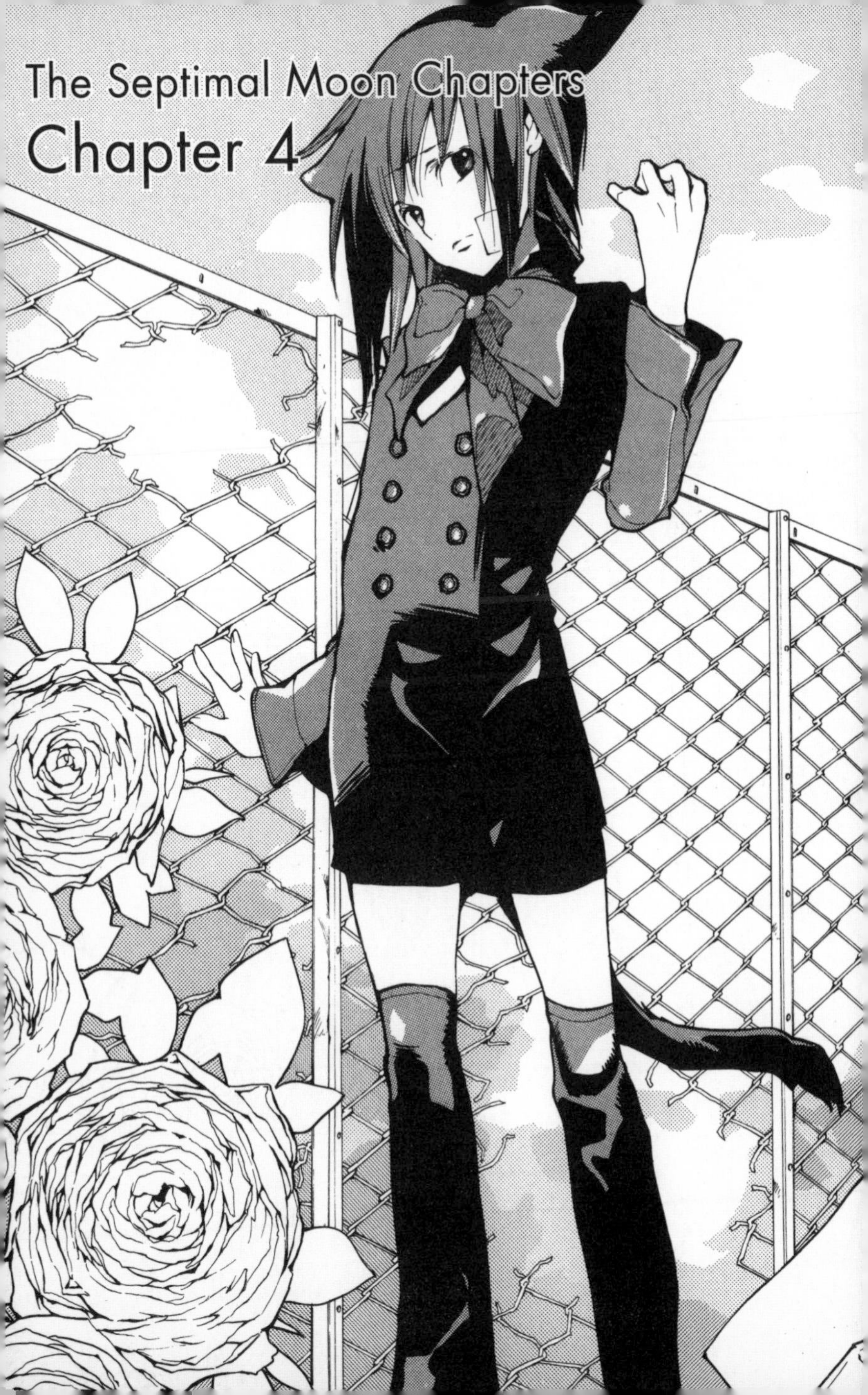

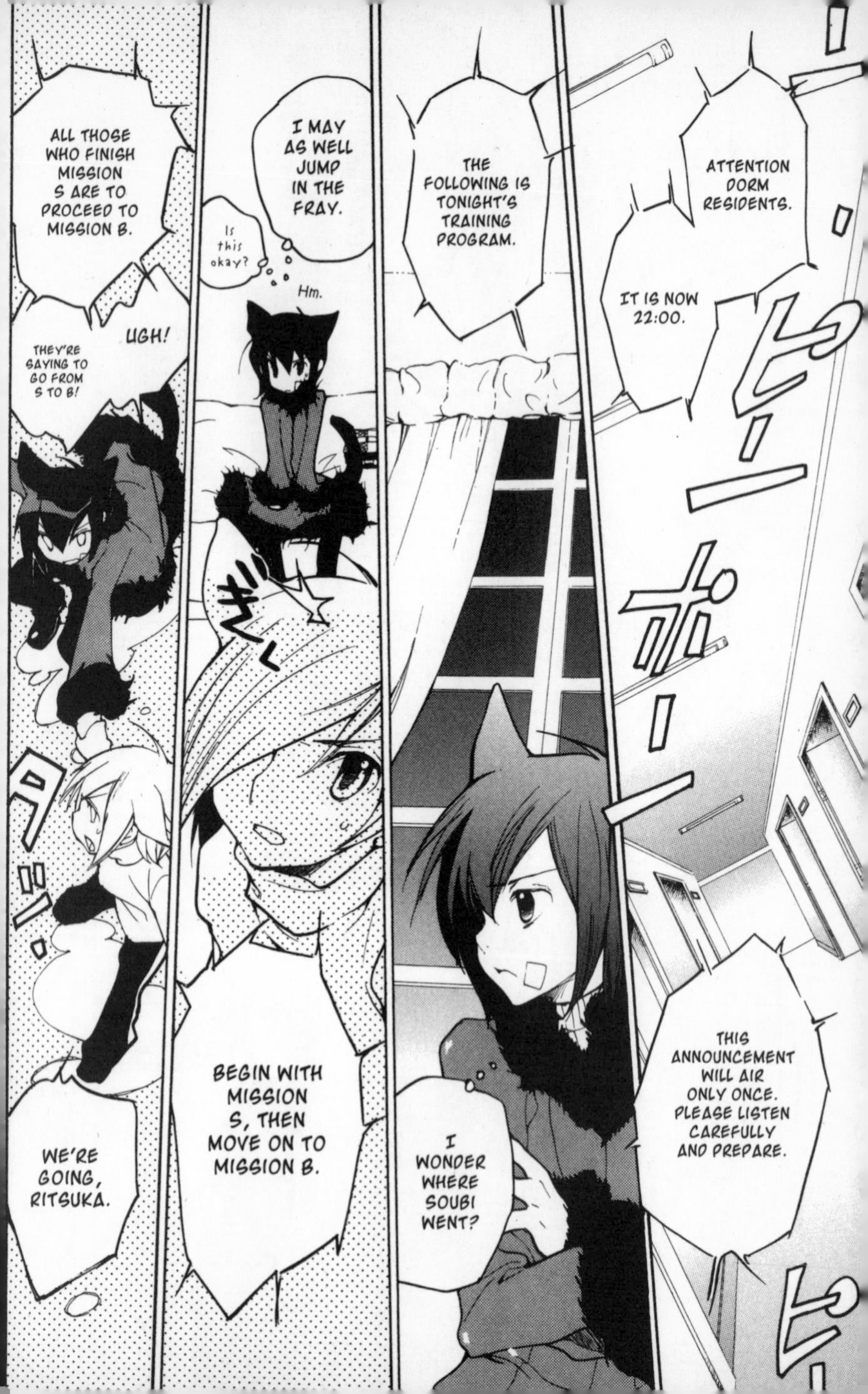
ATTENTION DORM RESIDENTS.
IT IS NOW 22:00.
THIS ANNOUNCEMENT WILL AIR ONLY ONCE. PLEASE LISTEN CAREFULLY AND PREPARE.
THE FOLLOWING IS TONIGHT'S TRAINING PROGRAM.
I WONDER WHERE SOUBI WENT?
I MAY AS WELL JUMP IN THE FRAY.
Is this okay?
Hm.
BEGIN WITH MISSION S, THEN MOVE ON TO MISSION B.
ALL THOSE WHO FINISH MISSION S ARE TO PROCEED TO MISSION B.
UGH!
THEY'RE SAYING TO GO FROM S TO B!
WE'RE GOING, RITSUKA.

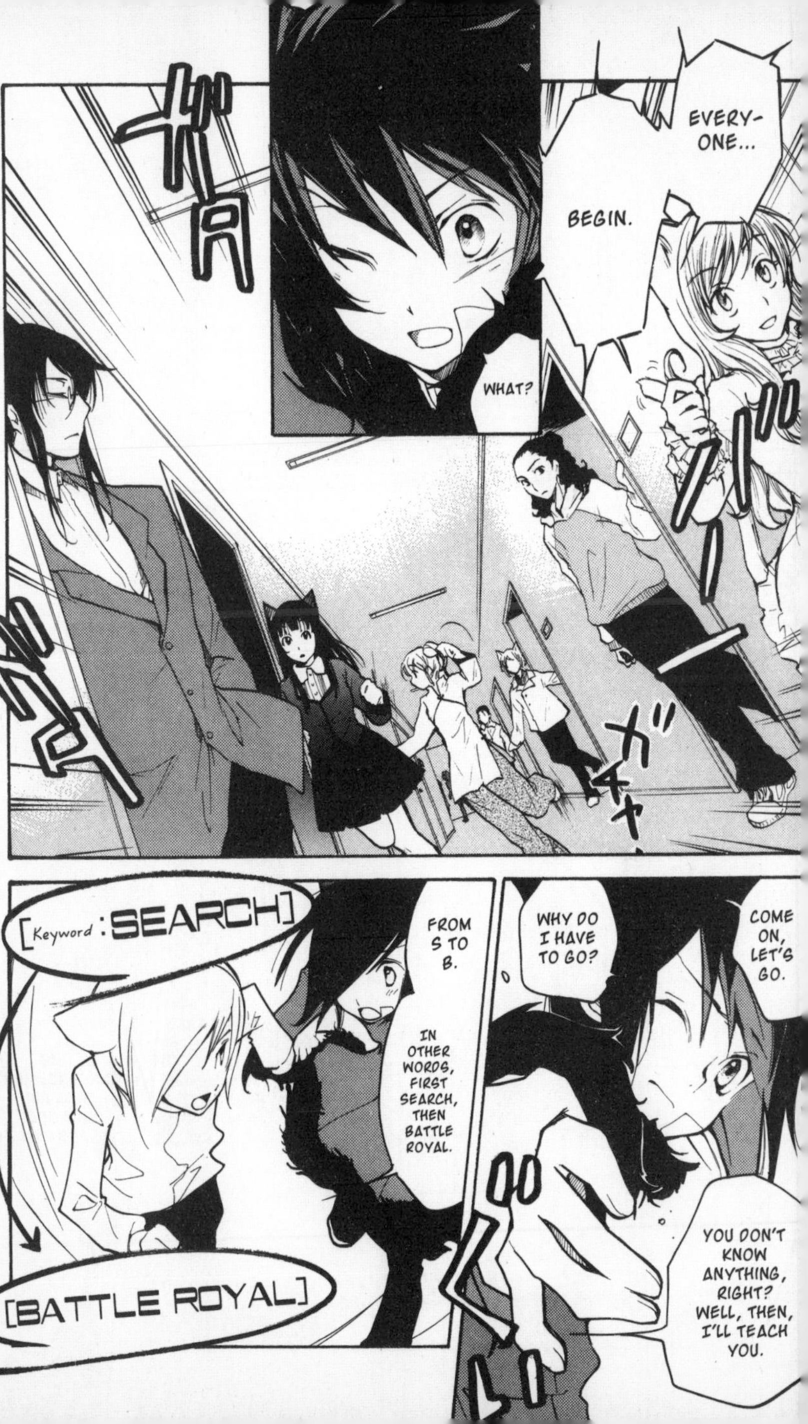
EVERY-ONE...
BEGIN.
WHAT?
COME ON, LET'S GO.
WHY DO I HAVE TO GO?
YOU DON'T KNOW ANYTHING, RIGHT? WELL, THEN, I'LL TEACH YOU.
FROM S TO B.
IN OTHER WORDS, FIRST SEARCH, THEN BATTLE ROYAL.
[Keyword : SEARCH]
[BATTLE ROYAL]

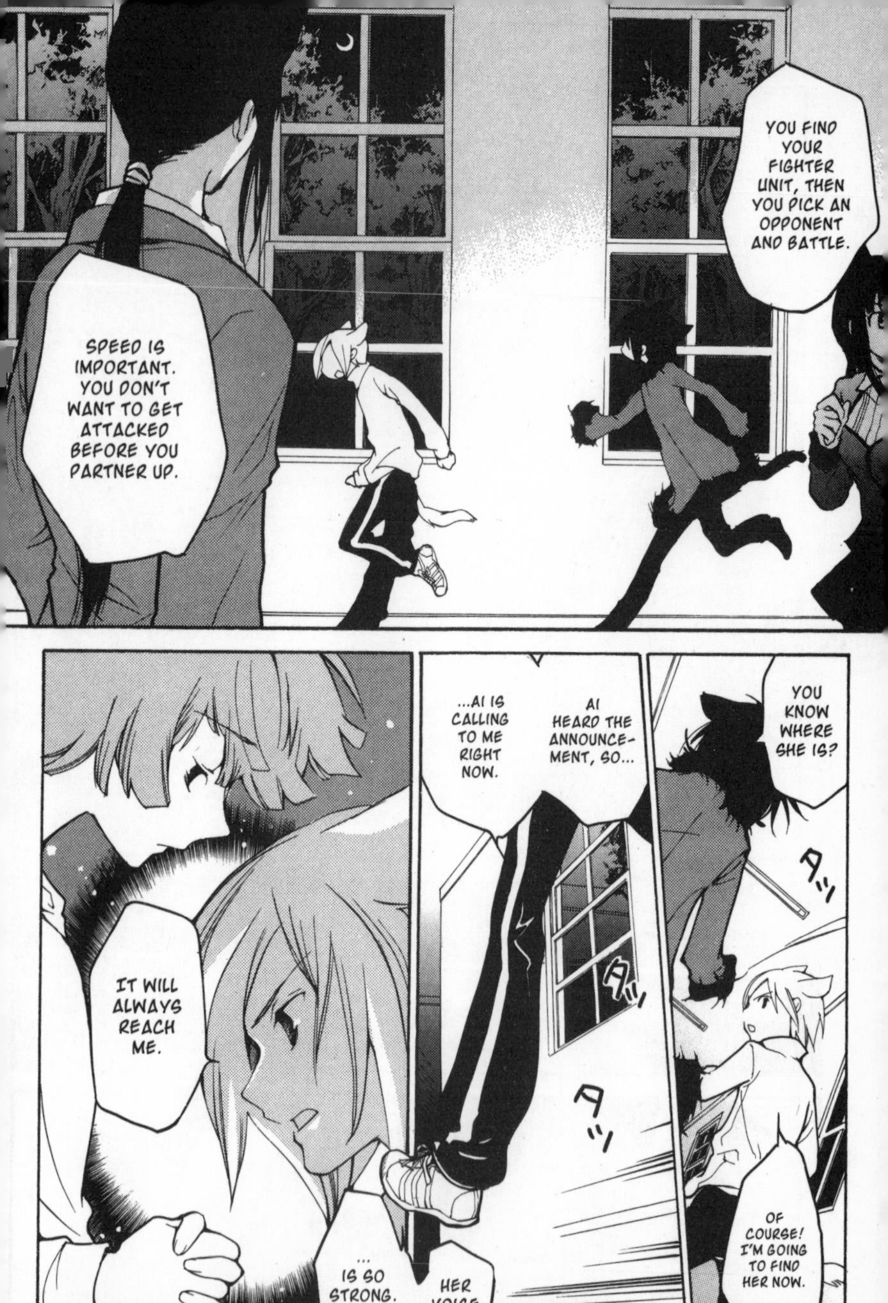

YOU FIND YOUR FIGHTER UNIT, THEN YOU PICK AN OPPONENT AND BATTLE.
SPEED IS IMPORTANT. YOU DON'T WANT TO GET ATTACKED BEFORE YOU PARTNER UP.
YOU KNOW WHERE SHE IS?
タッ
OF COURSE! I'M GOING TO FIND HER NOW.
AI HEARD THE ANNOUNCEMENT, SO...
...AI IS CALLING TO ME RIGHT NOW.
タッ
タッ
IT WILL ALWAYS REACH ME.
HER VOICE ...
... IS SO STRONG.

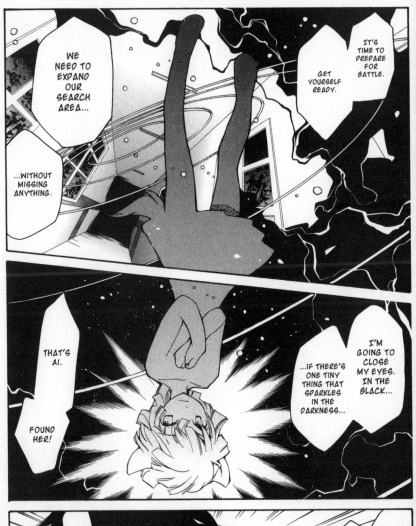

IT'S TIME TO PREPARE FOR BATTLE.
GET YOURSELF READY.
WE NEED TO EXPAND OUR SEARCH AREA...
...WITHOUT MISSING ANYTHING.
I'M GOING TO CLOSE MY EYES. IN THE BLACK...
...IF THERE'S ONE TINY THING THAT SPARKLES IN THE DARKNESS...
THAT'S AI.
FOUND HER!
YOU CALL OUT, TOO.
SOUBI WILL DEFINITELY HEAR YOU.
NO... REALLY?
HE'S HAD THE TRAINING.

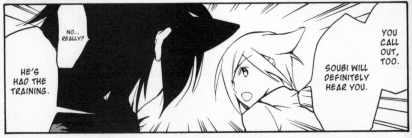

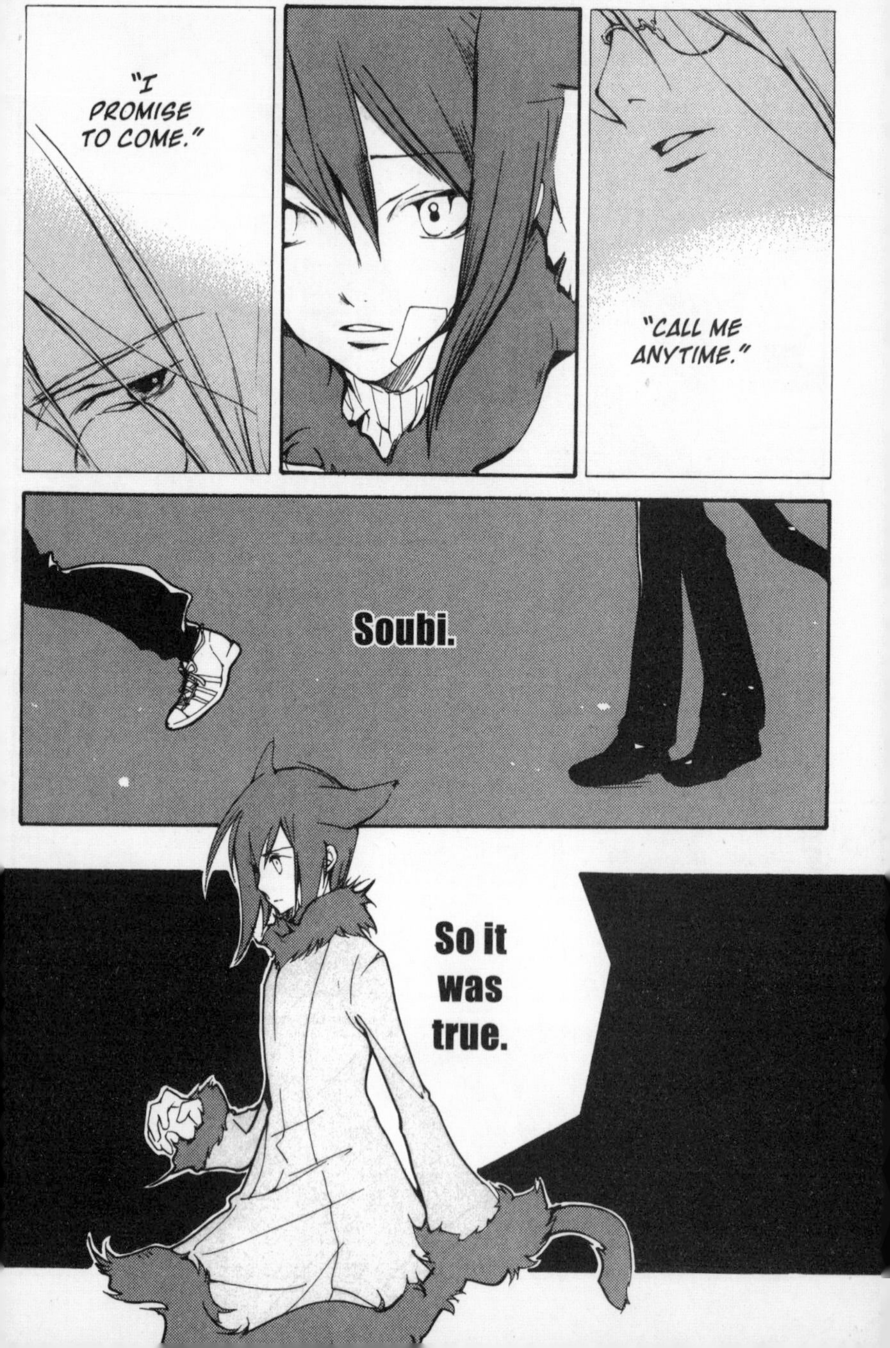
"CALL ME ANYTIME."
"I PROMISE TO COME."
Soubi.
So it was true.

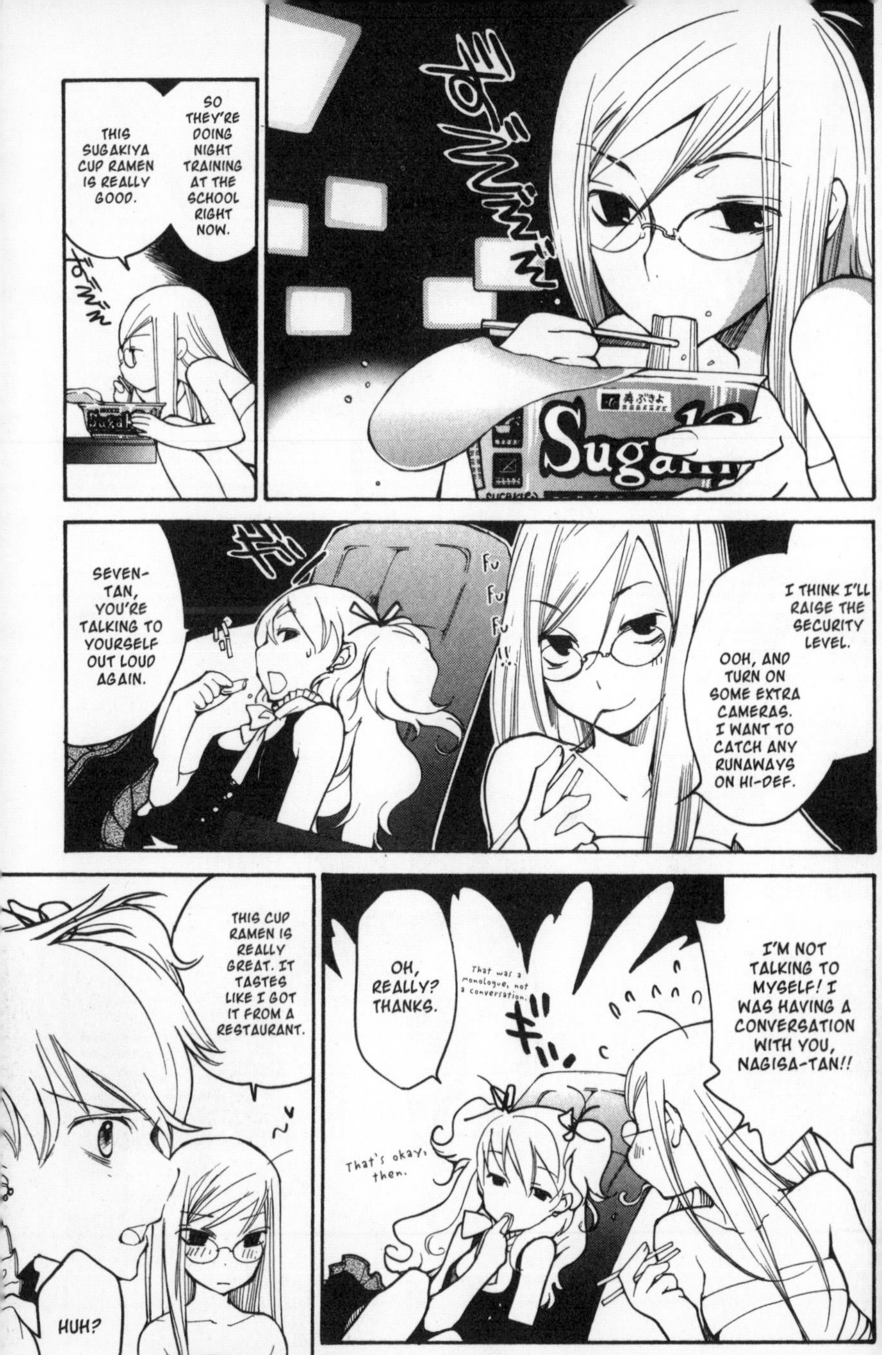
SO THEY'RE DOING NIGHT TRAINING AT THE SCHOOL RIGHT NOW.
THIS SUGAKIYA CUP RAMEN IS REALLY GOOD.
I THINK I'LL RAISE THE SECURITY LEVEL.
OOH, AND TURN ON SOME EXTRA CAMERAS. I WANT TO CATCH ANY RUNAWAYS ON HI-DEF.
Fu Fu Fu
SEVEN-TAN, YOU'RE TALKING TO YOURSELF OUT LOUD AGAIN.
I'M NOT TALKING TO MYSELF! I WAS HAVING A CONVERSATION WITH YOU, NAGISA-TAN!!
That was a monologue, not a conversation.
OH, REALLY? THANKS.
That's okay, then.
THIS CUP RAMEN IS REALLY GREAT. IT TASTES LIKE I GOT IT FROM A RESTAURANT.
HUH?

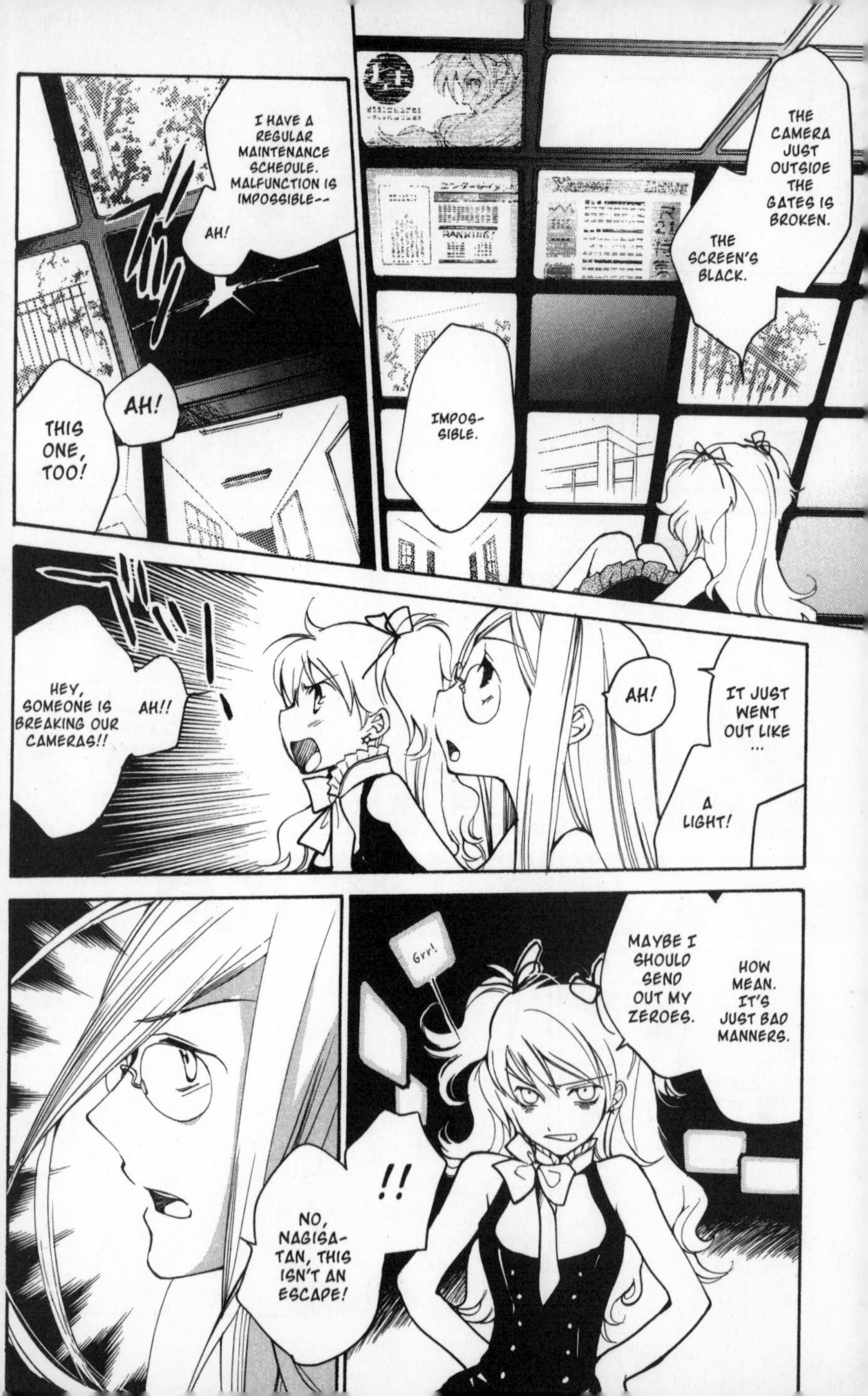
THE CAMERA JUST OUTSIDE THE GATES IS BROKEN.
THE SCREEN'S BLACK.
IMPOS-SIBLE.
I HAVE A REGULAR MAINTENANCE SCHEDULE. MALFUNCTION IS IMPOSSIBLE--
AH!
AH!
THIS ONE, TOO!
IT JUST WENT OUT LIKE ...
A LIGHT!
AH!
AH!!
HEY, SOMEONE IS BREAKING OUR CAMERAS!!
HOW MEAN. IT'S JUST BAD MANNERS.
MAYBE I SHOULD SEND OUT MY ZEROES.
Grr!
!!
NO, NAGISA-TAN, THIS ISN'T AN ESCAPE!

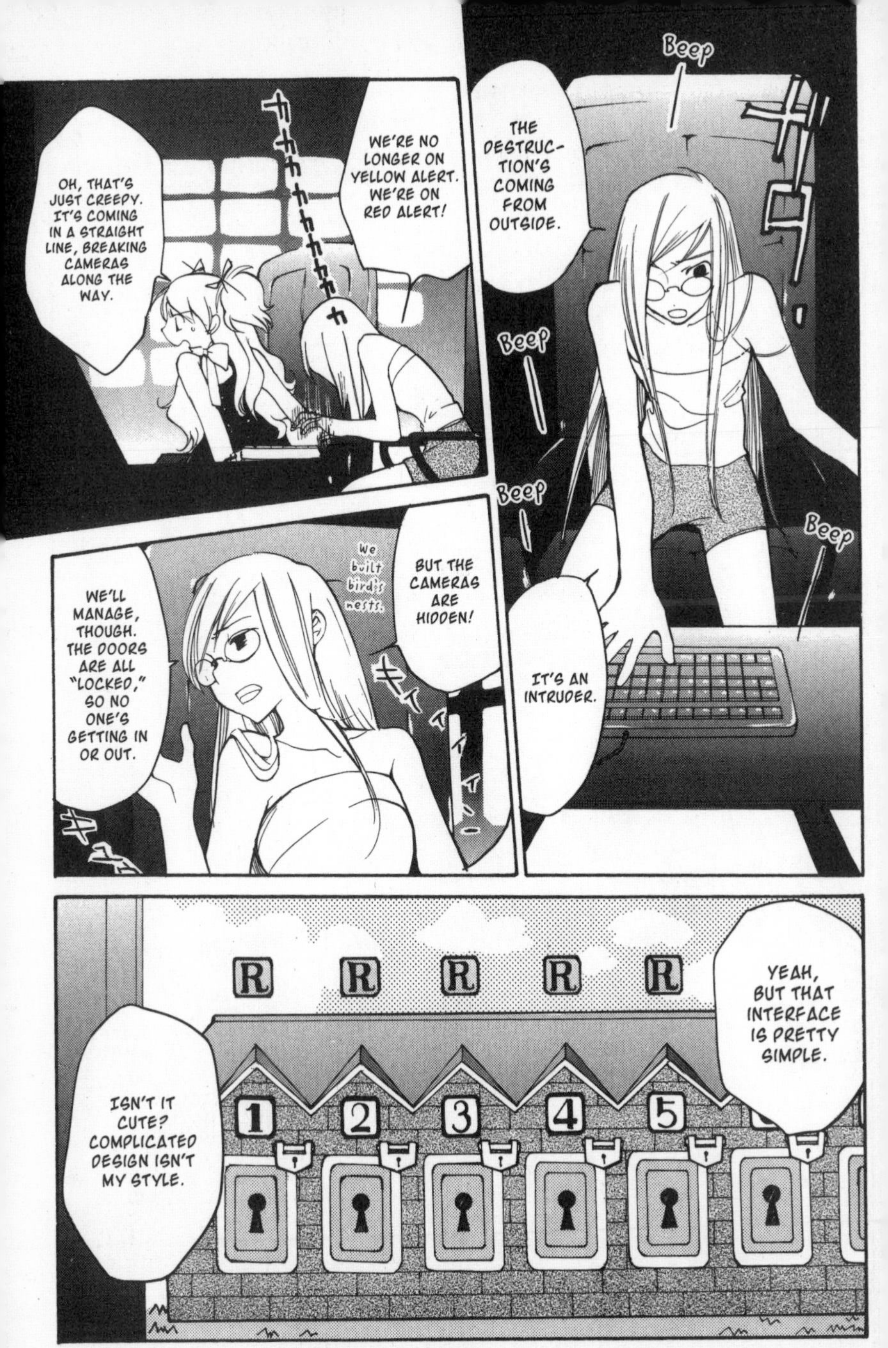
Beep
THE DESTRUCTION'S COMING FROM OUTSIDE.
Beep
Beep
Beep
IT'S AN INTRUDER.
WE'RE NO LONGER ON YELLOW ALERT. WE'RE ON RED ALERT!
OH, THAT'S JUST CREEPY. IT'S COMING IN A STRAIGHT LINE, BREAKING CAMERAS ALONG THE WAY.
BUT THE CAMERAS ARE HIDDEN!
We built bird's nests.
WE'LL MANAGE, THOUGH. THE DOORS ARE ALL "LOCKED," SO NO ONE'S GETTING IN OR OUT.
YEAH, BUT THAT INTERFACE IS PRETTY SIMPLE.
R R R R R
1 2 3 4 5
ISN'T IT CUTE? COMPLICATED DESIGN ISN'T MY STYLE.

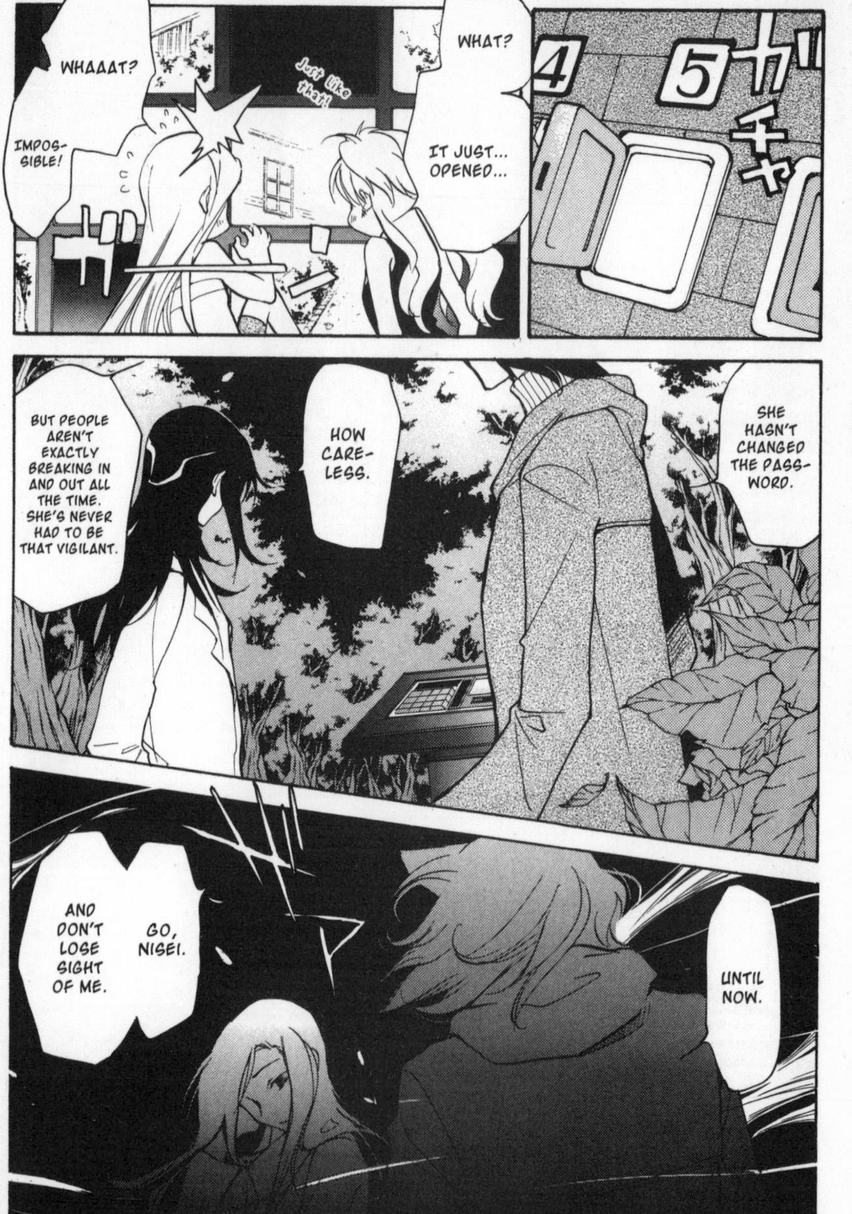
4
5
ガチャ
WHAT?
IT JUST... OPENED...
Just like that!
WHAAAT?
IMPOSSIBLE!
SHE HASN'T CHANGED THE PASSWORD.
HOW CARELESS.
BUT PEOPLE AREN'T EXACTLY BREAKING IN AND OUT ALL THE TIME. SHE'S NEVER HAD TO BE THAT VIGILANT.
UNTIL NOW.
GO, NISEI.
AND DON'T LOSE SIGHT OF ME.

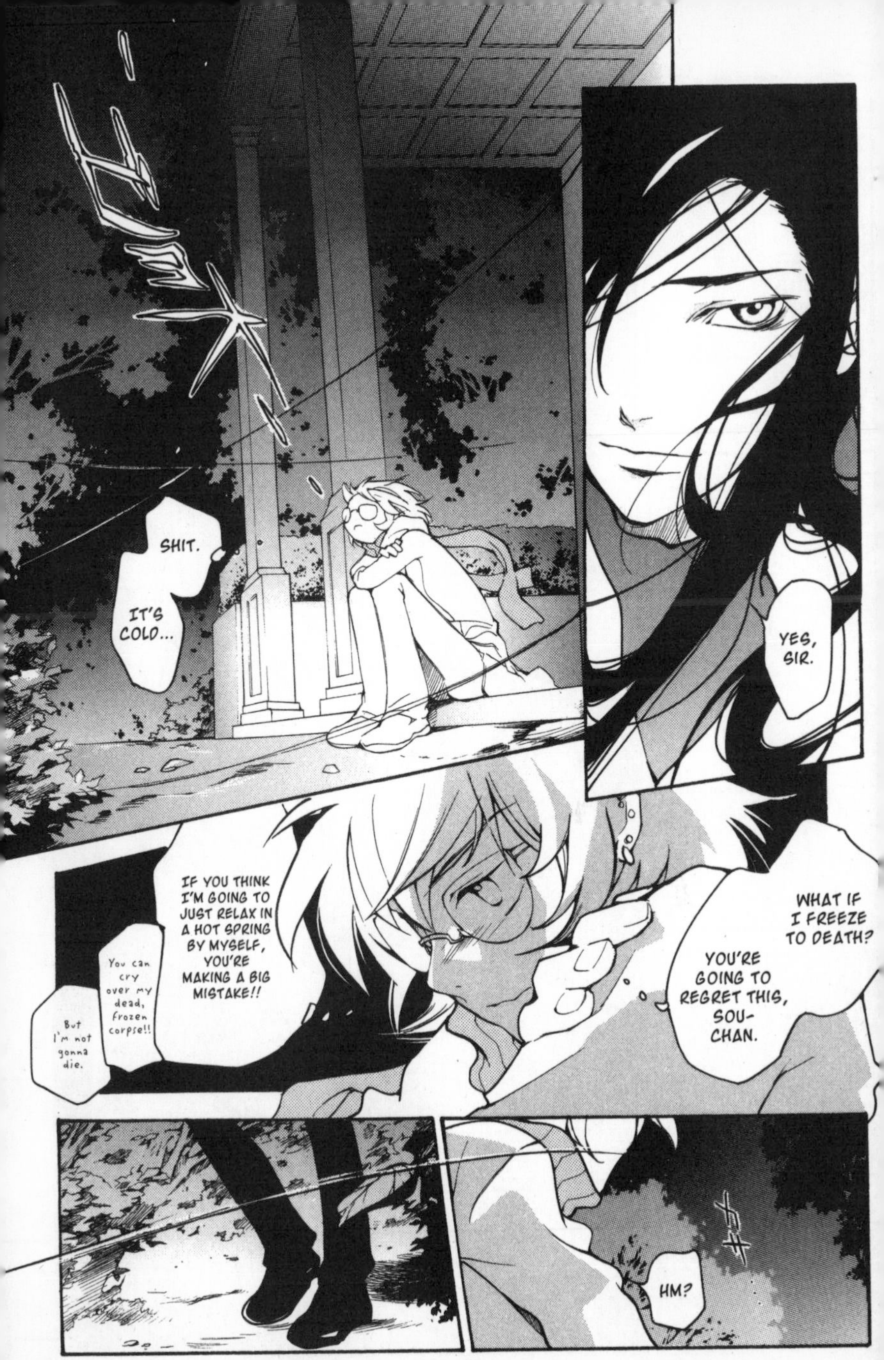
YES, SIR.
SHIT.
IT'S COLD...
WHAT IF I FREEZE TO DEATH?
YOU'RE GOING TO REGRET THIS, SOU-CHAN.
IF YOU THINK I'M GOING TO JUST RELAX IN A HOT SPRING BY MYSELF, YOU'RE MAKING A BIG MISTAKE!!
You can cry over my dead, frozen corpse!!
But I'm not gonna die.
HM?

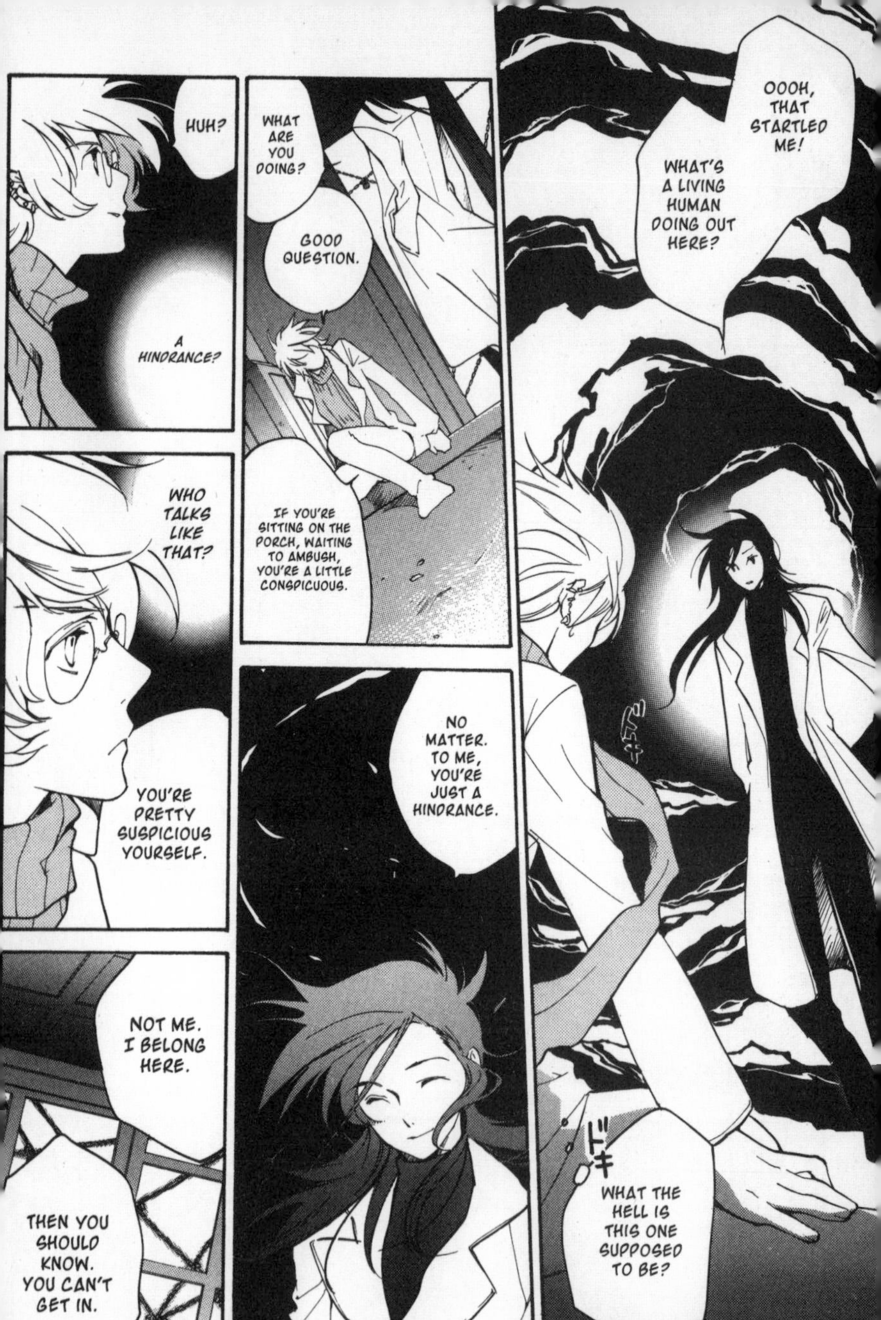
OOOH, THAT STARTLED ME!
WHAT'S A LIVING HUMAN DOING OUT HERE?
ドキ
ドキ
WHAT THE HELL IS THIS ONE SUPPOSED TO BE?
WHAT ARE YOU DOING?
GOOD QUESTION.
IF YOU'RE SITTING ON THE PORCH, WAITING TO AMBUSH, YOU'RE A LITTLE CONSPICUOUS.
NO MATTER. TO ME, YOU'RE JUST A HINDRANCE.
HUH?
A HINDRANCE?
WHO TALKS LIKE THAT?
YOU'RE PRETTY SUSPICIOUS YOURSELF.
NOT ME. I BELONG HERE.
THEN YOU SHOULD KNOW. YOU CAN'T GET IN.

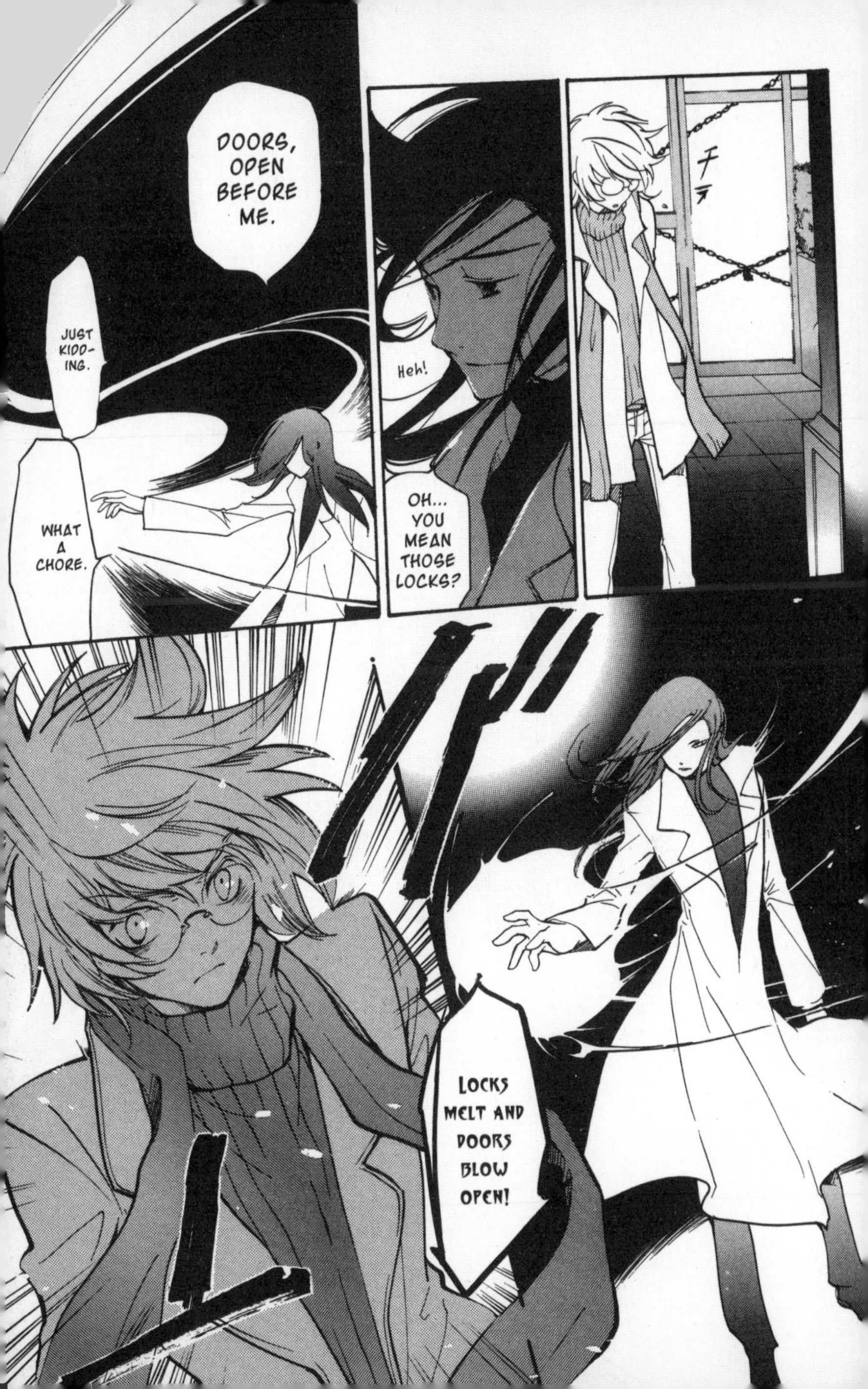
Heh!
OH... YOU MEAN THOSE LOCKS?
DOORS, OPEN BEFORE ME.
JUST KIDD-ING.
WHAT A CHORE.
LOCKS MELT AND DOORS BLOW OPEN!

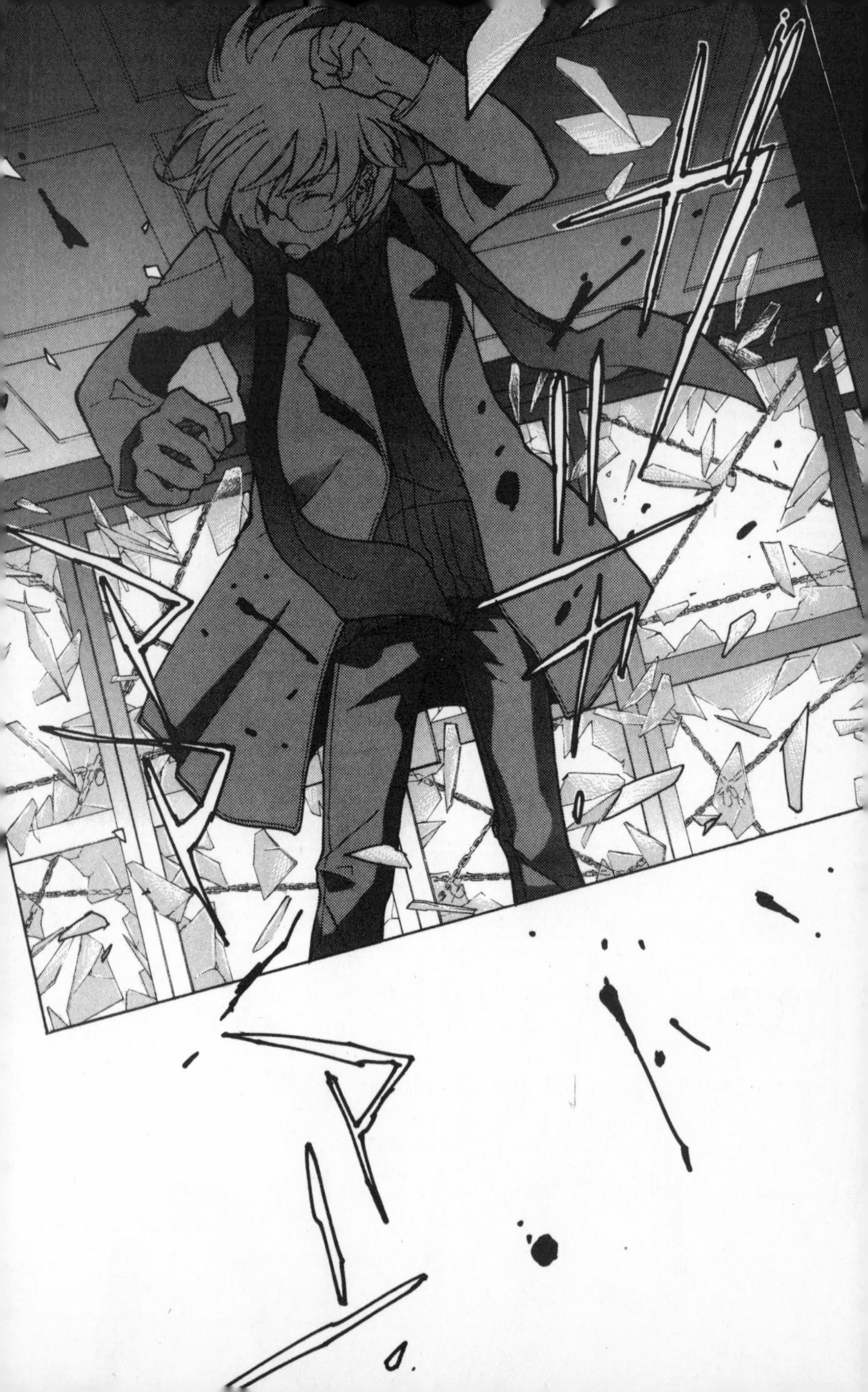

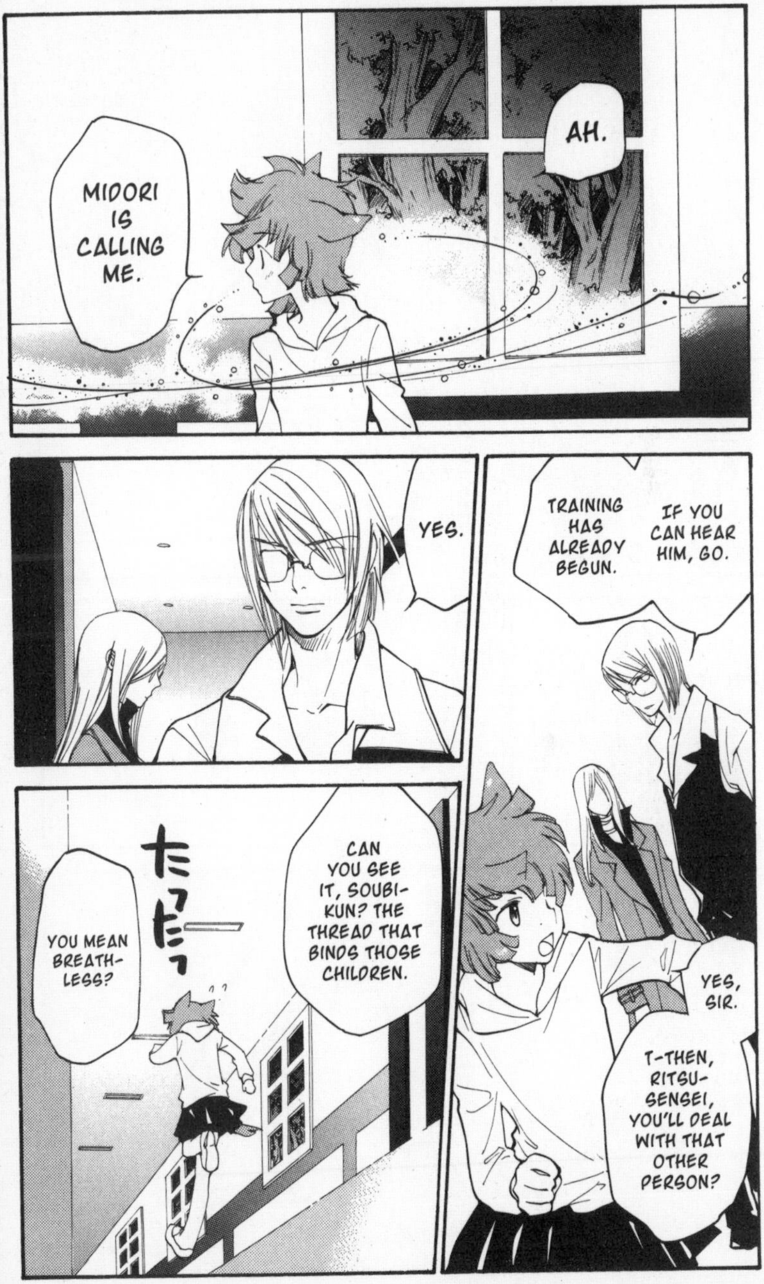
AH.
MIDORI IS CALLING ME.
IF YOU CAN HEAR HIM, GO.
TRAINING HAS ALREADY BEGUN.
YES.
YES, SIR.
T-THEN, RITSU-SENSEI, YOU'LL DEAL WITH THAT OTHER PERSON?
CAN YOU SEE IT, SOUBI-KUN? THE THREAD THAT BINDS THOSE CHILDREN.
たったっ
YOU MEAN BREATH-LESS?

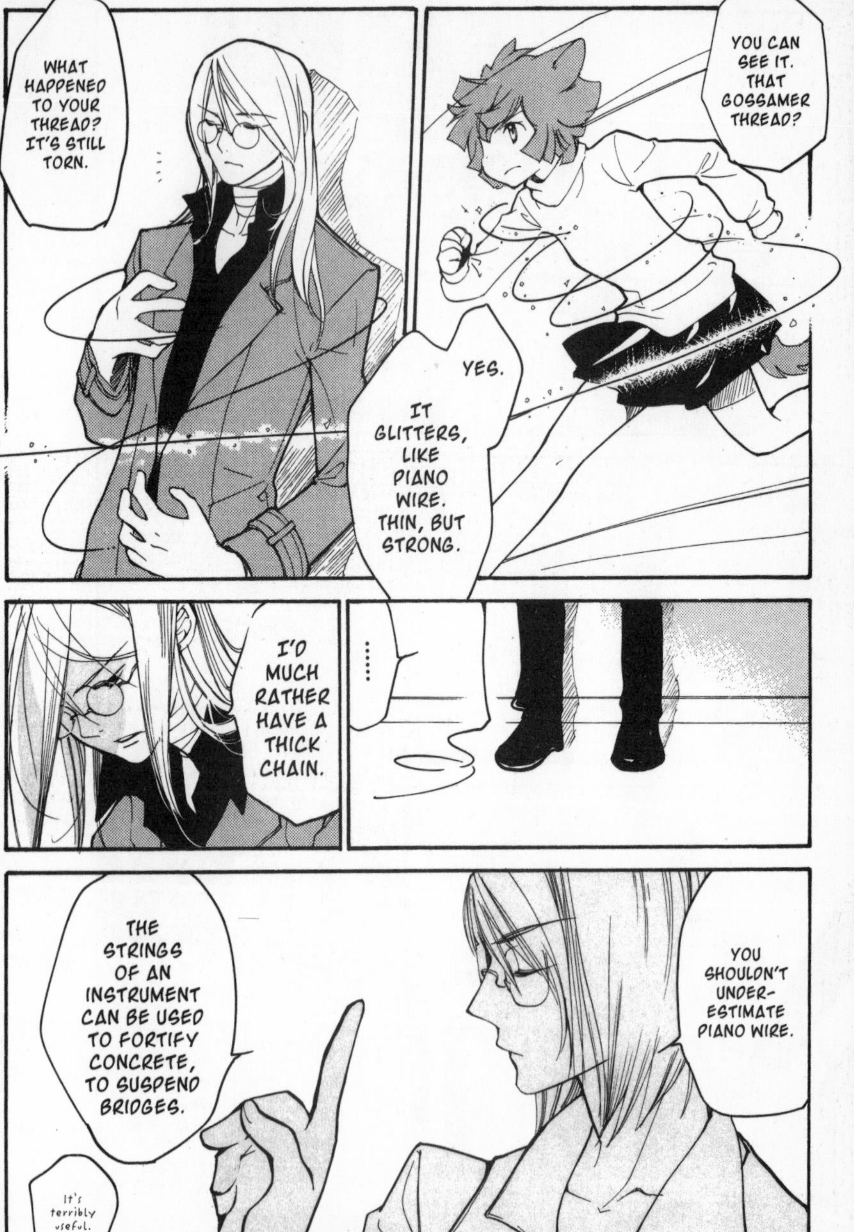

YOU CAN SEE IT. THAT GOSSAMER THREAD?
YES.
IT GLITTERS, LIKE PIANO WIRE. THIN, BUT STRONG.
WHAT HAPPENED TO YOUR THREAD? IT'S STILL TORN.
......
I'D MUCH RATHER HAVE A THICK CHAIN.
YOU SHOULDN'T UNDER-ESTIMATE PIANO WIRE.
THE STRINGS OF AN INSTRUMENT CAN BE USED TO FORTIFY CONCRETE, TO SUSPEND BRIDGES.
It's terribly useful.

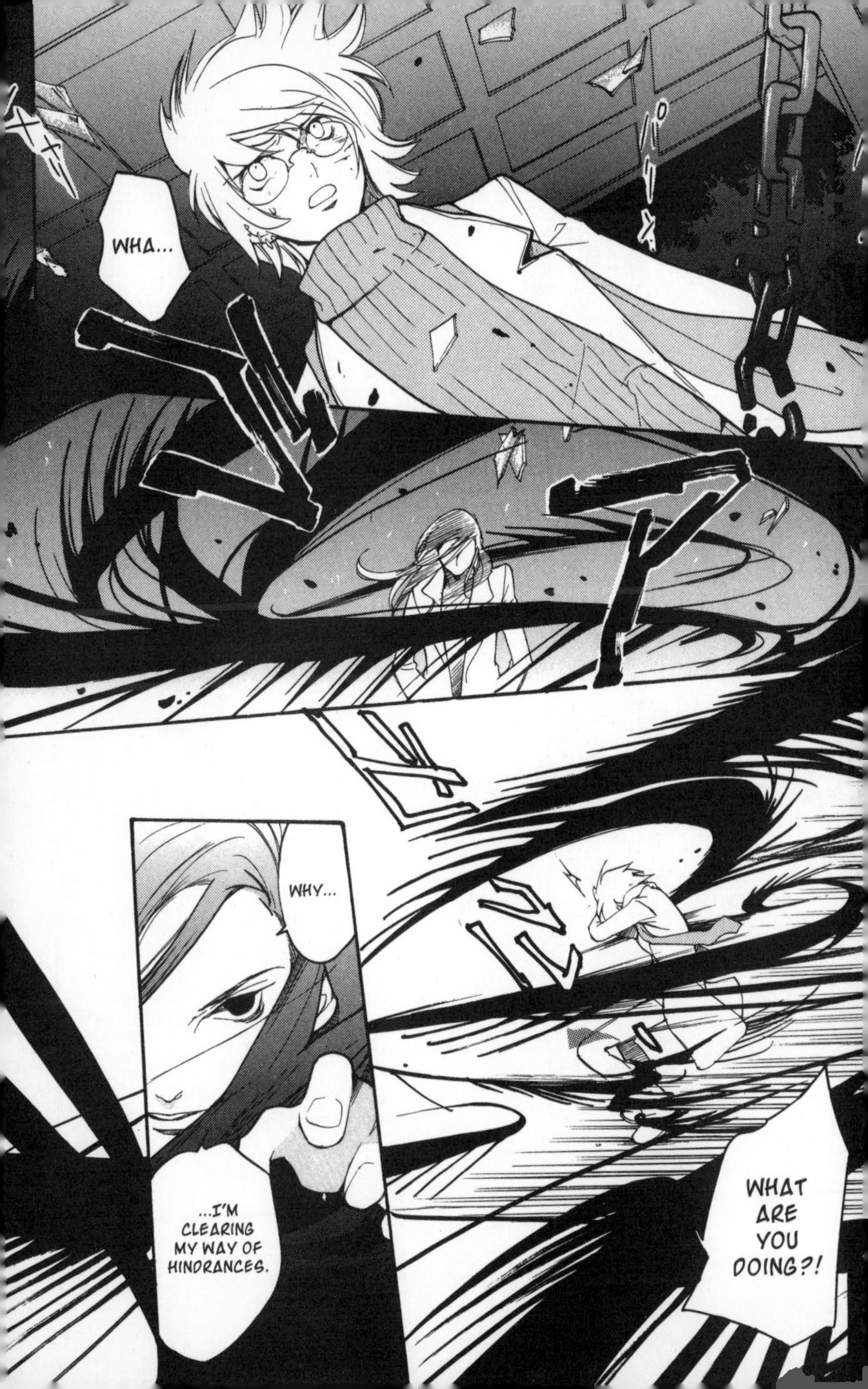
WHA...
WHAT ARE YOU DOING?!
WHY...
...I'M CLEARING MY WAY OF HINDRANCES.

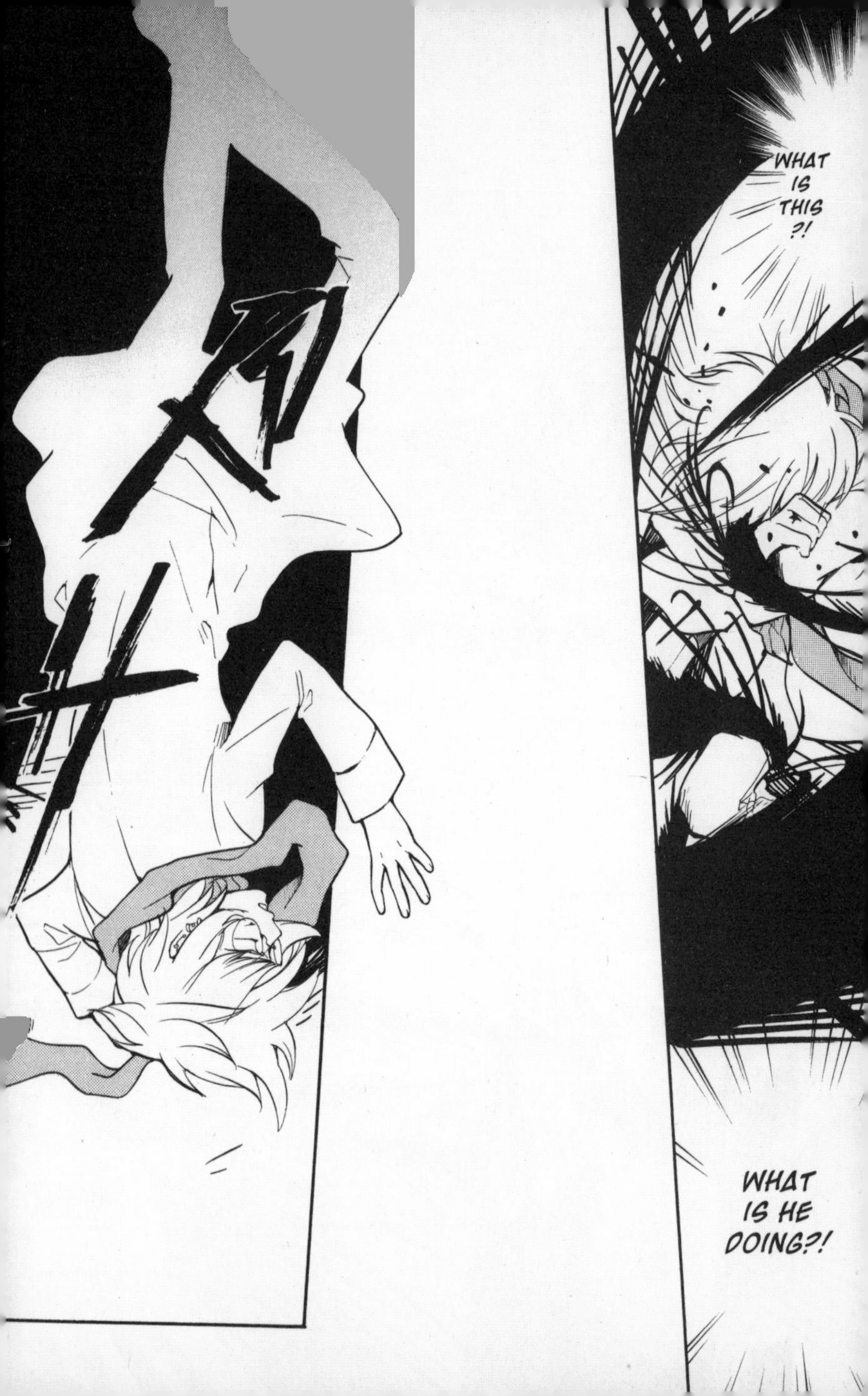
WHAT IS THIS ?!
WHAT IS HE DOING?!

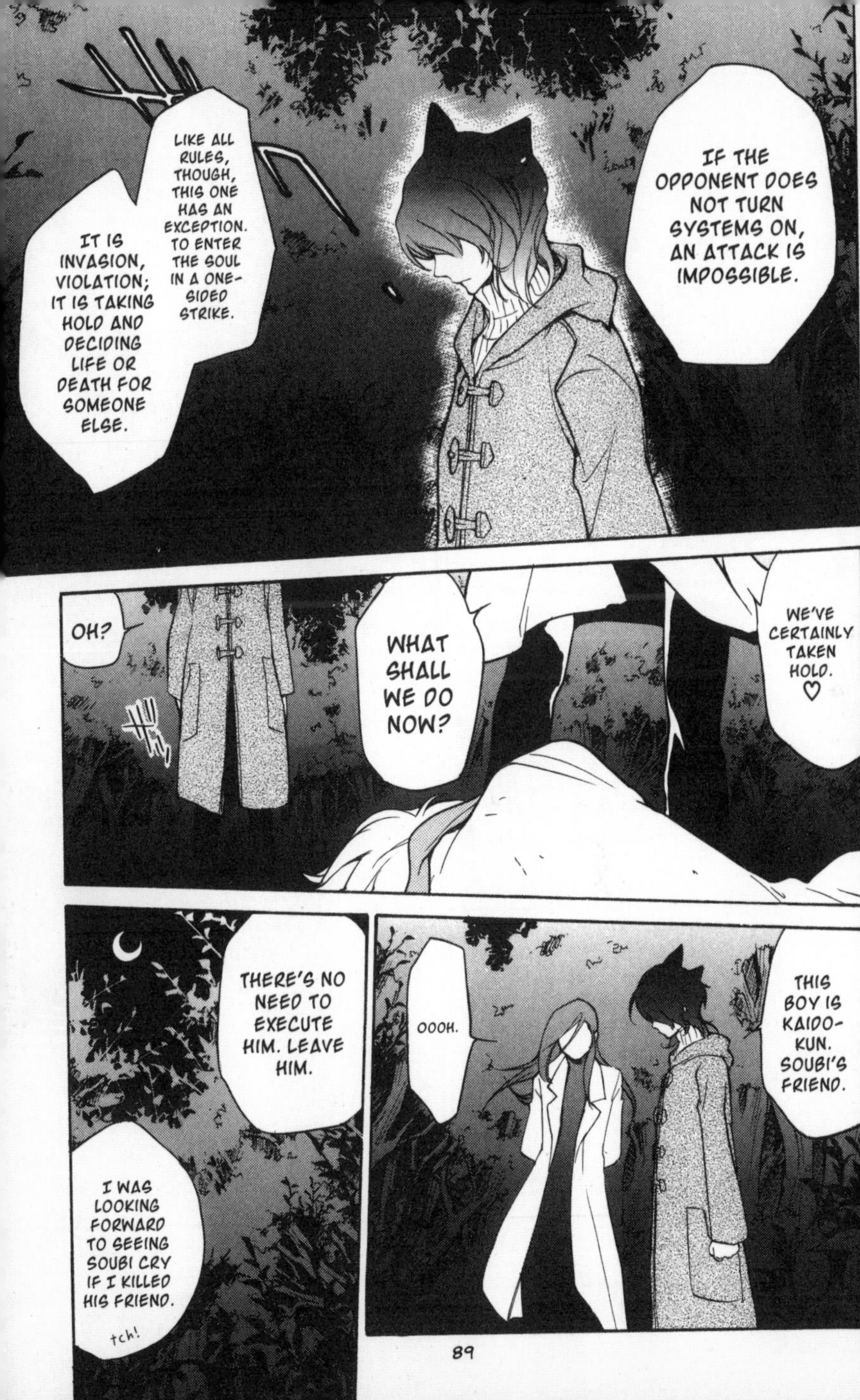
IF THE OPPONENT DOES NOT TURN SYSTEMS ON, AN ATTACK IS IMPOSSIBLE.
LIKE ALL RULES, THOUGH, THIS ONE HAS AN EXCEPTION. TO ENTER THE SOUL IN A ONE-SIDED STRIKE.
IT IS INVASION, VIOLATION; IT IS TAKING HOLD AND DECIDING LIFE OR DEATH FOR SOMEONE ELSE.
WE'VE CERTAINLY TAKEN HOLD. ♡
WHAT SHALL WE DO NOW?
OH?
THIS BOY IS KAIDO-KUN. SOUBI'S FRIEND.
OOOH.
THERE'S NO NEED TO EXECUTE HIM. LEAVE HIM.
I WAS LOOKING FORWARD TO SEEING SOUBI CRY IF I KILLED HIS FRIEND.
tch!

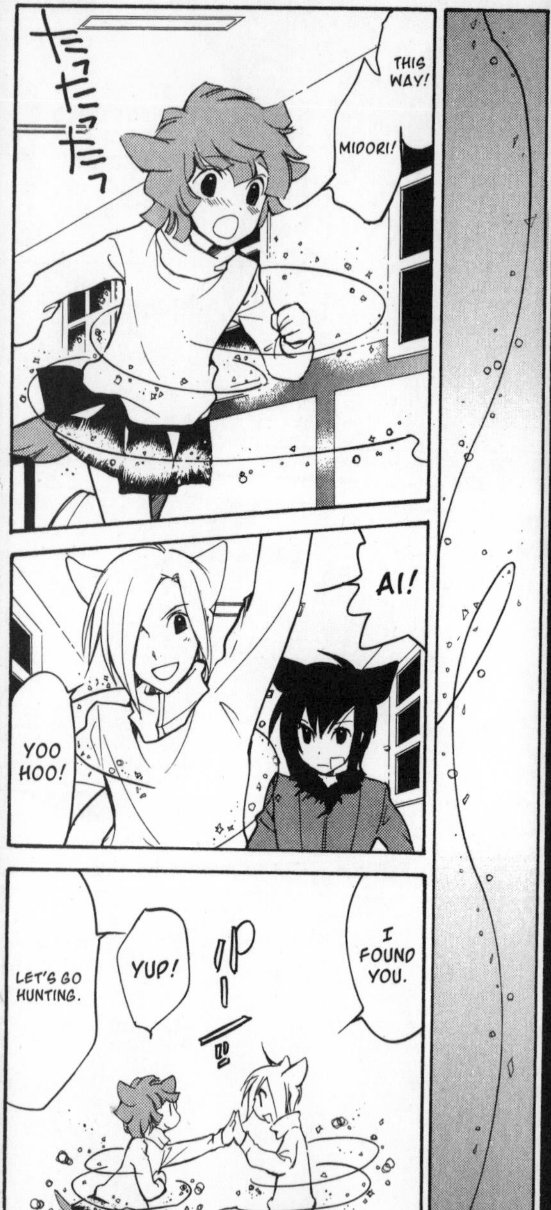
IF WE KEEP KAIDO-KUN ALIVE NOW...
...WE COULD HAVE MORE FUN LATER ON.
THIS WAY!
MIDORI!
たったったっ
AI!
YOO HOO!
I FOUND YOU.
YUP!
LET'S GO HUNTING.

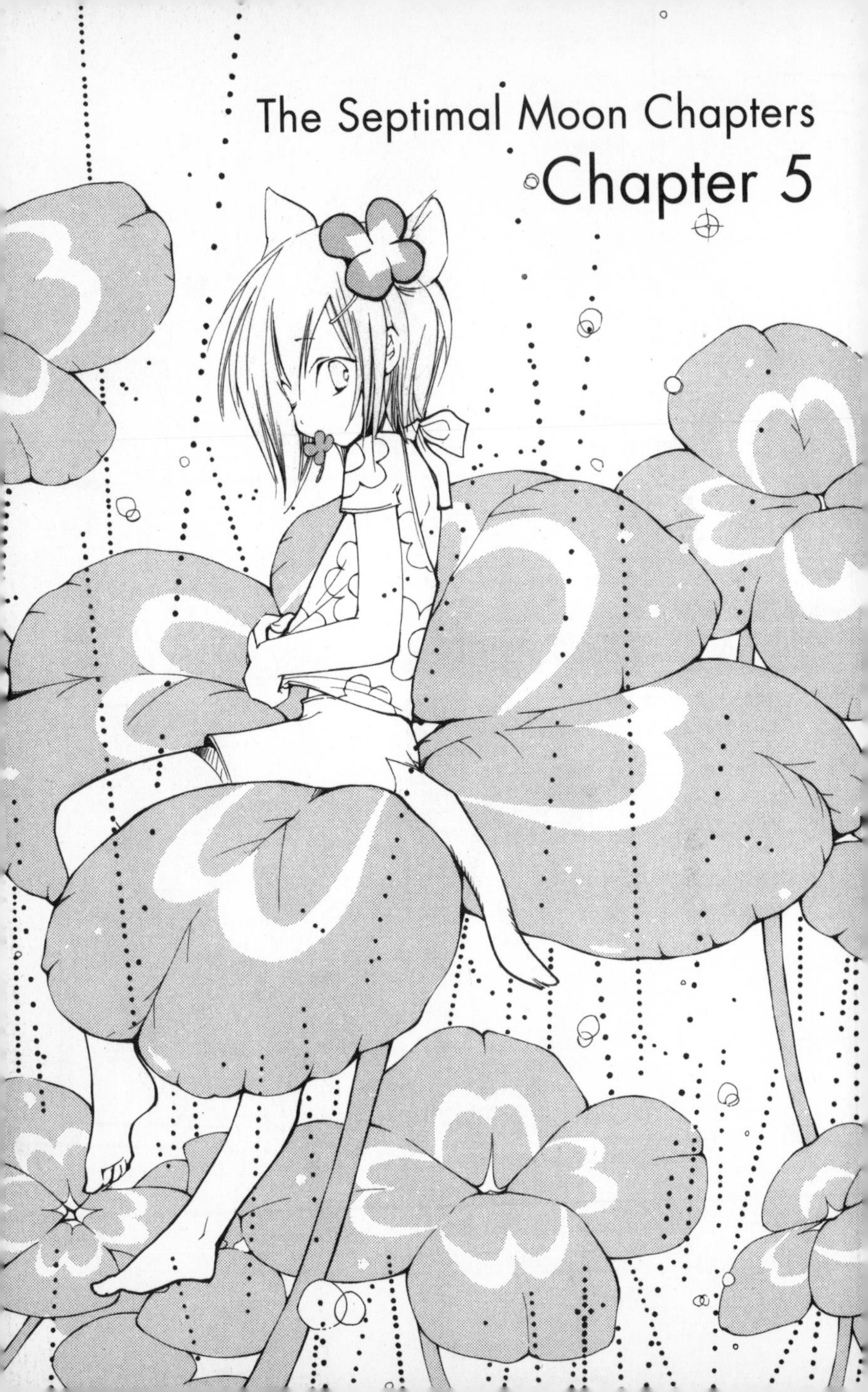
The Septimal Moon Chapters
Chapter 5

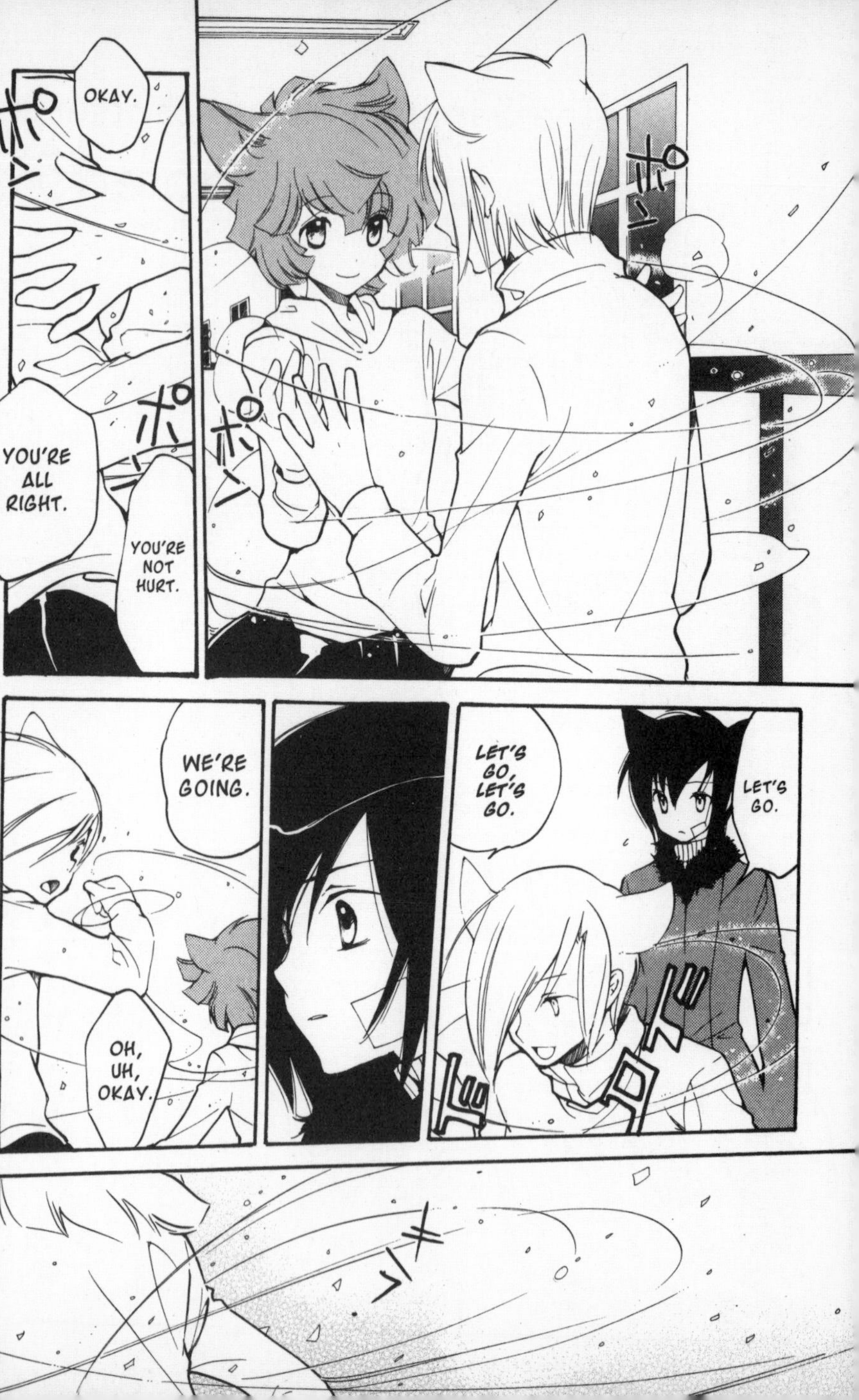
ポン
ポン
ポン
OKAY.
ポン
YOU'RE ALL RIGHT.
YOU'RE NOT HURT.
LET'S GO.
LET'S GO, LET'S GO.
WE'RE GOING.
OH, UH, OKAY.

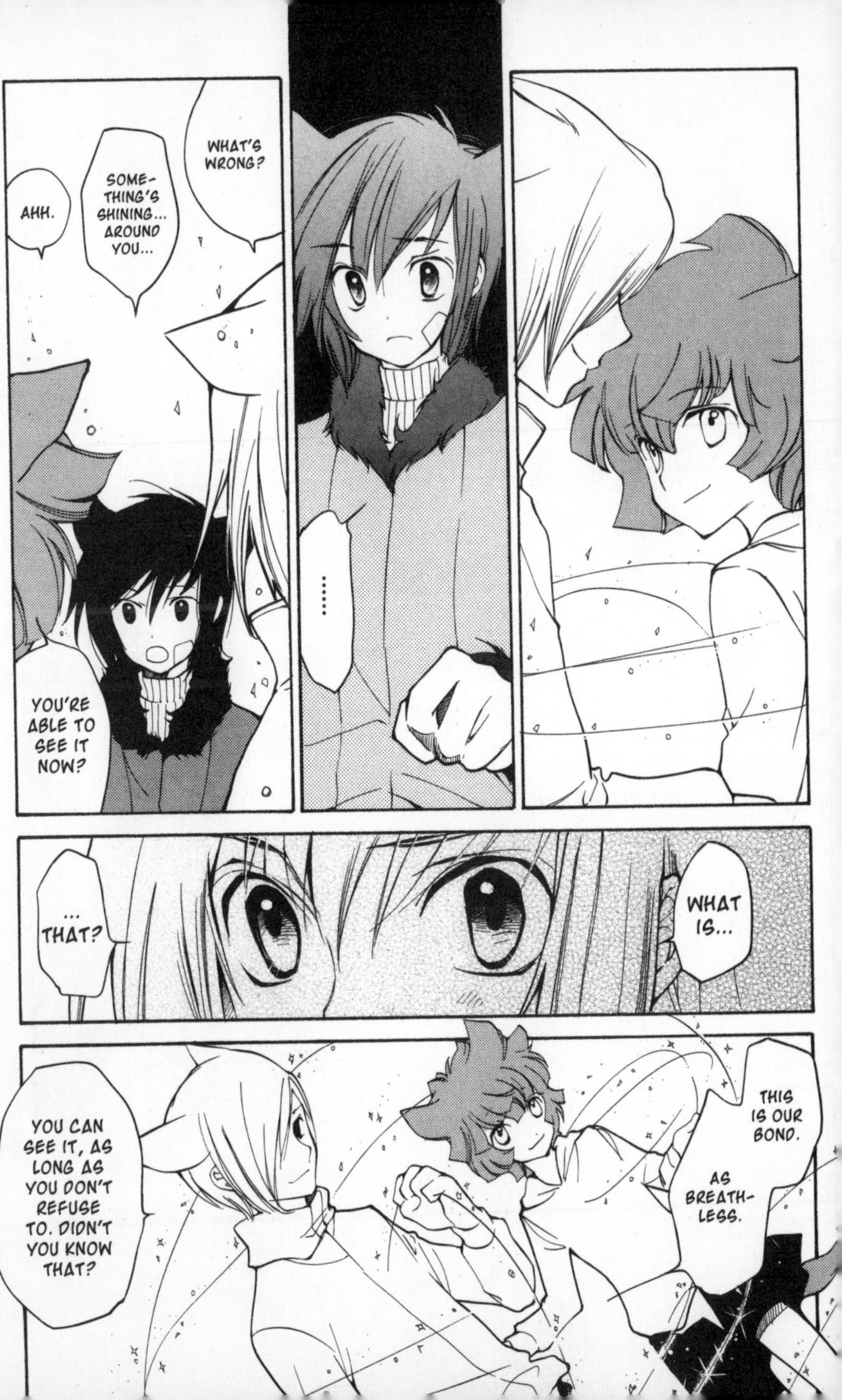
......
WHAT'S WRONG?
SOME-THING'S SHINING... AROUND YOU...
AHH.
YOU'RE ABLE TO SEE IT NOW?
WHAT IS...
...THAT?
THIS IS OUR BOND.
AS BREATH-LESS.
YOU CAN SEE IT, AS LONG AS YOU DON'T REFUSE TO. DIDN'T YOU KNOW THAT?

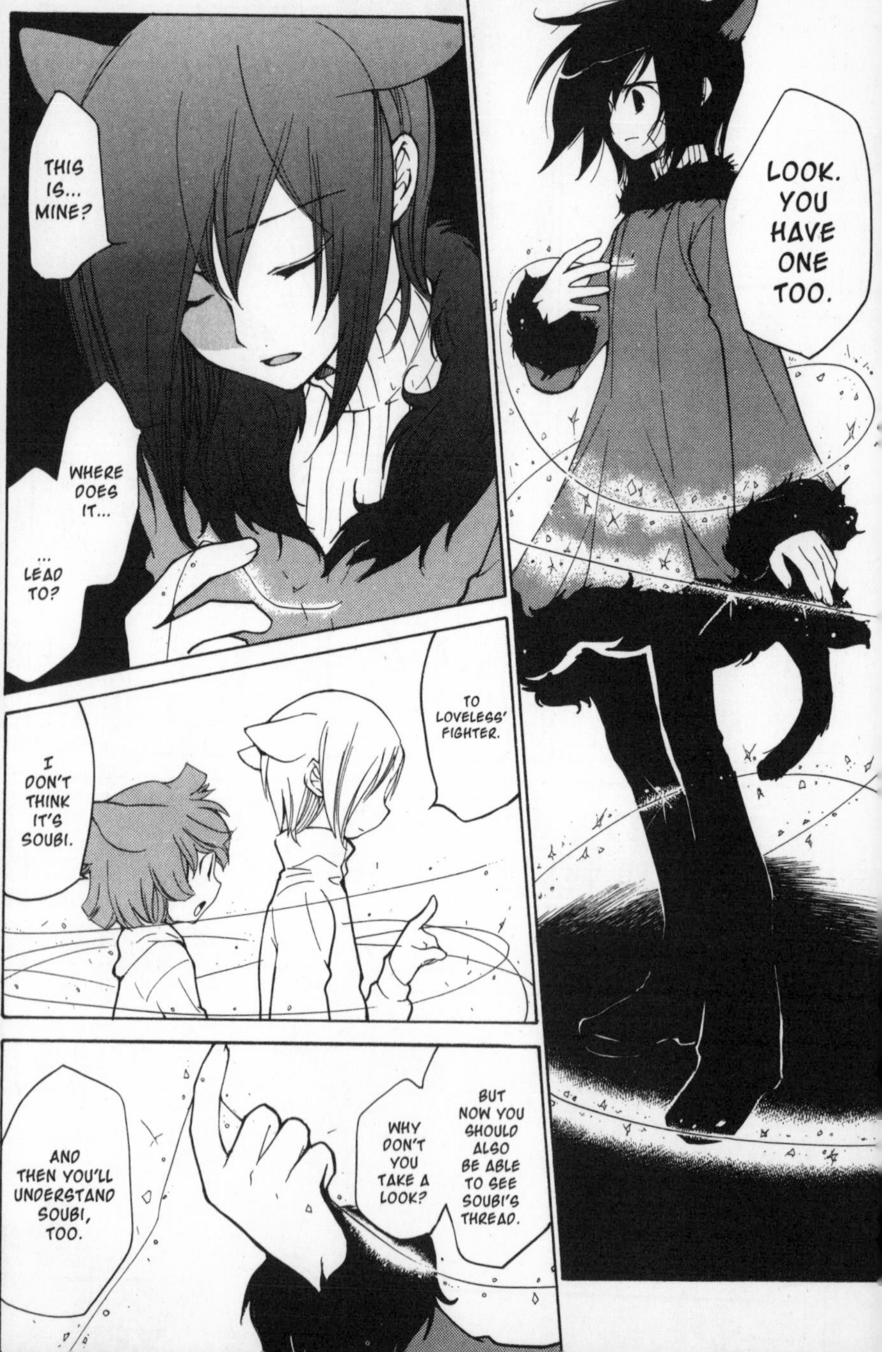
LOOK. YOU HAVE ONE TOO.
THIS IS... MINE?
WHERE DOES IT...
...LEAD TO?
TO LOVELESS' FIGHTER.
I DON'T THINK IT'S SOUBI.
BUT NOW YOU SHOULD ALSO BE ABLE TO SEE SOUBI'S THREAD.
WHY DON'T YOU TAKE A LOOK?
AND THEN YOU'LL UNDERSTAND SOUBI, TOO.

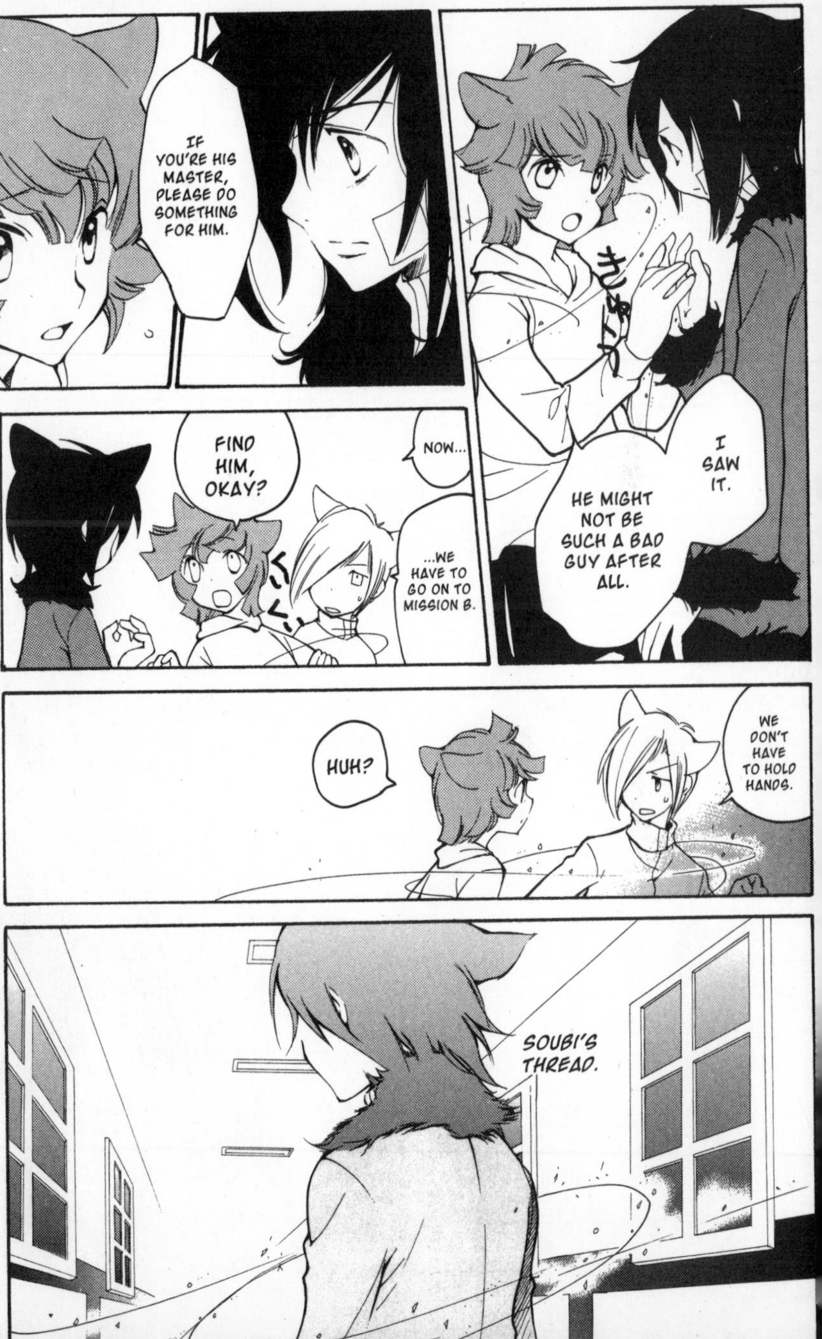
I SAW IT.
HE MIGHT NOT BE SUCH A BAD GUY AFTER ALL.
IF YOU'RE HIS MASTER, PLEASE DO SOMETHING FOR HIM.
NOW...
...WE HAVE TO GO ON TO MISSION B.
FIND HIM, OKAY?
WE DON'T HAVE TO HOLD HANDS.
HUH?
SOUBI'S THREAD.

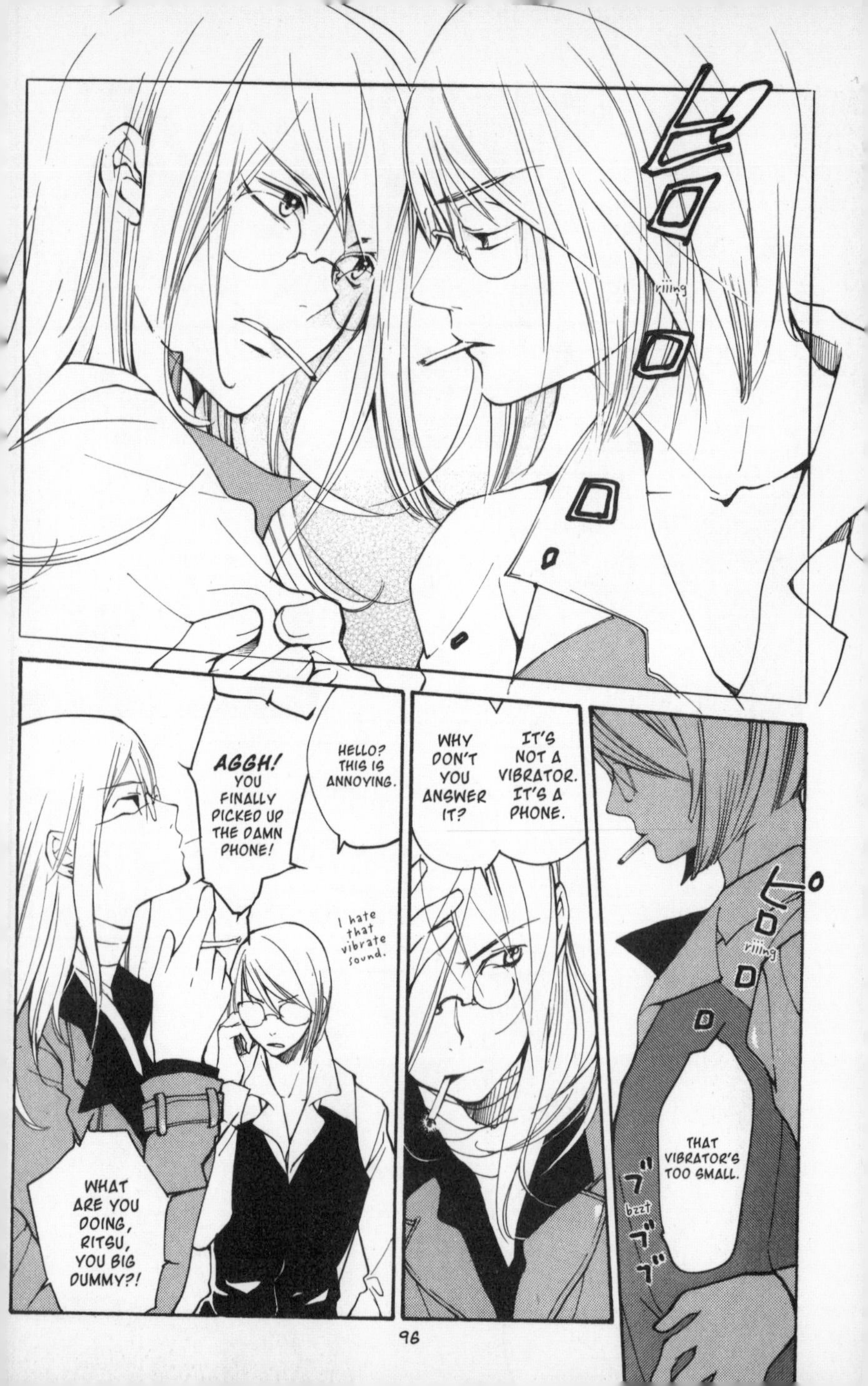
riiing
riiing
THAT VIBRATOR'S TOO SMALL.
ブブブ
bzzt
IT'S NOT A VIBRATOR. IT'S A PHONE.
WHY DON'T YOU ANSWER IT?
HELLO? THIS IS ANNOYING.
AGGH! YOU FINALLY PICKED UP THE DAMN PHONE!
I hate that vibrate sound.
WHAT ARE YOU DOING, RITSU, YOU BIG DUMMY?!

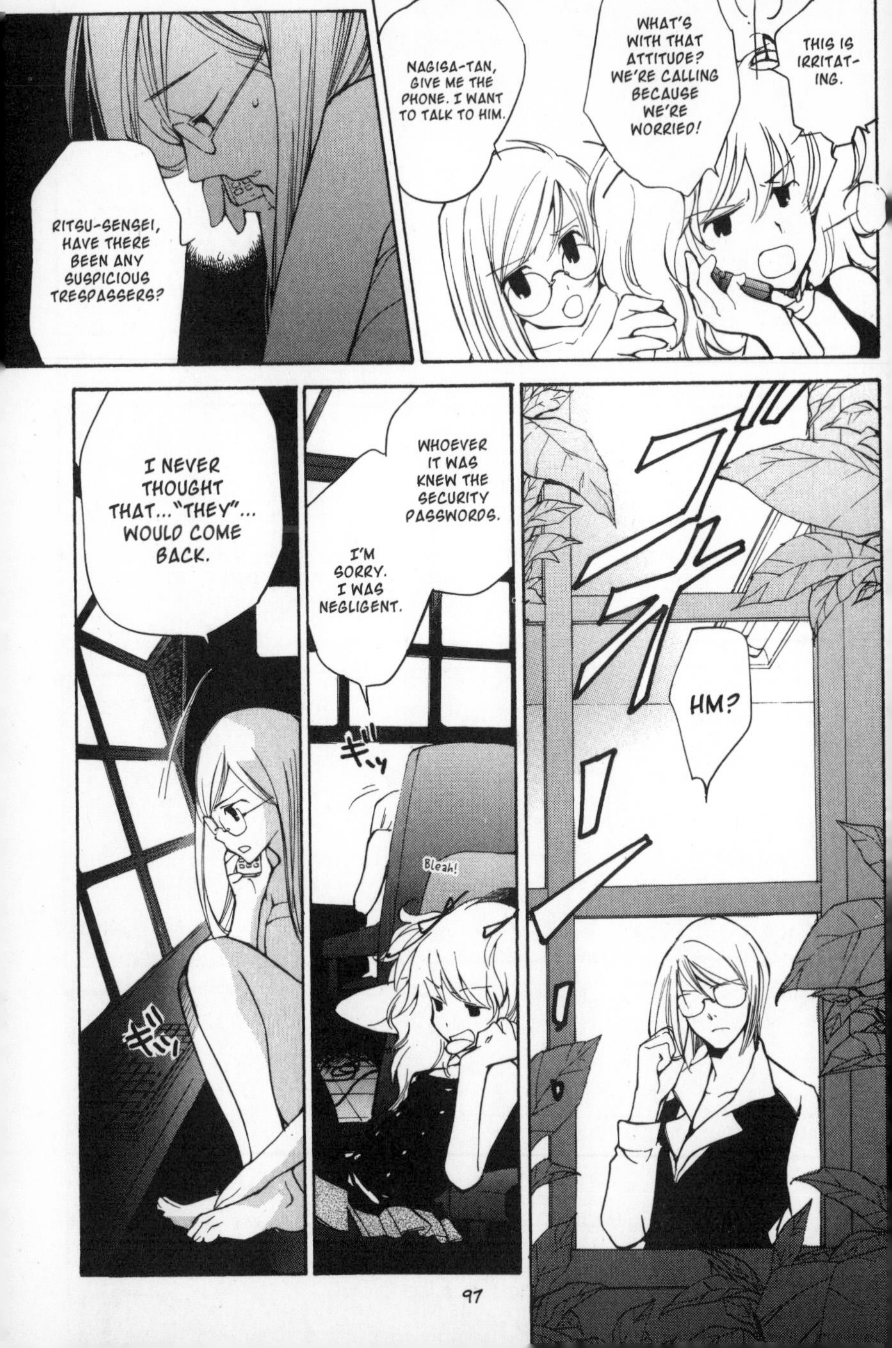

THIS IS IRRITAT-ING.
WHAT'S WITH THAT ATTITUDE? WE'RE CALLING BECAUSE WE'RE WORRIED!
NAGISA-TAN, GIVE ME THE PHONE. I WANT TO TALK TO HIM.
RITSU-SENSEI, HAVE THERE BEEN ANY SUSPICIOUS TRESPASSERS?
HM?
WHOEVER IT WAS KNEW THE SECURITY PASSWORDS.
I'M SORRY. I WAS NEGLIGENT.
Bleah!
I NEVER THOUGHT THAT..."THEY"... WOULD COME BACK.

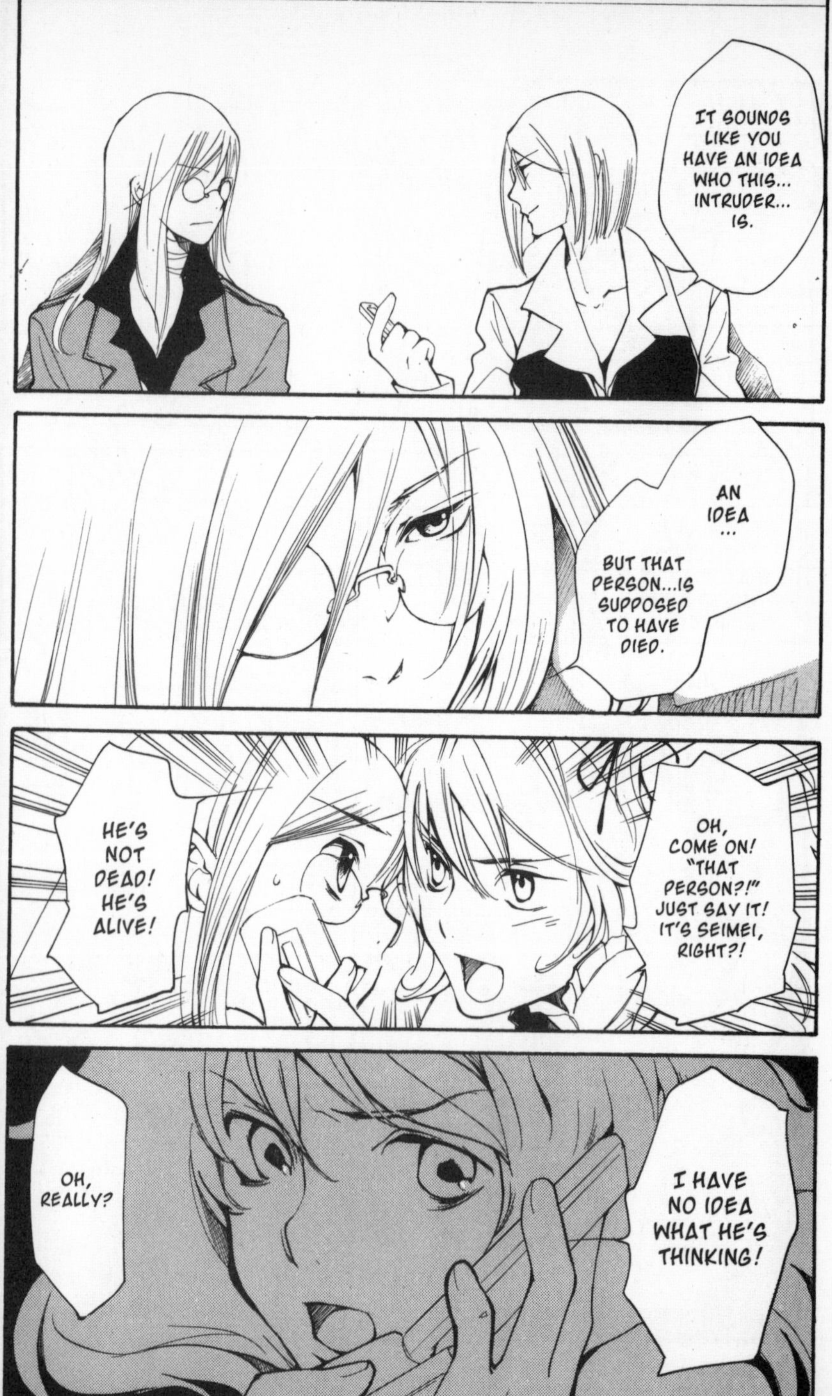
IT SOUNDS LIKE YOU HAVE AN IDEA WHO THIS... INTRUDER... IS.
AN IDEA ...
BUT THAT PERSON...IS SUPPOSED TO HAVE DIED.
OH, COME ON! "THAT PERSON?!" JUST SAY IT! IT'S SEIMEI, RIGHT?!
HE'S NOT DEAD! HE'S ALIVE!
I HAVE NO IDEA WHAT HE'S THINKING!
OH, REALLY?

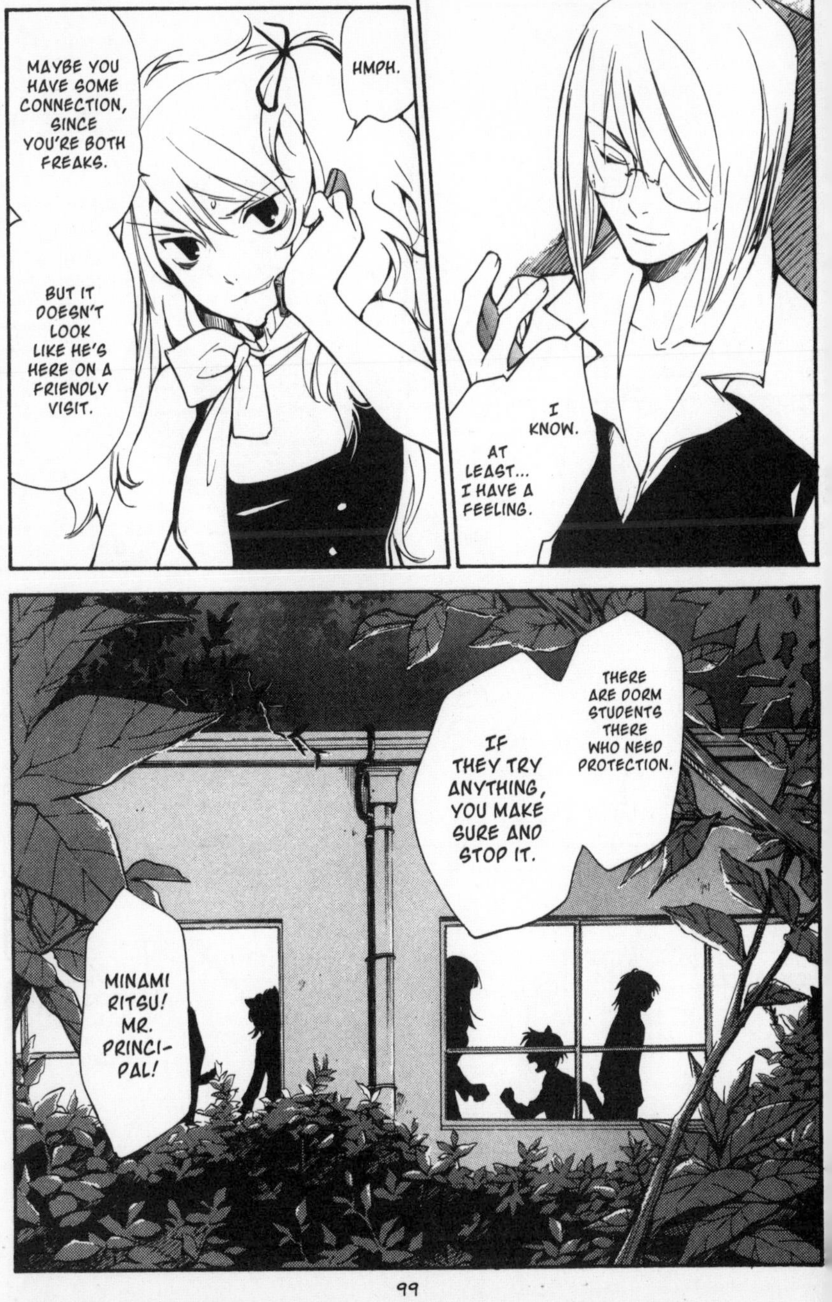
I KNOW.
AT LEAST... I HAVE A FEELING.
HMPH.
MAYBE YOU HAVE SOME CONNECTION, SINCE YOU'RE BOTH FREAKS.
BUT IT DOESN'T LOOK LIKE HE'S HERE ON A FRIENDLY VISIT.
THERE ARE DORM STUDENTS THERE WHO NEED PROTECTION.
IF THEY TRY ANYTHING, YOU MAKE SURE AND STOP IT.
MINAMI RITSU! MR. PRINCI-PAL!

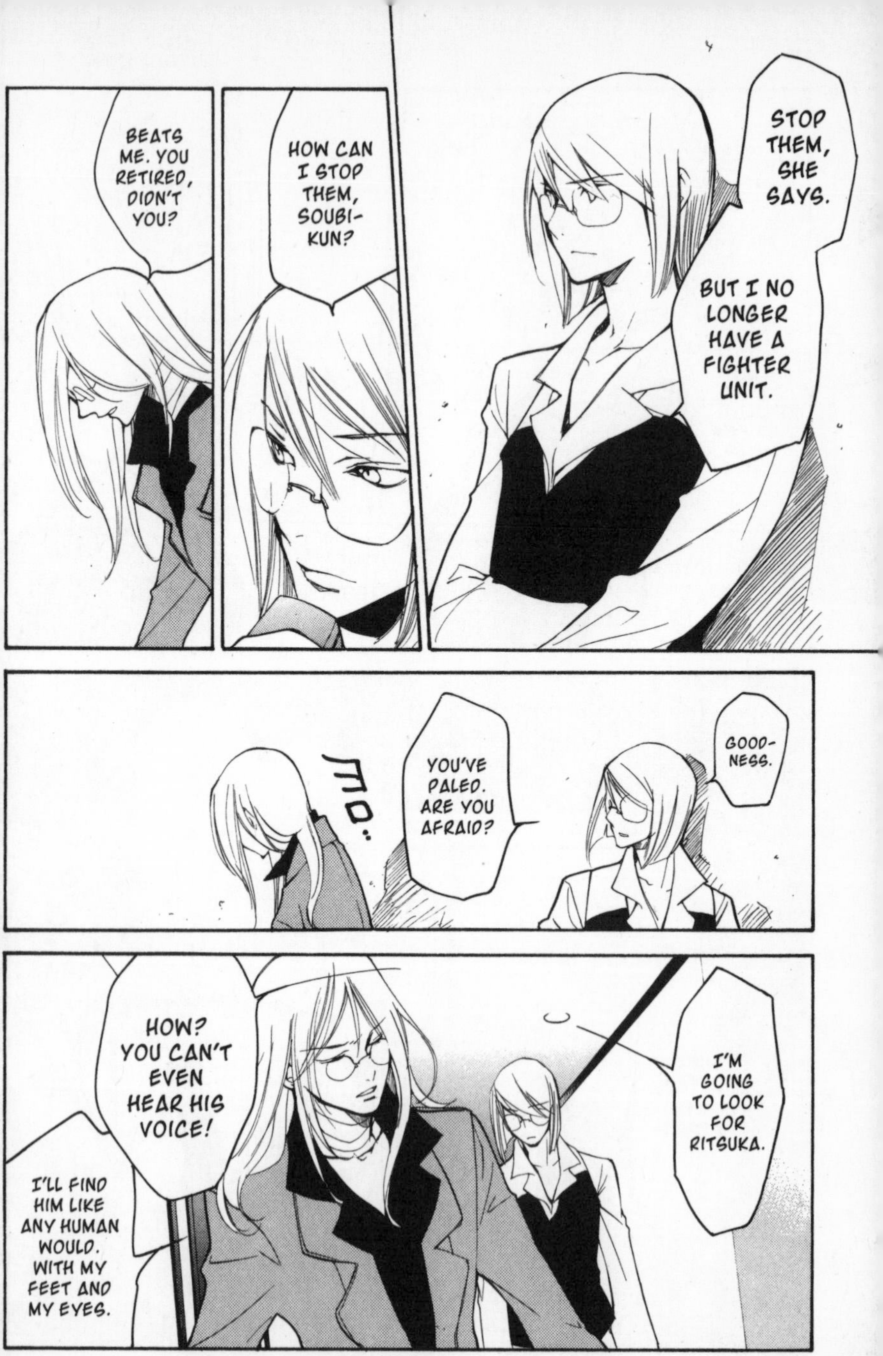
STOP THEM, SHE SAYS.
BUT I NO LONGER HAVE A FIGHTER UNIT.
HOW CAN I STOP THEM, SOUBI-KUN?
BEATS ME. YOU RETIRED, DIDN'T YOU?
GOOD-NESS.
YOU'VE PALED. ARE YOU AFRAID?
I'M GOING TO LOOK FOR RITSUKA.
HOW? YOU CAN'T EVEN HEAR HIS VOICE!
I'LL FIND HIM LIKE ANY HUMAN WOULD. WITH MY FEET AND MY EYES.

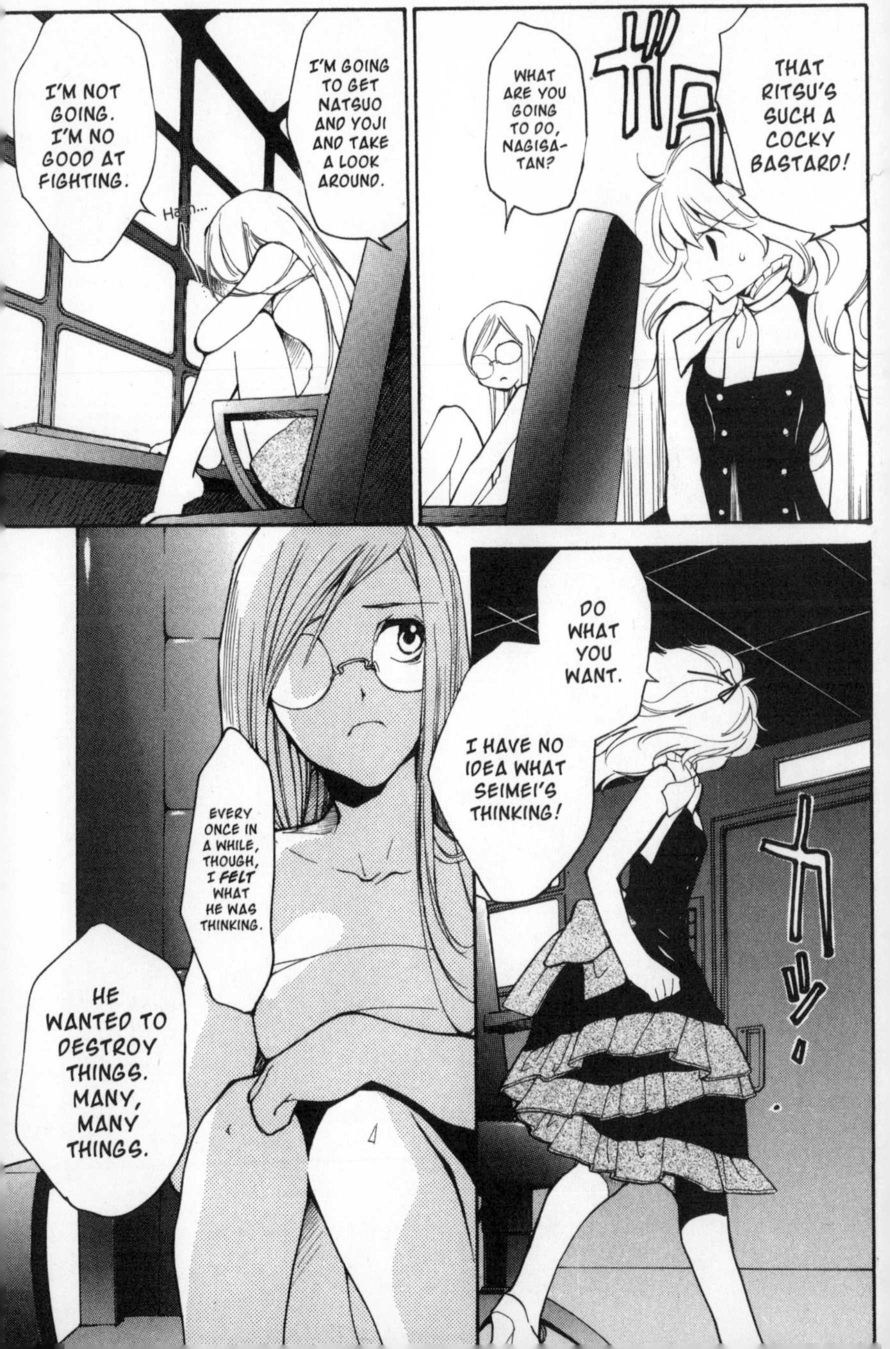
THAT RITSU'S SUCH A COCKY BASTARD!
WHAT ARE YOU GOING TO DO, NAGISA-TAN?
I'M GOING TO GET NATSUO AND YOJI AND TAKE A LOOK AROUND.
I'M NOT GOING. I'M NO GOOD AT FIGHTING.
Haan...
DO WHAT YOU WANT.
I HAVE NO IDEA WHAT SEIMEI'S THINKING!
EVERY ONCE IN A WHILE, THOUGH, I FELT WHAT HE WAS THINKING.
HE WANTED TO DESTROY THINGS. MANY, MANY THINGS.

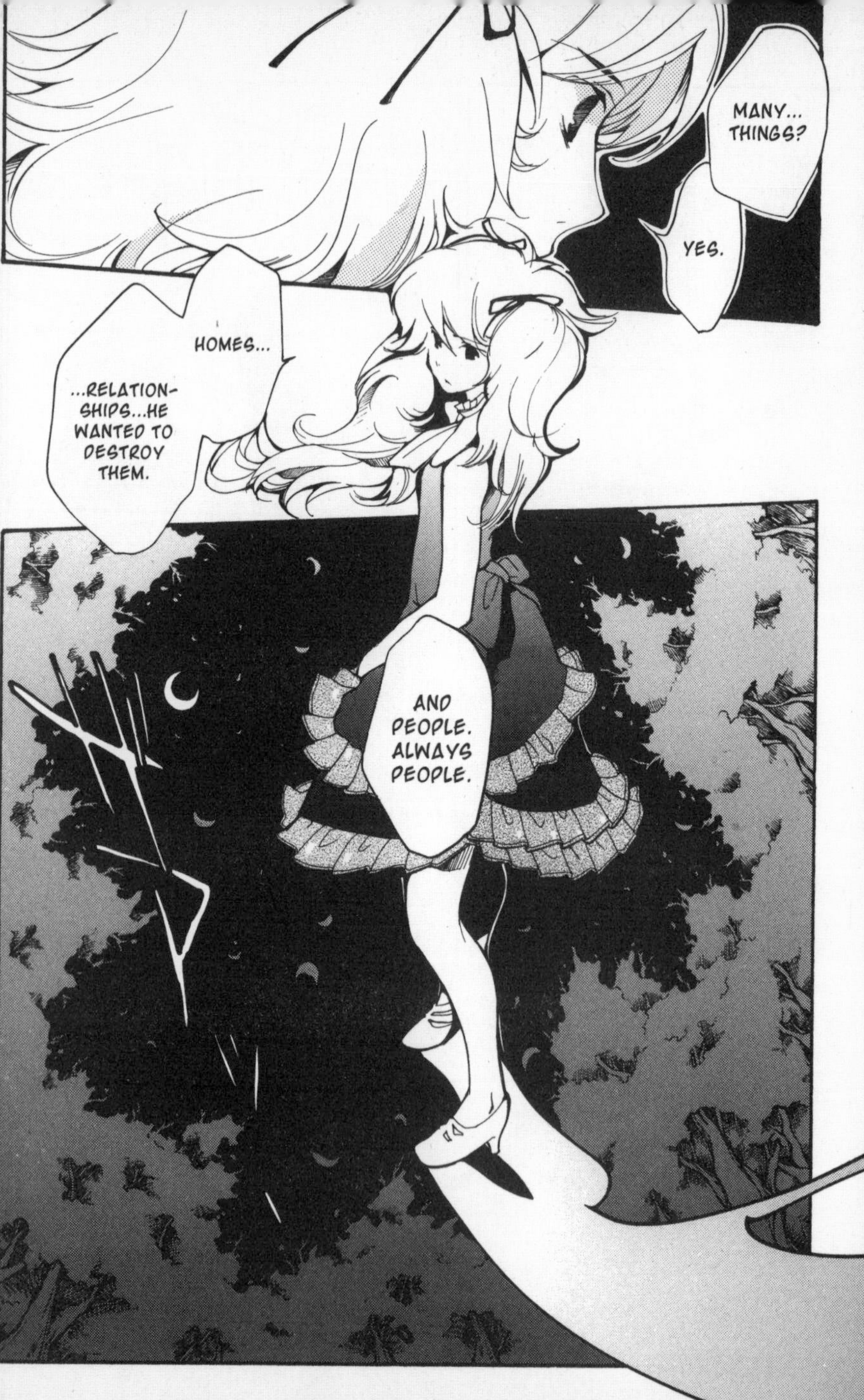
MANY... THINGS?
YES.
HOMES...
...RELATION-SHIPS...HE WANTED TO DESTROY THEM.
AND PEOPLE. ALWAYS PEOPLE.

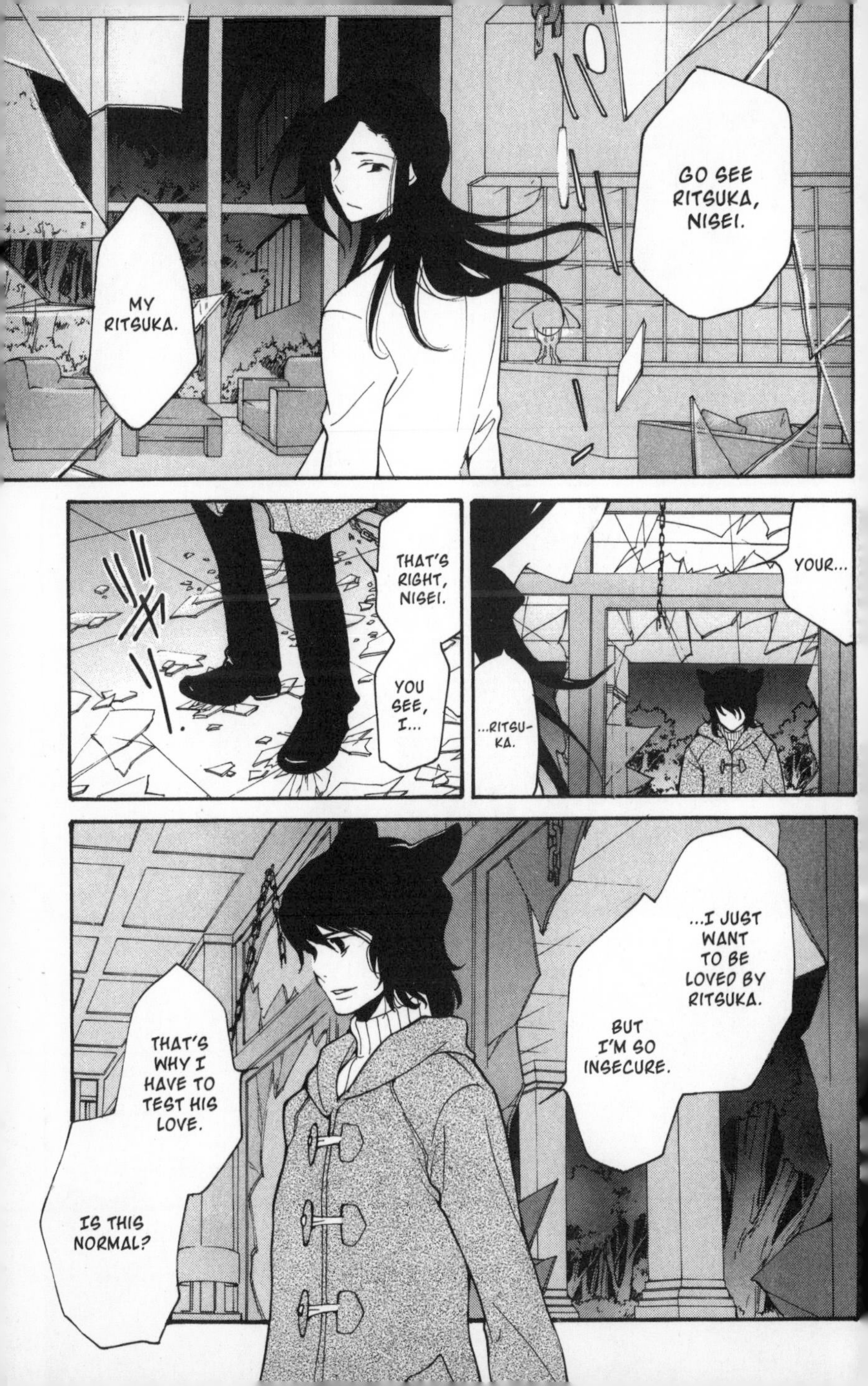
GO SEE RITSUKA, NISEI.
MY RITSUKA.
YOUR...
...RITSU-KA.
THAT'S RIGHT, NISEI.
YOU SEE, I...
...I JUST WANT TO BE LOVED BY RITSUKA.
BUT I'M SO INSECURE.
THAT'S WHY I HAVE TO TEST HIS LOVE.
IS THIS NORMAL?

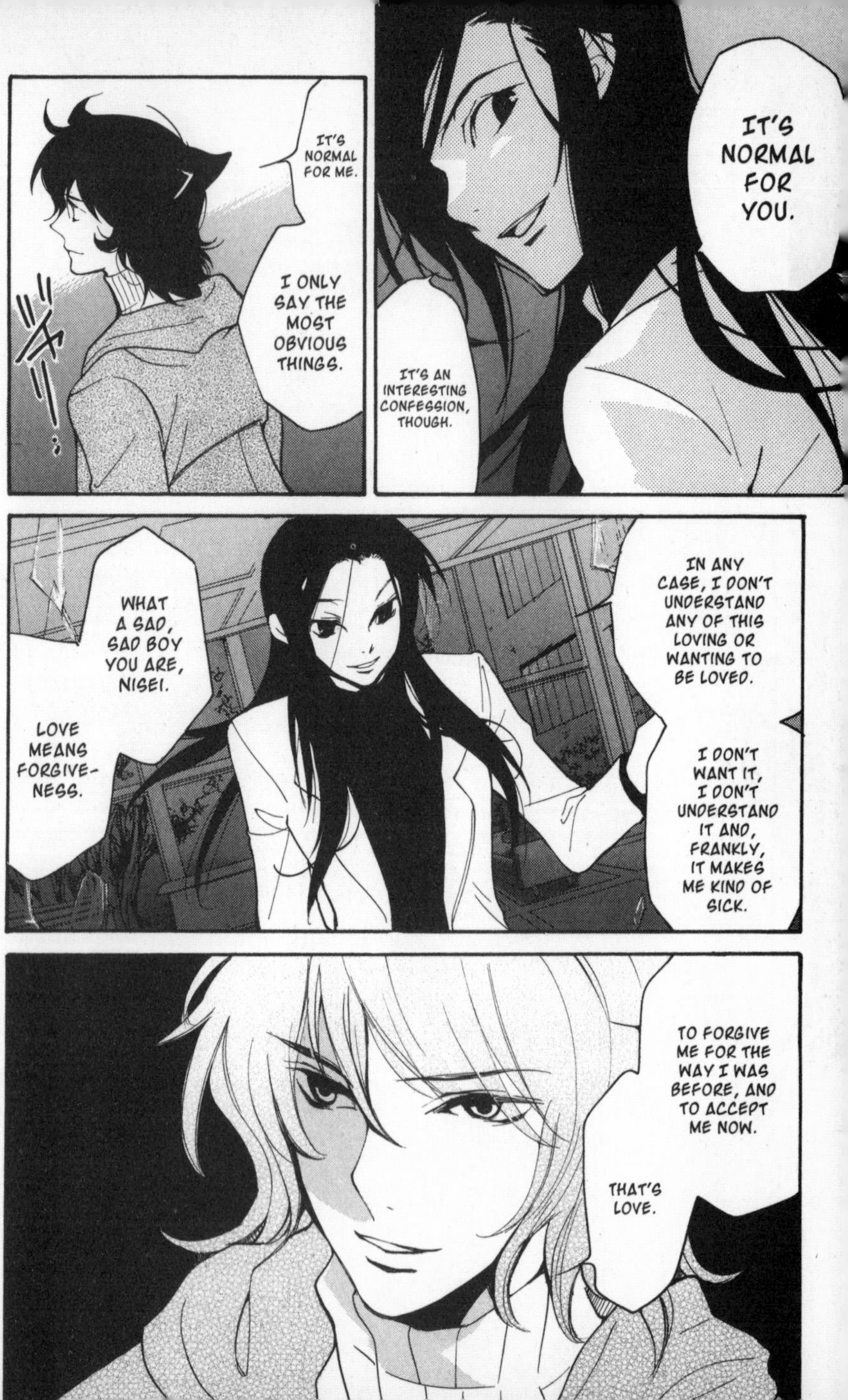
IT'S NORMAL FOR YOU.
IT'S AN INTERESTING CONFESSION, THOUGH.
IT'S NORMAL FOR ME.
I ONLY SAY THE MOST OBVIOUS THINGS.
IN ANY CASE, I DON'T UNDERSTAND ANY OF THIS LOVING OR WANTING TO BE LOVED.
I DON'T WANT IT, I DON'T UNDERSTAND IT AND, FRANKLY, IT MAKES ME KIND OF SICK.
WHAT A SAD, SAD BOY YOU ARE, NISEI.
LOVE MEANS FORGIVE-NESS.
TO FORGIVE ME FOR THE WAY I WAS BEFORE, AND TO ACCEPT ME NOW.
THAT'S LOVE.

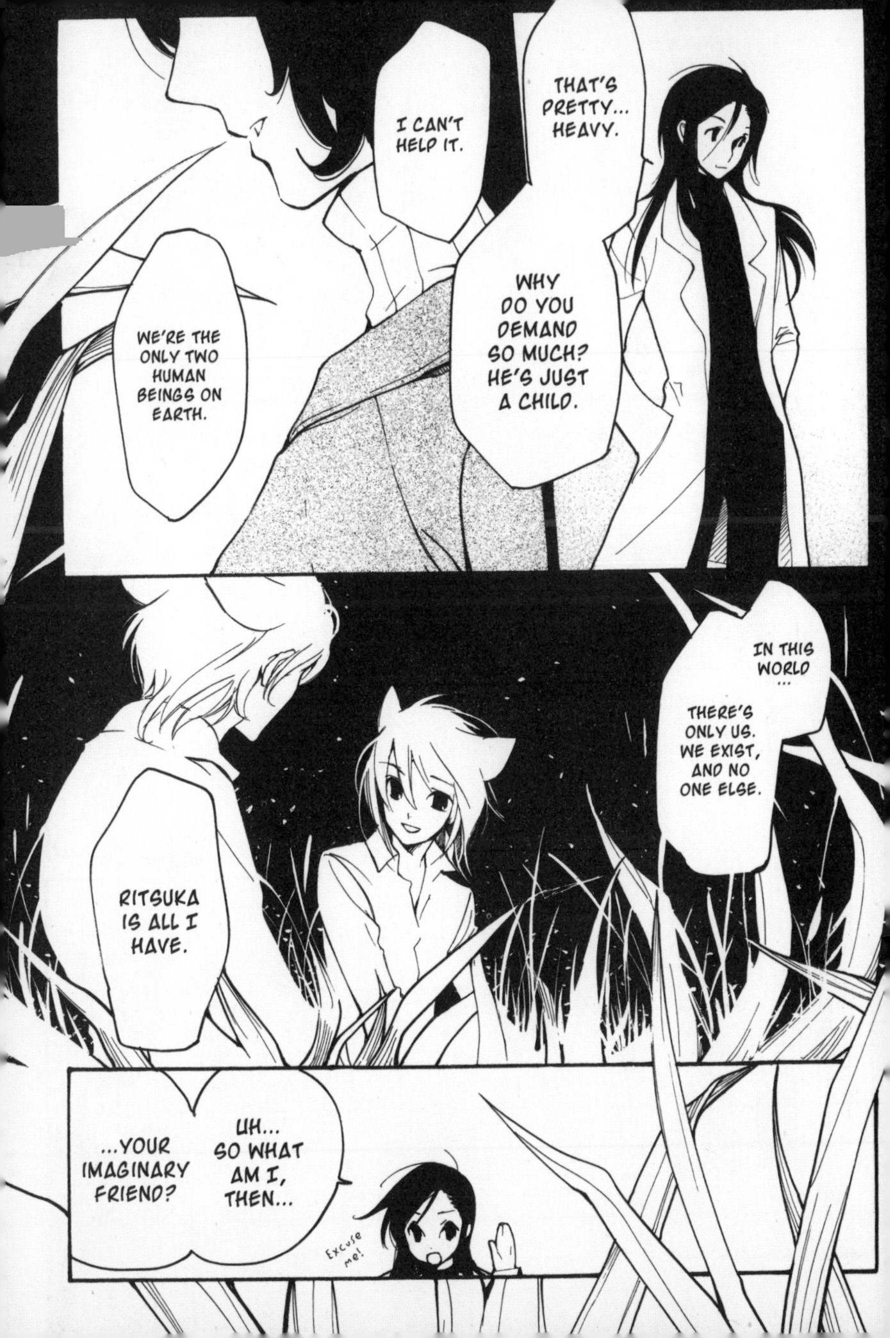
THAT'S PRETTY... HEAVY.
WHY DO YOU DEMAND SO MUCH? HE'S JUST A CHILD.
I CAN'T HELP IT.
WE'RE THE ONLY TWO HUMAN BEINGS ON EARTH.
IN THIS WORLD ...
THERE'S ONLY US. WE EXIST, AND NO ONE ELSE.
RITSUKA IS ALL I HAVE.
UH... SO WHAT AM I, THEN...
...YOUR IMAGINARY FRIEND?
Excuse me!

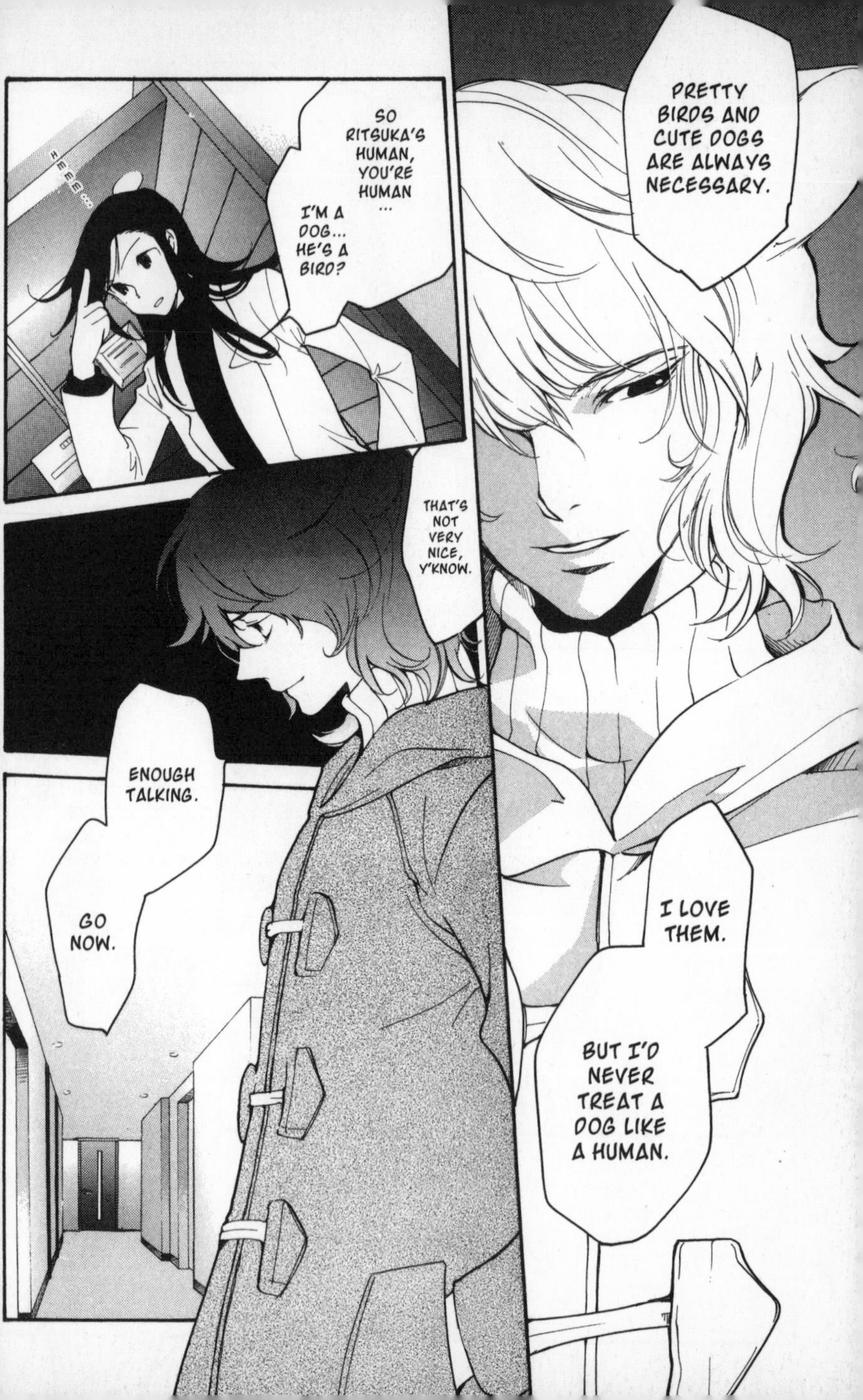
PRETTY BIRDS AND CUTE DOGS ARE ALWAYS NECESSARY.
I LOVE THEM.
BUT I'D NEVER TREAT A DOG LIKE A HUMAN.
SO RITSUKA'S HUMAN, YOU'RE HUMAN ...
I'M A DOG... HE'S A BIRD?
HEEE...
THAT'S NOT VERY NICE, Y'KNOW.
ENOUGH TALKING.
GO NOW.

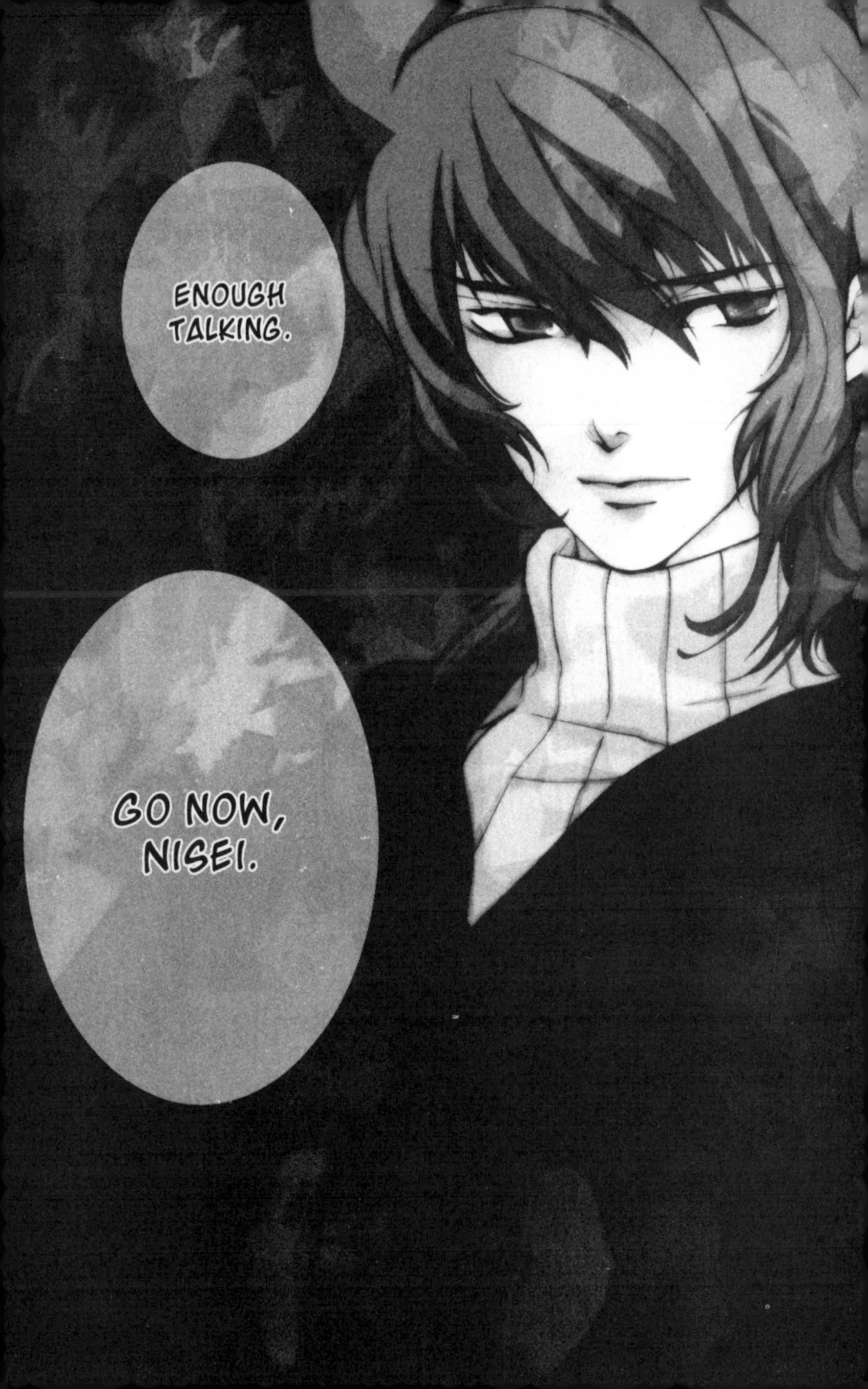
ENOUGH TALKING.
GO NOW, NISEI.

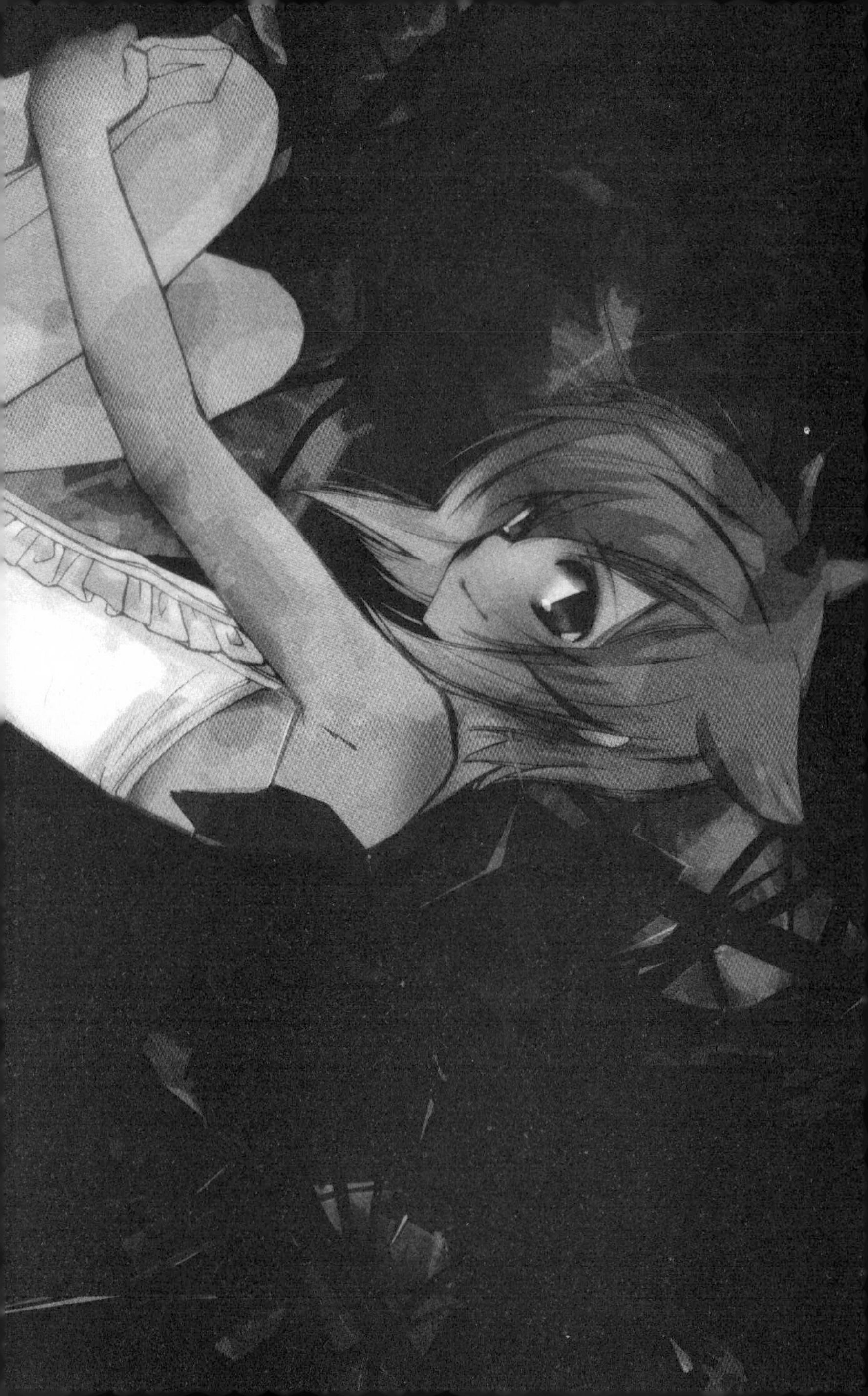

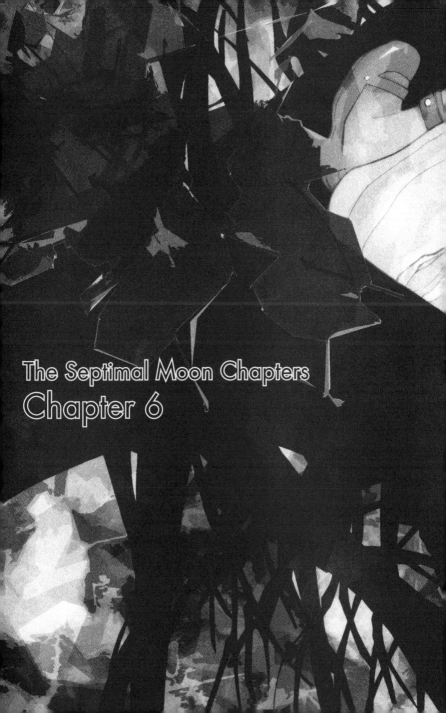

The Septimal Moon Chapters
Chapter 6

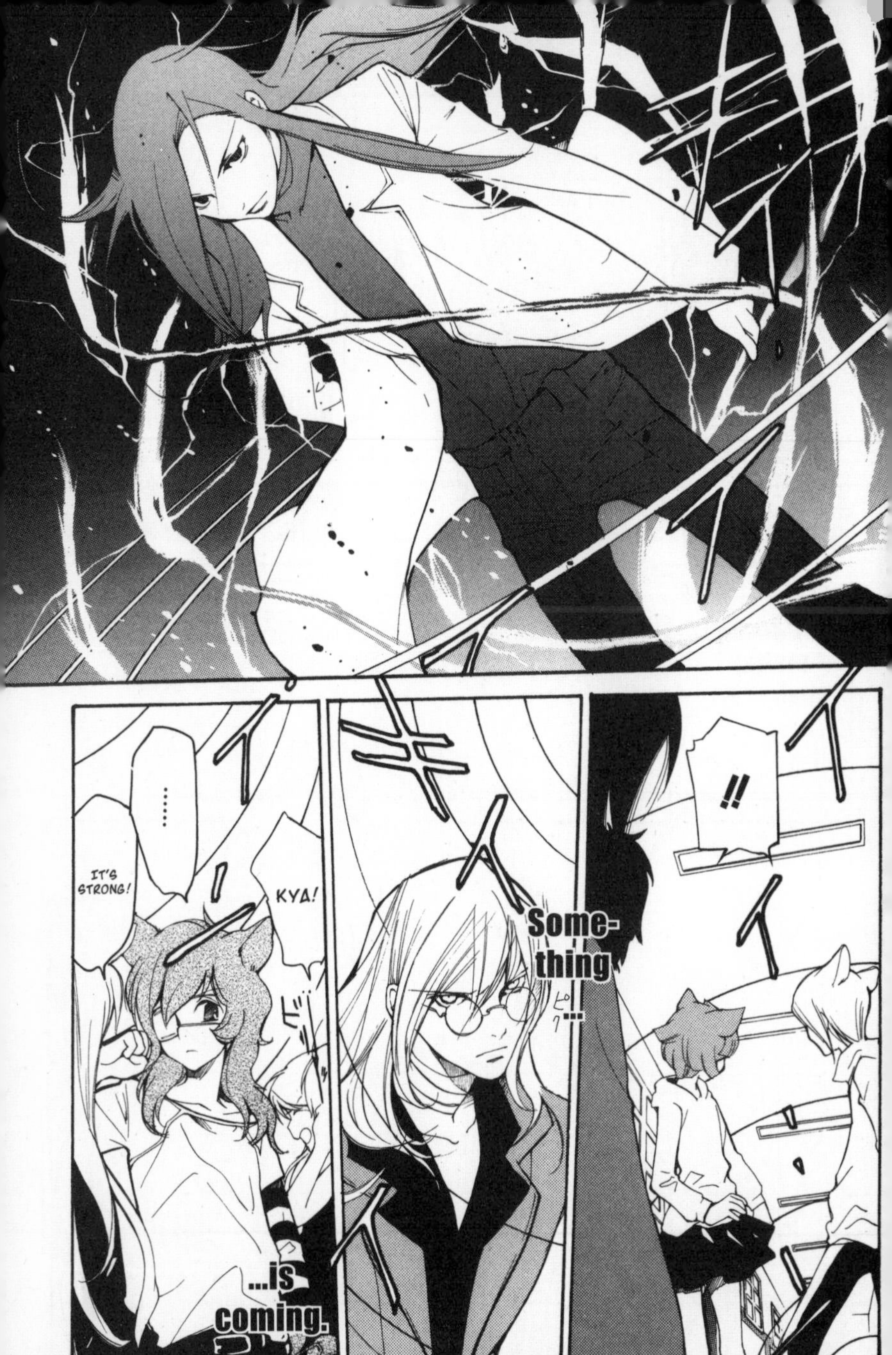
!!
Some-
thing
......
KYA!
IT'S STRONG!
...is
coming.

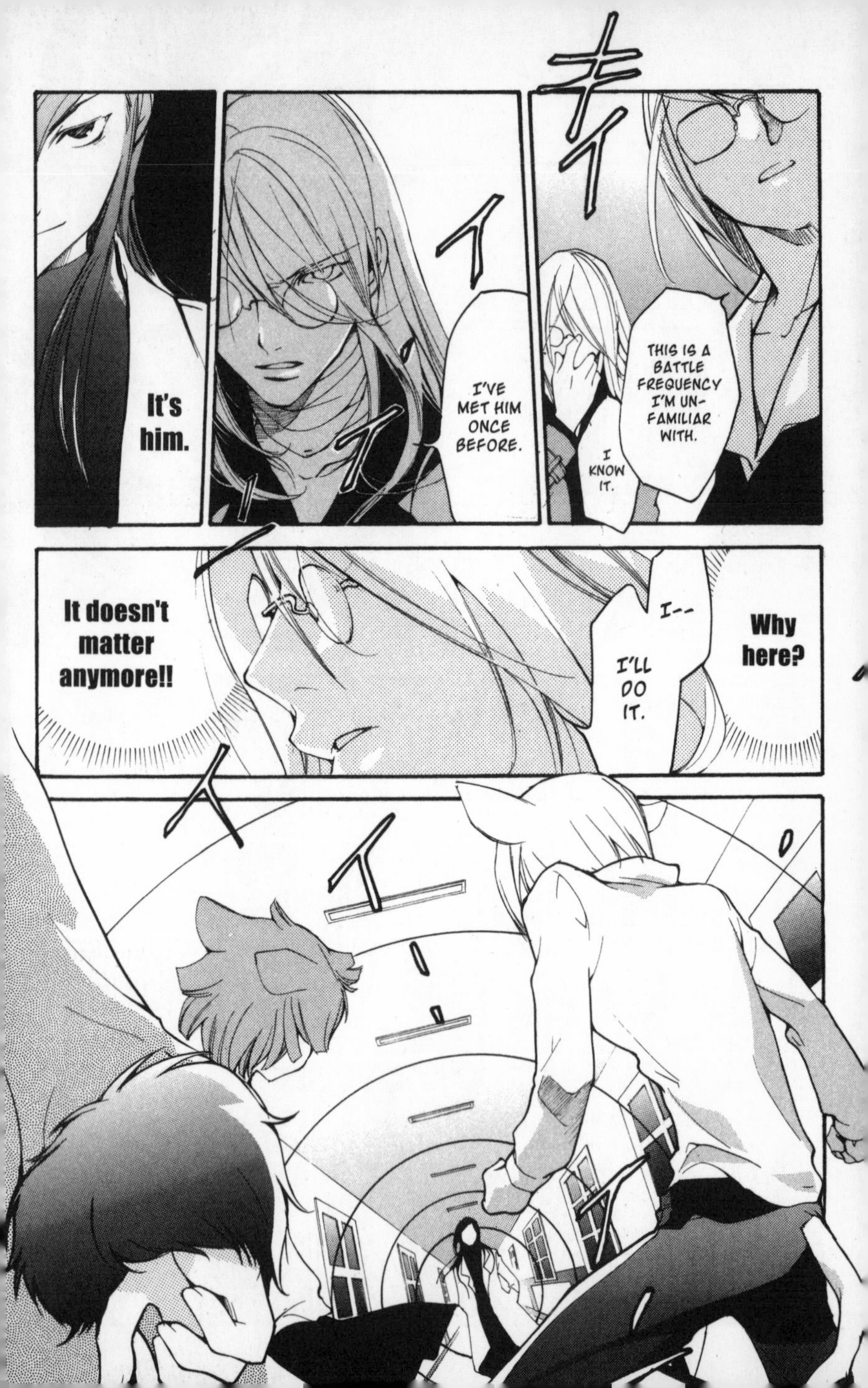

THIS IS A BATTLE FREQUENCY I'M UN-FAMILIAR WITH.
I KNOW IT.
I'VE MET HIM ONCE BEFORE.
It's him.
Why here?
I--
I'LL DO IT.
It doesn't matter anymore!!

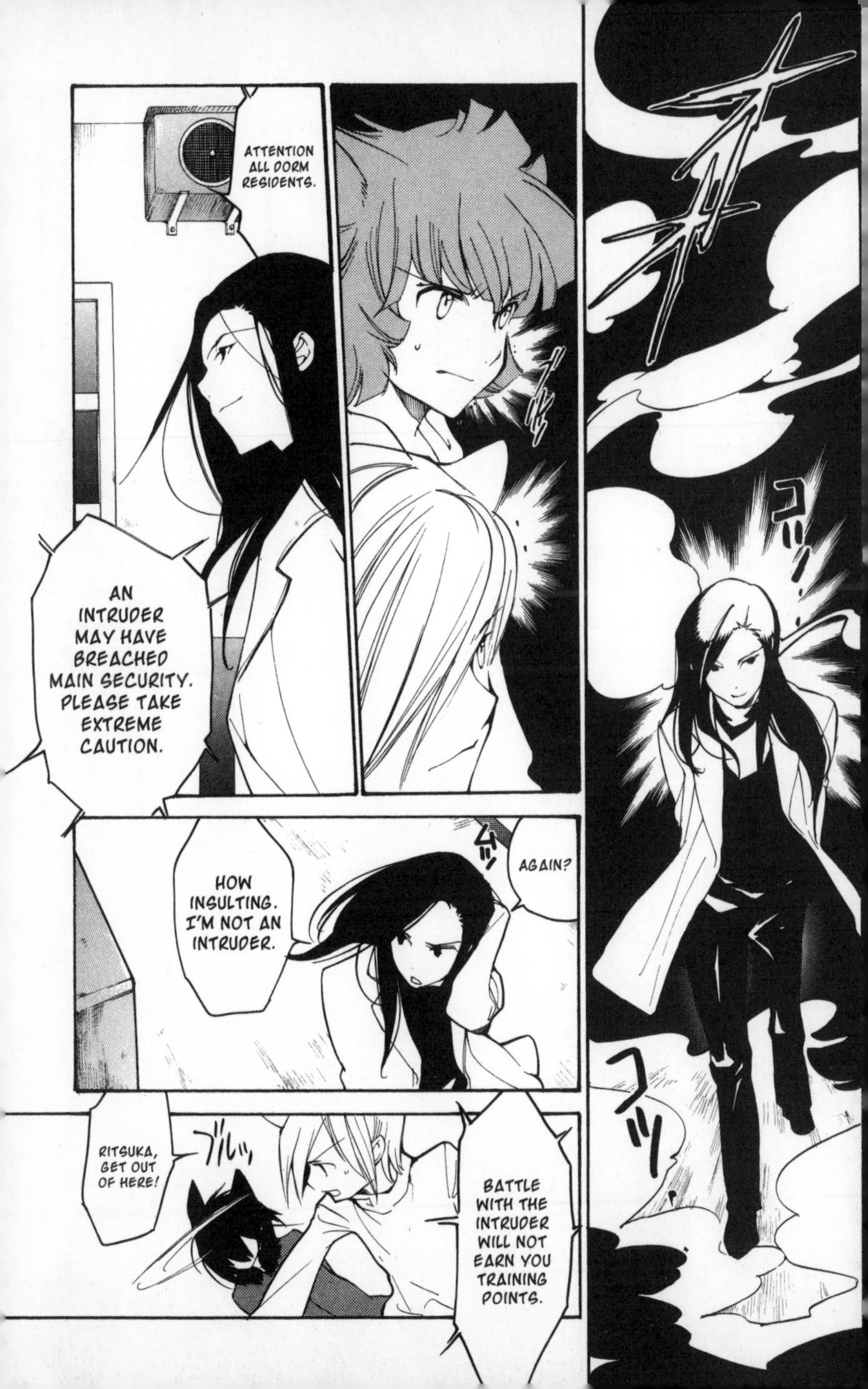
ATTENTION ALL DORM RESIDENTS.
AN INTRUDER MAY HAVE BREACHED MAIN SECURITY. PLEASE TAKE EXTREME CAUTION.
AGAIN?
HOW INSULTING. I'M NOT AN INTRUDER.
BATTLE WITH THE INTRUDER WILL NOT EARN YOU TRAINING POINTS.
RITSUKA, GET OUT OF HERE!

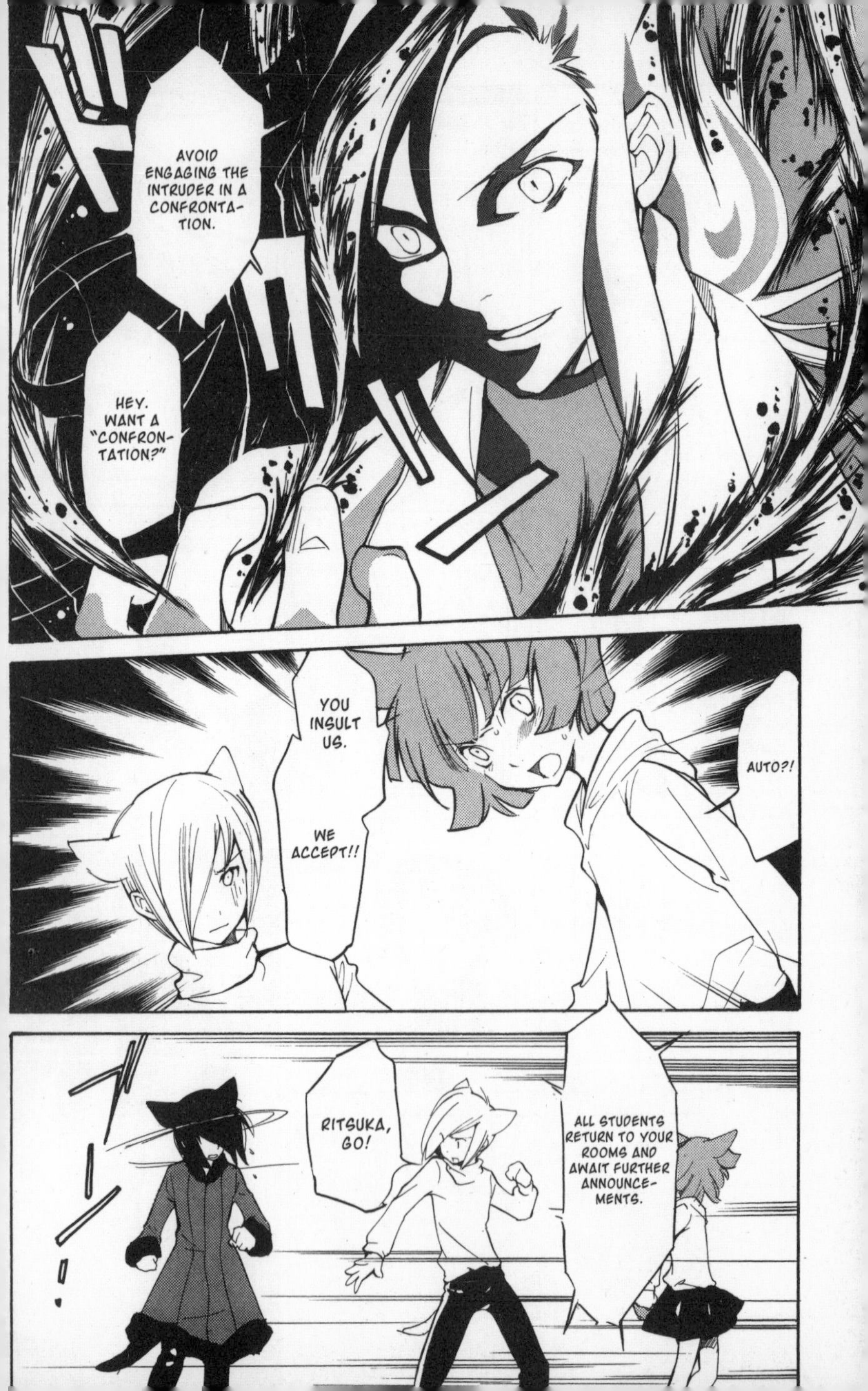
AVOID ENGAGING THE INTRUDER IN A CONFRONTA-TION.
HEY. WANT A "CONFRON-TATION?"
AUTO?!
YOU INSULT US.
WE ACCEPT!!
ALL STUDENTS RETURN TO YOUR ROOMS AND AWAIT FURTHER ANNOUNCE-MENTS.
RITSUKA, GO!

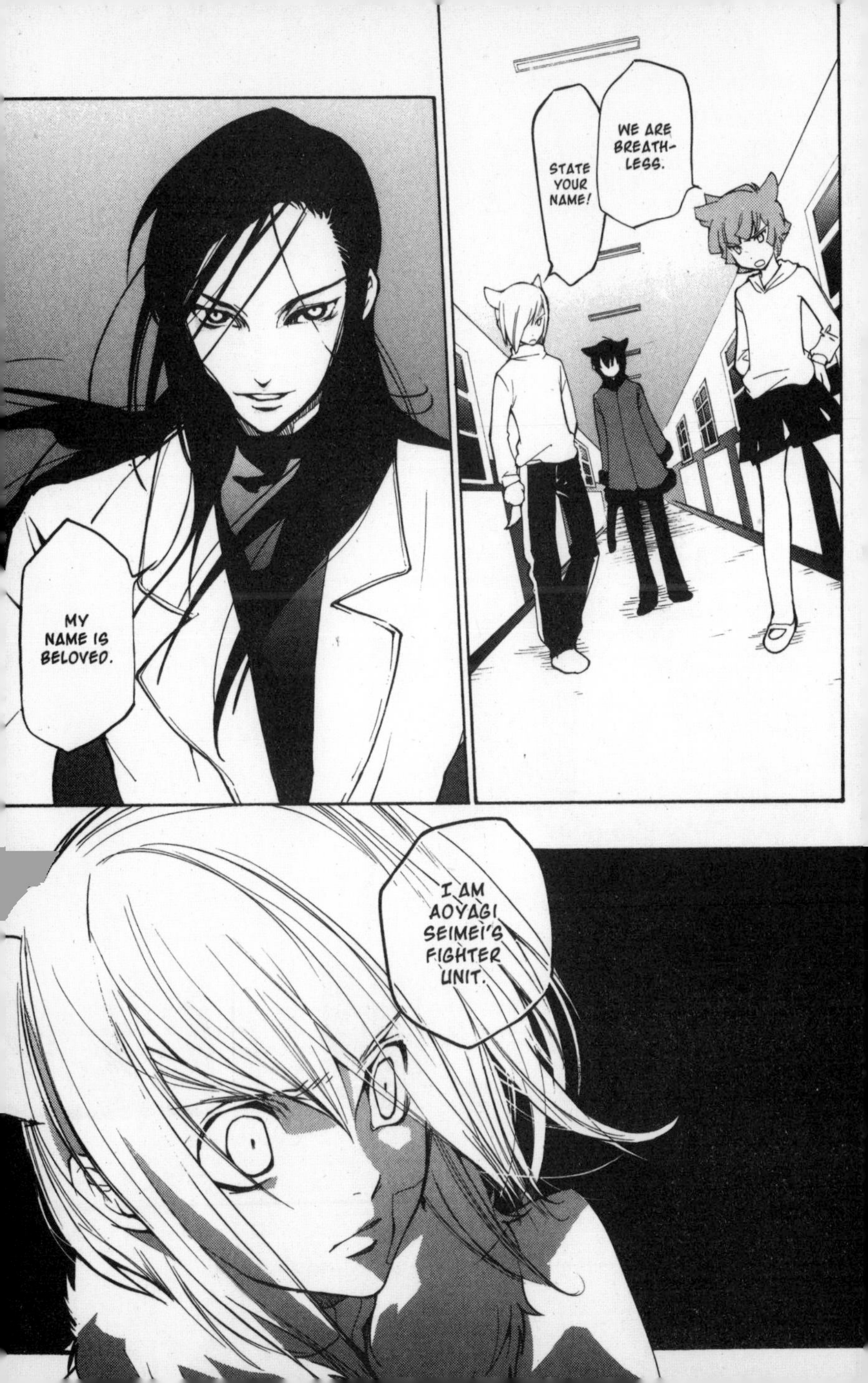
WE ARE BREATHLESS.
STATE YOUR NAME!
MY NAME IS BELOVED.
I AM AOYAGI SEIMEI'S FIGHTER UNIT.

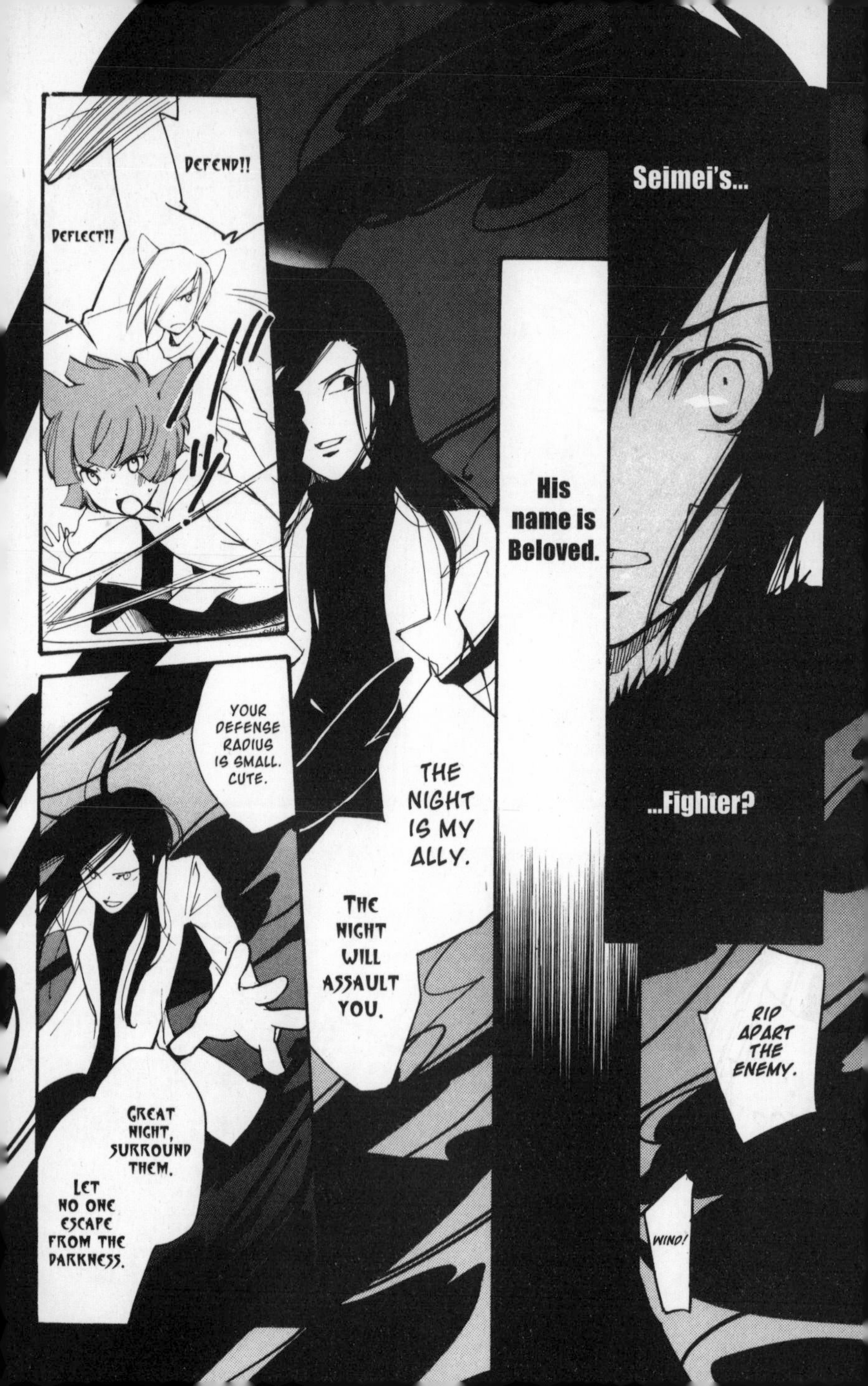
Seimei's...
...Fighter?
His name is Beloved.
RIP APART THE ENEMY.
WIND!
DEFEND!!
DEFLECT!!
THE NIGHT IS MY ALLY.
THE NIGHT WILL ASSAULT YOU.
YOUR DEFENSE RADIUS IS SMALL. CUTE.
GREAT NIGHT, SURROUND THEM.
LET NO ONE ESCAPE FROM THE DARKNESS.

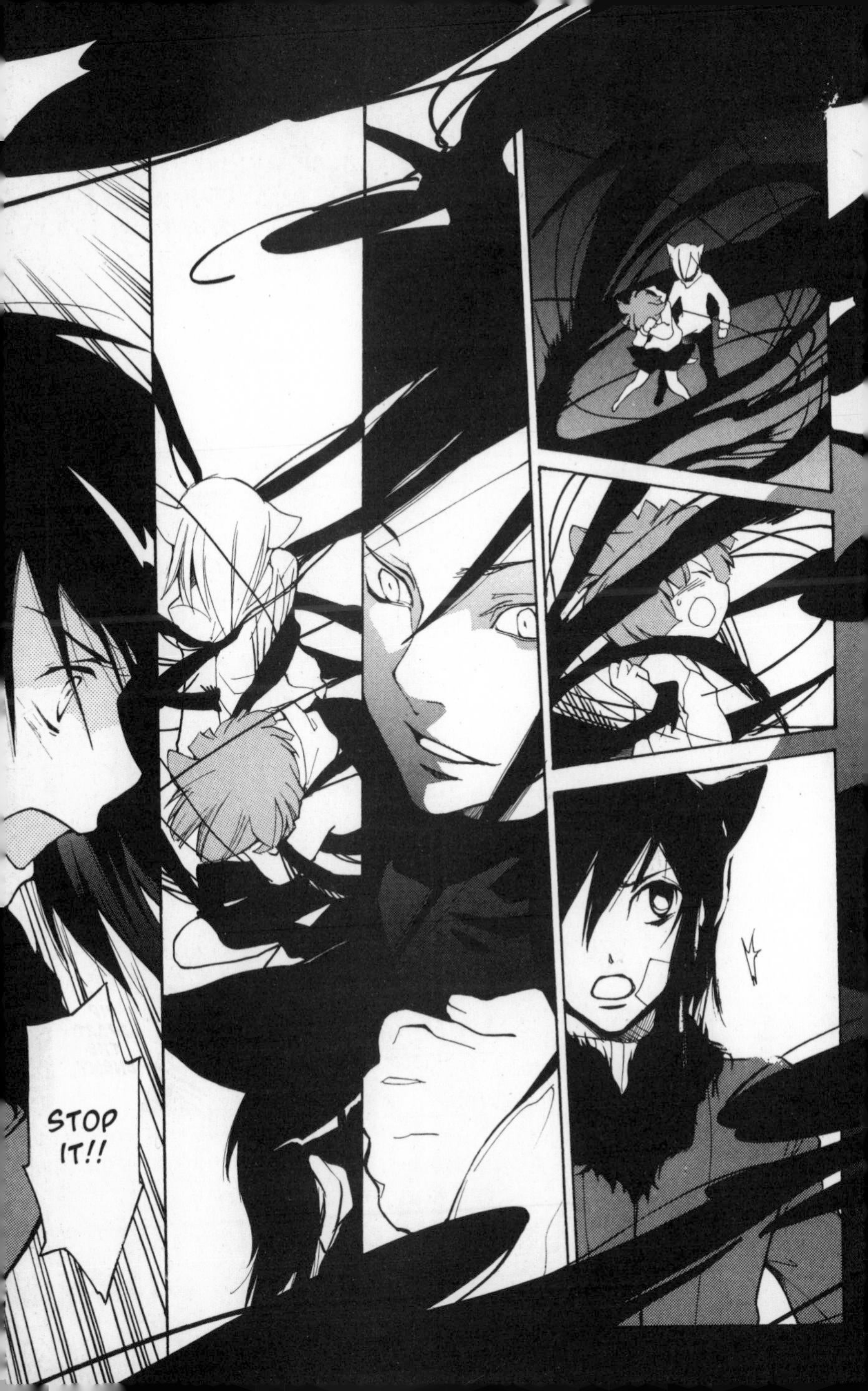
STOP IT!!

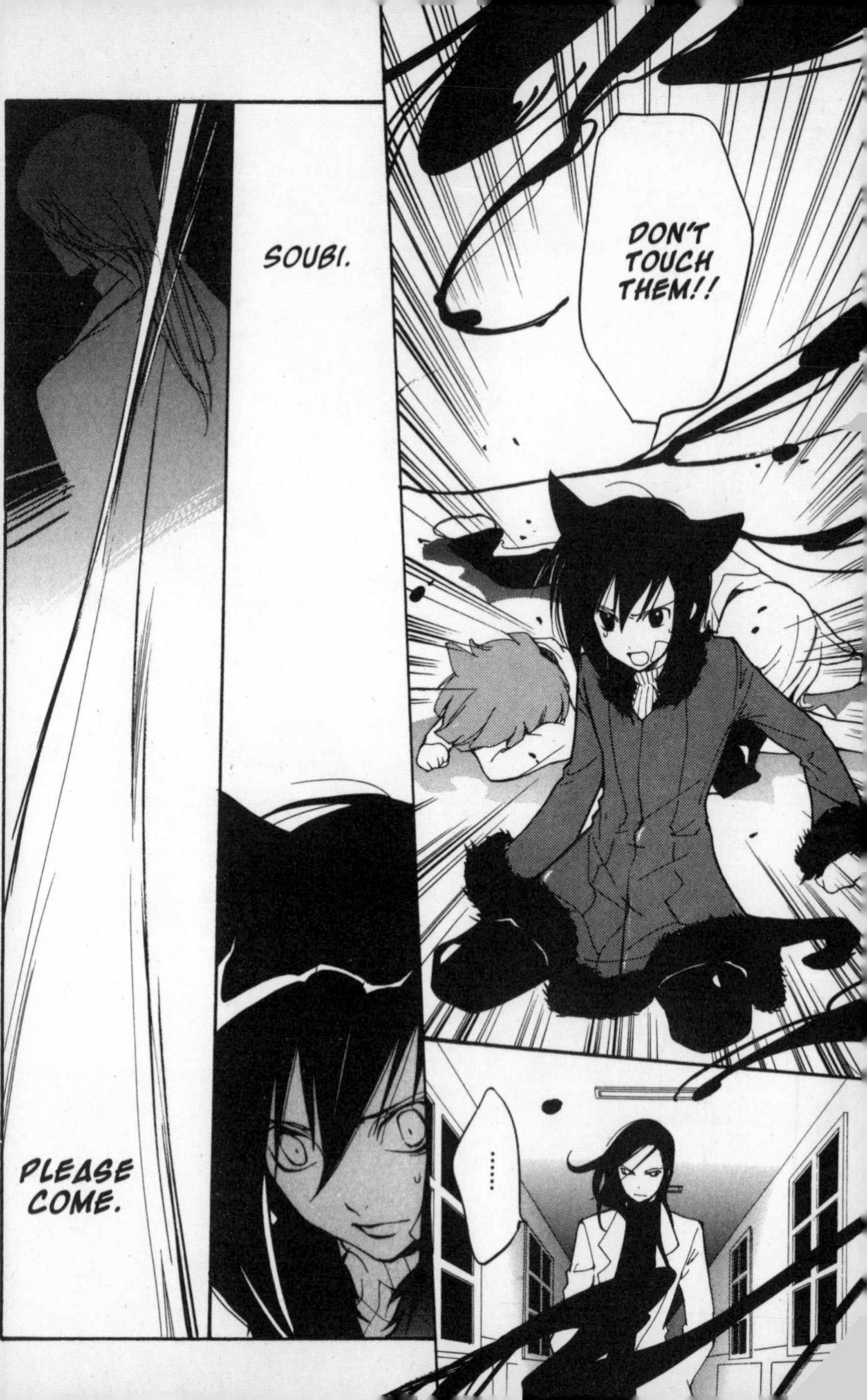
DON'T TOUCH THEM!!
......
SOUBI.
PLEASE COME.

I NEED YOU NOW, SOUBI.

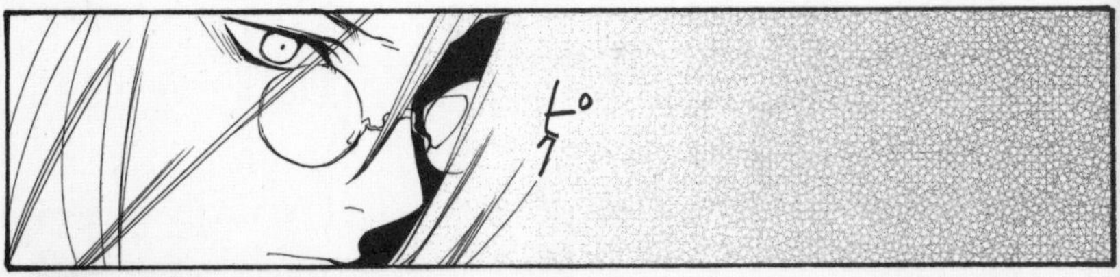

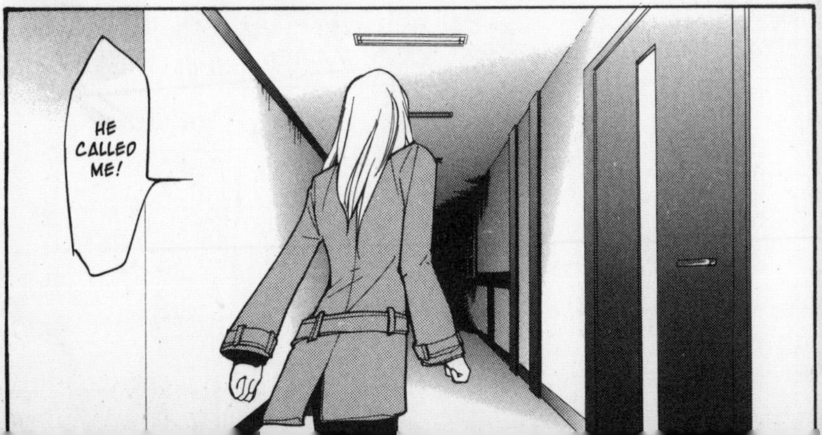
HE CALLED ME!

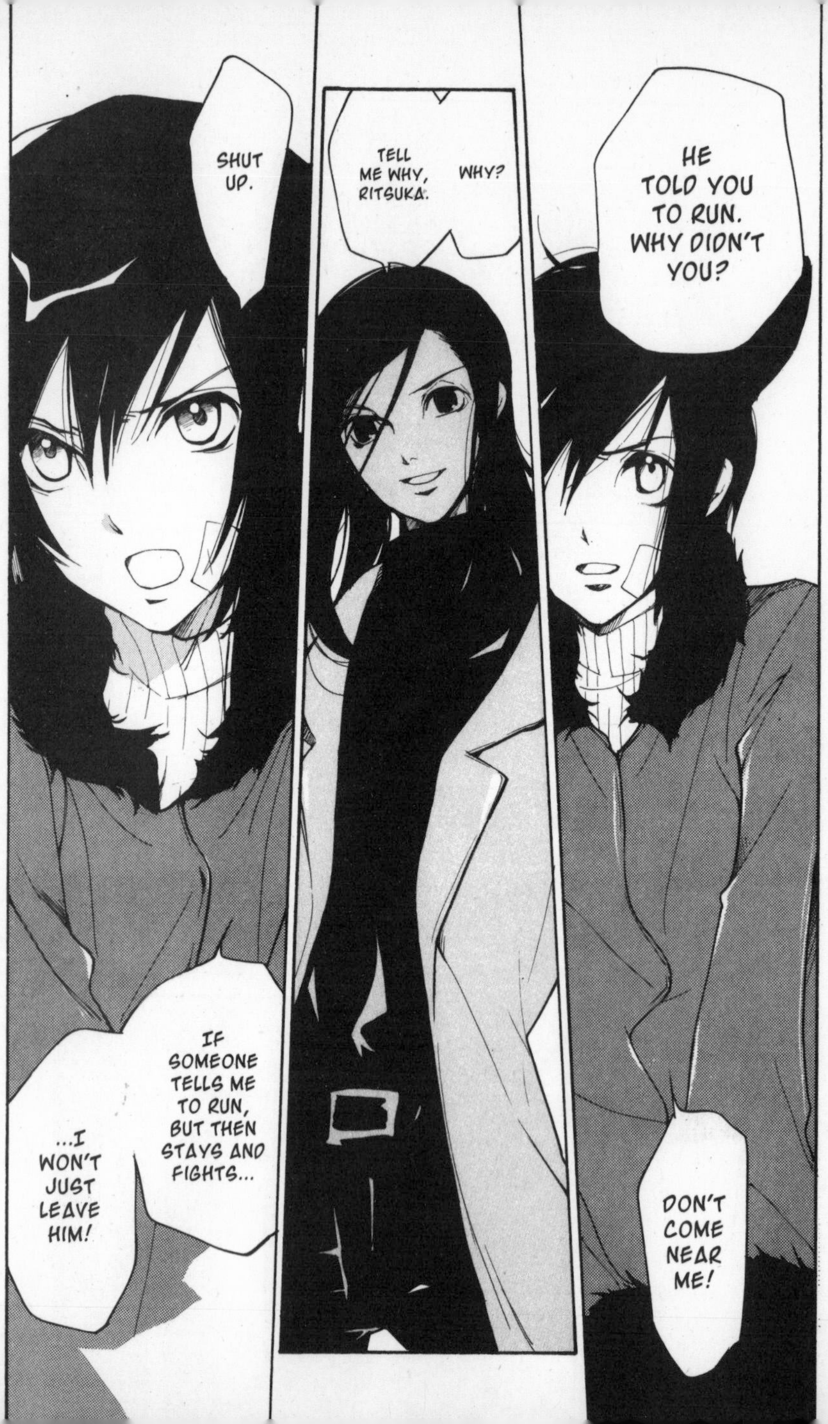
HE TOLD YOU TO RUN. WHY DIDN'T YOU?
DON'T COME NEAR ME!
TELL ME WHY, RITSUKA. WHY?
SHUT UP.
IF SOMEONE TELLS ME TO RUN, BUT THEN STAYS AND FIGHTS...
...I WON'T JUST LEAVE HIM!

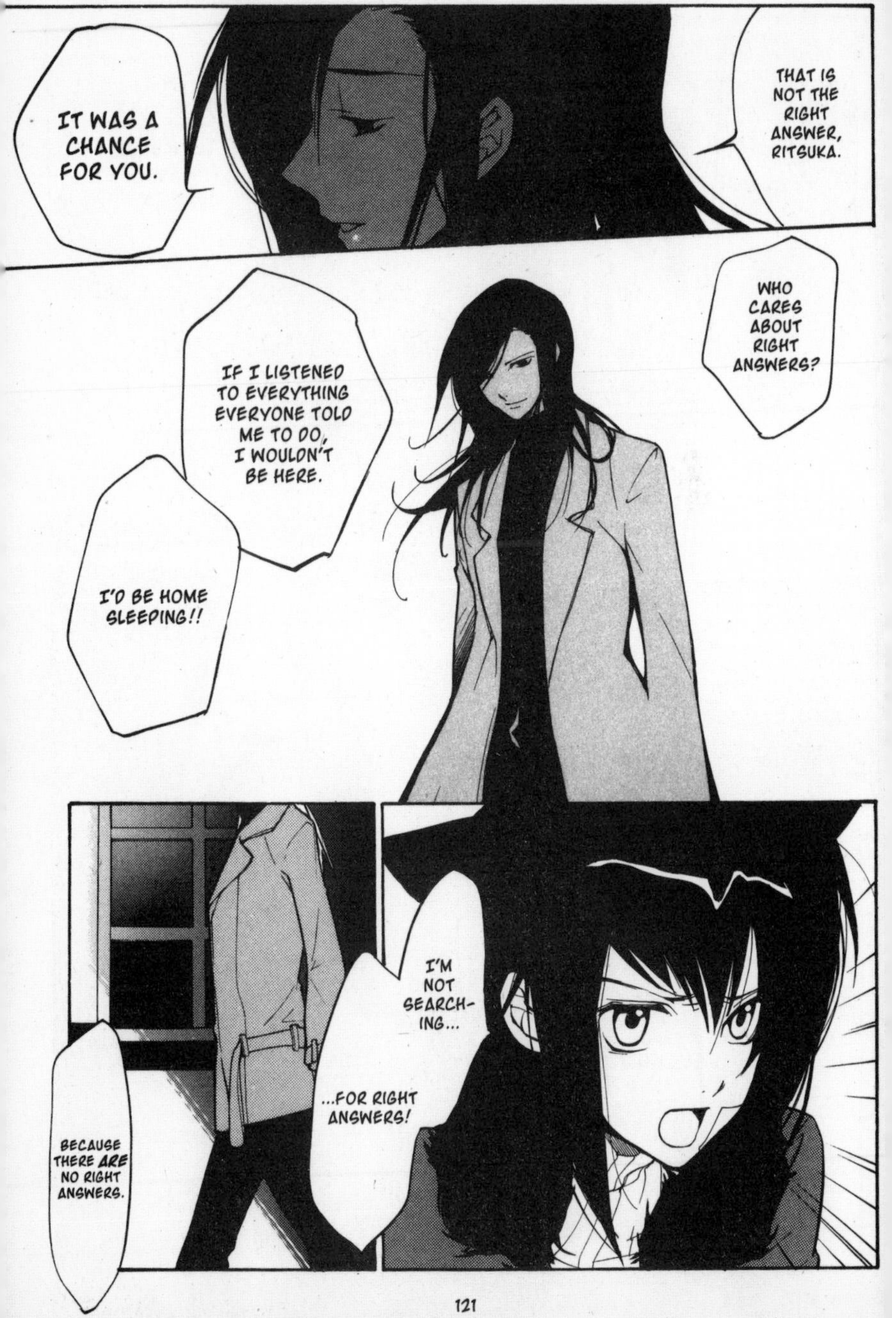
THAT IS NOT THE RIGHT ANSWER, RITSUKA.
IT WAS A CHANCE FOR YOU.
WHO CARES ABOUT RIGHT ANSWERS?
IF I LISTENED TO EVERYTHING EVERYONE TOLD ME TO DO, I WOULDN'T BE HERE.
I'D BE HOME SLEEPING!!
I'M NOT SEARCHING...
...FOR RIGHT ANSWERS!
BECAUSE THERE *ARE* NO RIGHT ANSWERS.

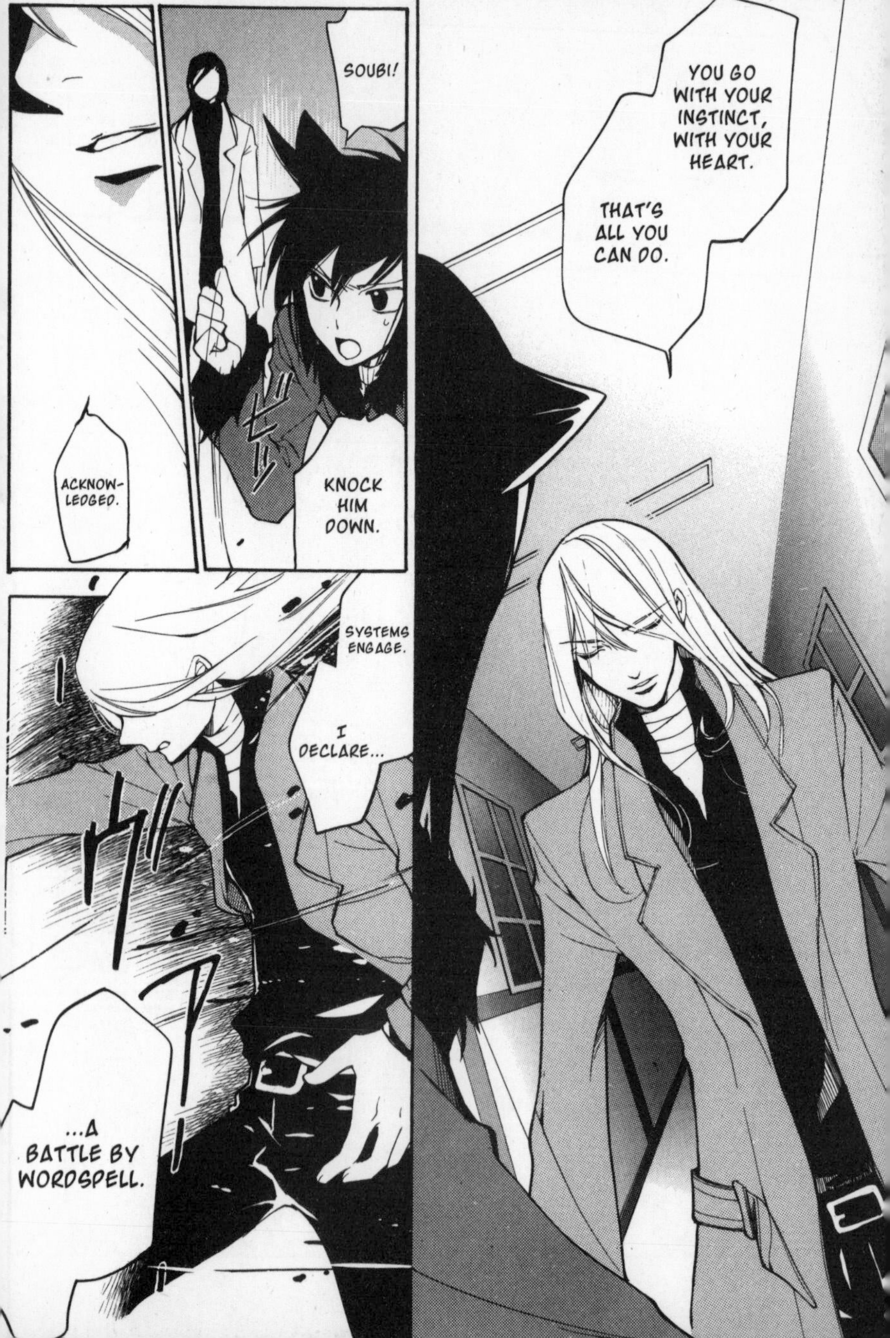
YOU GO WITH YOUR INSTINCT, WITH YOUR HEART.
THAT'S ALL YOU CAN DO.
SOUBI!
KNOCK HIM DOWN.
ACKNOW-LEDGED.
SYSTEMS ENGAGE.
I DECLARE...
...A BATTLE BY WORDSPELL.

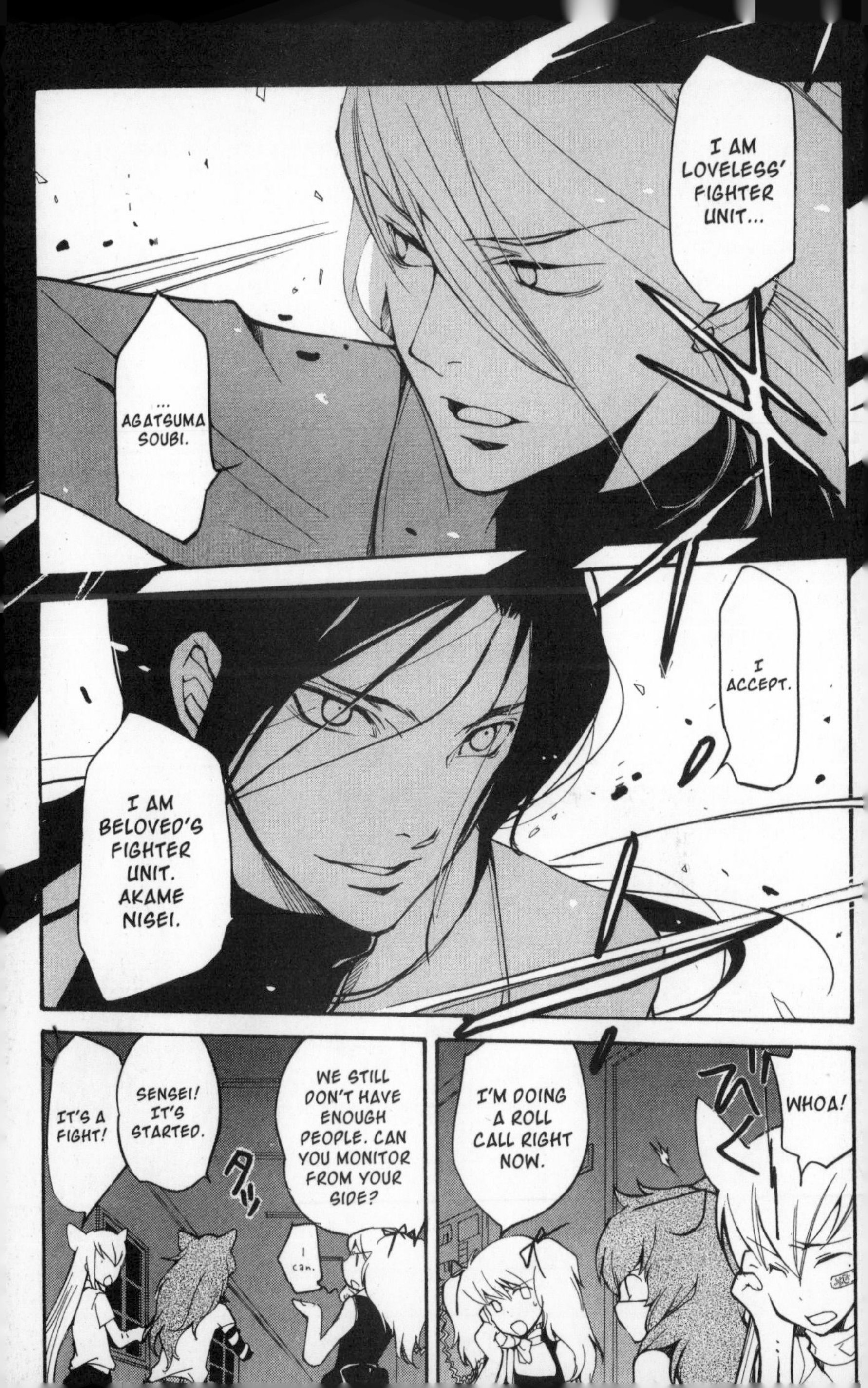
I AM LOVELESS' FIGHTER UNIT...
...AGATSUMA SOUBI.
I ACCEPT.
I AM BELOVED'S FIGHTER UNIT. AKAME NISEI.
WHOA!
I'M DOING A ROLL CALL RIGHT NOW.
WE STILL DON'T HAVE ENOUGH PEOPLE. CAN YOU MONITOR FROM YOUR SIDE?
SENSEI! IT'S STARTED.
IT'S A FIGHT!
I can.

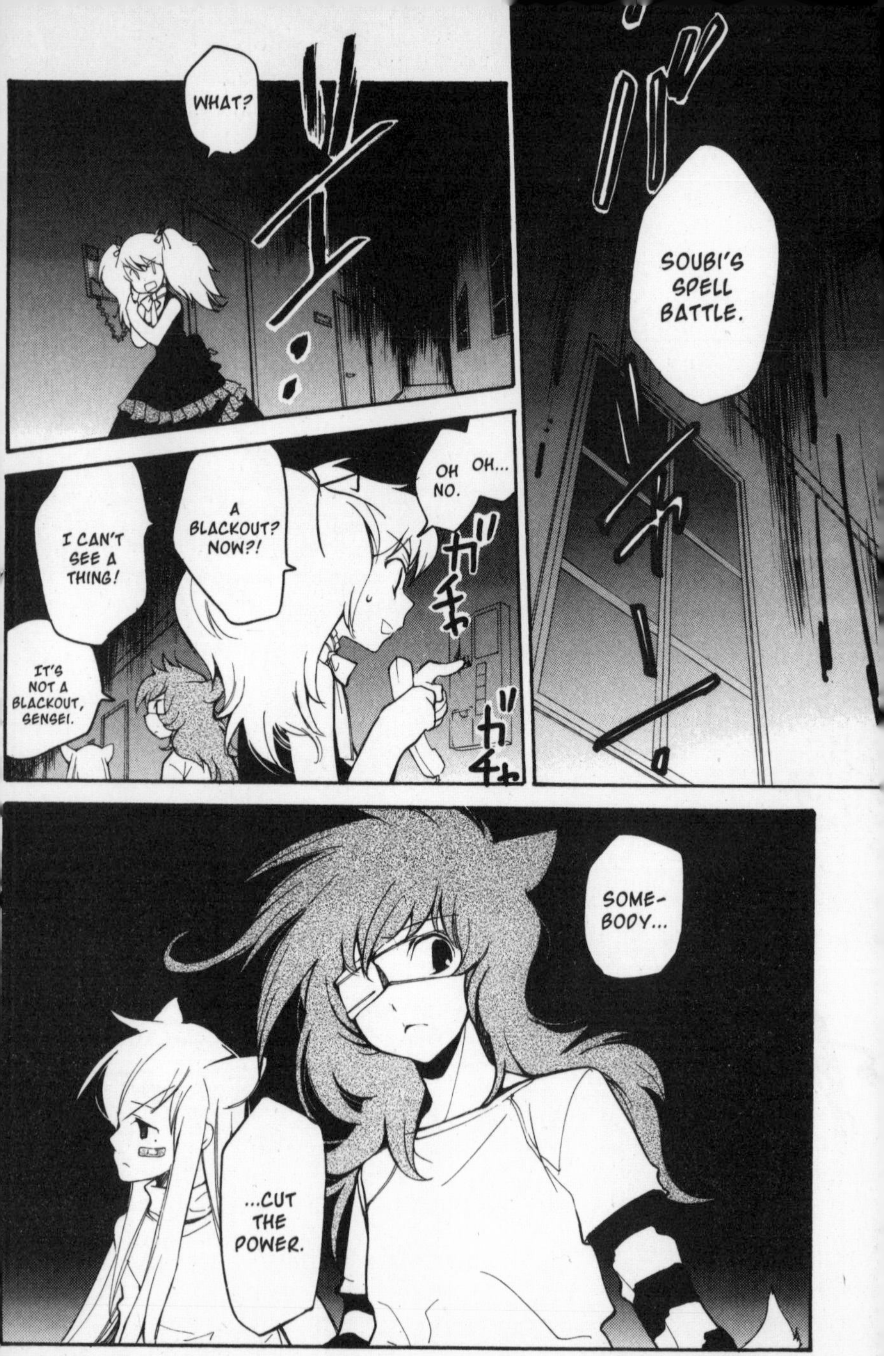
SOUBI'S SPELL BATTLE.
WHAT?
OH... OH NO.
A BLACKOUT? NOW?!
I CAN'T SEE A THING!
IT'S NOT A BLACKOUT, SENSEI.
SOME-BODY...
...CUT THE POWER.

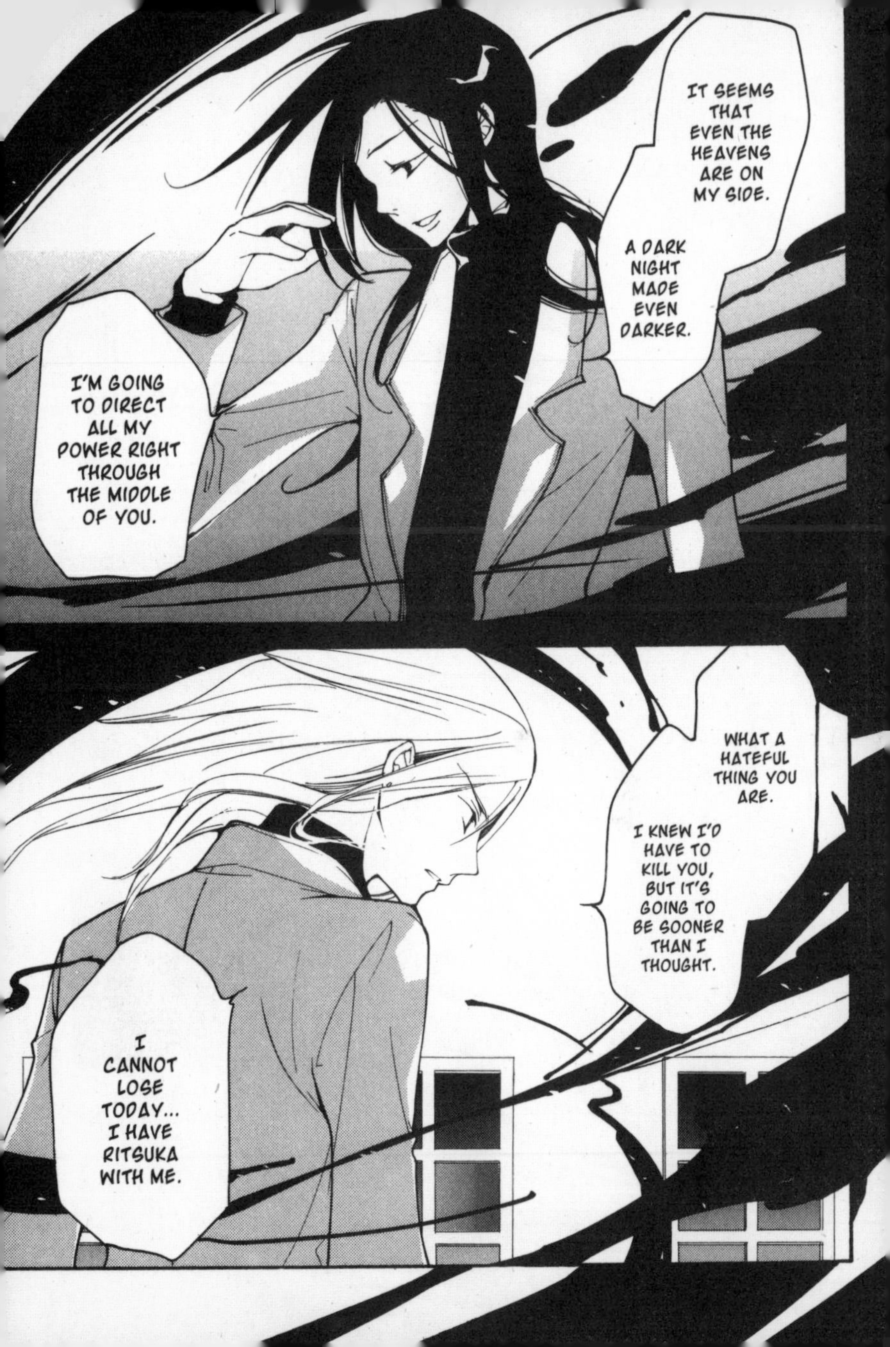
IT SEEMS THAT EVEN THE HEAVENS ARE ON MY SIDE.
A DARK NIGHT MADE EVEN DARKER.
I'M GOING TO DIRECT ALL MY POWER RIGHT THROUGH THE MIDDLE OF YOU.
WHAT A HATEFUL THING YOU ARE.
I KNEW I'D HAVE TO KILL YOU, BUT IT'S GOING TO BE SOONER THAN I THOUGHT.
I CANNOT LOSE TODAY... I HAVE RITSUKA WITH ME.

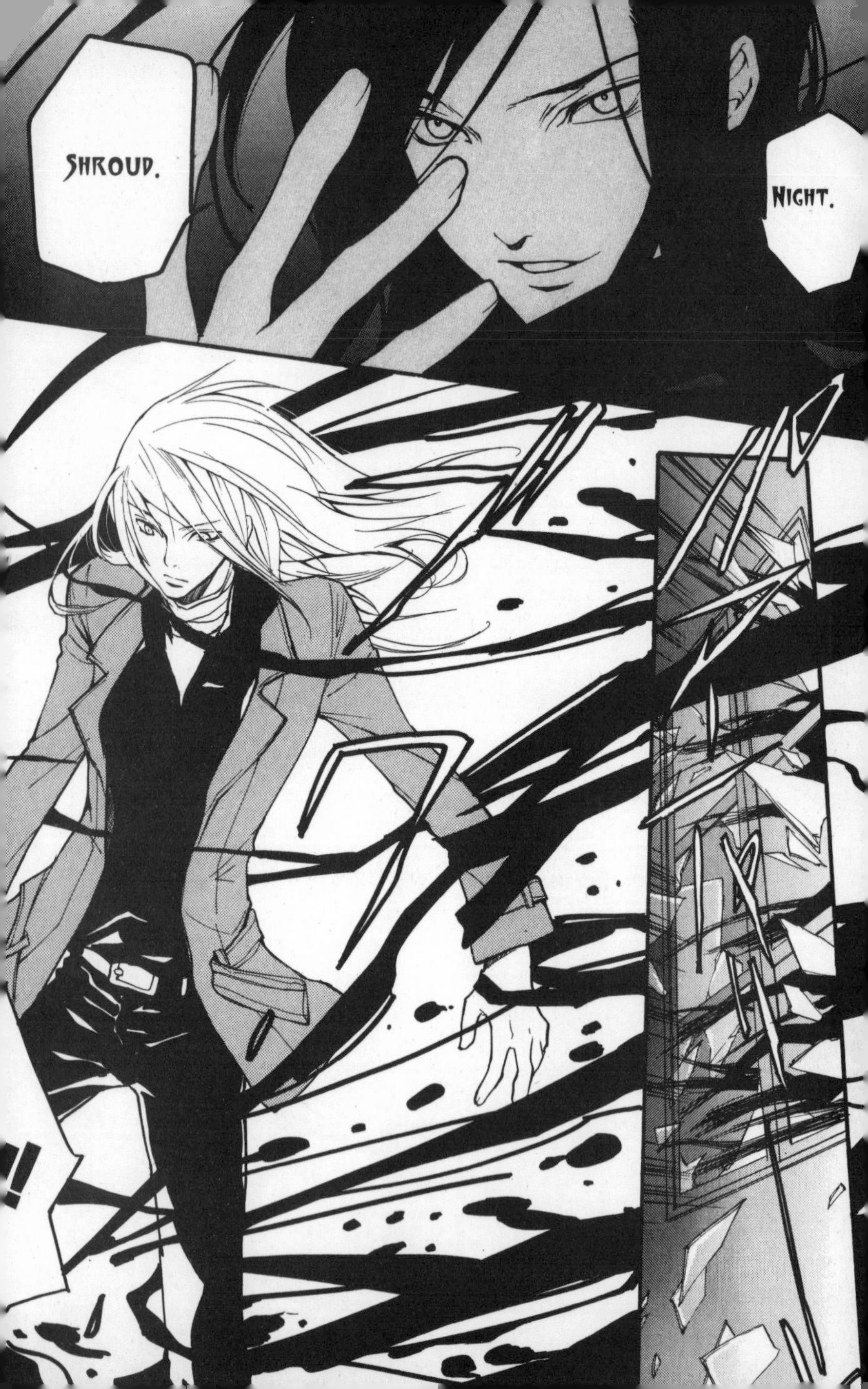
NIGHT.
SHROUD.
!!

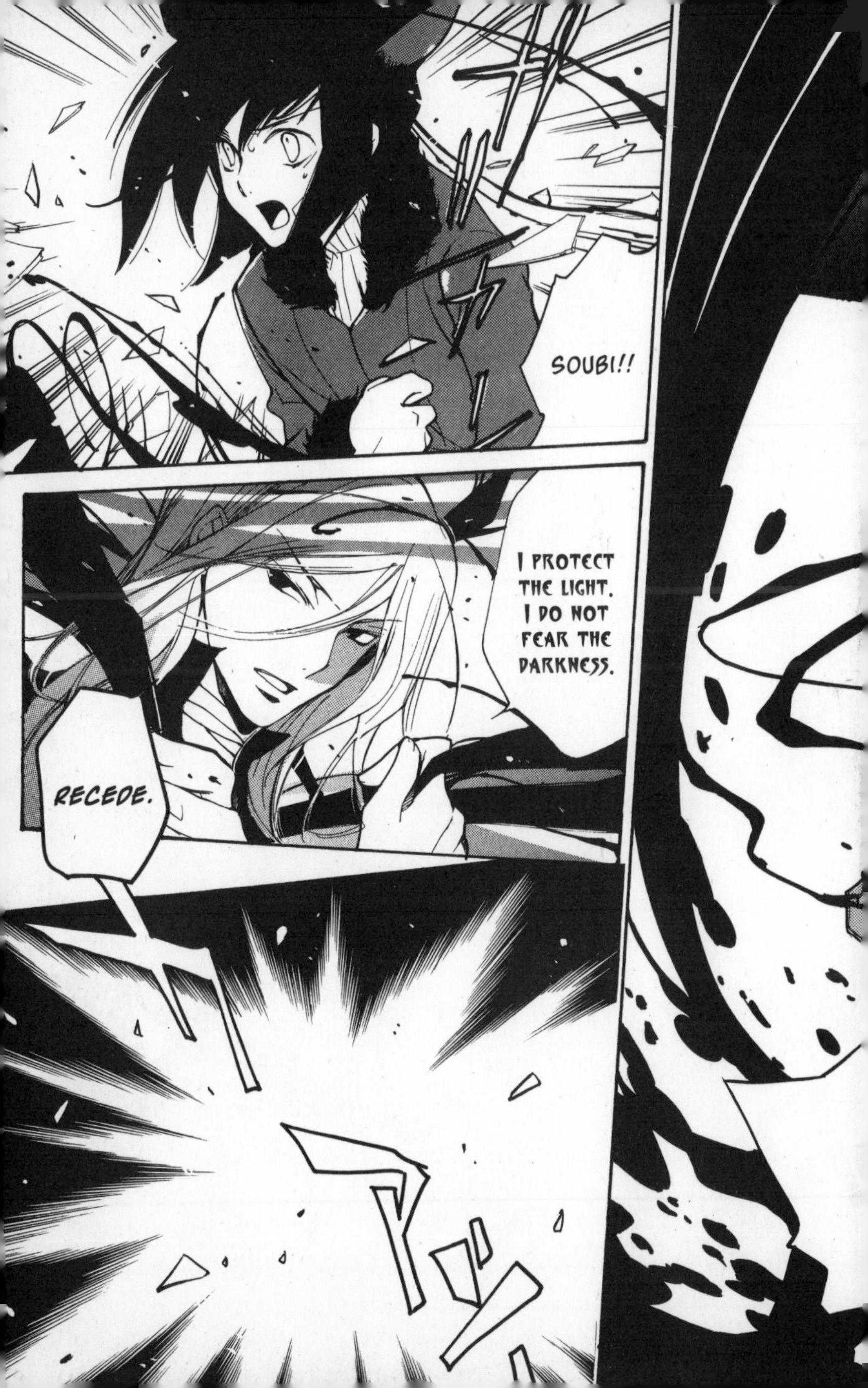
SOUBI!!
I PROTECT THE LIGHT. I DO NOT FEAR THE DARKNESS.
RECEDE.

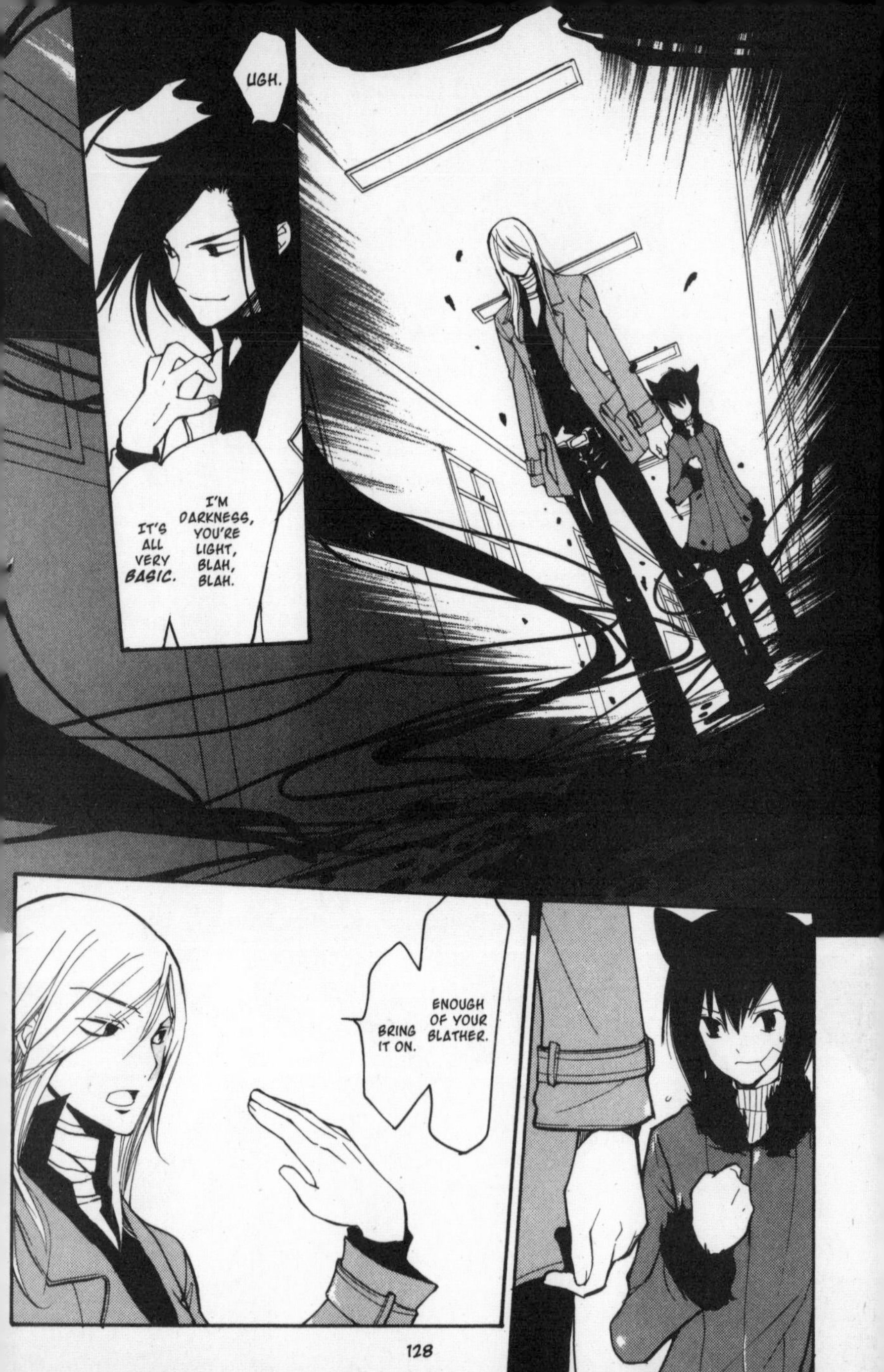
UGH.
I'M DARKNESS, YOU'RE LIGHT, BLAH, BLAH.
IT'S ALL VERY BASIC.
ENOUGH OF YOUR BLATHER.
BRING IT ON.

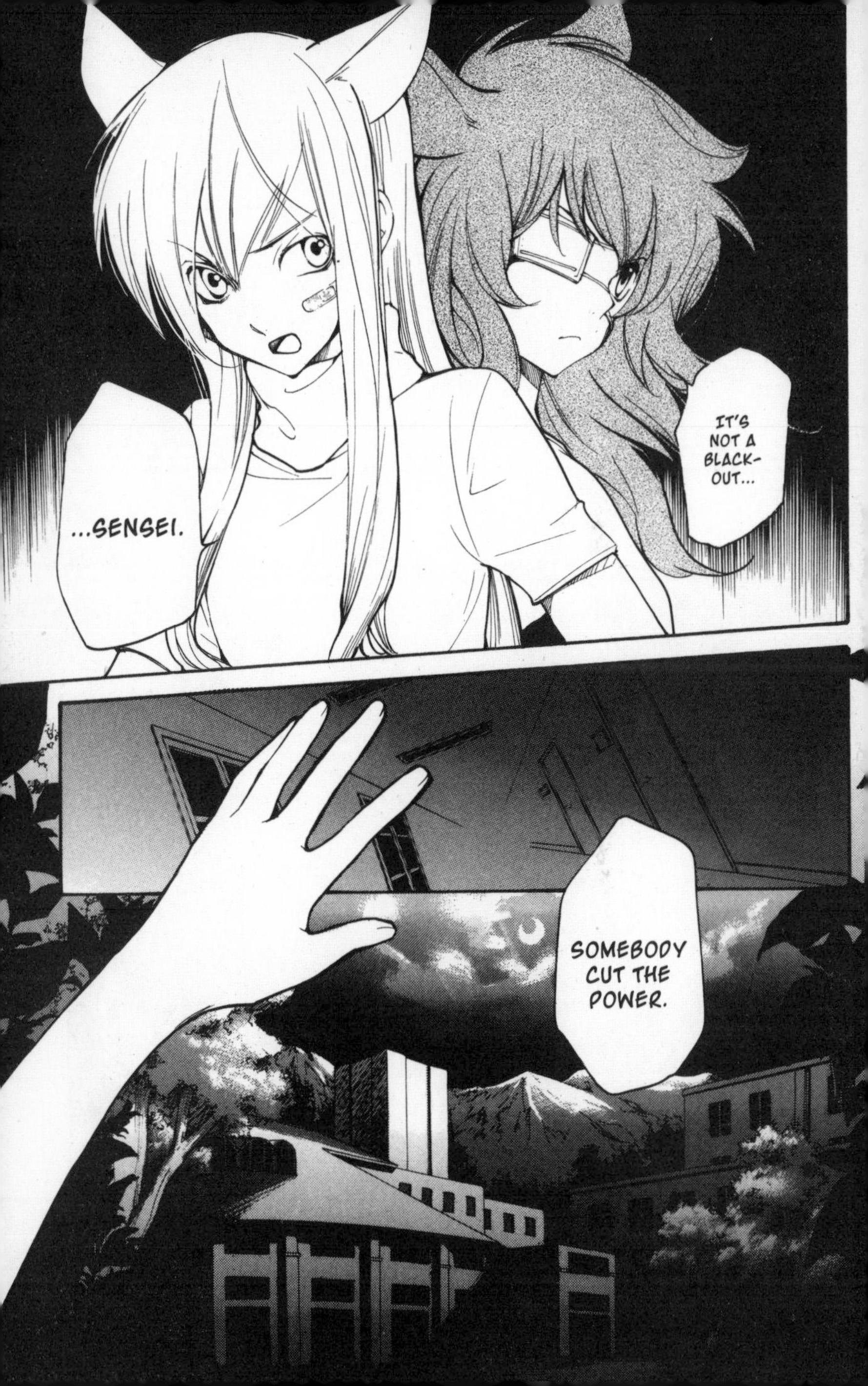
IT'S NOT A BLACK-OUT...
...SENSEI.
SOMEBODY CUT THE POWER.

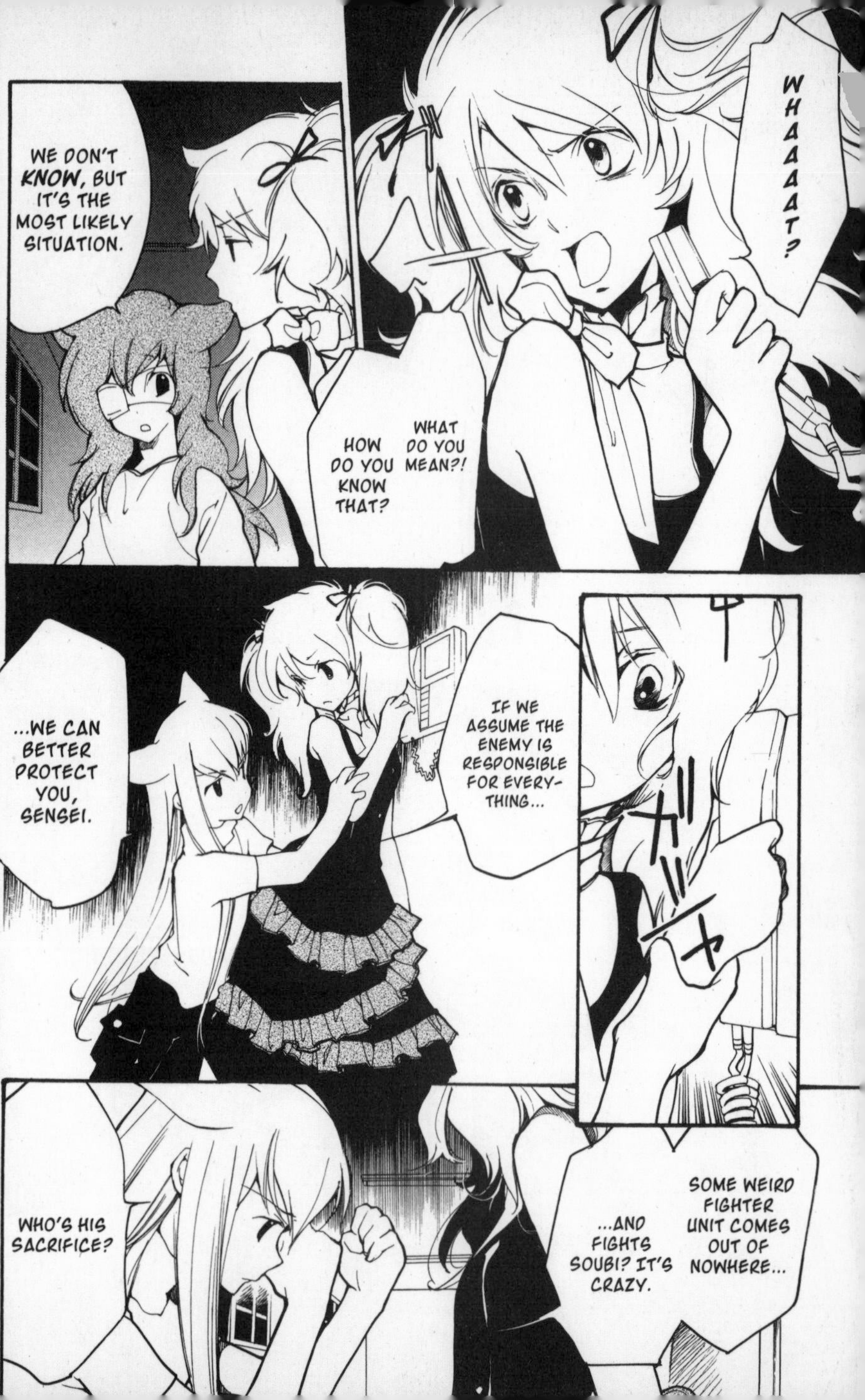
WHAAAAAT?
WHAT DO YOU MEAN?!
HOW DO YOU KNOW THAT?
WE DON'T **KNOW**, BUT IT'S THE MOST LIKELY SITUATION.
IF WE ASSUME THE ENEMY IS RESPONSIBLE FOR EVERY-THING...
...WE CAN BETTER PROTECT YOU, SENSEI.
SOME WEIRD FIGHTER UNIT COMES OUT OF NOWHERE...
...AND FIGHTS SOUBI? IT'S CRAZY.
WHO'S HIS SACRIFICE?

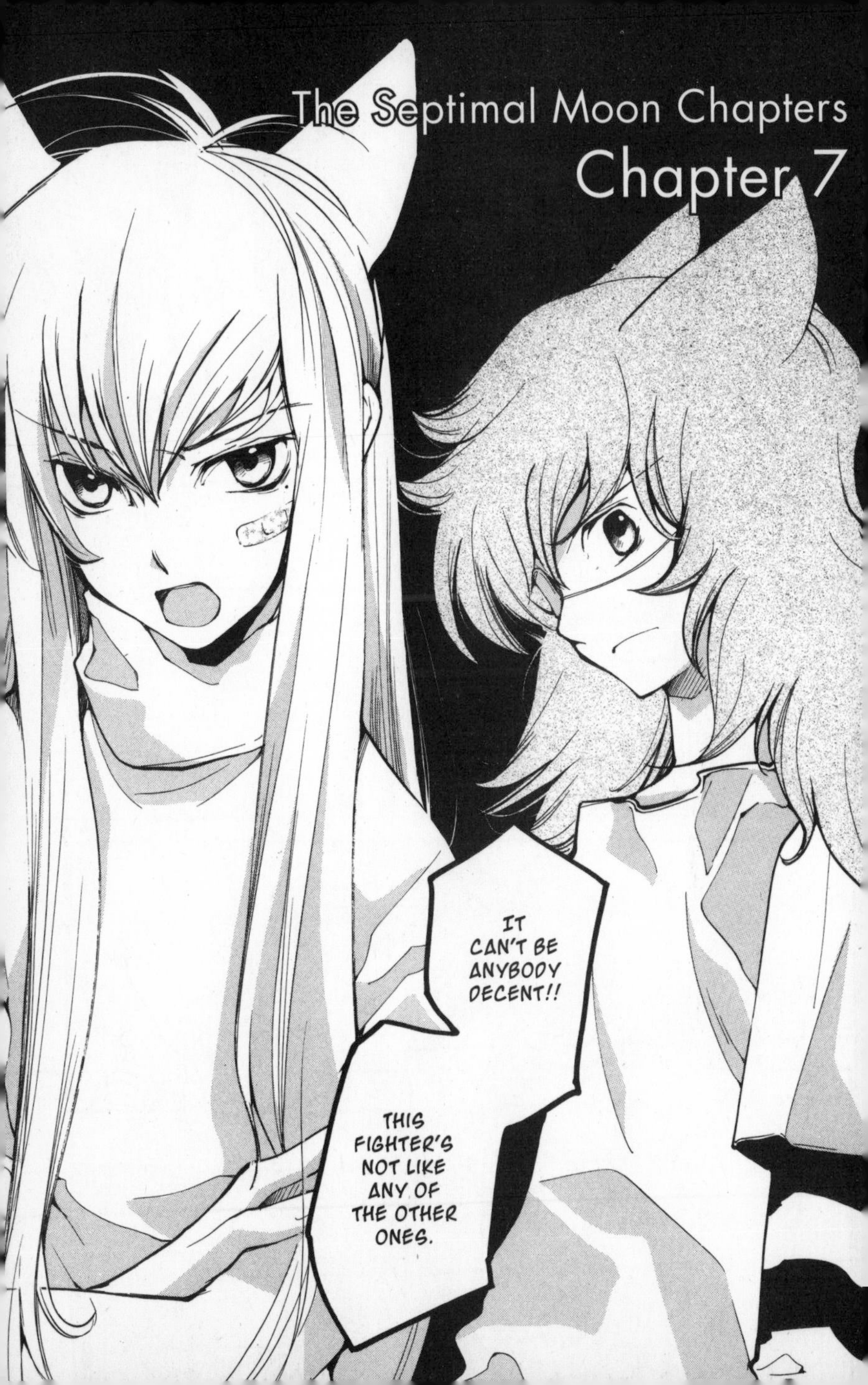
The Septimal Moon Chapters
Chapter 7
IT CAN'T BE ANYBODY DECENT!!
THIS FIGHTER'S NOT LIKE ANY OF THE OTHER ONES.

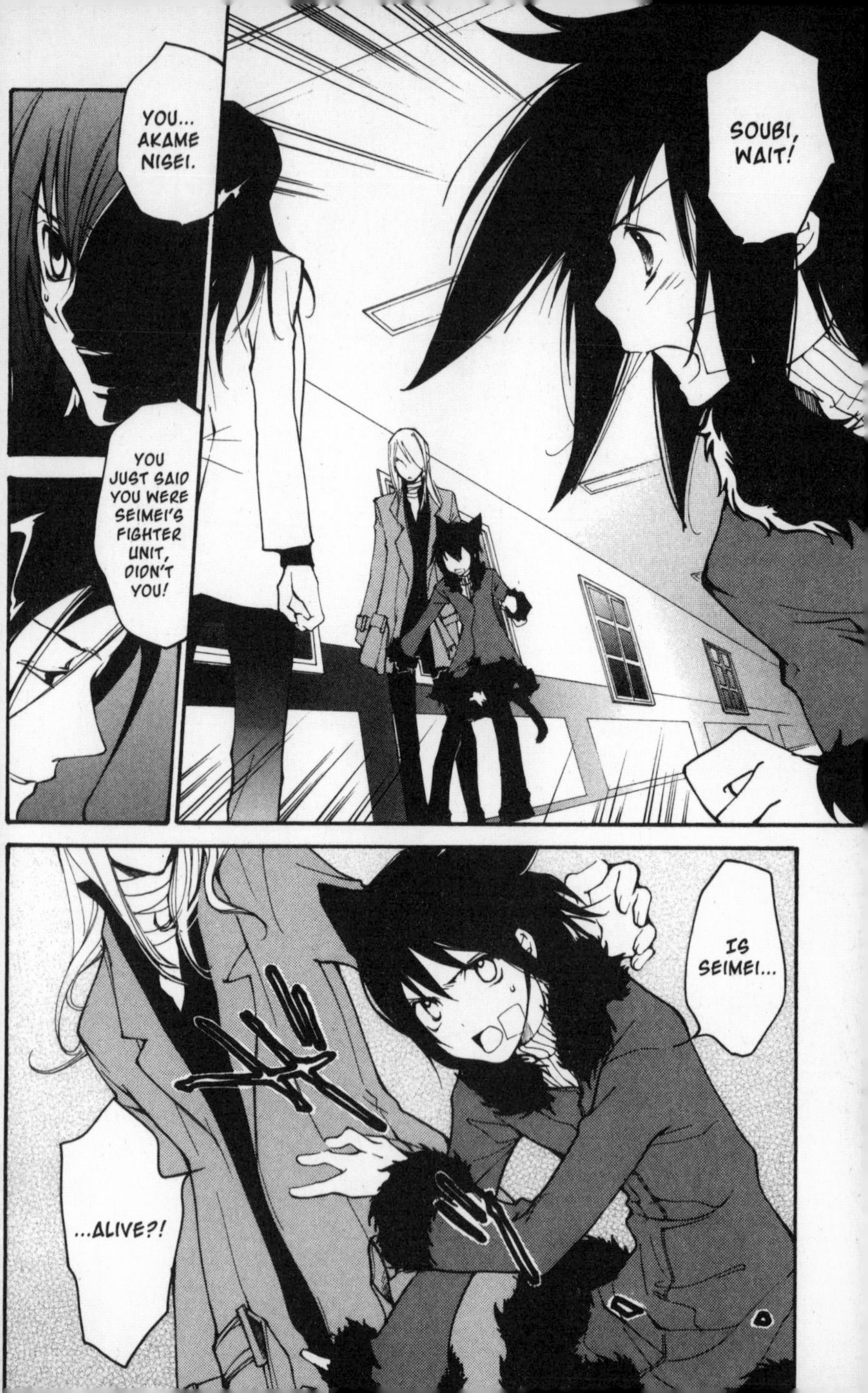
SOUBI, WAIT!
YOU... AKAME NISEI.
YOU JUST SAID YOU WERE SEIMEI'S FIGHTER UNIT, DIDN'T YOU!
IS SEIMEI...
...ALIVE?!

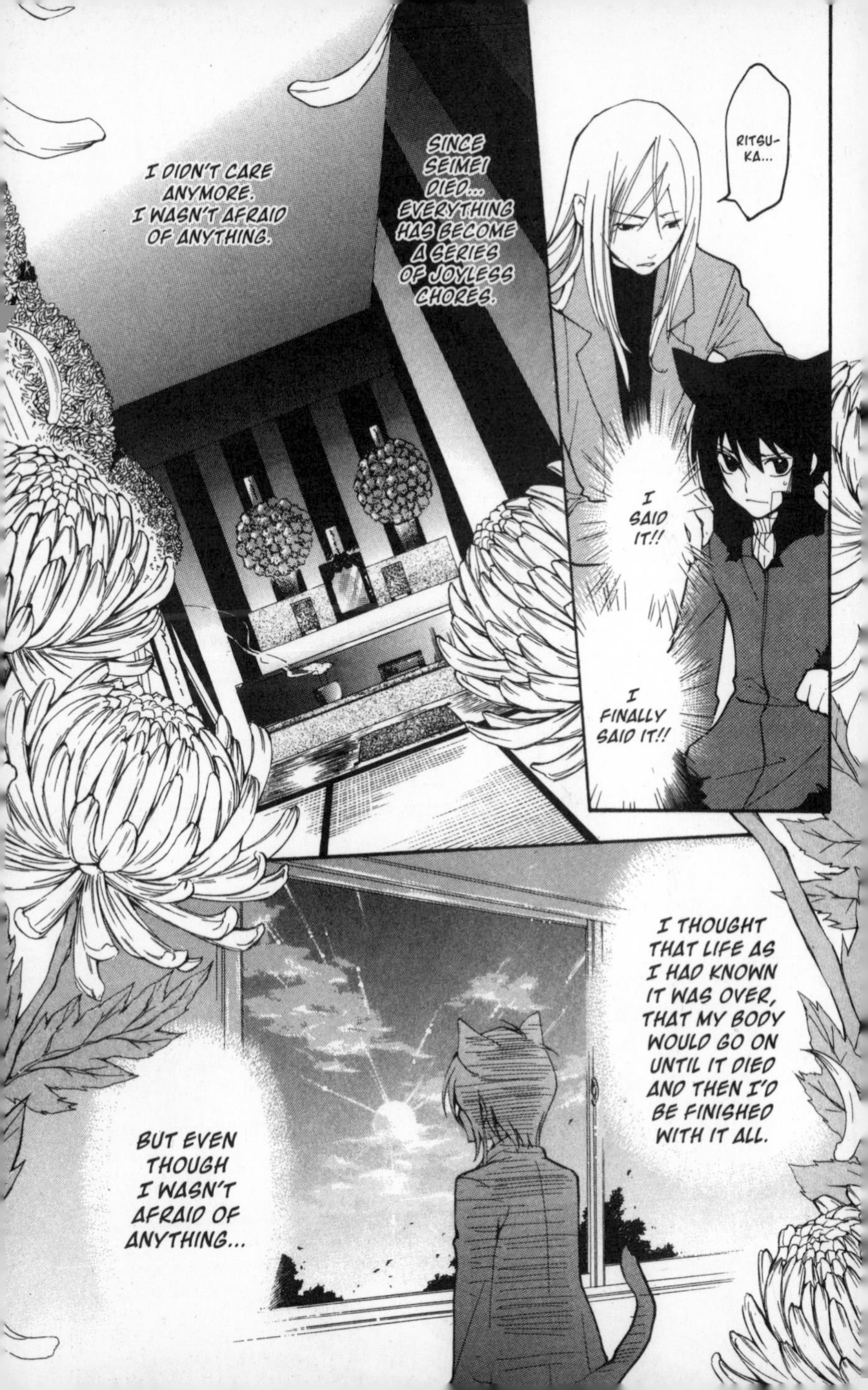
RITSU-KA...
I SAID IT!!
I FINALLY SAID IT!!
SINCE SEIMEI DIED... EVERYTHING HAS BECOME A SERIES OF JOYLESS CHORES.
I DIDN'T CARE ANYMORE. I WASN'T AFRAID OF ANYTHING.
I THOUGHT THAT LIFE AS I HAD KNOWN IT WAS OVER, THAT MY BODY WOULD GO ON UNTIL IT DIED AND THEN I'D BE FINISHED WITH IT ALL.
BUT EVEN THOUGH I WASN'T AFRAID OF ANYTHING...

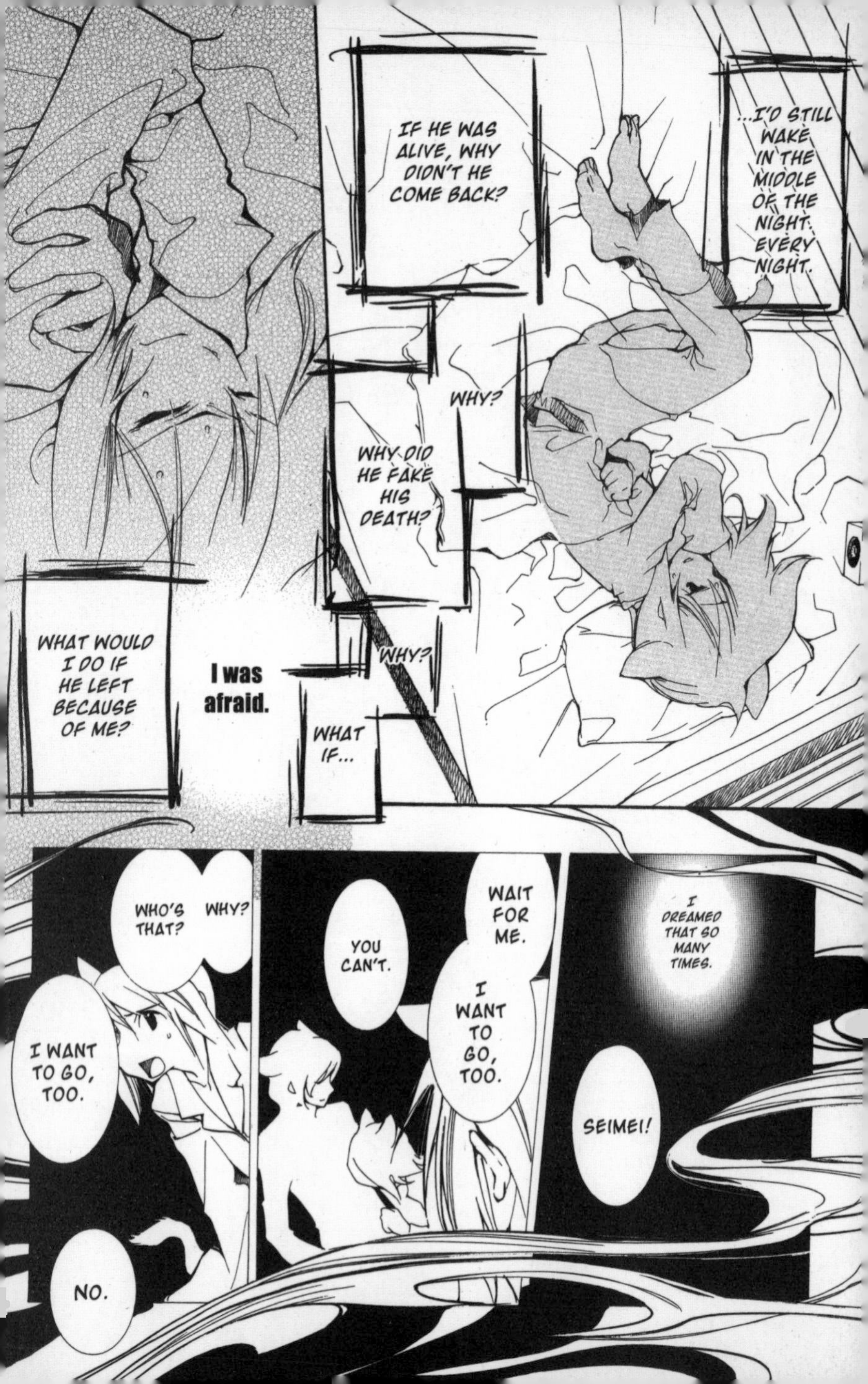
...I'D STILL WAKE IN THE MIDDLE OF THE NIGHT EVERY NIGHT.
IF HE WAS ALIVE, WHY DIDN'T HE COME BACK?
WHY?
WHY DID HE FAKE HIS DEATH?
WHY?
WHAT IF...
I was afraid.
WHAT WOULD I DO IF HE LEFT BECAUSE OF ME?
I DREAMED THAT SO MANY TIMES.
SEIMEI!
WAIT FOR ME.
YOU CAN'T.
I WANT TO GO, TOO.
WHY?
WHO'S THAT?
I WANT TO GO, TOO.
NO.

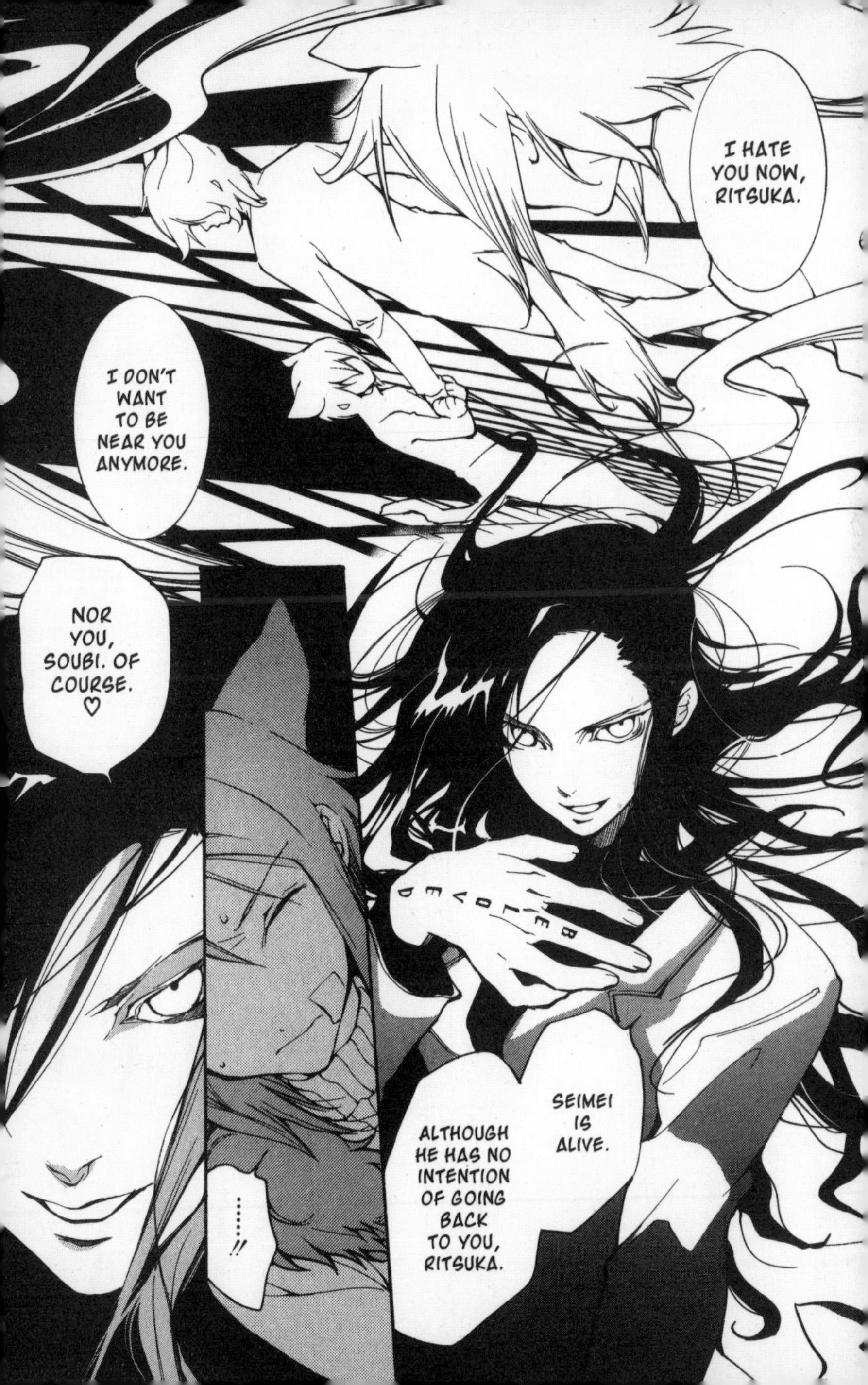
I HATE YOU NOW, RITSUKA.
I DON'T WANT TO BE NEAR YOU ANYMORE.
NOR YOU, SOUBI. OF COURSE. ♡
SEIMEI IS ALIVE.
ALTHOUGH HE HAS NO INTENTION OF GOING BACK TO YOU, RITSUKA.
......!!

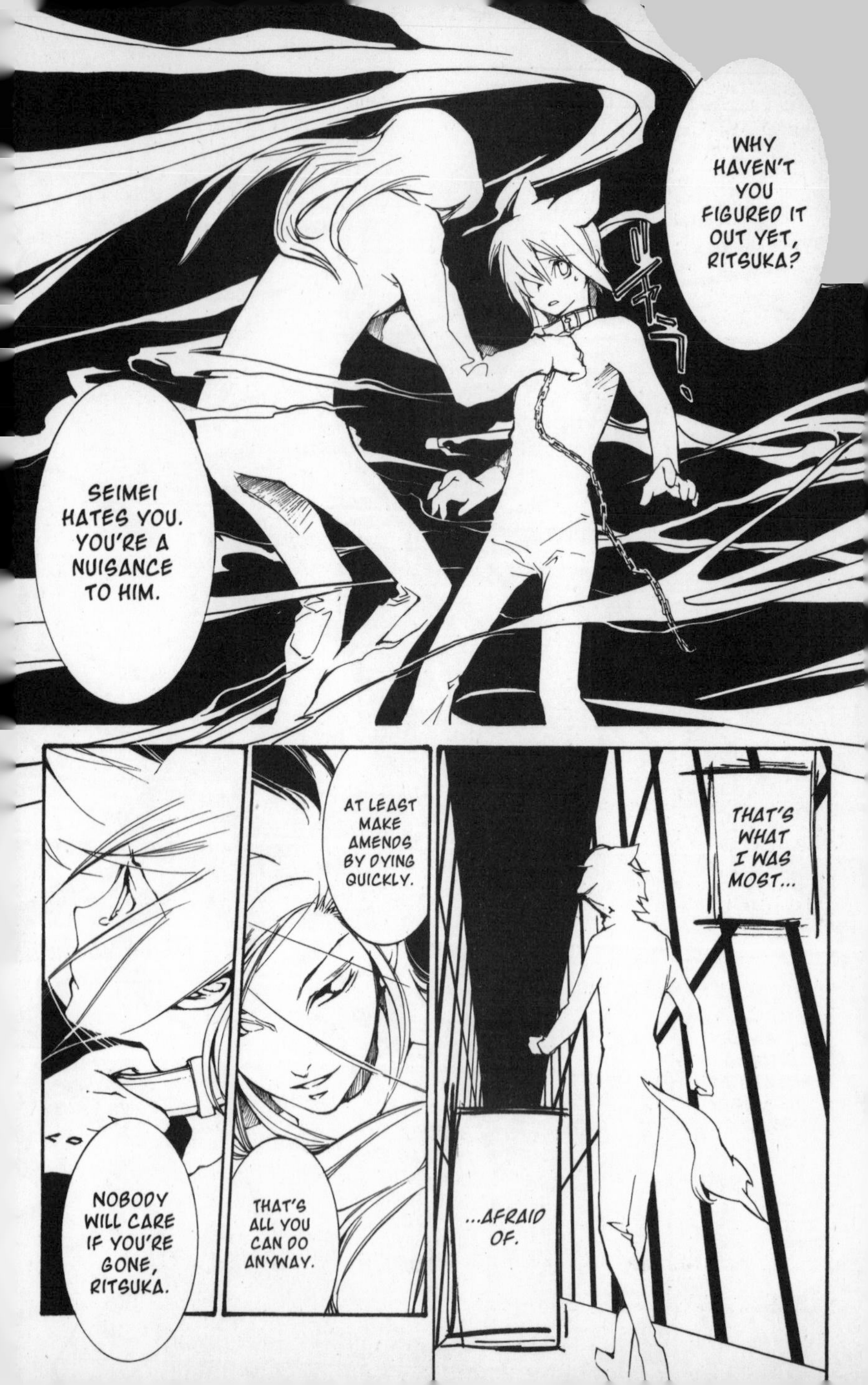
WHY HAVEN'T YOU FIGURED IT OUT YET, RITSUKA?
SEIMEI HATES YOU. YOU'RE A NUISANCE TO HIM.
THAT'S WHAT I WAS MOST...
...AFRAID OF.
AT LEAST MAKE AMENDS BY DYING QUICKLY.
THAT'S ALL YOU CAN DO ANYWAY.
NOBODY WILL CARE IF YOU'RE GONE, RITSUKA.

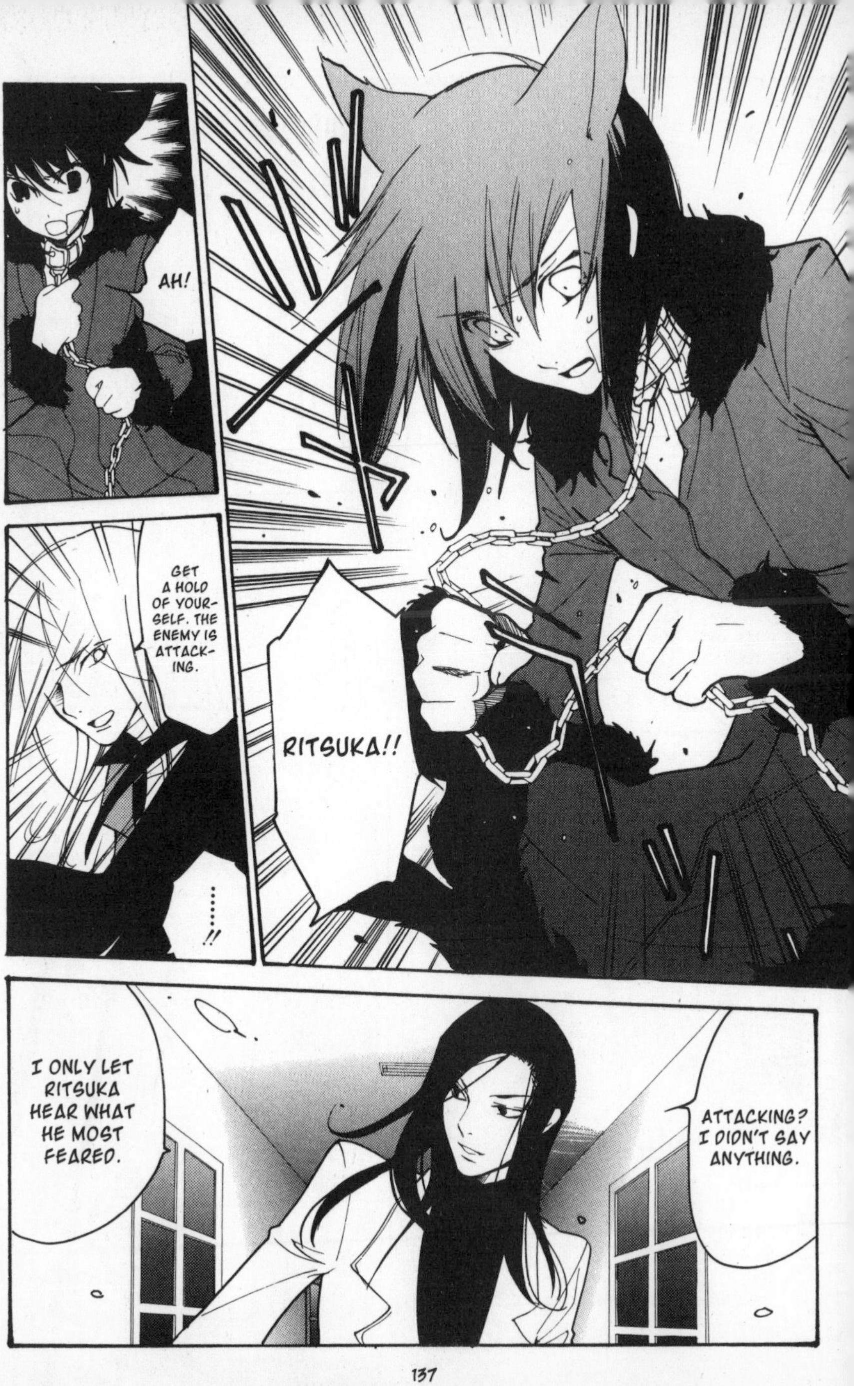
RITSUKA!!
AH!
GET A HOLD OF YOURSELF. THE ENEMY IS ATTACKING.
......!!
ATTACKING? I DIDN'T SAY ANYTHING.
I ONLY LET RITSUKA HEAR WHAT HE MOST FEARED.

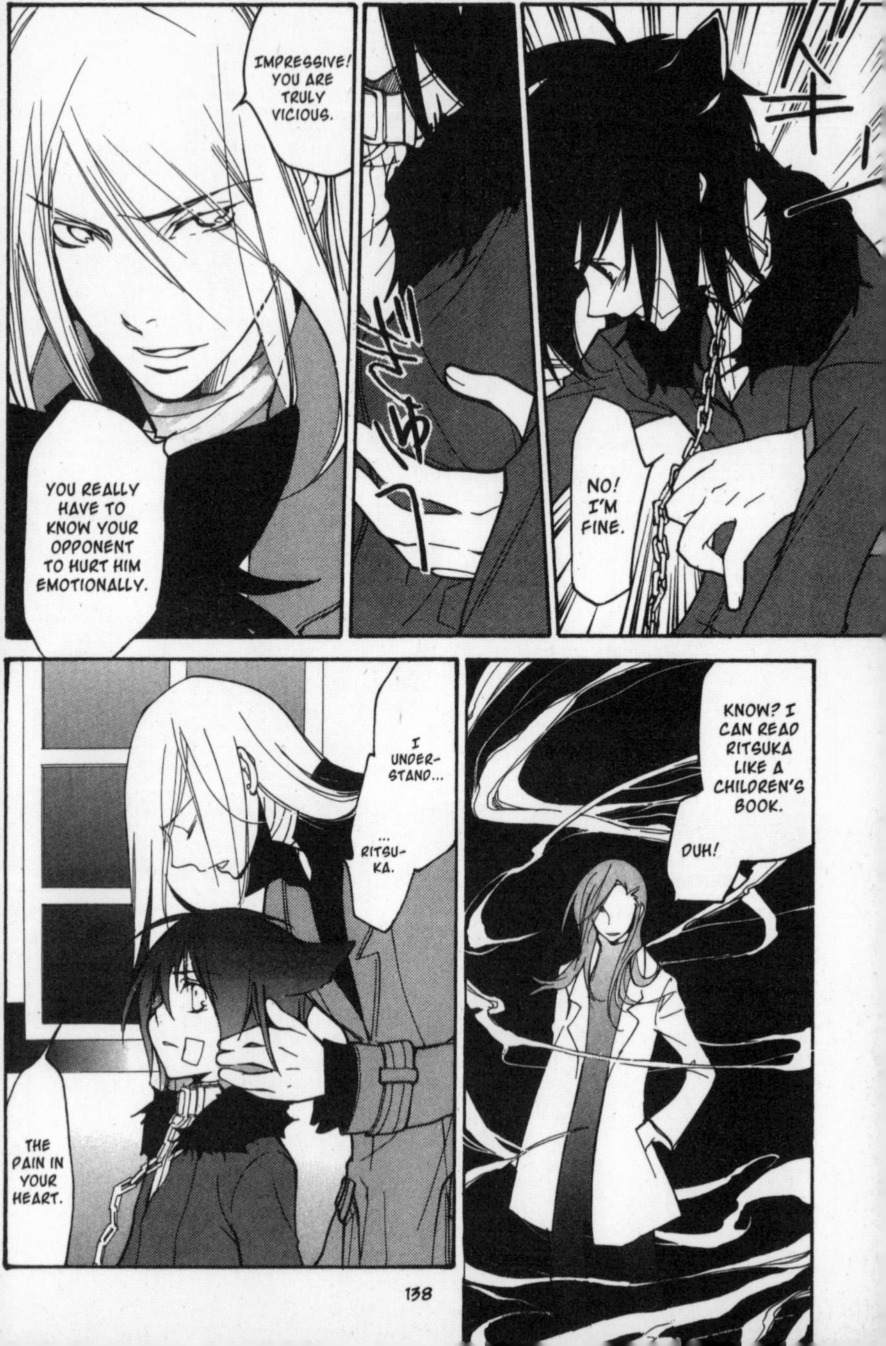
NO! I'M FINE.
IMPRESSIVE! YOU ARE TRULY VICIOUS.
YOU REALLY HAVE TO KNOW YOUR OPPONENT TO HURT HIM EMOTIONALLY.
KNOW? I CAN READ RITSUKA LIKE A CHILDREN'S BOOK.
DUH!
I UNDER-STAND...
...RITSU-KA.
THE PAIN IN YOUR HEART.

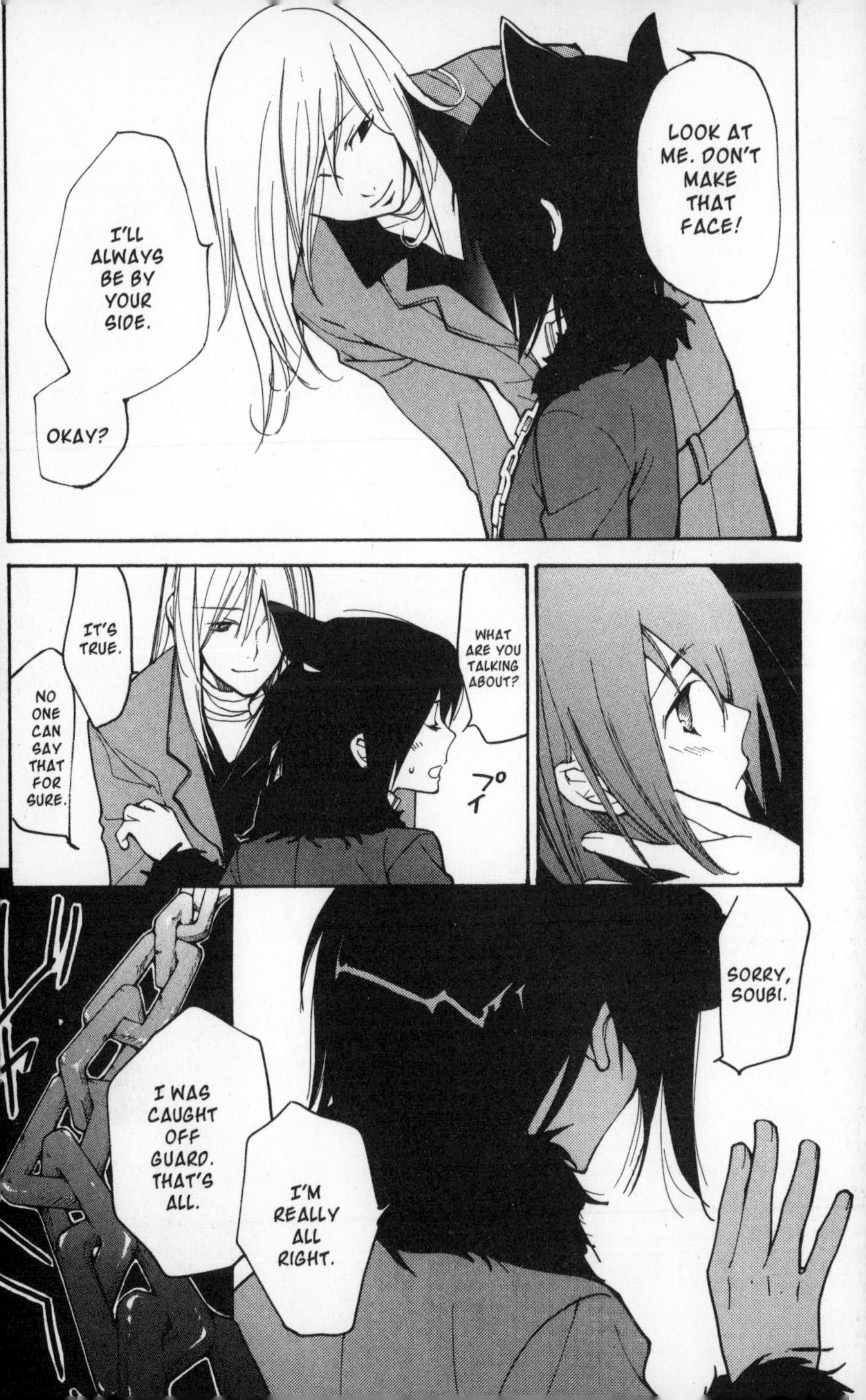
LOOK AT ME. DON'T MAKE THAT FACE!
I'LL ALWAYS BE BY YOUR SIDE.
OKAY?
WHAT ARE YOU TALKING ABOUT?
プイ
IT'S TRUE.
NO ONE CAN SAY THAT FOR SURE.
SORRY, SOUBI.
I'M REALLY ALL RIGHT.
I WAS CAUGHT OFF GUARD. THAT'S ALL.

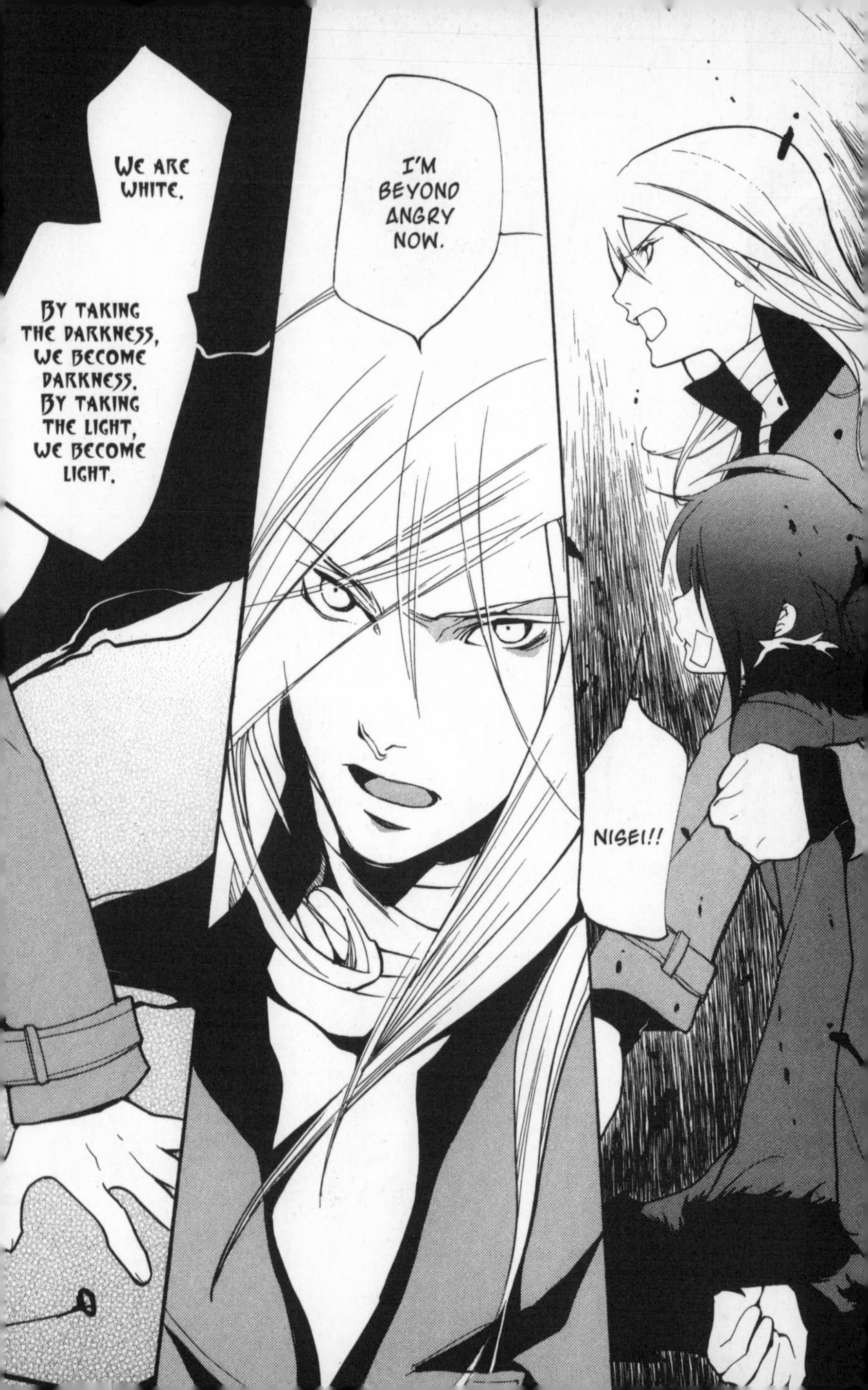
NISEI!!
I'M BEYOND ANGRY NOW.
WE ARE WHITE.
BY TAKING THE DARKNESS, WE BECOME DARKNESS. BY TAKING THE LIGHT, WE BECOME LIGHT.

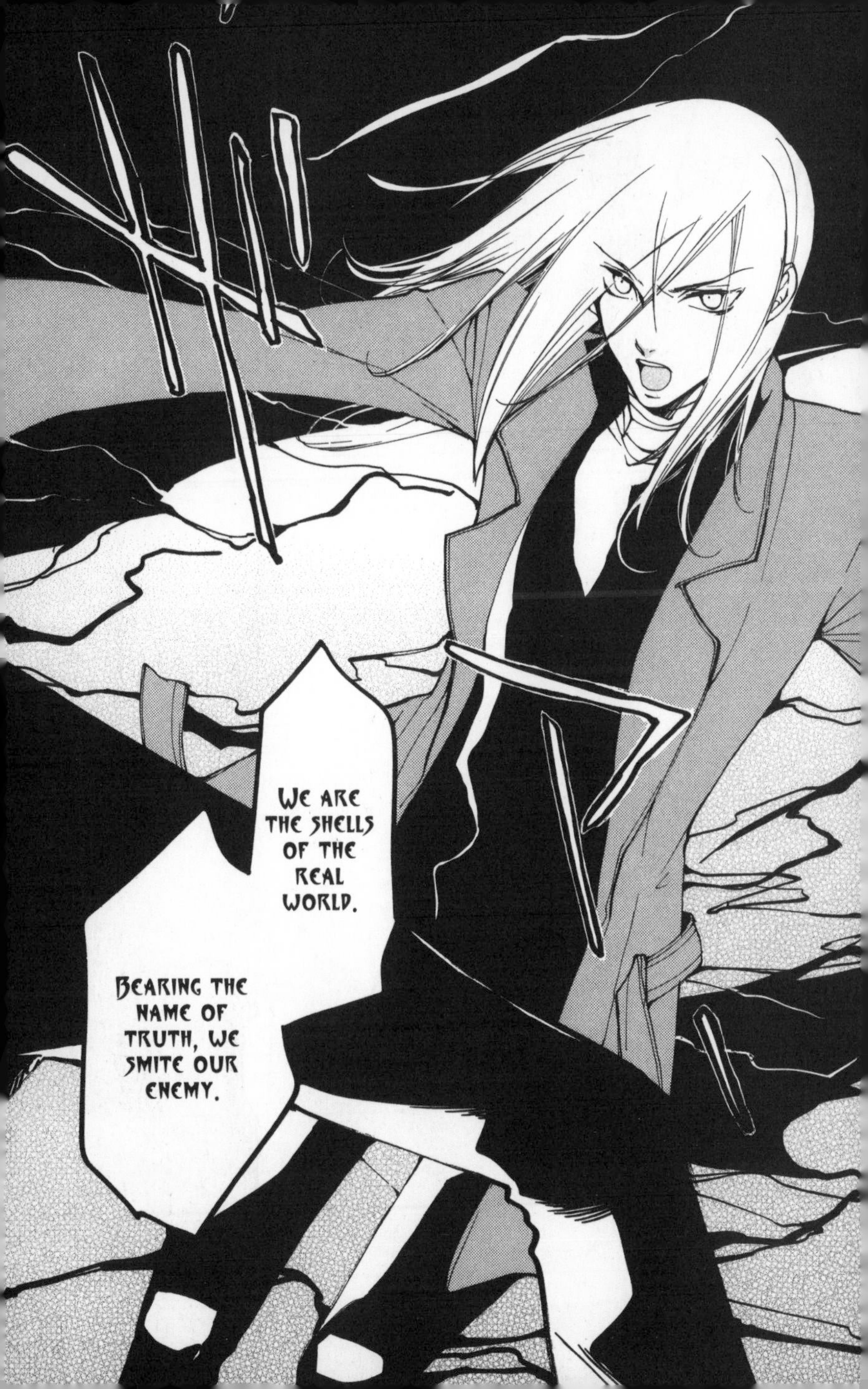
WE ARE THE SHELLS OF THE REAL WORLD.
BEARING THE NAME OF TRUTH, WE SMITE OUR ENEMY.

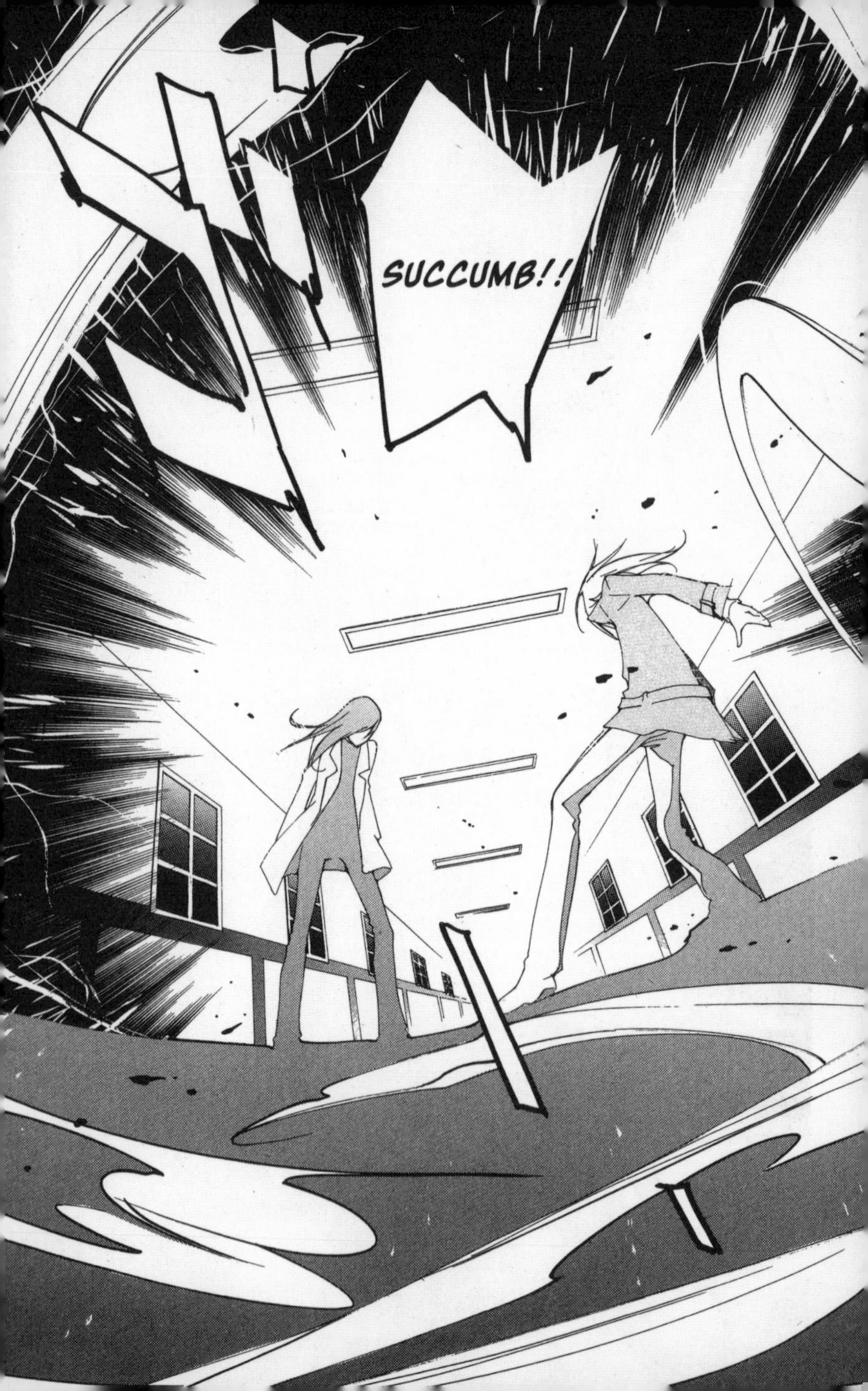
SUCCUMB!!

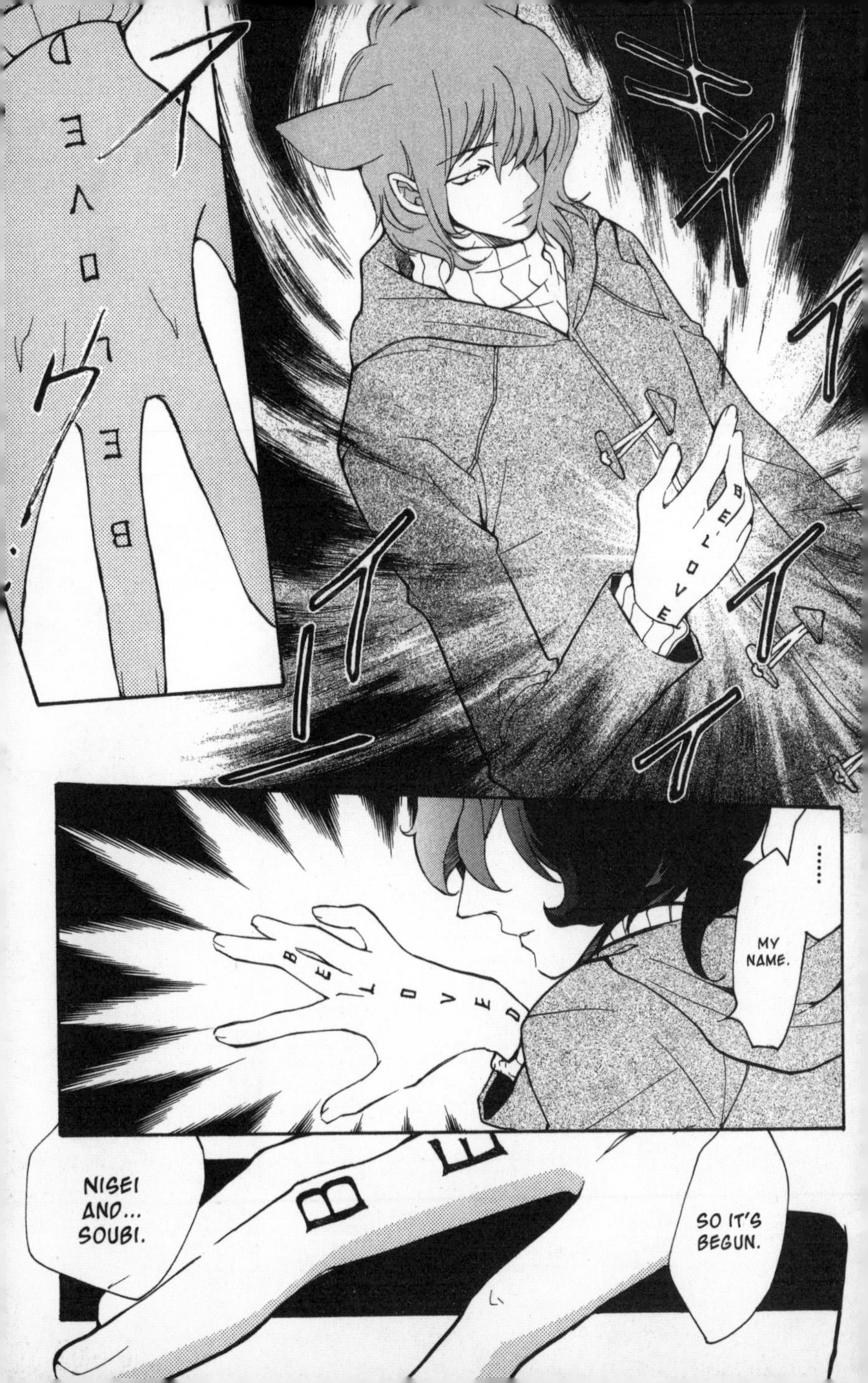
......
MY NAME.
SO IT'S BEGUN.
NISEI AND... SOUBI.

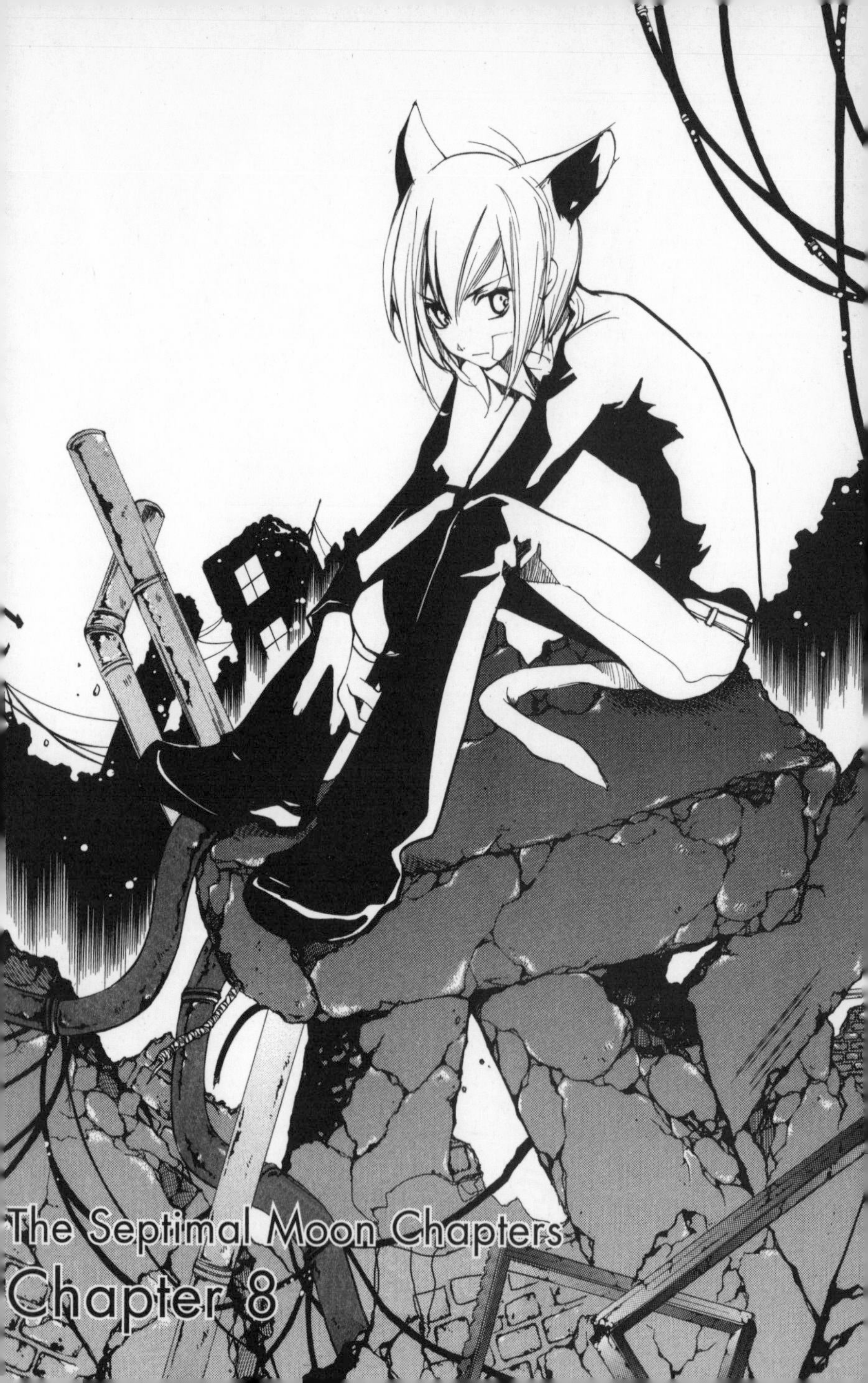
The Septimal Moon Chapters
Chapter 8

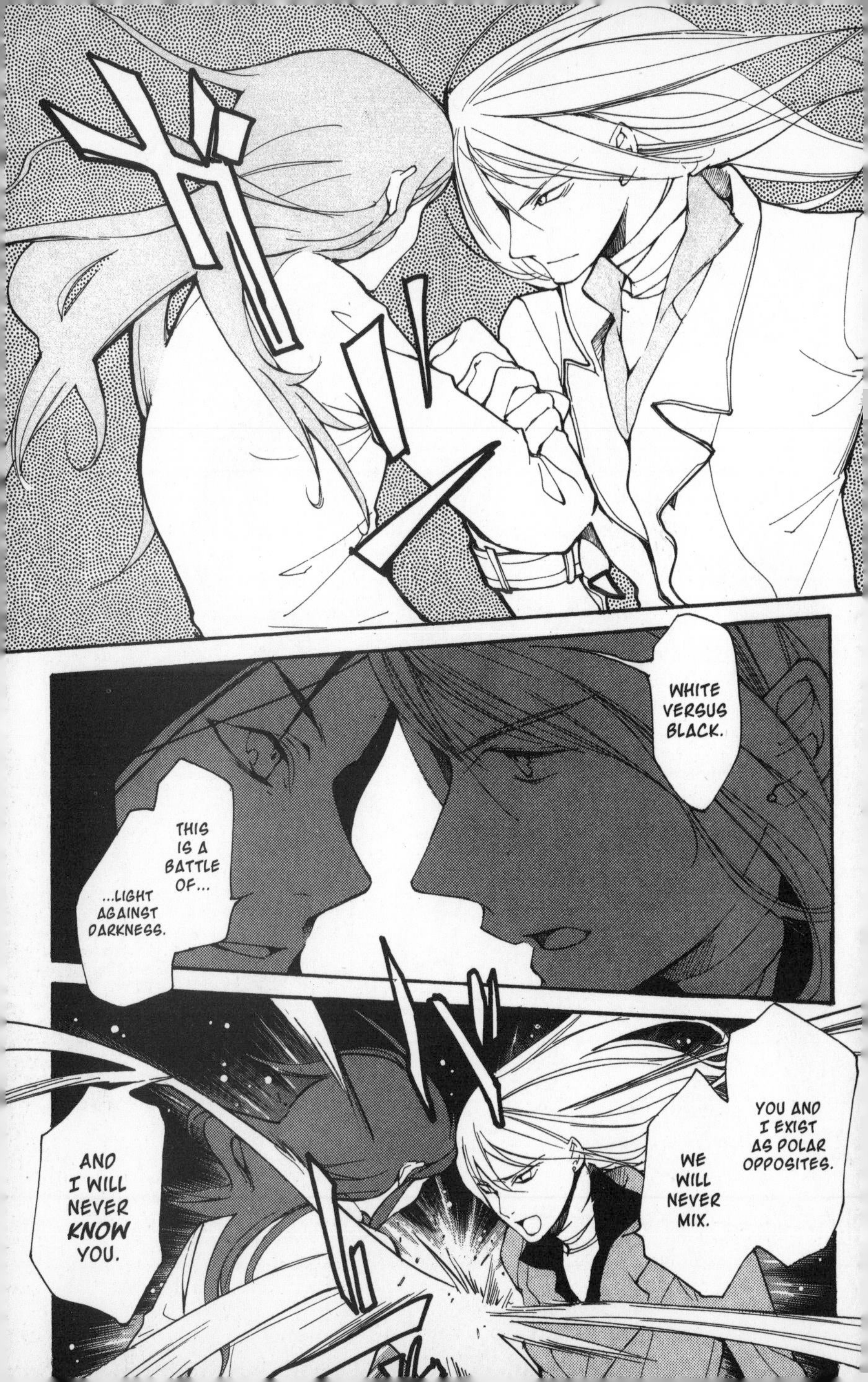
WHITE VERSUS BLACK.
THIS IS A BATTLE OF...
...LIGHT AGAINST DARKNESS.
YOU AND I EXIST AS POLAR OPPOSITES.
WE WILL NEVER MIX.
AND I WILL NEVER KNOW YOU.

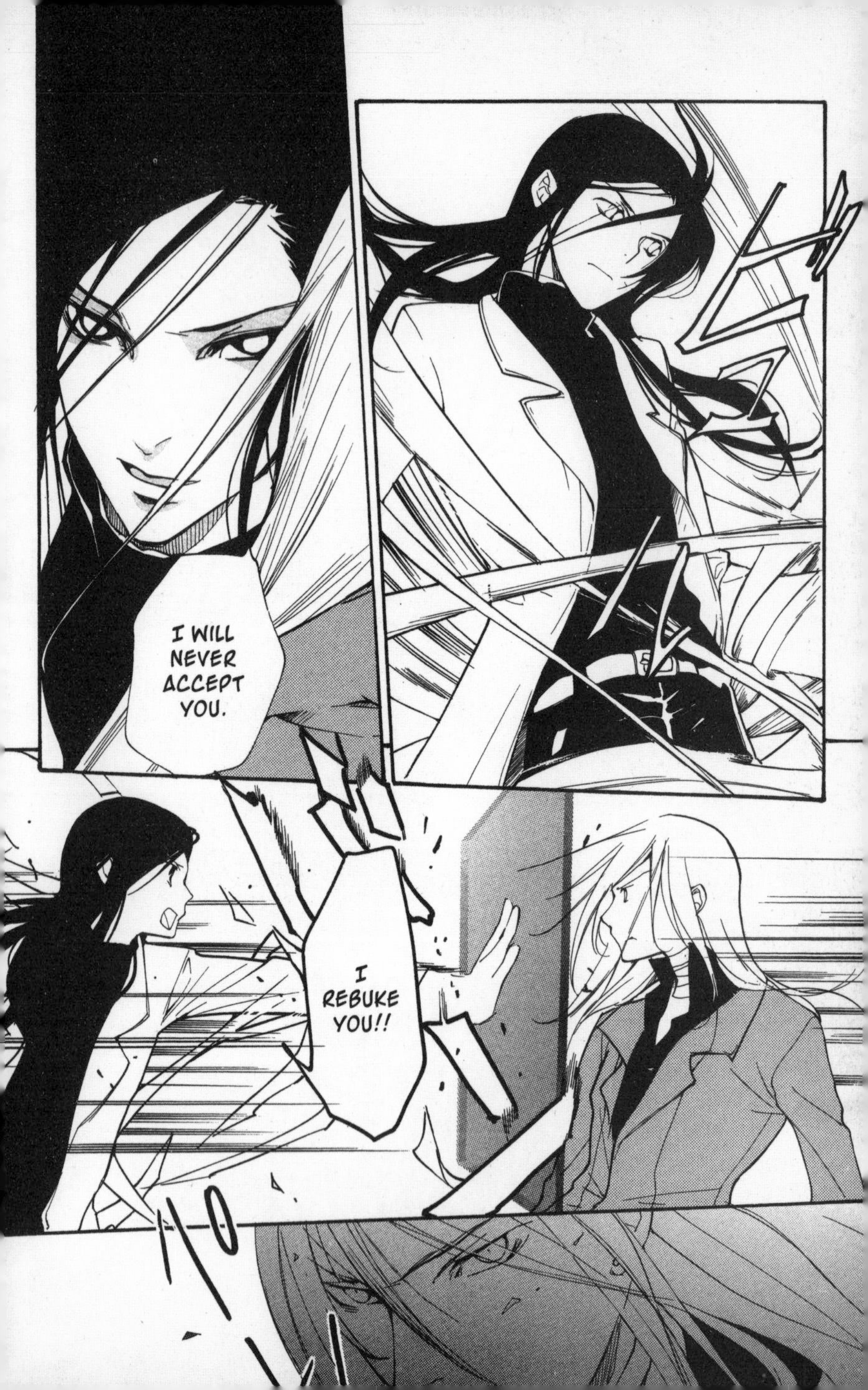
I WILL NEVER ACCEPT YOU.
I REBUKE YOU!!

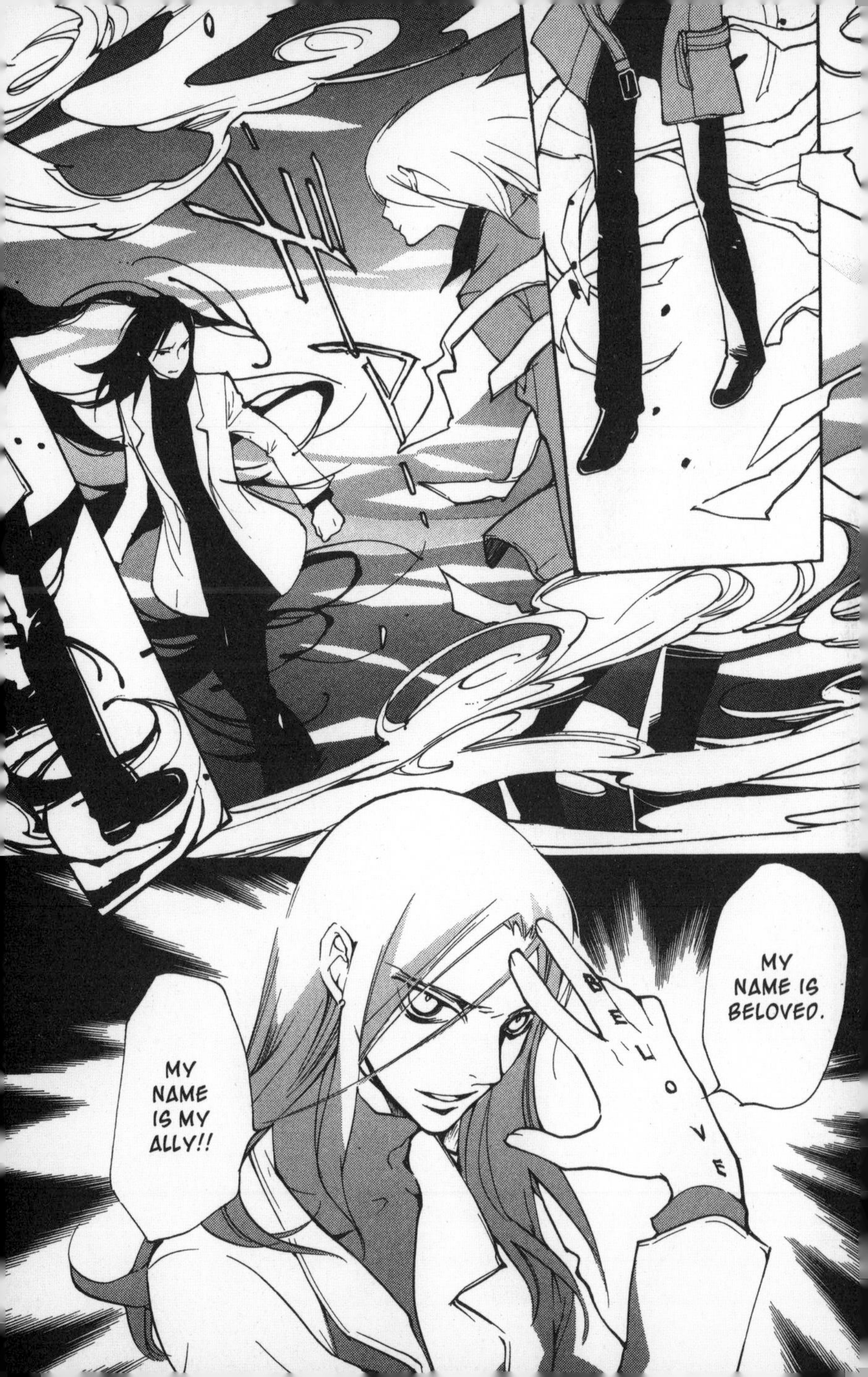
MY NAME IS BELOVED.
BELOVE
MY NAME IS MY ALLY!!

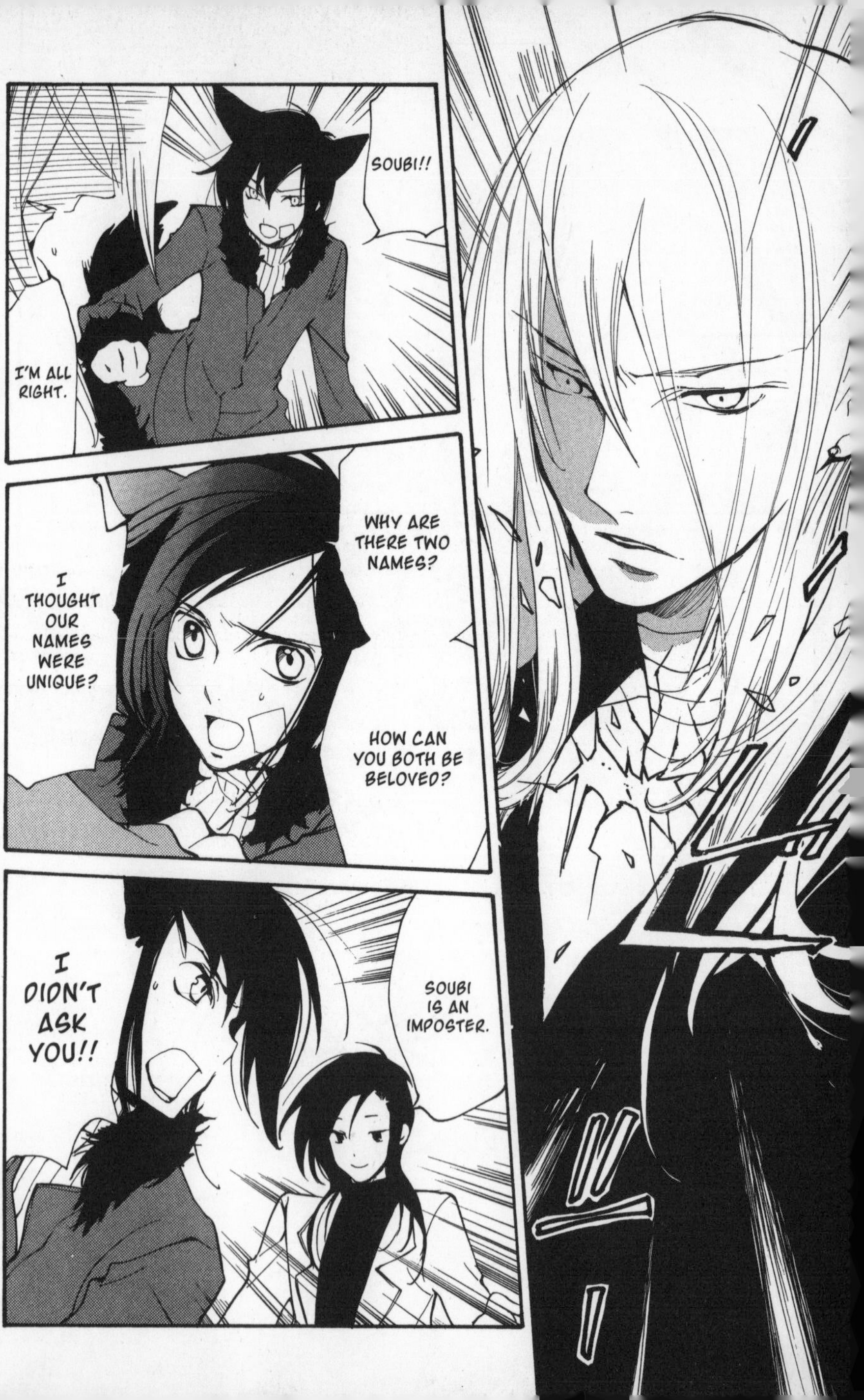
SOUBI!!
I'M ALL RIGHT.
WHY ARE THERE TWO NAMES?
I THOUGHT OUR NAMES WERE UNIQUE?
HOW CAN YOU BOTH BE BELOVED?
SOUBI IS AN IMPOSTER.
I DIDN'T ASK YOU!!

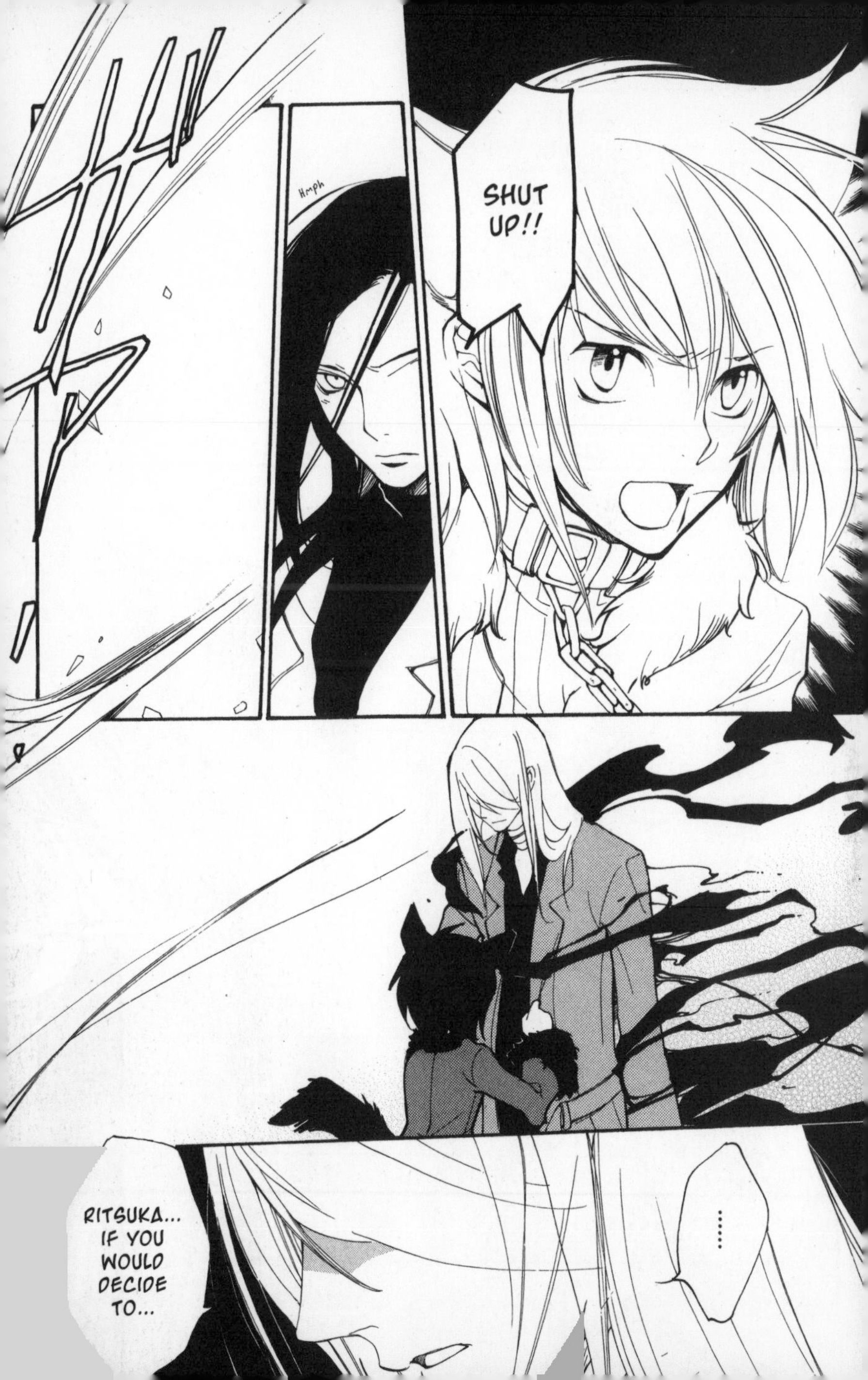
SHUT UP!!
Hmph
......
RITSUKA... IF YOU WOULD DECIDE TO...

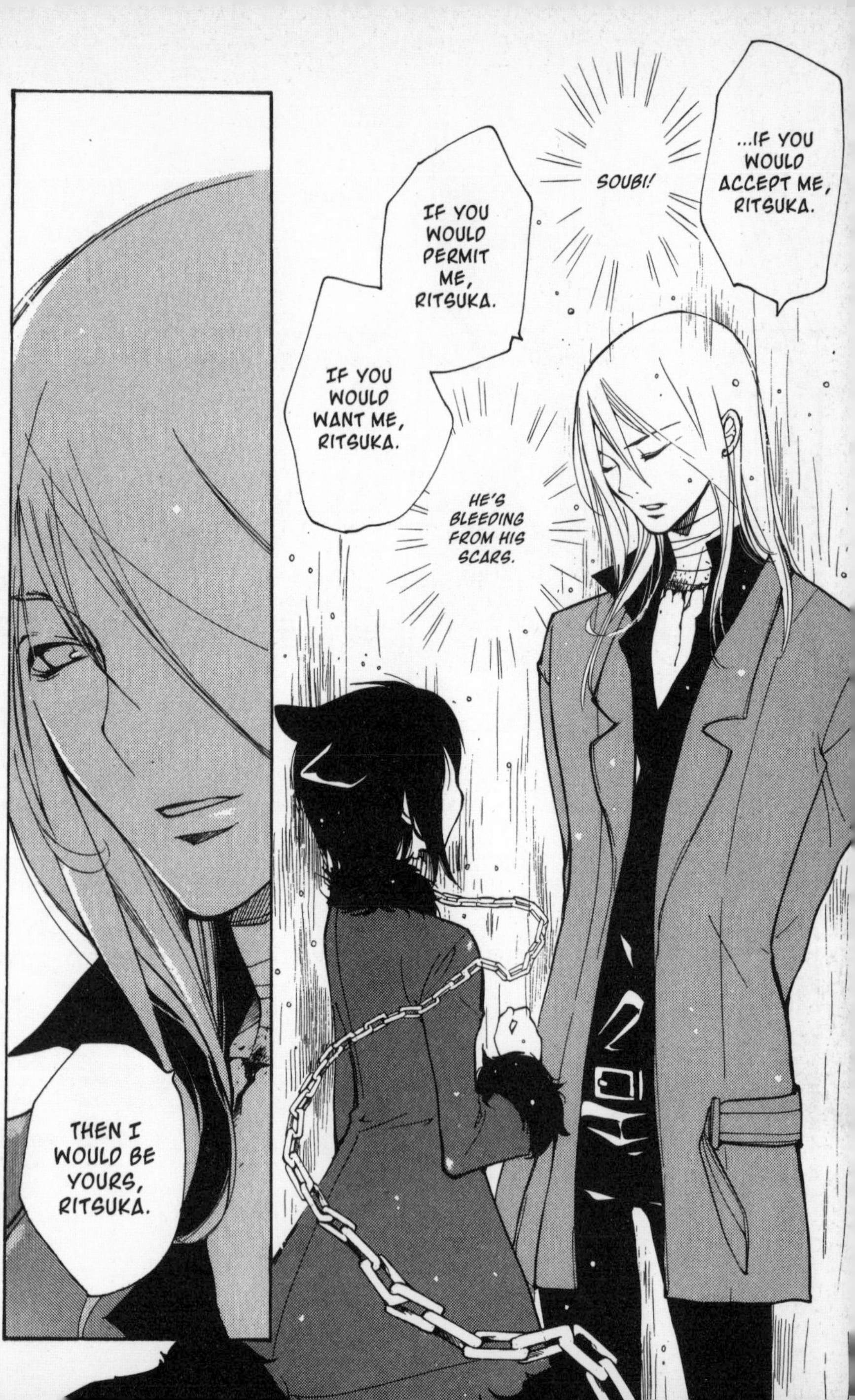
...IF YOU WOULD ACCEPT ME, RITSUKA.
SOUBI!
IF YOU WOULD PERMIT ME, RITSUKA.
IF YOU WOULD WANT ME, RITSUKA.
HE'S BLEEDING FROM HIS SCARS.
THEN I WOULD BE YOURS, RITSUKA.

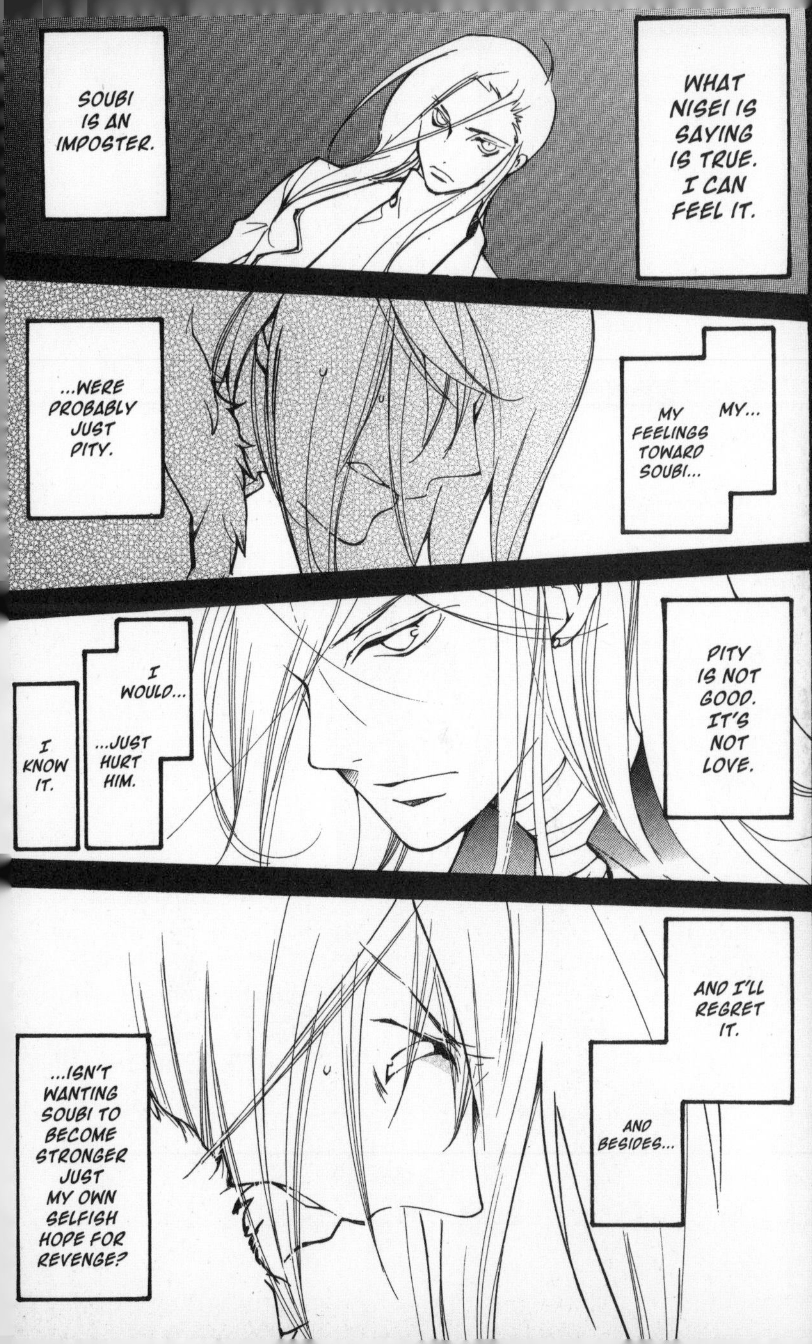
WHAT NISEI IS SAYING IS TRUE. I CAN FEEL IT.
SOUBI IS AN IMPOSTER.
MY...
MY FEELINGS TOWARD SOUBI...
...WERE PROBABLY JUST PITY.
PITY IS NOT GOOD. IT'S NOT LOVE.
I WOULD...
...JUST HURT HIM.
I KNOW IT.
AND I'LL REGRET IT.
AND BESIDES...
...ISN'T WANTING SOUBI TO BECOME STRONGER JUST MY OWN SELFISH HOPE FOR REVENGE?

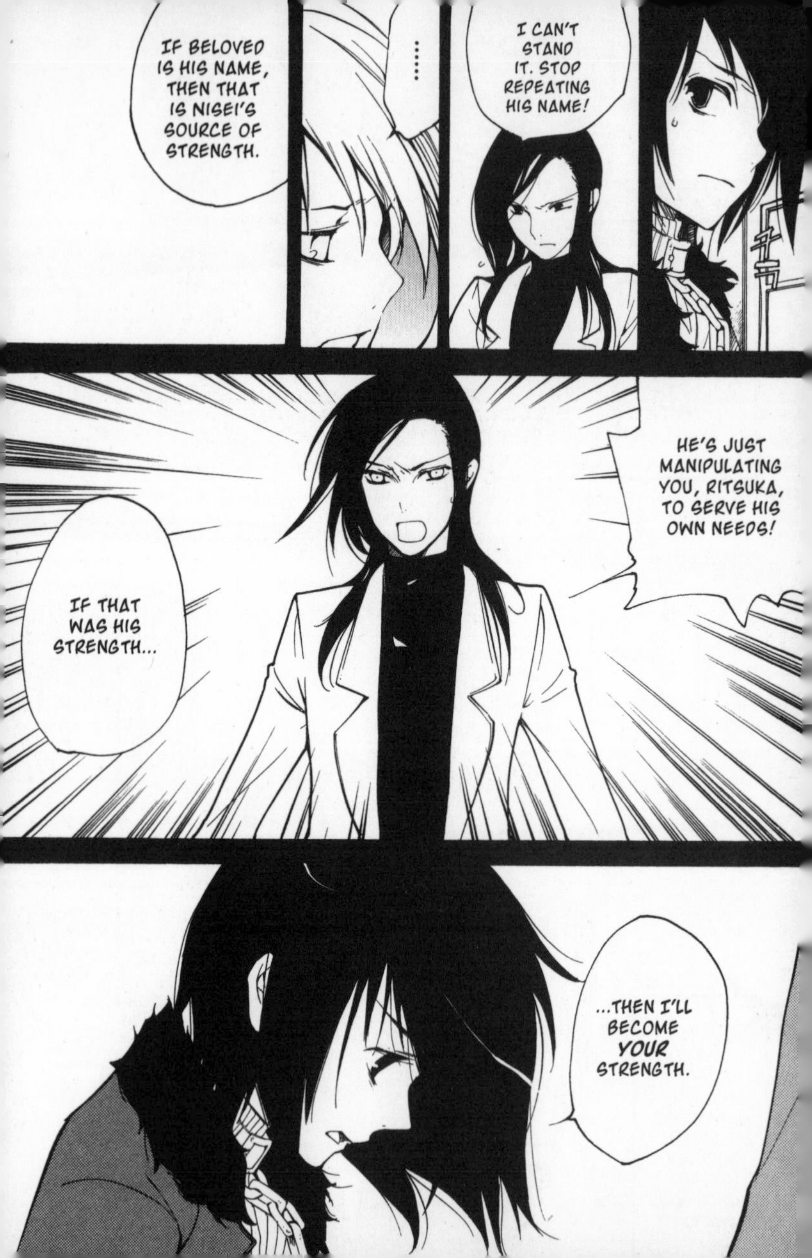
I CAN'T STAND IT. STOP REPEATING HIS NAME!
......
IF BELOVED IS HIS NAME, THEN THAT IS NISEI'S SOURCE OF STRENGTH.
HE'S JUST MANIPULATING YOU, RITSUKA, TO SERVE HIS OWN NEEDS!
IF THAT WAS HIS STRENGTH...
...THEN I'LL BECOME *YOUR* STRENGTH.

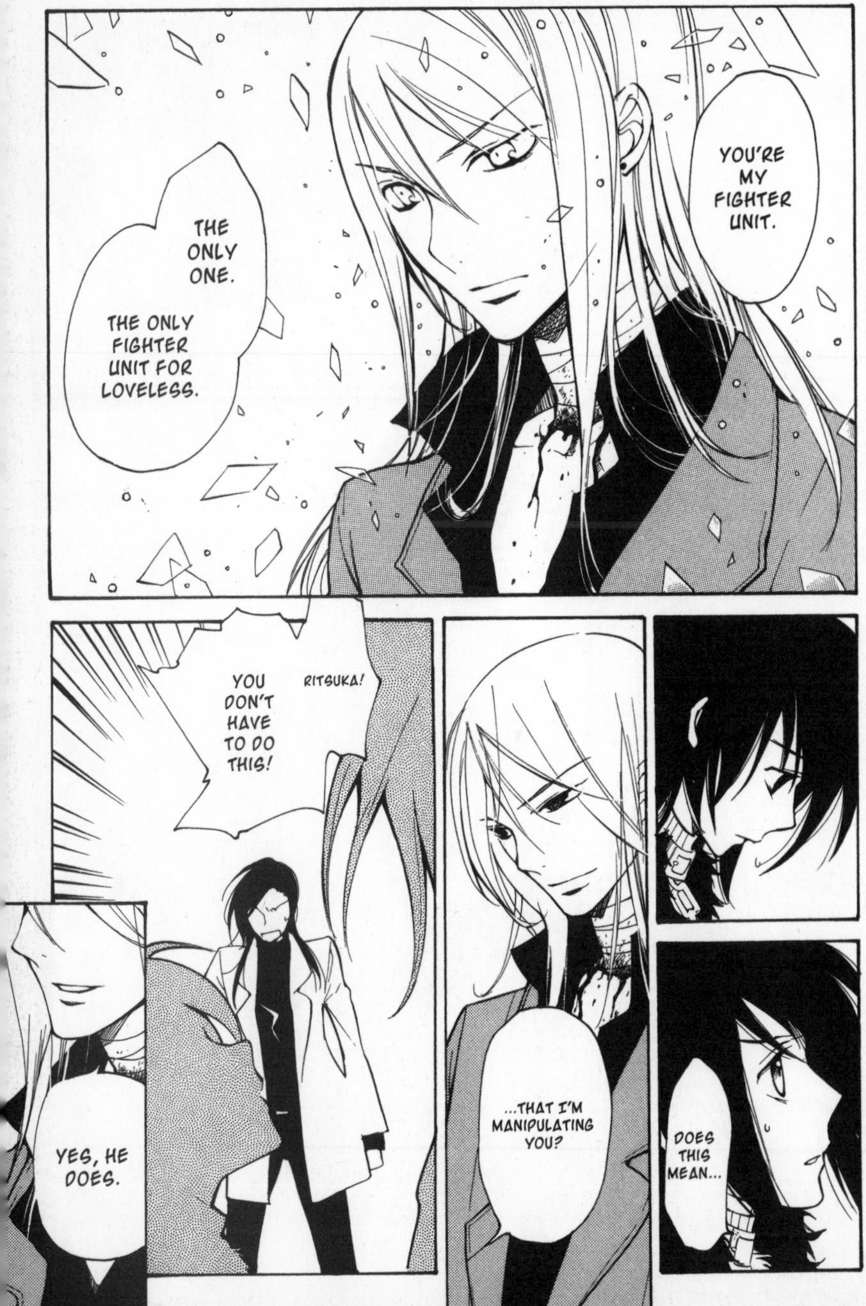
YOU'RE MY FIGHTER UNIT.
THE ONLY ONE.
THE ONLY FIGHTER UNIT FOR LOVELESS.
DOES THIS MEAN...
...THAT I'M MANIPULATING YOU?
RITSUKA!
YOU DON'T HAVE TO DO THIS!
YES, HE DOES.

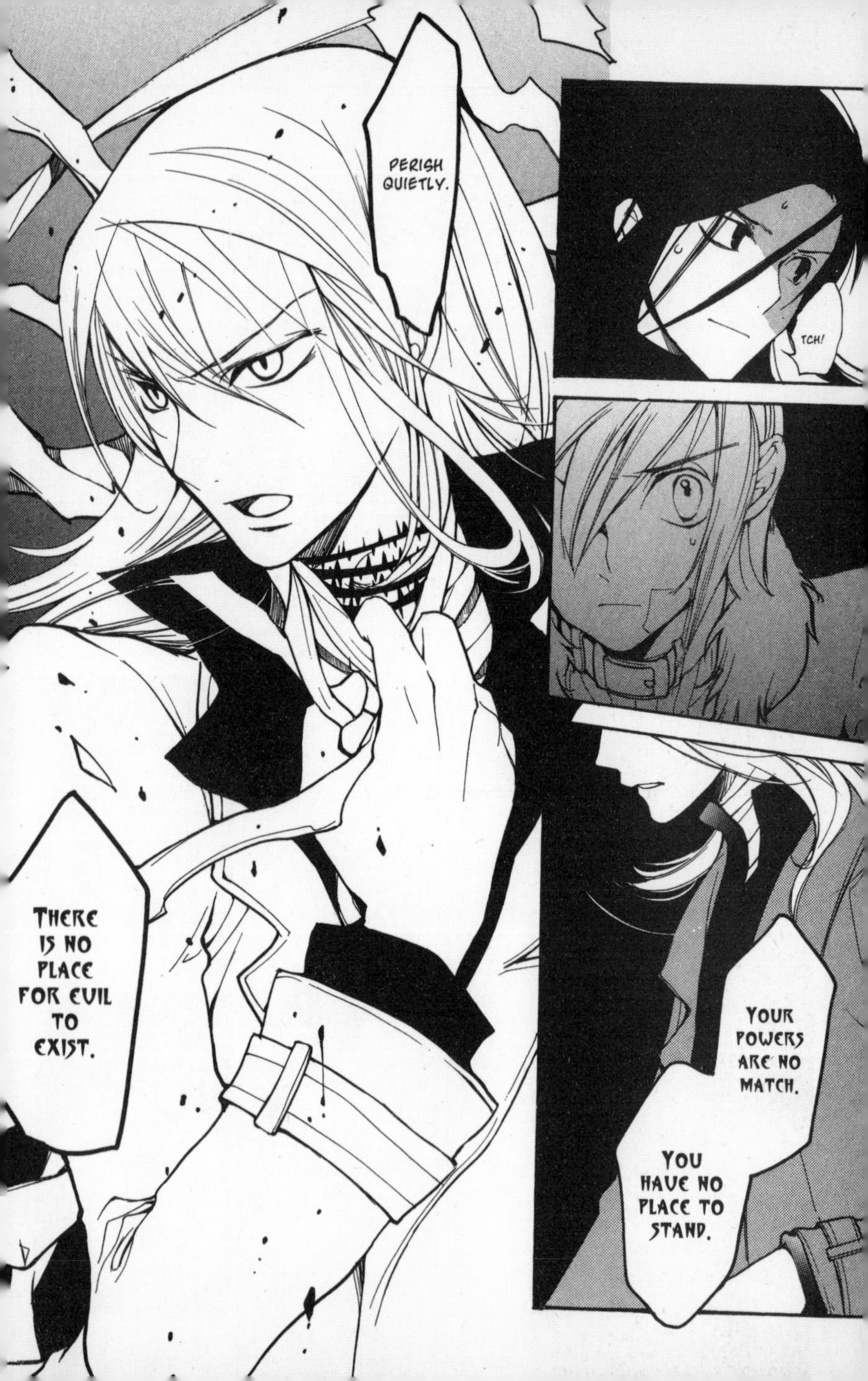
TCH!
YOUR POWERS ARE NO MATCH.
YOU HAVE NO PLACE TO STAND.
PERISH QUIETLY.
THERE IS NO PLACE FOR EVIL TO EXIST.

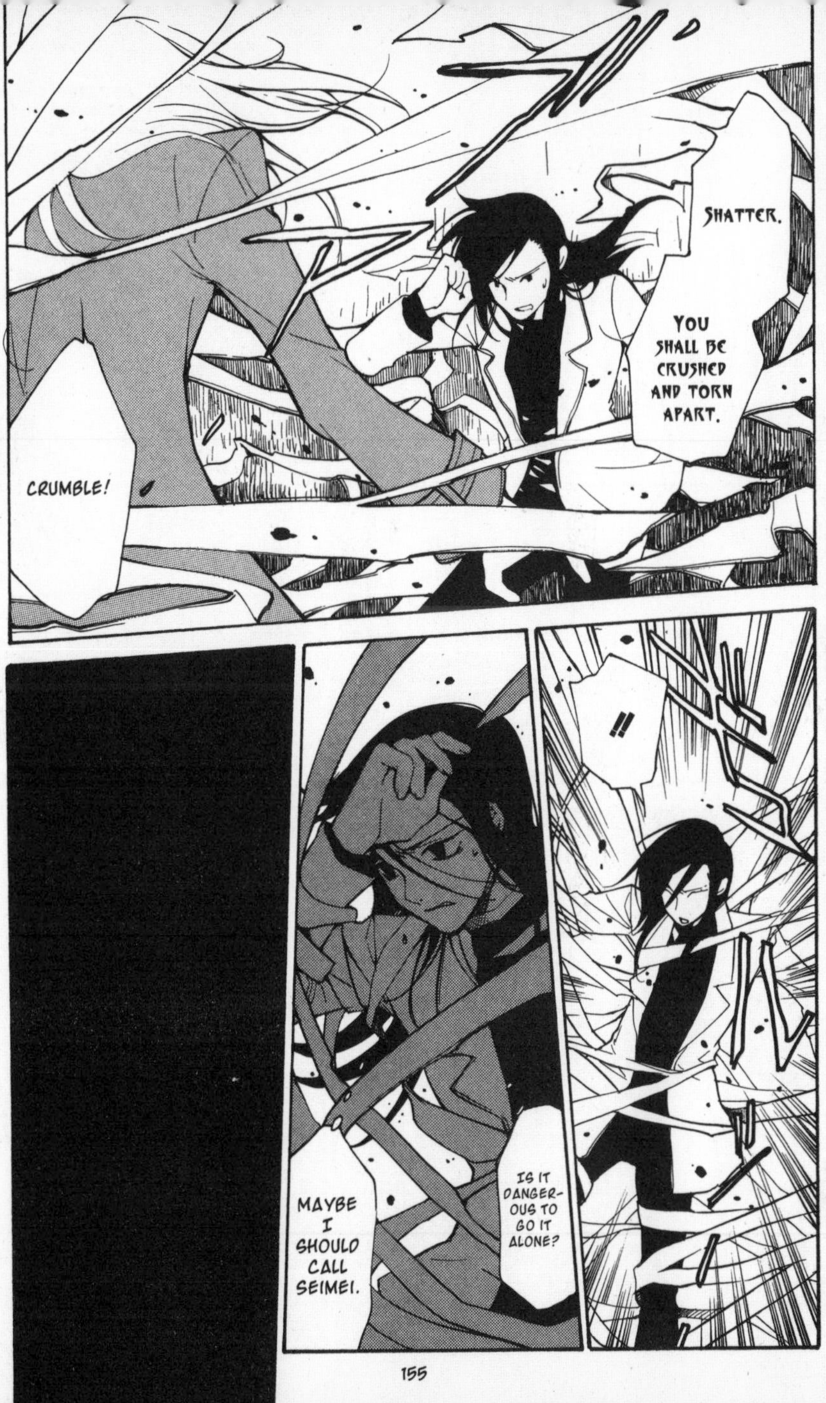
SHATTER.
YOU SHALL BE CRUSHED AND TORN APART.
CRUMBLE!
!!
IS IT DANGER-OUS TO GO IT ALONE?
MAYBE I SHOULD CALL SEIMEI.

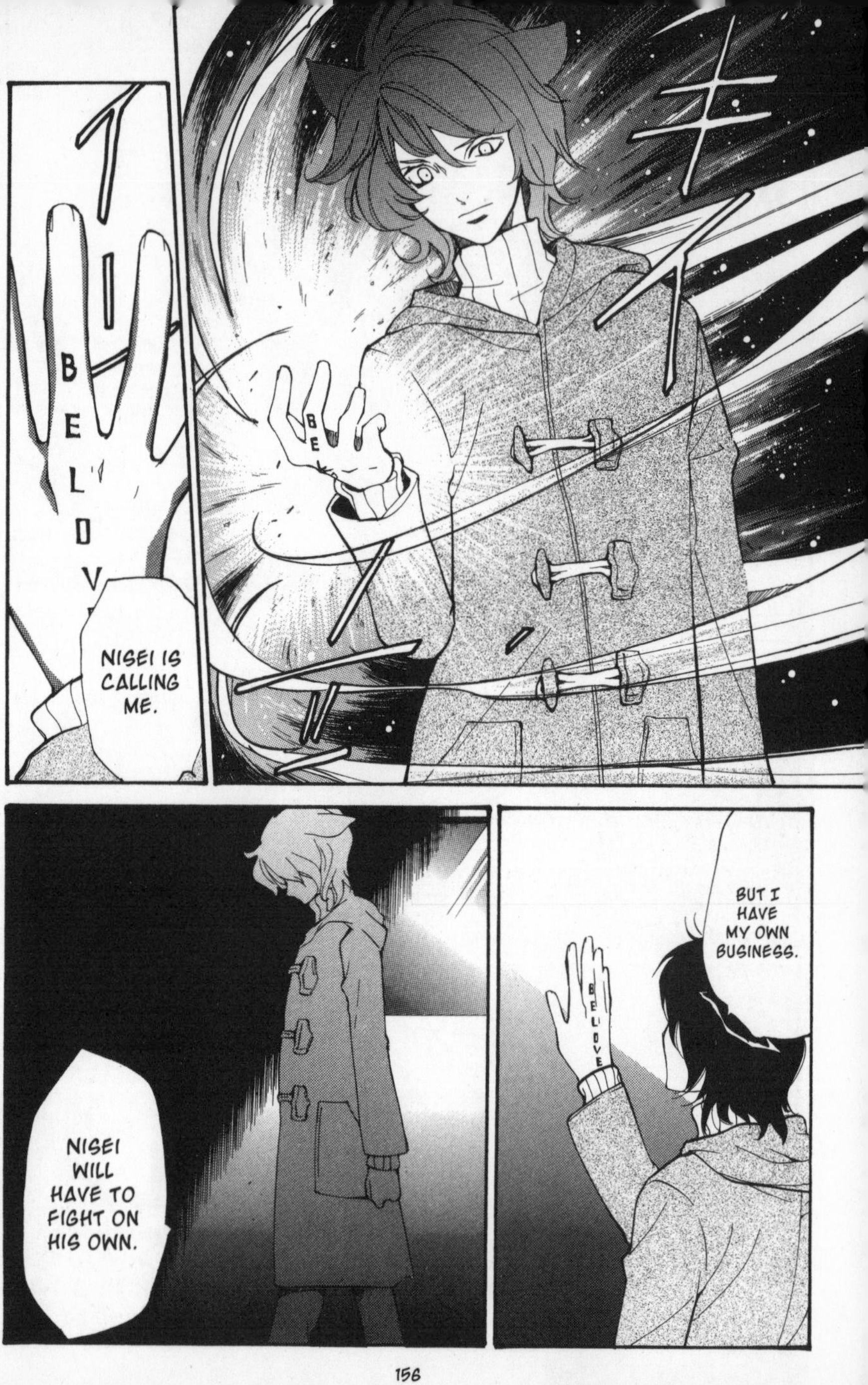
NISEI IS CALLING ME.
BUT I HAVE MY OWN BUSINESS.
NISEI WILL HAVE TO FIGHT ON HIS OWN.

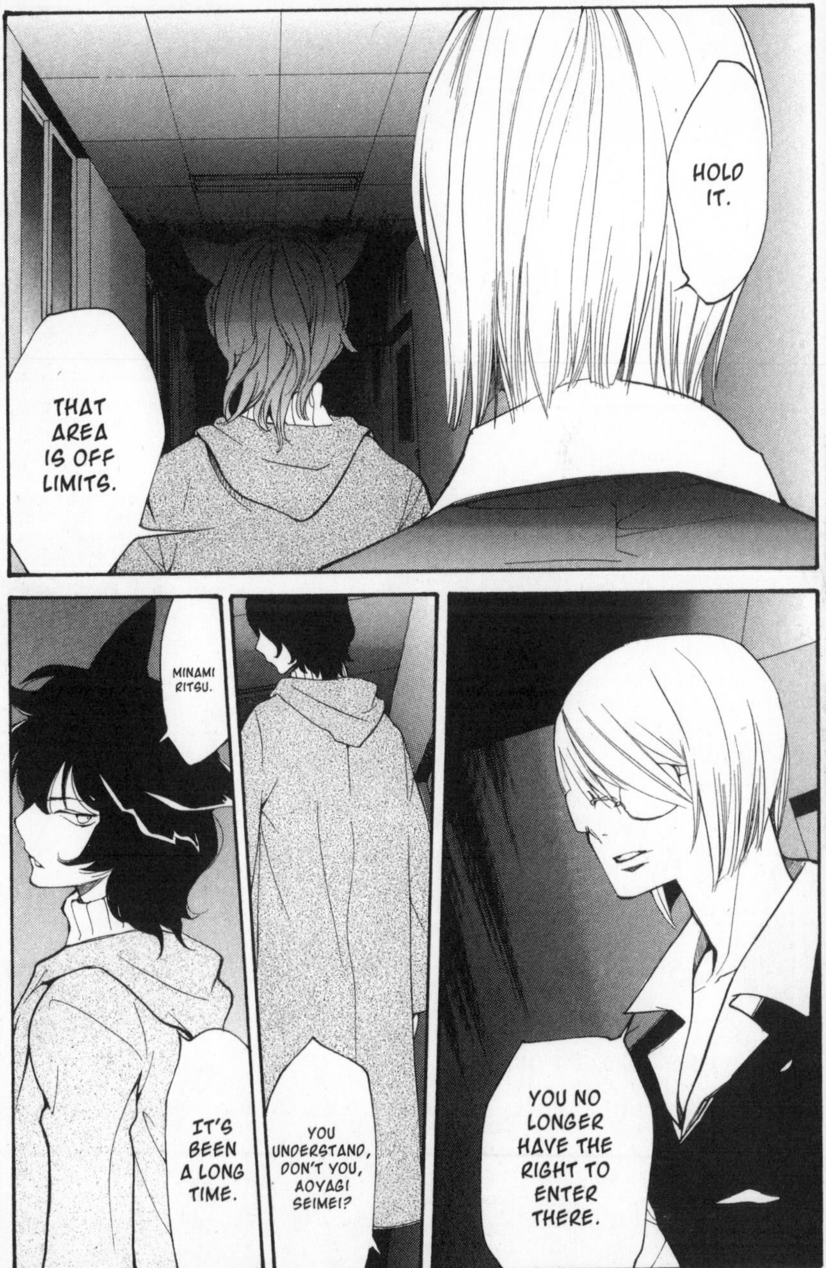
HOLD IT.
THAT AREA IS OFF LIMITS.
YOU NO LONGER HAVE THE RIGHT TO ENTER THERE.
YOU UNDERSTAND, DON'T YOU, AOYAGI SEIMEI?
MINAMI RITSU.
IT'S BEEN A LONG TIME.

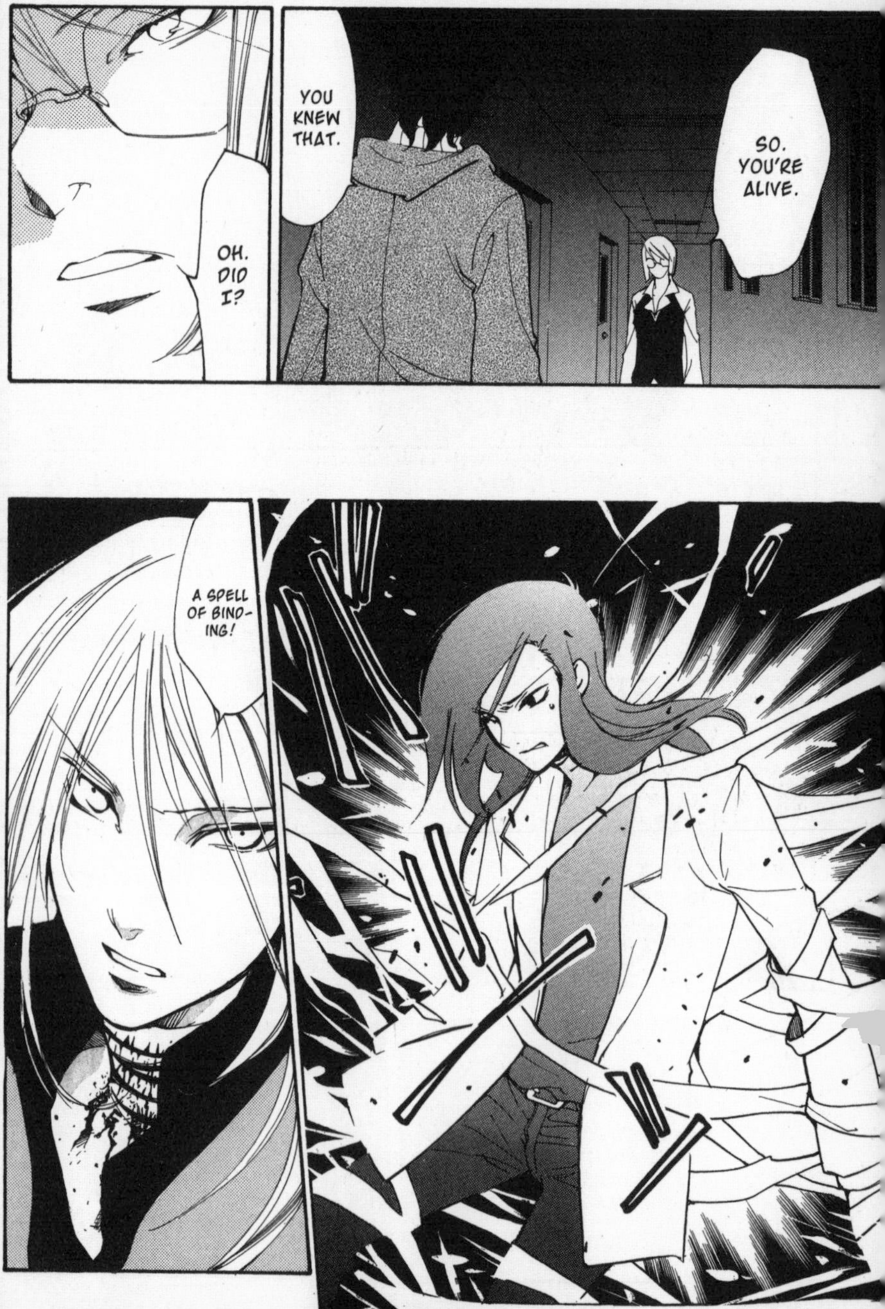
SO. YOU'RE ALIVE.
YOU KNEW THAT.
OH. DID I?
A SPELL OF BIND-ING!

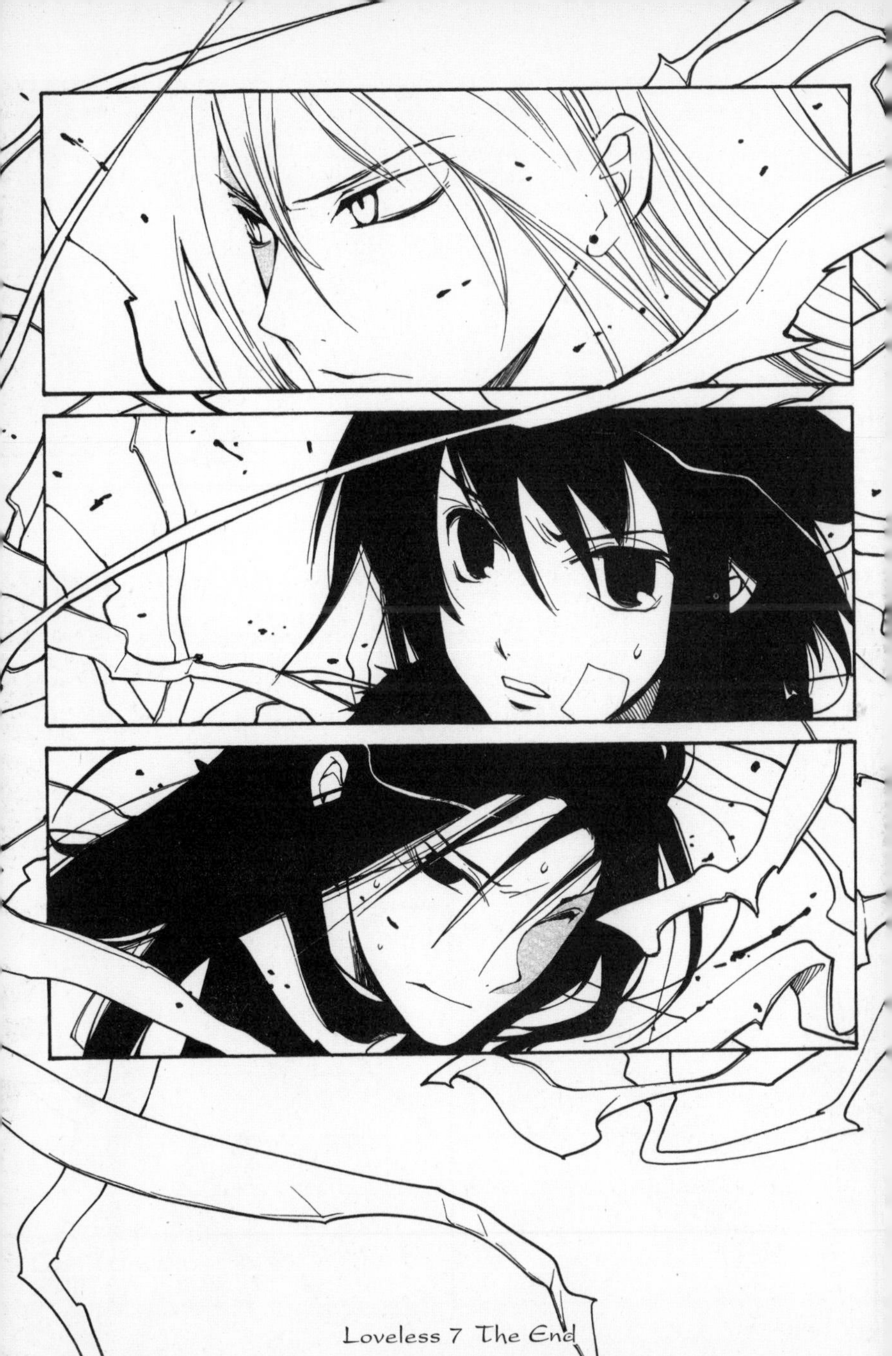

Loveless 7 The End

Hah.

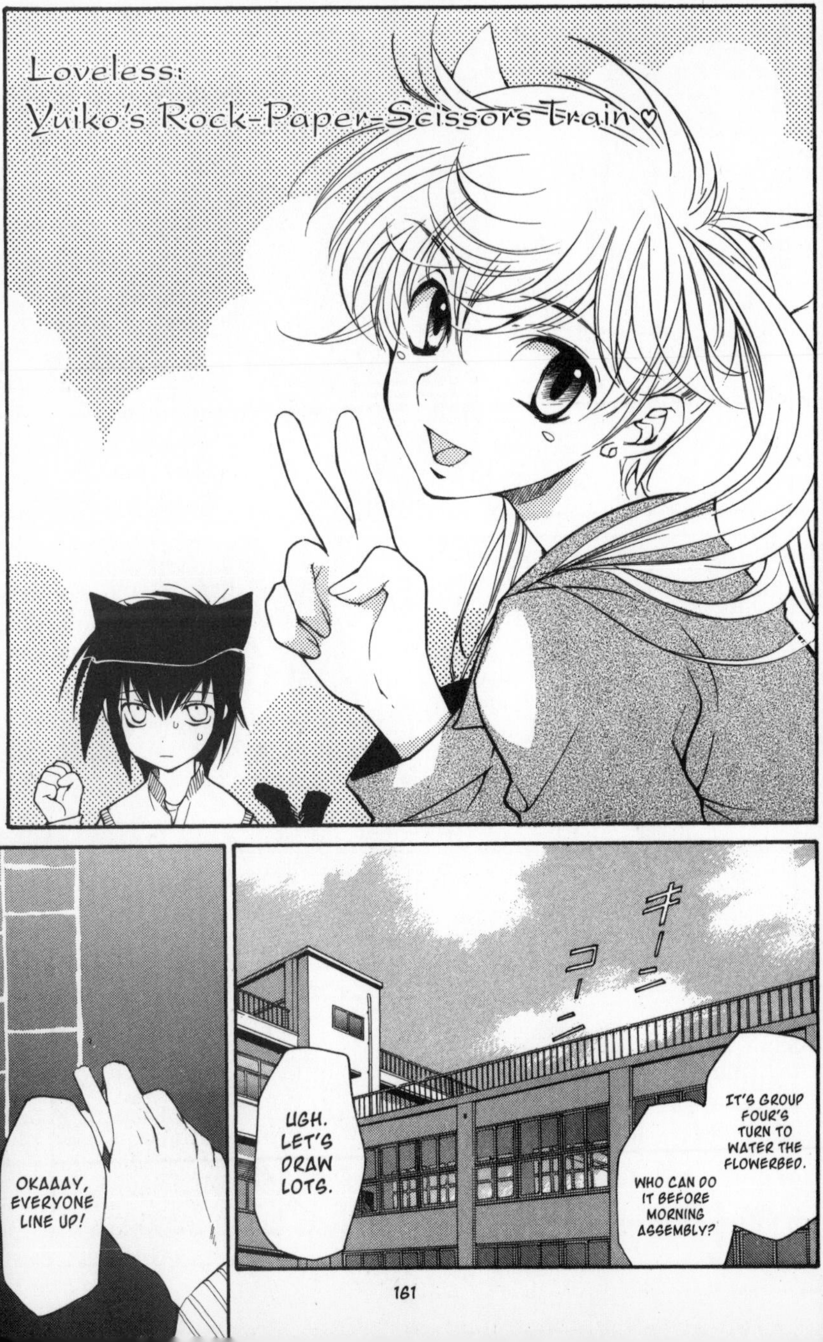
Loveless:
Yuiko's Rock-Paper-Scissors Train ♡
キーン
コーン
IT'S GROUP FOUR'S TURN TO WATER THE FLOWERBED.
WHO CAN DO IT BEFORE MORNING ASSEMBLY?
UGH. LET'S DRAW LOTS.
OKAAAY, EVERYONE LINE UP!

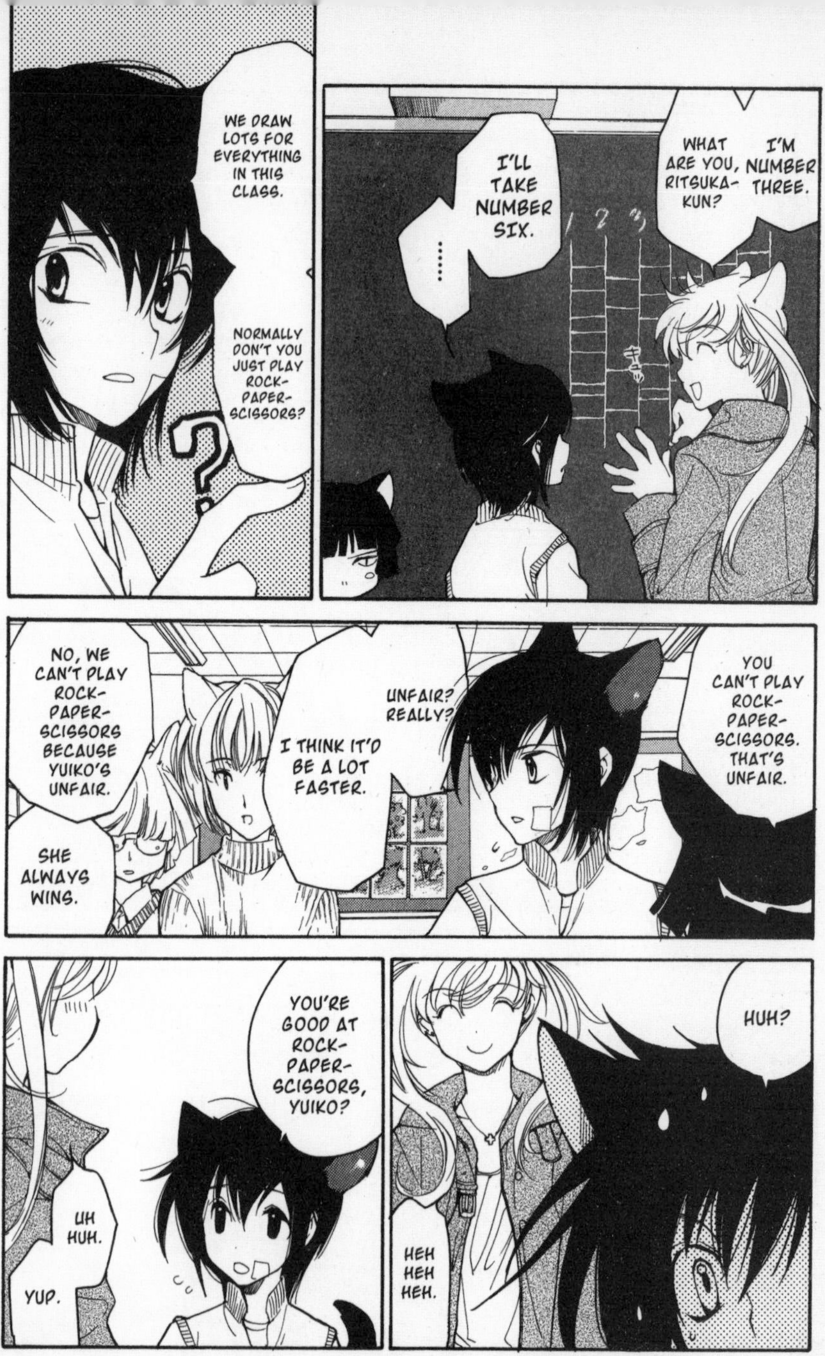
I'M NUMBER THREE.
WHAT ARE YOU, RITSUKA-KUN?
I'LL TAKE NUMBER SIX.
......
WE DRAW LOTS FOR EVERYTHING IN THIS CLASS.
NORMALLY DON'T YOU JUST PLAY ROCK-PAPER-SCISSORS?
YOU CAN'T PLAY ROCK-PAPER-SCISSORS. THAT'S UNFAIR.
UNFAIR? REALLY?
I THINK IT'D BE A LOT FASTER.
NO, WE CAN'T PLAY ROCK-PAPER-SCISSORS BECAUSE YUIKO'S UNFAIR.
SHE ALWAYS WINS.
HUH?
HEH HEH HEH.
YOU'RE GOOD AT ROCK-PAPER-SCISSORS, YUIKO?
UH HUH.
YUP.

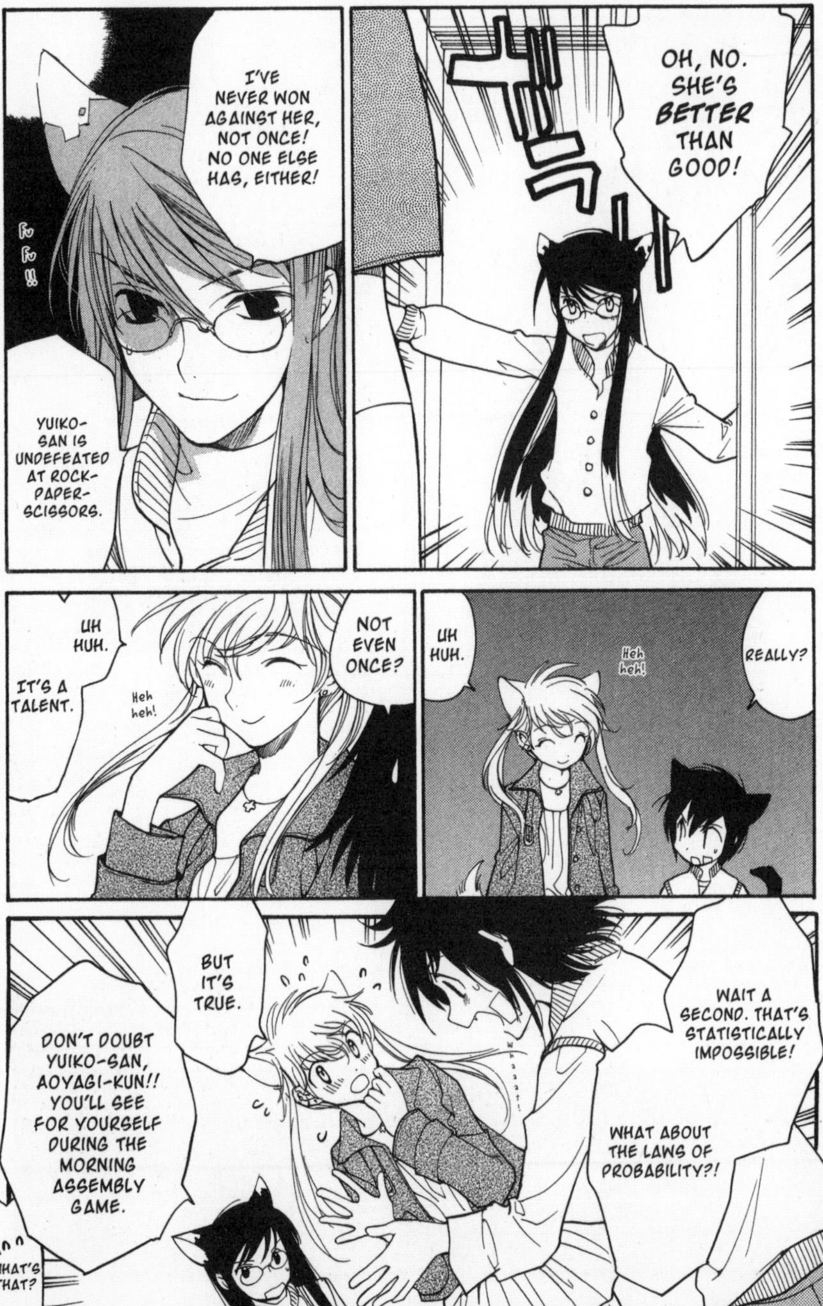
OH, NO. SHE'S BETTER THAN GOOD!
I'VE NEVER WON AGAINST HER, NOT ONCE! NO ONE ELSE HAS, EITHER!
YUIKO-SAN IS UNDEFEATED AT ROCK-PAPER-SCISSORS.
REALLY?
Heh heh!
UH HUH.
NOT EVEN ONCE?
Heh heh!
UH HUH.
IT'S A TALENT.
WAIT A SECOND. THAT'S STATISTICALLY IMPOSSIBLE!
WHAT ABOUT THE LAWS OF PROBABILITY?!
whaaat!
BUT IT'S TRUE.
DON'T DOUBT YUIKO-SAN, AOYAGI-KUN!! YOU'LL SEE FOR YOURSELF DURING THE MORNING ASSEMBLY GAME.
WHAT'S THAT?

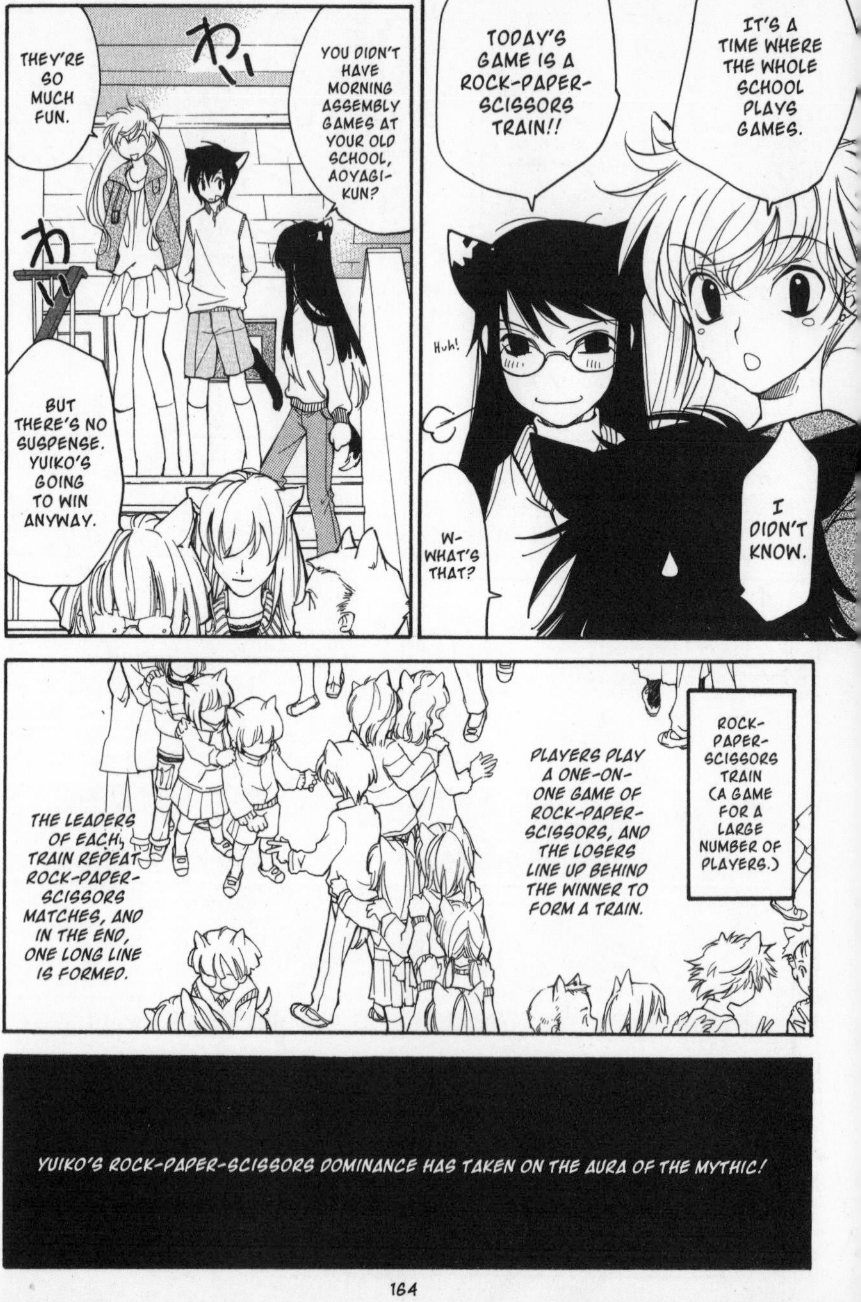
IT'S A TIME WHERE THE WHOLE SCHOOL PLAYS GAMES.
TODAY'S GAME IS A ROCK-PAPER-SCISSORS TRAIN!!
I DIDN'T KNOW.
Huh!
W-WHAT'S THAT?
わい
YOU DIDN'T HAVE MORNING ASSEMBLY GAMES AT YOUR OLD SCHOOL, AOYAGI-KUN?
THEY'RE SO MUCH FUN.
わい
BUT THERE'S NO SUSPENSE. YUIKO'S GOING TO WIN ANYWAY.
ROCK-PAPER-SCISSORS TRAIN (A GAME FOR A LARGE NUMBER OF PLAYERS.)
PLAYERS PLAY A ONE-ON-ONE GAME OF ROCK-PAPER-SCISSORS, AND THE LOSERS LINE UP BEHIND THE WINNER TO FORM A TRAIN.
THE LEADERS OF EACH TRAIN REPEAT ROCK-PAPER-SCISSORS MATCHES, AND IN THE END, ONE LONG LINE IS FORMED.
YUIKO'S ROCK-PAPER-SCISSORS DOMINANCE HAS TAKEN ON THE AURA OF THE MYTHIC!

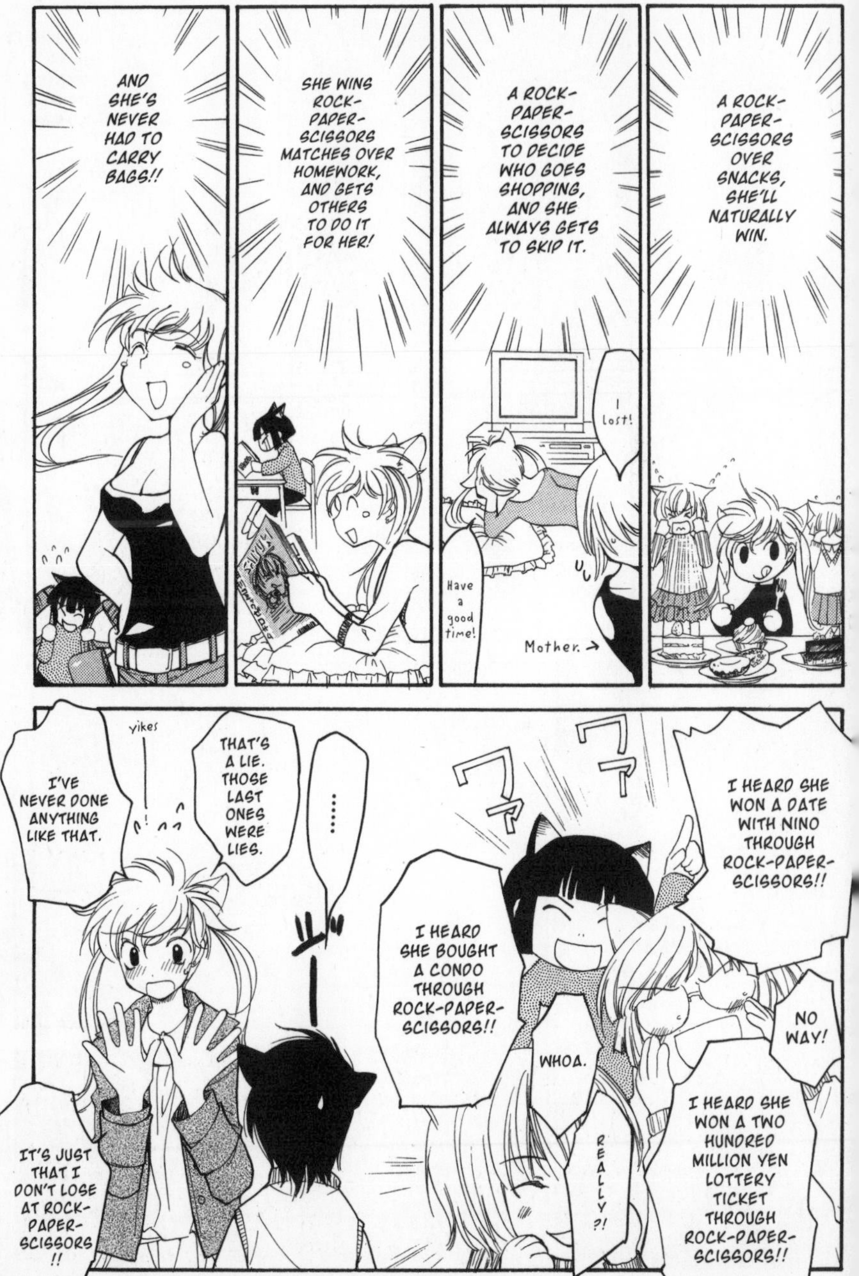
A ROCK-PAPER-SCISSORS OVER SNACKS, SHE'LL NATURALLY WIN.
A ROCK-PAPER-SCISSORS TO DECIDE WHO GOES SHOPPING, AND SHE ALWAYS GETS TO SKIP IT.
I lost!
Have a good time!
Mother. →
SHE WINS ROCK-PAPER-SCISSORS MATCHES OVER HOMEWORK, AND GETS OTHERS TO DO IT FOR HER!
AND SHE'S NEVER HAD TO CARRY BAGS!!
I HEARD SHE WON A DATE WITH NINO THROUGH ROCK-PAPER-SCISSORS!!
ワァ
ワァ
NO WAY!
I HEARD SHE BOUGHT A CONDO THROUGH ROCK-PAPER-SCISSORS!!
WHOA.
I HEARD SHE WON A TWO HUNDRED MILLION YEN LOTTERY TICKET THROUGH ROCK-PAPER-SCISSORS!!
REALLY?!
......
THAT'S A LIE. THOSE LAST ONES WERE LIES.
yikes
I'VE NEVER DONE ANYTHING LIKE THAT.
IT'S JUST THAT I DON'T LOSE AT ROCK-PAPER-SCISSORS!!

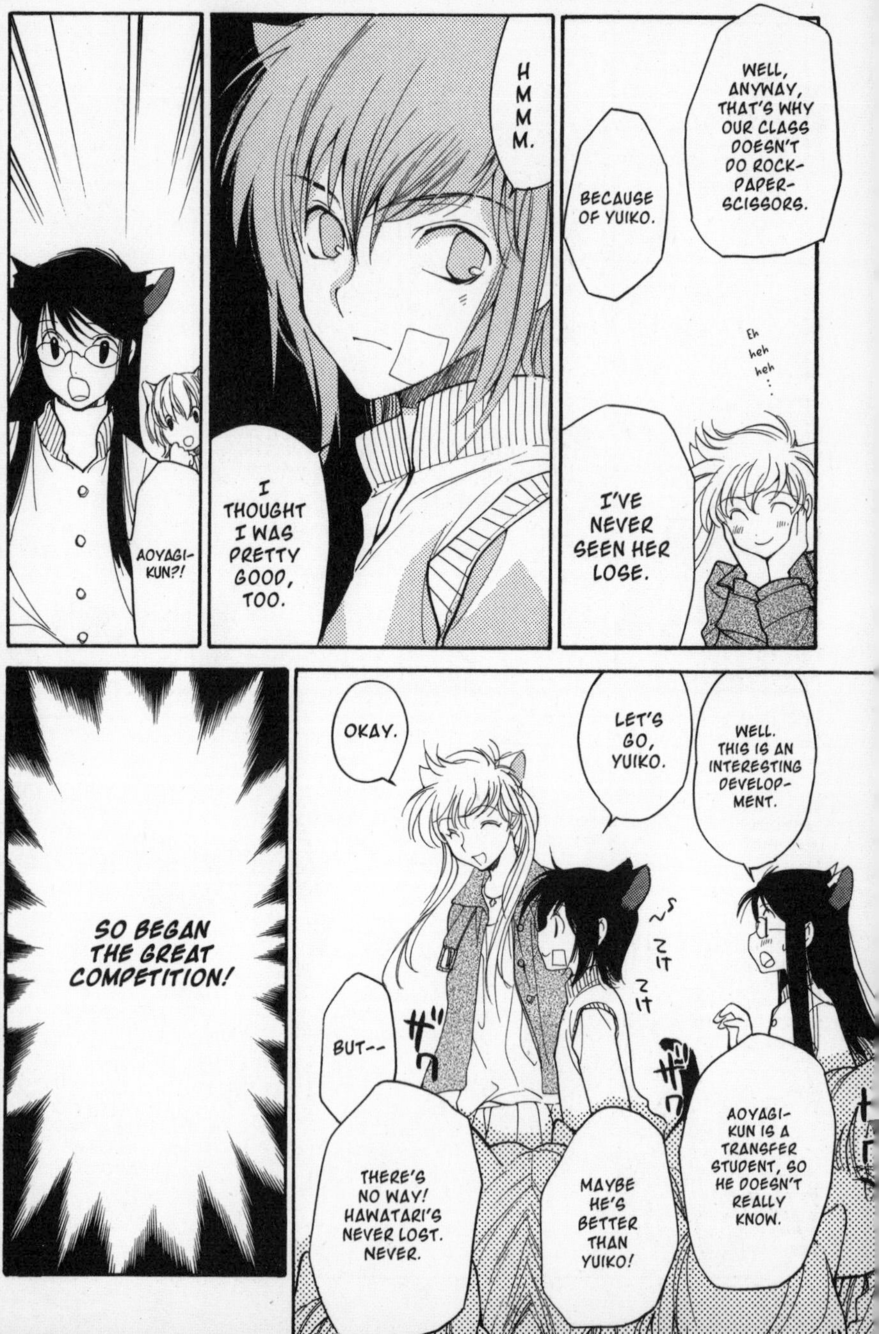
WELL, ANYWAY, THAT'S WHY OUR CLASS DOESN'T DO ROCK-PAPER-SCISSORS.
BECAUSE OF YUIKO.
Eh heh heh...
I'VE NEVER SEEN HER LOSE.
HMMM.
I THOUGHT I WAS PRETTY GOOD, TOO.
AOYAGI-KUN?!
WELL. THIS IS AN INTERESTING DEVELOPMENT.
LET'S GO, YUIKO.
OKAY.
AOYAGI-KUN IS A TRANSFER STUDENT, SO HE DOESN'T REALLY KNOW.
MAYBE HE'S BETTER THAN YUIKO!
THERE'S NO WAY! HAWATARI'S NEVER LOST. NEVER.
BUT--
SO BEGAN THE GREAT COMPETITION!

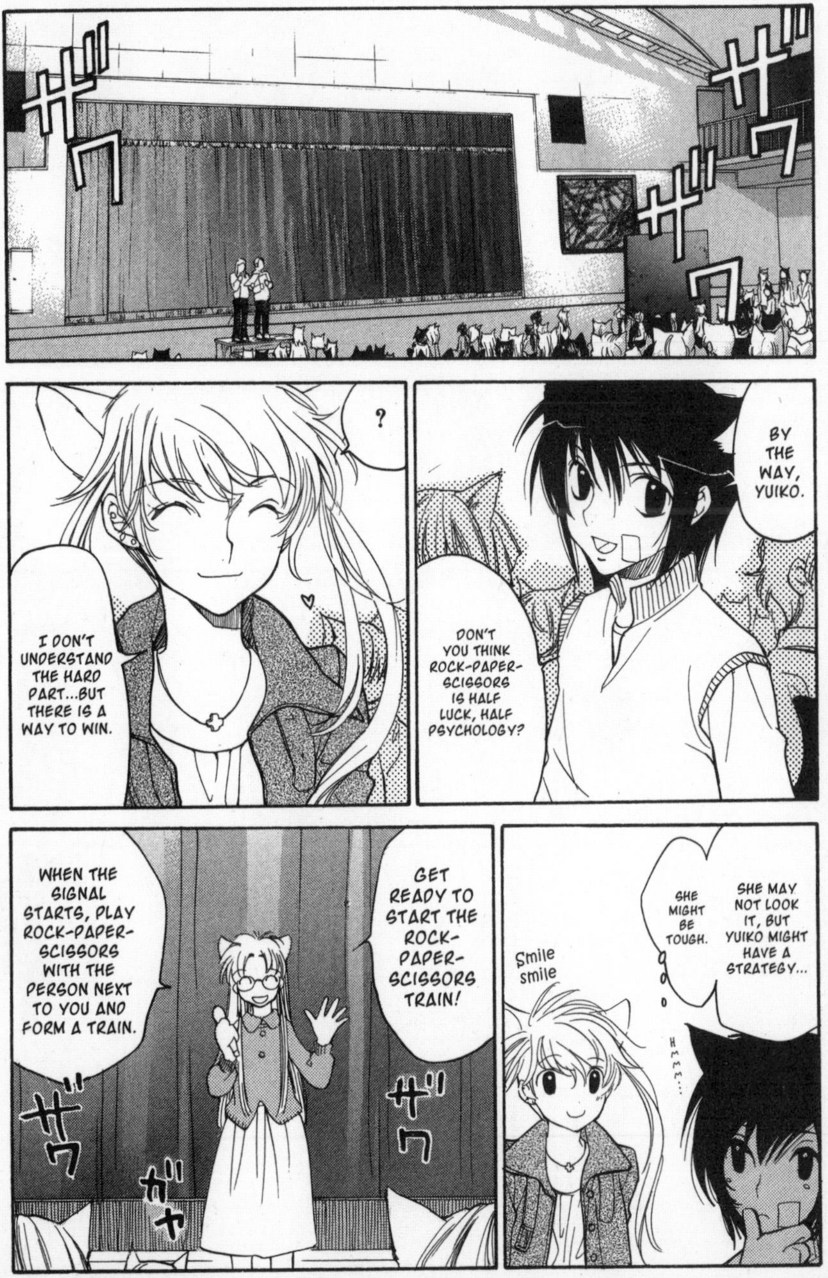
ザワ
ザワ
ザワ
BY THE WAY, YUIKO.
DON'T YOU THINK ROCK-PAPER-SCISSORS IS HALF LUCK, HALF PSYCHOLOGY?
?
I DON'T UNDERSTAND THE HARD PART...BUT THERE IS A WAY TO WIN.
SHE MAY NOT LOOK IT, BUT YUIKO MIGHT HAVE A STRATEGY...
SHE MIGHT BE TOUGH.
Smile smile
HMMM...
GET READY TO START THE ROCK-PAPER-SCISSORS TRAIN!
WHEN THE SIGNAL STARTS, PLAY ROCK-PAPER-SCISSORS WITH THE PERSON NEXT TO YOU AND FORM A TRAIN.
ザワ
ガヤ
ザワ

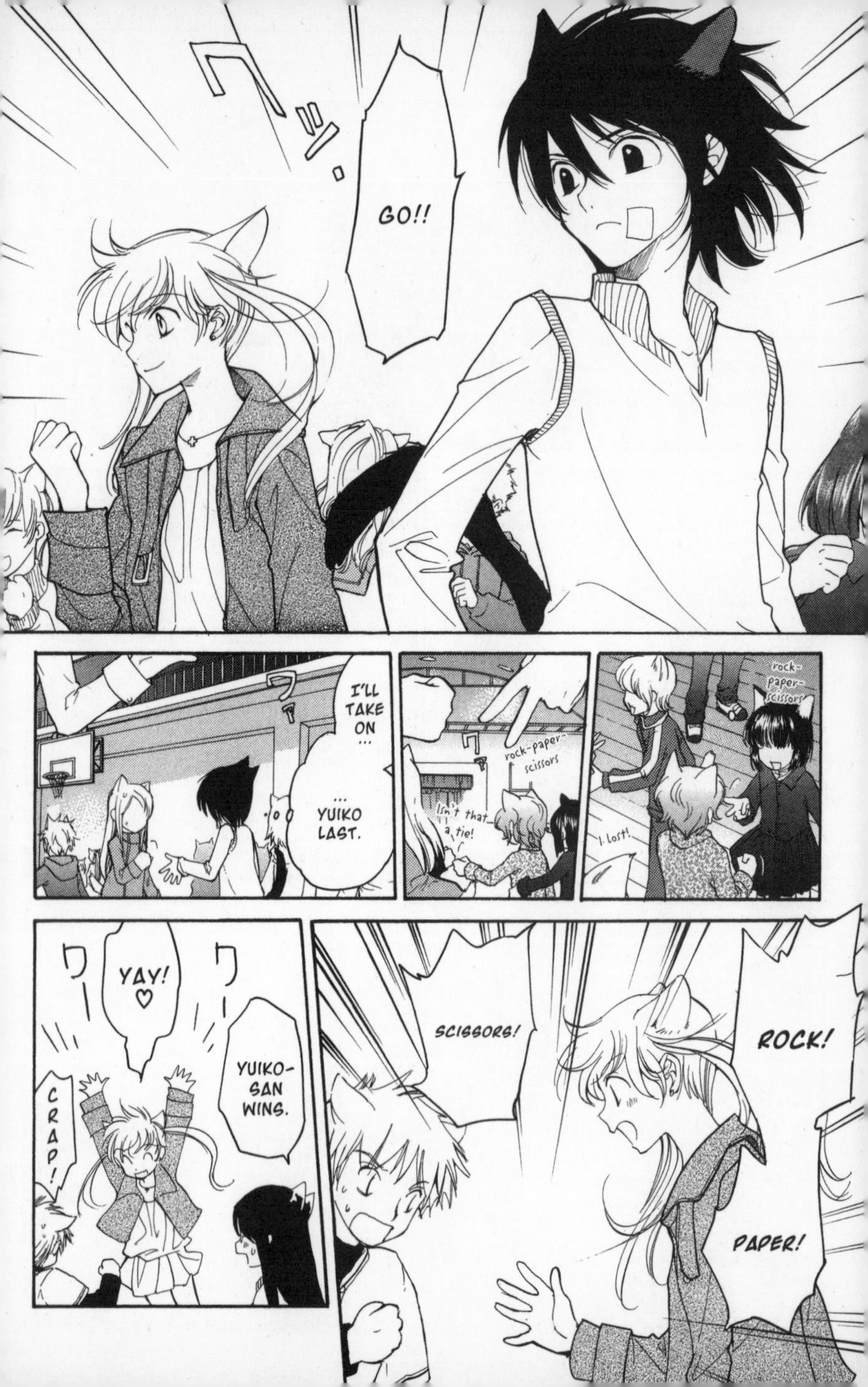
GO!!
-rock-paper-scissors
I. Lost!
rock-paper-scissors
Isn't that a tie!
I'LL TAKE ON ...
... YUIKO LAST.
ROCK!
SCISSORS!
PAPER!
ワー
YUIKO-SAN WINS.
YAY! ♡
ワー
CRAP!

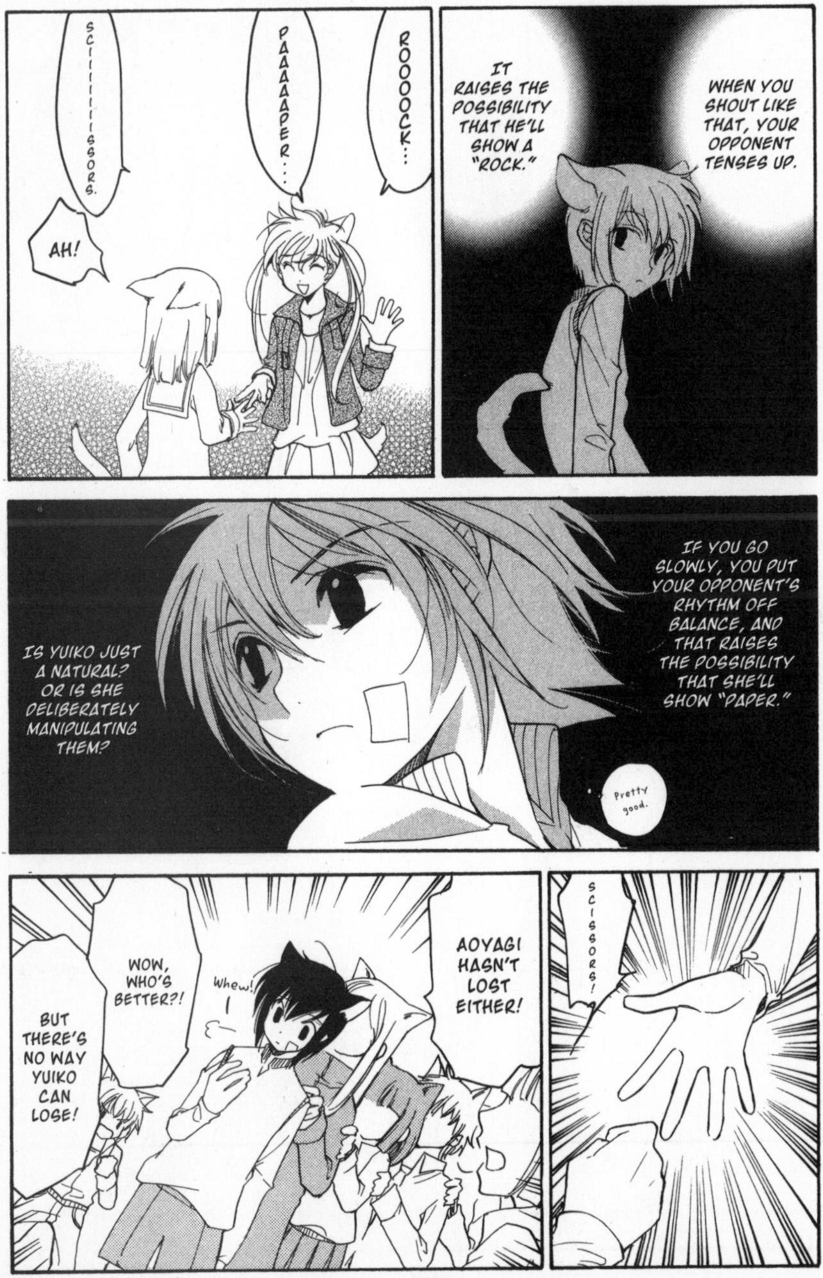
WHEN YOU SHOUT LIKE THAT, YOUR OPPONENT TENSES UP.
IT RAISES THE POSSIBILITY THAT HE'LL SHOW A "ROCK."
ROOOOOCK...
PAAAAAAPER...
SCIIIIIIIISSORS.
AH!
IF YOU GO SLOWLY, YOU PUT YOUR OPPONENT'S RHYTHM OFF BALANCE, AND THAT RAISES THE POSSIBILITY THAT SHE'LL SHOW "PAPER."
Pretty good.
IS YUIKO JUST A NATURAL? OR IS SHE DELIBERATELY MANIPULATING THEM?
SCISSORS!
AOYAGI HASN'T LOST EITHER!
Whew!
WOW, WHO'S BETTER?!
BUT THERE'S NO WAY YUIKO CAN LOSE!

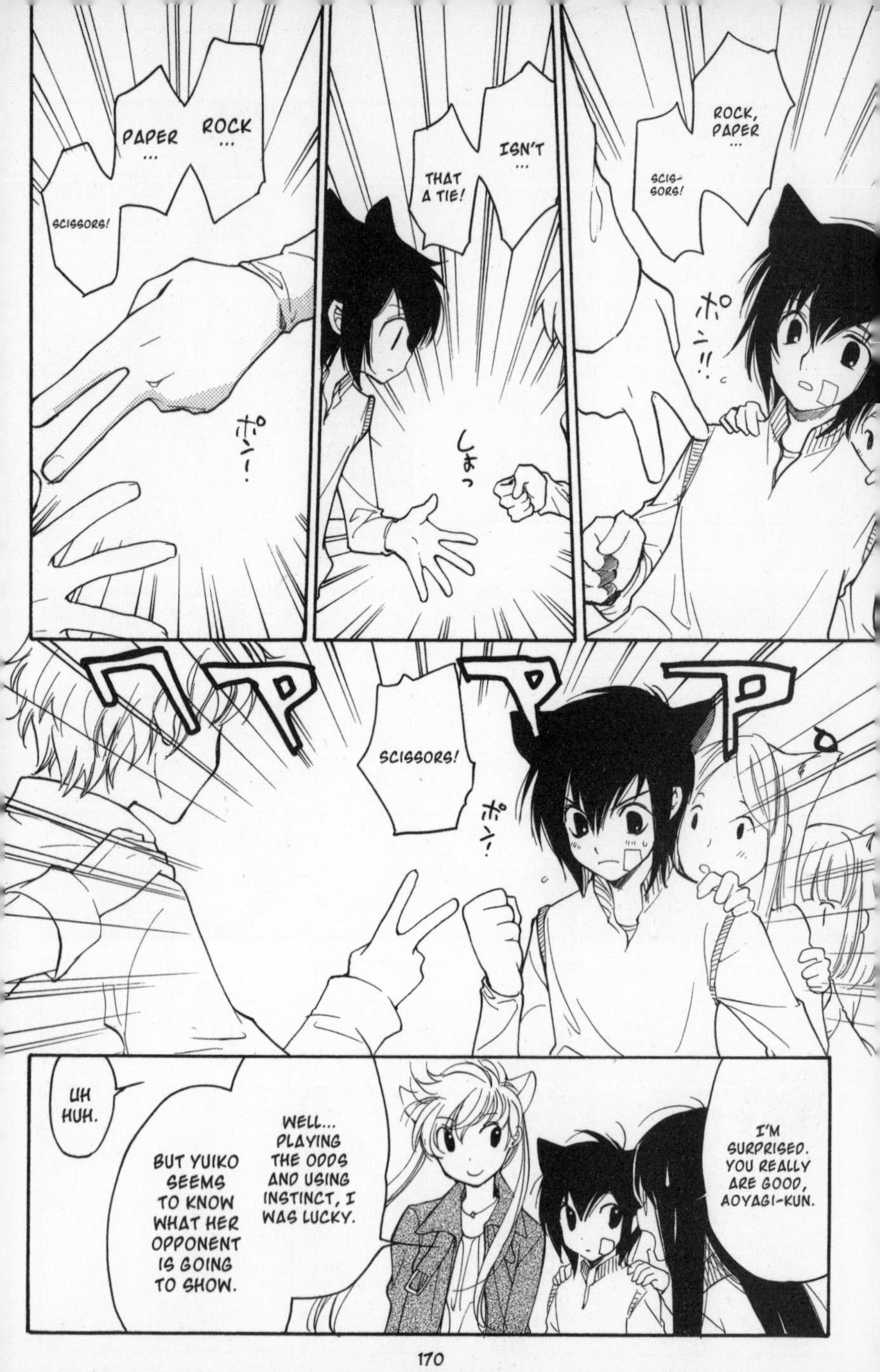
ROCK, PAPER ...
SCIS-SORS!
ポン!!
ISN'T ...
THAT A TIE!
しょっ
ROCK ...
PAPER ...
SCISSORS!
ポン!
SCISSORS!
ポン!
I'M SURPRISED. YOU REALLY ARE GOOD, AOYAGI-KUN.
WELL... PLAYING THE ODDS AND USING INSTINCT, I WAS LUCKY.
UH HUH.
BUT YUIKO SEEMS TO KNOW WHAT HER OPPONENT IS GOING TO SHOW.

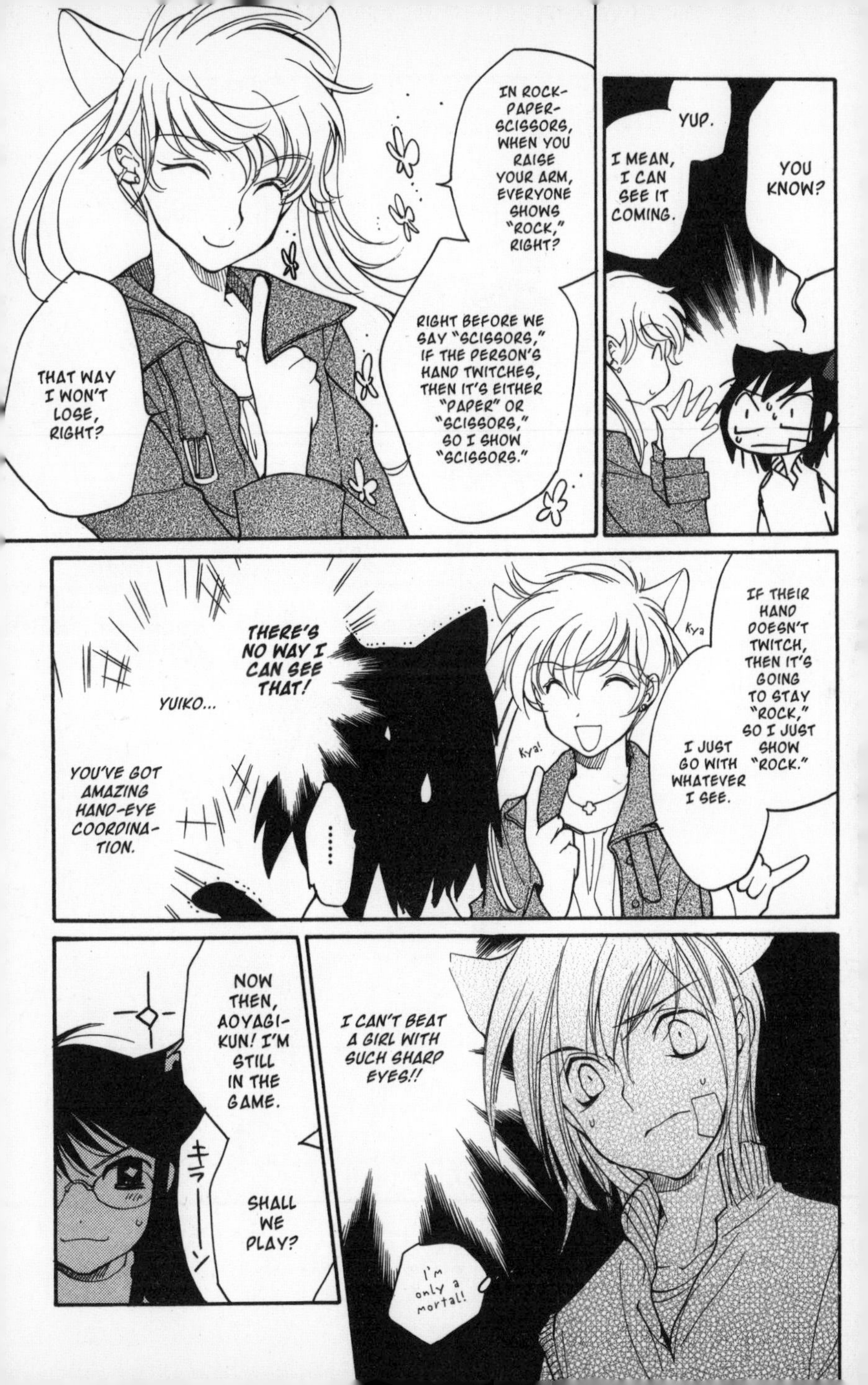
YUP.
YOU KNOW?
I MEAN, I CAN SEE IT COMING.
IN ROCK-PAPER-SCISSORS, WHEN YOU RAISE YOUR ARM, EVERYONE SHOWS "ROCK," RIGHT?
RIGHT BEFORE WE SAY "SCISSORS," IF THE PERSON'S HAND TWITCHES, THEN IT'S EITHER "PAPER" OR "SCISSORS," SO I SHOW "SCISSORS."
THAT WAY I WON'T LOSE, RIGHT?
IF THEIR HAND DOESN'T TWITCH, THEN IT'S GOING TO STAY "ROCK," SO I JUST SHOW "ROCK."
I JUST GO WITH WHATEVER I SEE.
Kya
Kya!
THERE'S NO WAY I CAN SEE THAT!
YUIKO...
YOU'VE GOT AMAZING HAND-EYE COORDINA-TION.
......
I CAN'T BEAT A GIRL WITH SUCH SHARP EYES!!
I'm only a mortal!
NOW THEN, AOYAGI-KUN! I'M STILL IN THE GAME.
SHALL WE PLAY?

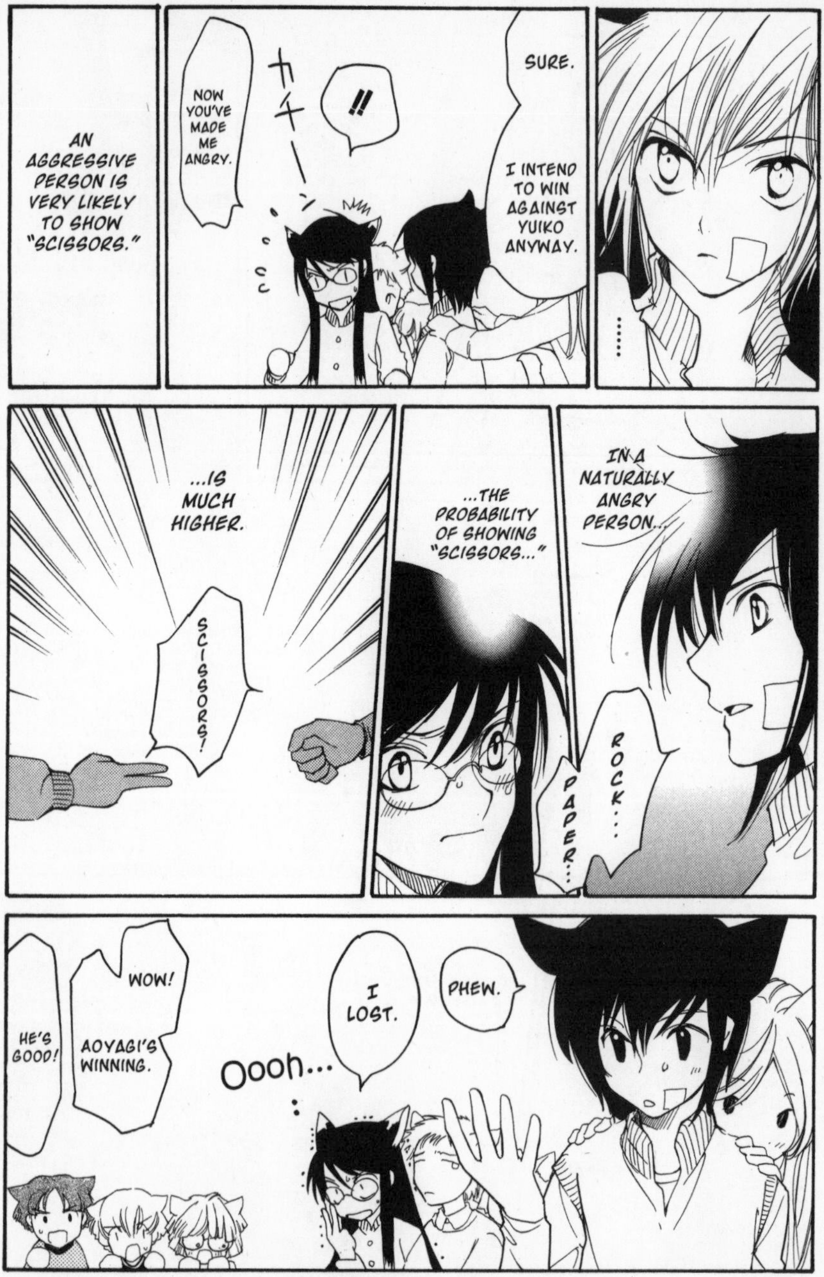
......
SURE.
I INTEND TO WIN AGAINST YUIKO ANYWAY.
!!
カチーン
NOW YOU'VE MADE ME ANGRY.
AN AGGRESSIVE PERSON IS VERY LIKELY TO SHOW "SCISSORS."
IN A NATURALLY ANGRY PERSON...
ROCK...
...THE PROBABILITY OF SHOWING "SCISSORS..."
PAPER...
...IS MUCH HIGHER.
SCISSORS!
PHEW.
I LOST.
Oooh...
WOW! AOYAGI'S WINNING.
HE'S GOOD!

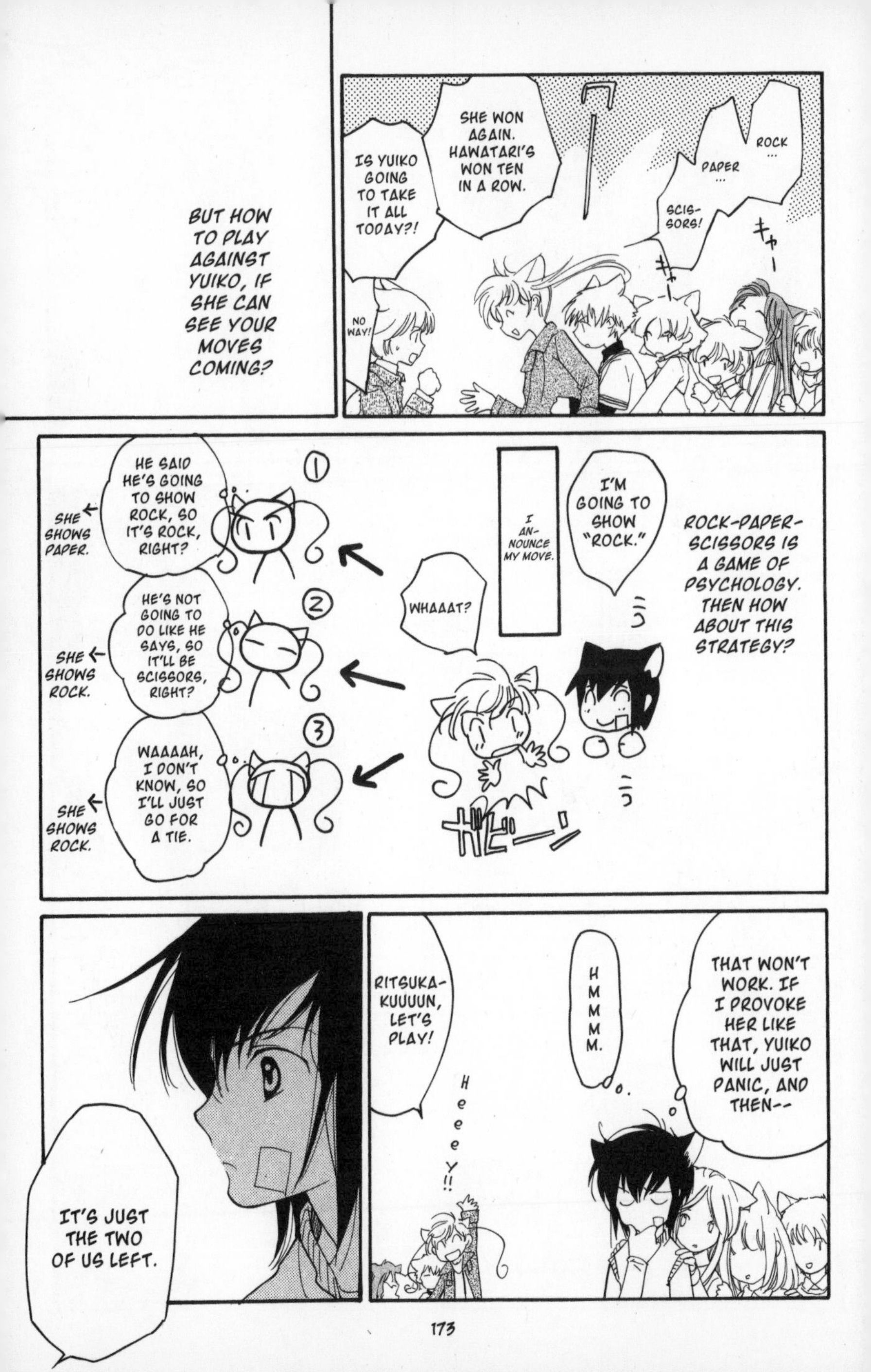
ROCK...
PAPER...
SCIS-SORS!
キャー
SHE WON AGAIN. HAWATARI'S WON TEN IN A ROW.
IS YUIKO GOING TO TAKE IT ALL TODAY?!
NO WAY!
BUT HOW TO PLAY AGAINST YUIKO, IF SHE CAN SEE YOUR MOVES COMING?
ROCK-PAPER-SCISSORS IS A GAME OF PSYCHOLOGY. THEN HOW ABOUT THIS STRATEGY?
I'M GOING TO SHOW "ROCK."
I AN-NOUNCE MY MOVE.
WHAAAT?
①
HE SAID HE'S GOING TO SHOW ROCK, SO IT'S ROCK, RIGHT?
SHE SHOWS PAPER.
②
HE'S NOT GOING TO DO LIKE HE SAYS, SO IT'LL BE SCISSORS, RIGHT?
SHE SHOWS ROCK.
③
WAAAAH, I DON'T KNOW, SO I'LL JUST GO FOR A TIE.
SHE SHOWS ROCK.
THAT WON'T WORK. IF I PROVOKE HER LIKE THAT, YUIKO WILL JUST PANIC, AND THEN--
HMMMM.
RITSUKA-KUUUUN, LET'S PLAY!
Heeey!!
IT'S JUST THE TWO OF US LEFT.

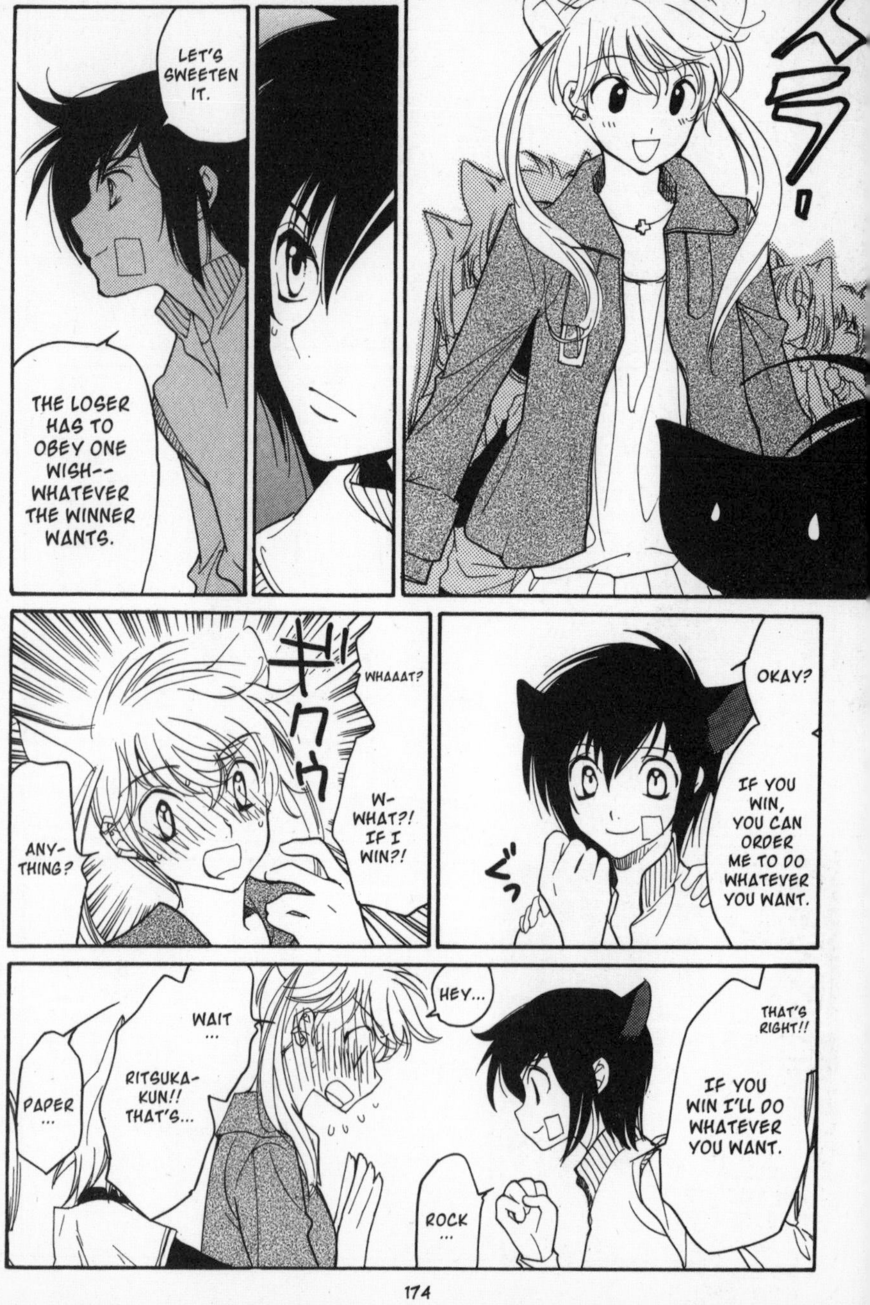
LET'S SWEETEN IT.
THE LOSER HAS TO OBEY ONE WISH--WHATEVER THE WINNER WANTS.
OKAY?
IF YOU WIN, YOU CAN ORDER ME TO DO WHATEVER YOU WANT.
ぐっ
WHAAAT?
W-WHAT?! IF I WIN?!
ANY-THING?
THAT'S RIGHT!!
IF YOU WIN I'LL DO WHATEVER YOU WANT.
HEY...
ROCK ...
WAIT ...
RITSUKA-KUN!! THAT'S...
PAPER ...

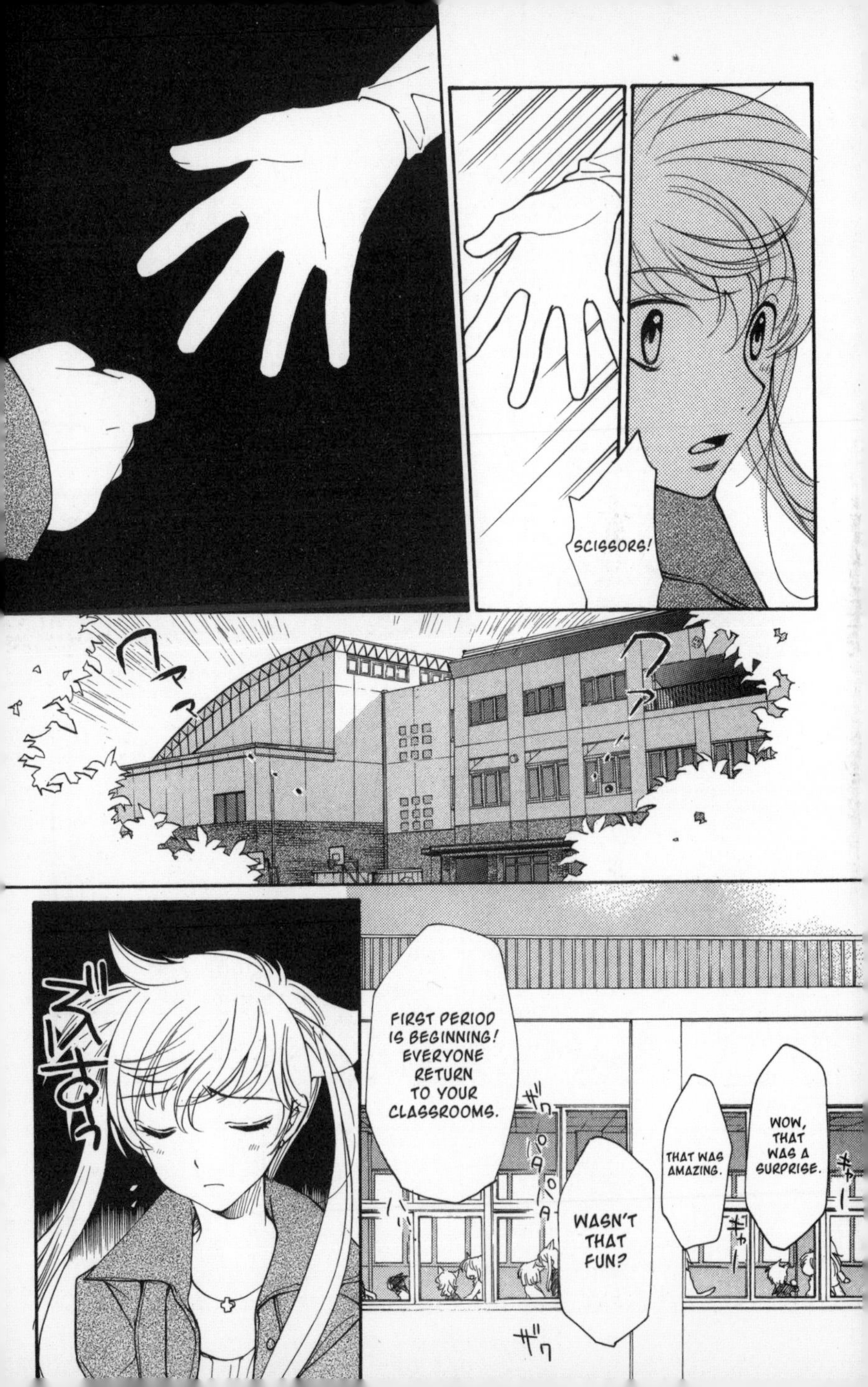
SCISSORS!
FIRST PERIOD IS BEGINNING! EVERYONE RETURN TO YOUR CLASSROOMS.
WOW, THAT WAS A SURPRISE.
THAT WAS AMAZING.
WASN'T THAT FUN?

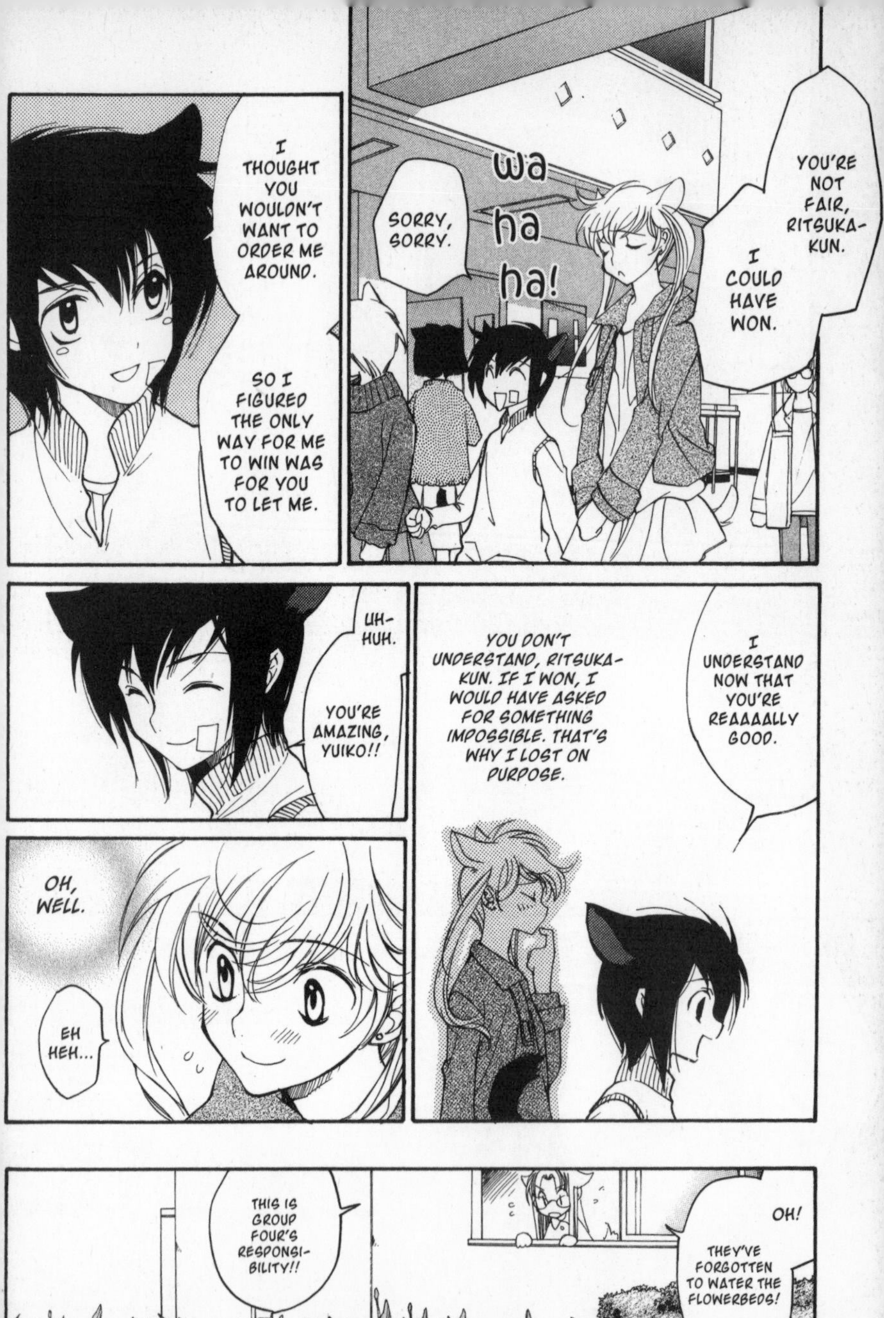
YOU'RE NOT FAIR, RITSUKA-KUN.
I COULD HAVE WON.
wa ha ha!
SORRY, SORRY.
I THOUGHT YOU WOULDN'T WANT TO ORDER ME AROUND.
SO I FIGURED THE ONLY WAY FOR ME TO WIN WAS FOR YOU TO LET ME.
I UNDERSTAND NOW THAT YOU'RE REAAAALLY GOOD.
YOU DON'T UNDERSTAND, RITSUKA-KUN. IF I WON, I WOULD HAVE ASKED FOR SOMETHING IMPOSSIBLE. THAT'S WHY I LOST ON PURPOSE.
UH-HUH.
YOU'RE AMAZING, YUIKO!!
OH, WELL.
EH HEH...
OH!
THEY'VE FORGOTTEN TO WATER THE FLOWERBEDS!
THIS IS GROUP FOUR'S RESPONSIBILITY!!

The End

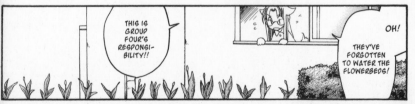

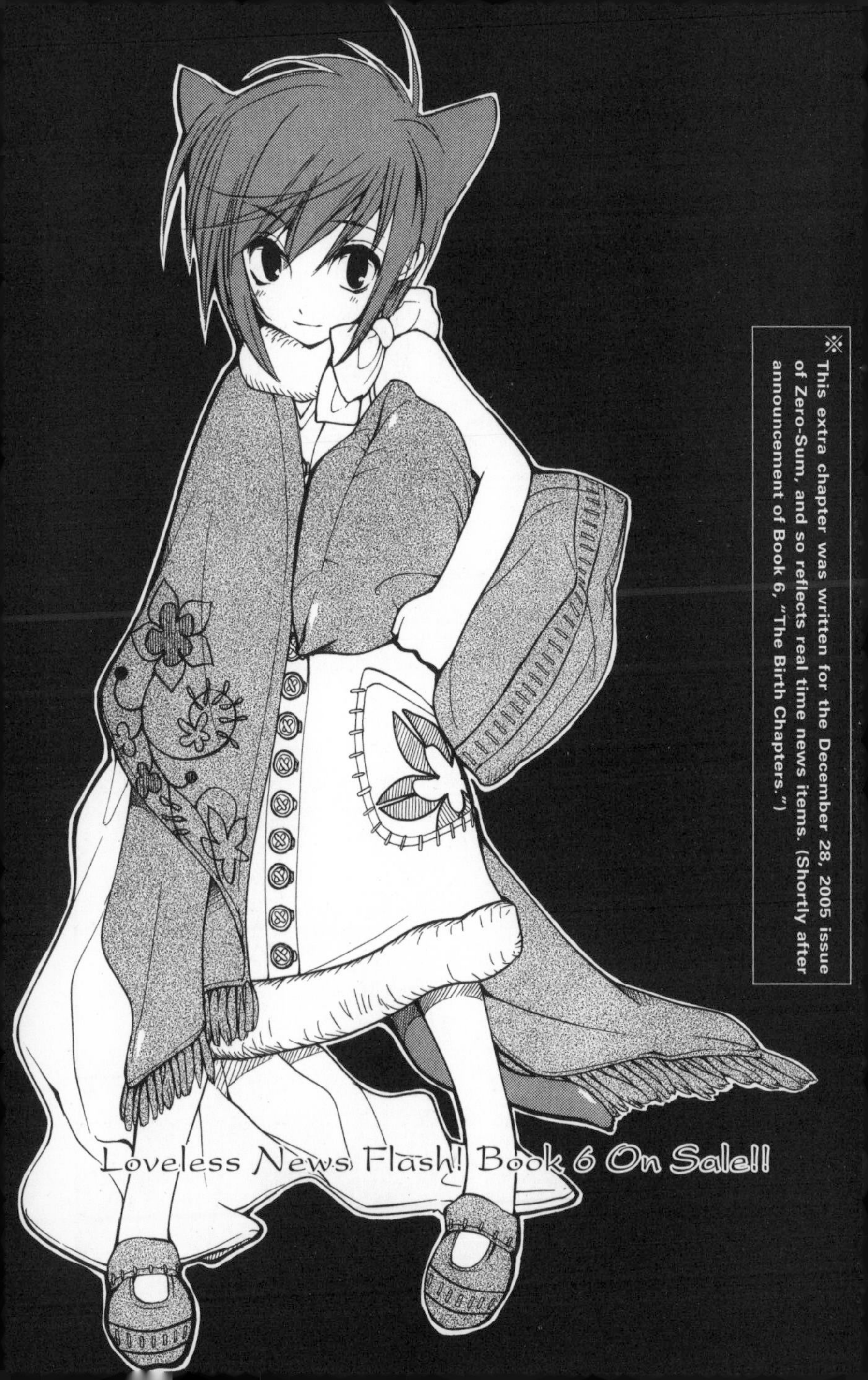
Loveless News Flash!! Book 6 On Sale!!

※ This extra chapter was written for the December 28, 2005 issue of Zero-Sum, and so reflects real time news items. (Shortly after announcement of Book 6, "The Birth Chapters.")

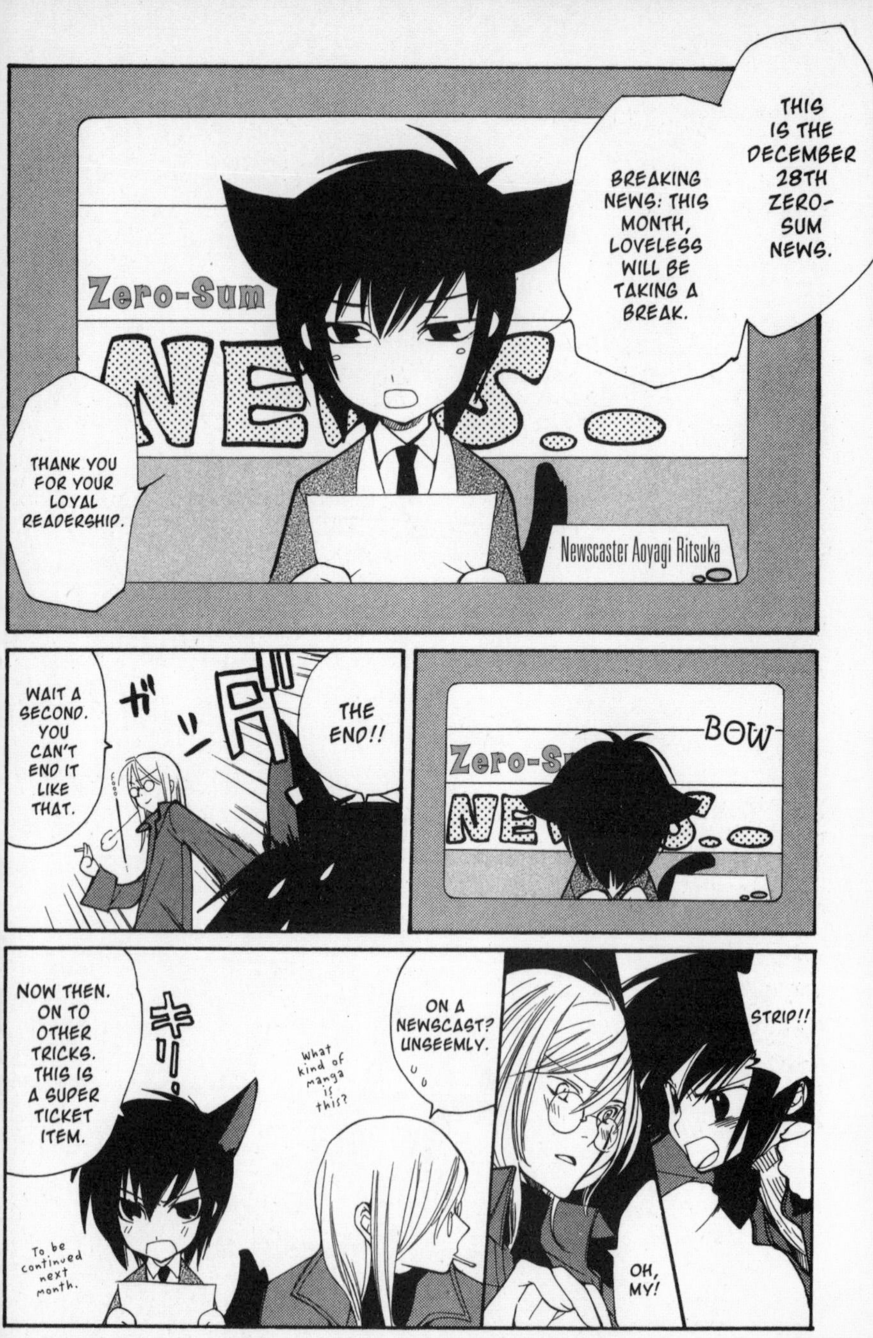
THIS IS THE DECEMBER 28TH ZERO-SUM NEWS.
BREAKING NEWS: THIS MONTH, LOVELESS WILL BE TAKING A BREAK.
Zero-Sum
NEWS
THANK YOU FOR YOUR LOYAL READERSHIP.
Newscaster Aoyagi Ritsuka
BOW
THE END!!
ガ
WAIT A SECOND. YOU CAN'T END IT LIKE THAT.
STRIP!!
OH, MY!
ON A NEWSCAST? UNSEEMLY.
What kind of manga is this?
キ
NOW THEN. ON TO OTHER TRICKS. THIS IS A SUPER TICKET ITEM.
To be continued next month.

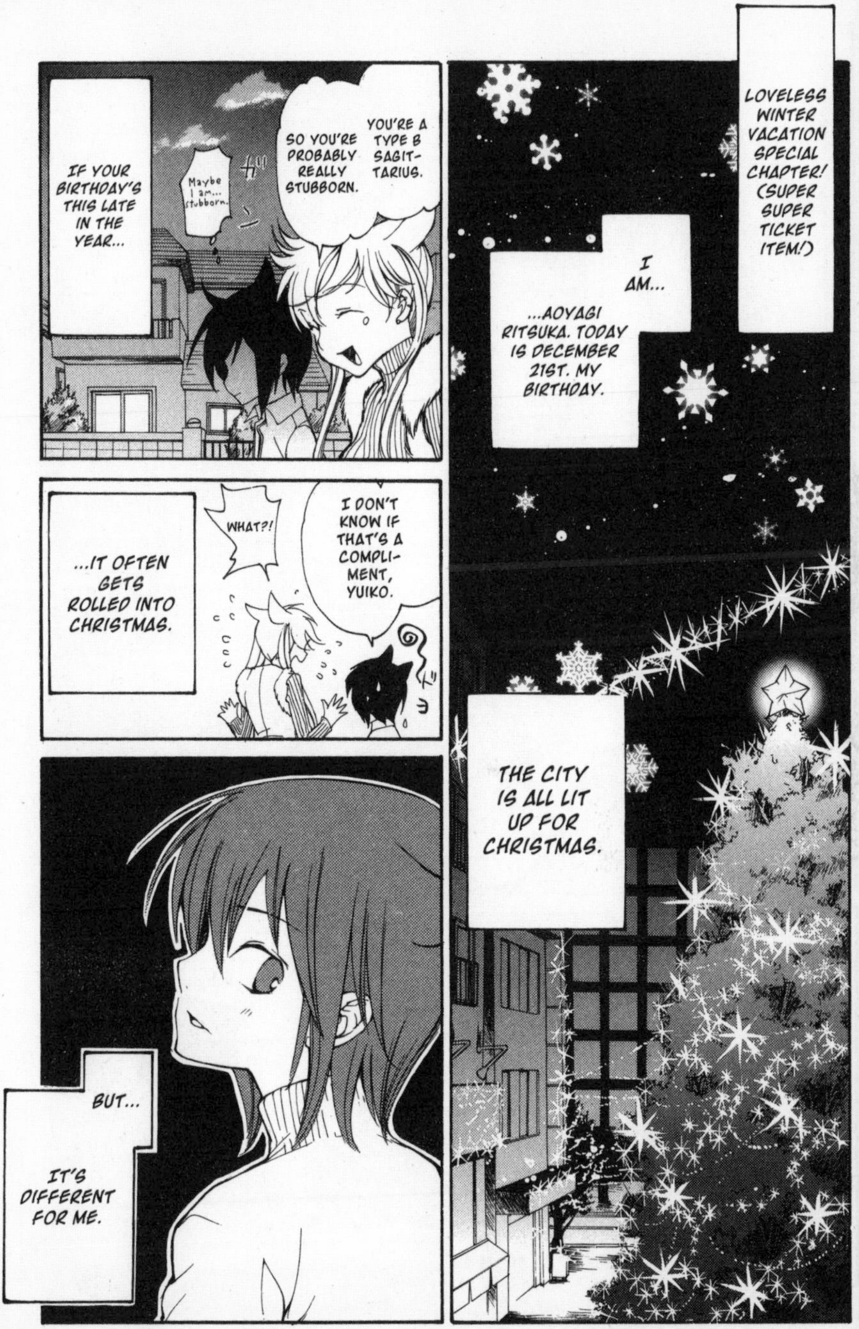
LOVELESS WINTER VACATION SPECIAL CHAPTER! (SUPER SUPER TICKET ITEM!)
I AM...
...AOYAGI RITSUKA. TODAY IS DECEMBER 21ST. MY BIRTHDAY.
THE CITY IS ALL LIT UP FOR CHRISTMAS.
YOU'RE A TYPE B SAGIT-TARIUS.
SO YOU'RE PROBABLY REALLY STUBBORN.
Maybe I am... stubborn.
IF YOUR BIRTHDAY'S THIS LATE IN THE YEAR...
I DON'T KNOW IF THAT'S A COMPLI-MENT, YUIKO.
WHAT?!
...IT OFTEN GETS ROLLED INTO CHRISTMAS.
BUT...
IT'S DIFFERENT FOR ME.

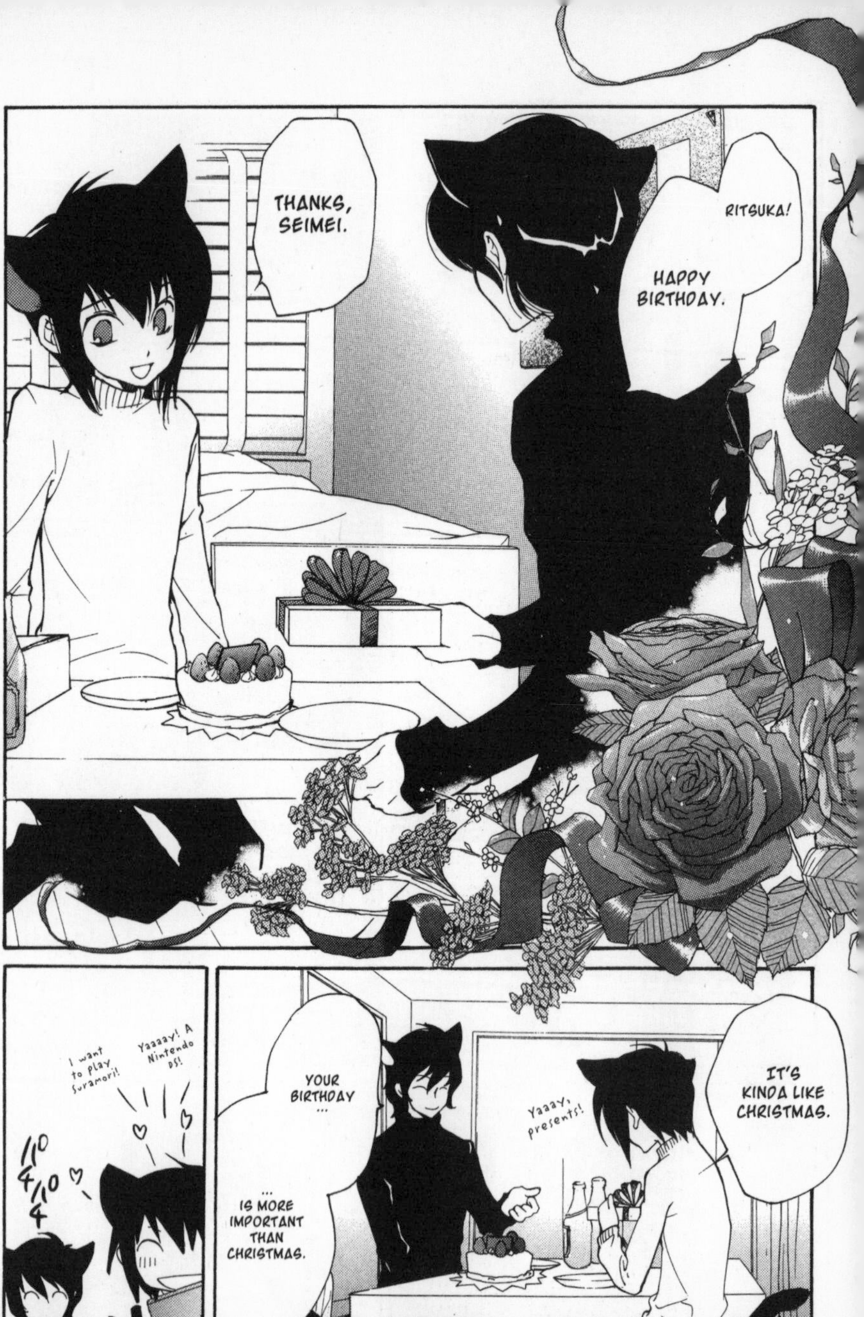
RITSUKA!
HAPPY BIRTHDAY.
THANKS, SEIMEI.
IT'S KINDA LIKE CHRISTMAS.
Yaaay, presents!
YOUR BIRTHDAY ...
... IS MORE IMPORTANT THAN CHRISTMAS.
Yaaaay! A Nintendo DS!
I want to play Suramori!

This year it would be the Diamond version.

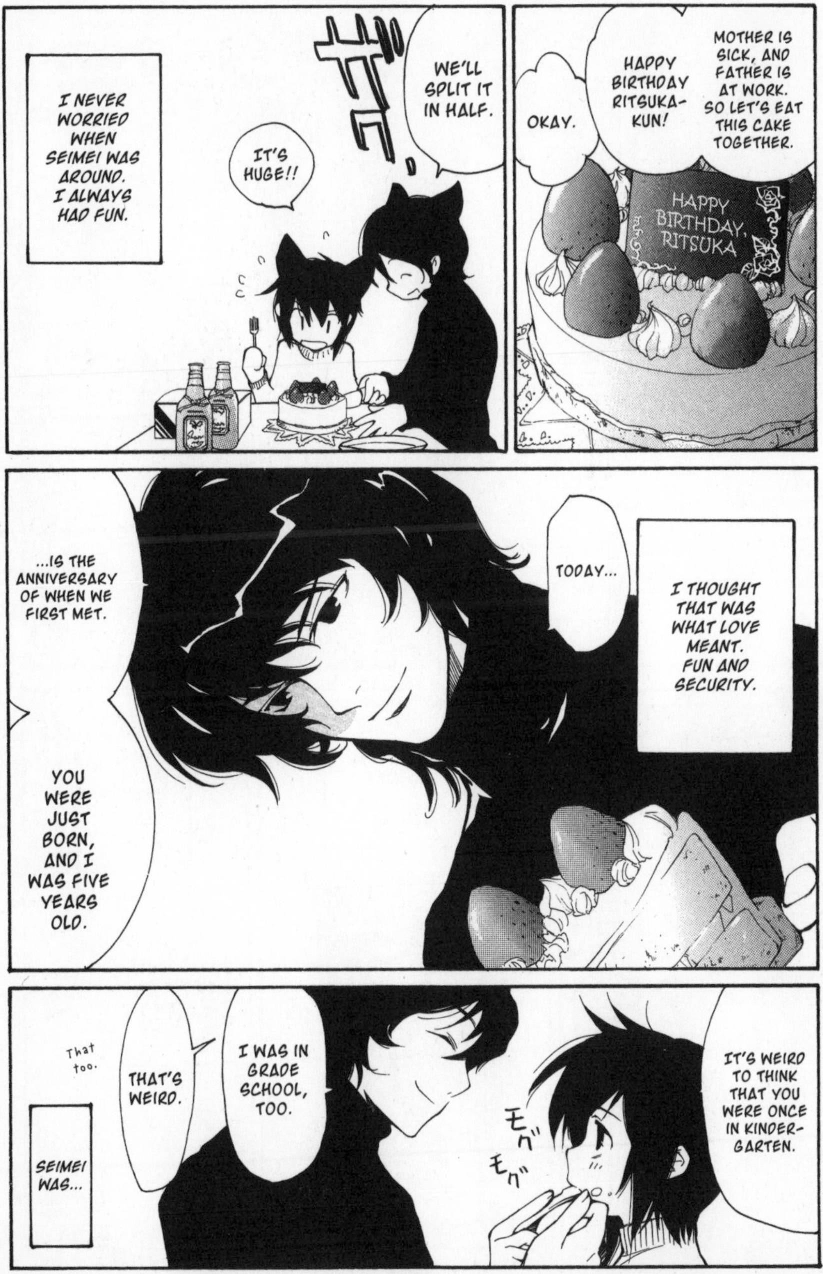
MOTHER IS SICK, AND FATHER IS AT WORK. SO LET'S EAT THIS CAKE TOGETHER.
HAPPY BIRTHDAY RITSUKA-KUN!
OKAY.
HAPPY BIRTHDAY, RITSUKA
WE'LL SPLIT IT IN HALF.
IT'S HUGE!!
I NEVER WORRIED WHEN SEIMEI WAS AROUND. I ALWAYS HAD FUN.
I THOUGHT THAT WAS WHAT LOVE MEANT. FUN AND SECURITY.
TODAY...
...IS THE ANNIVERSARY OF WHEN WE FIRST MET.
YOU WERE JUST BORN, AND I WAS FIVE YEARS OLD.
IT'S WEIRD TO THINK THAT YOU WERE ONCE IN KINDER-GARTEN.
モグ
モグ
I WAS IN GRADE SCHOOL, TOO.
THAT'S WEIRD.
That too.
SEIMEI WAS...

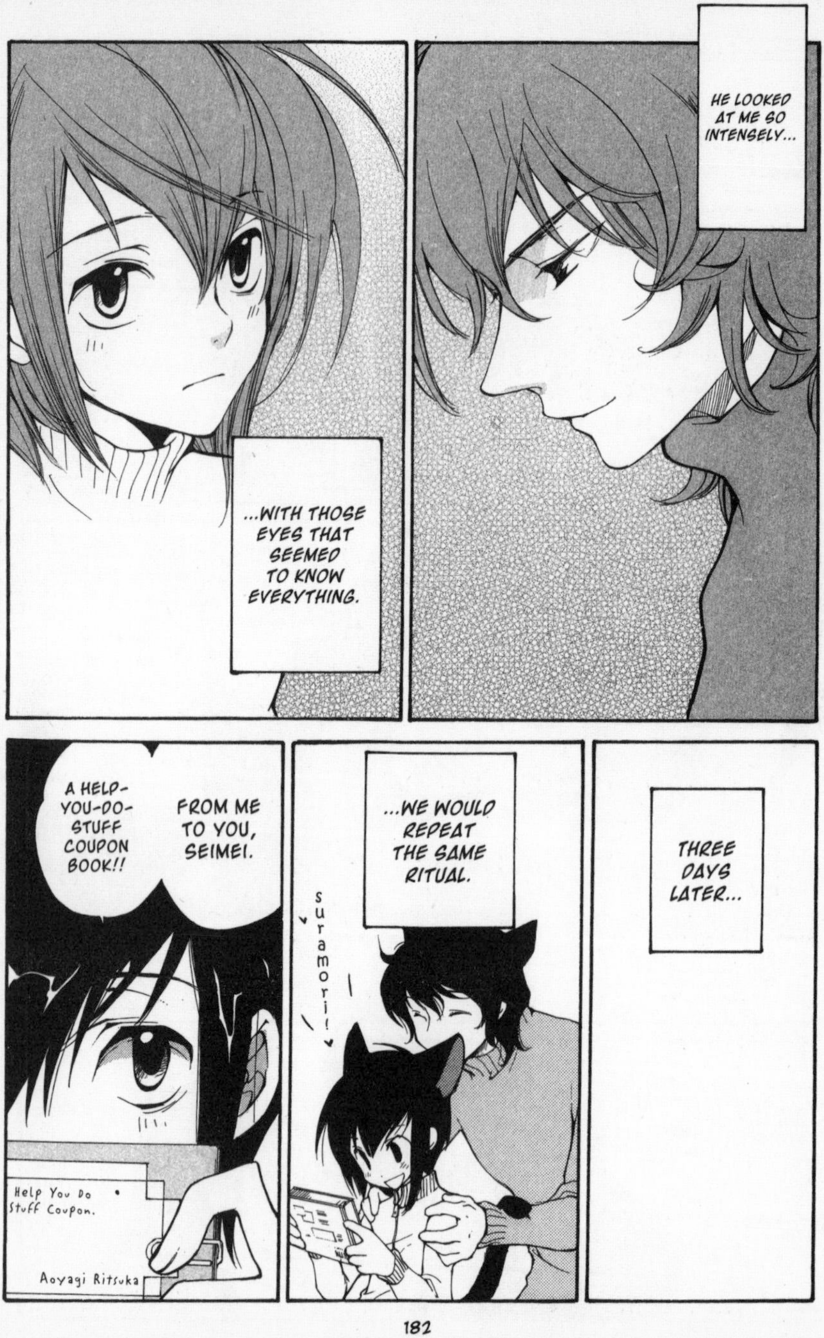
HE LOOKED AT ME SO INTENSELY...
...WITH THOSE EYES THAT SEEMED TO KNOW EVERYTHING.
THREE DAYS LATER...
...WE WOULD REPEAT THE SAME RITUAL.
suramori!
FROM ME TO YOU, SEIMEI.
A HELP-YOU-DO-STUFF COUPON BOOK!!
Help You Do Stuff Coupon.
Aoyagi Ritsuka

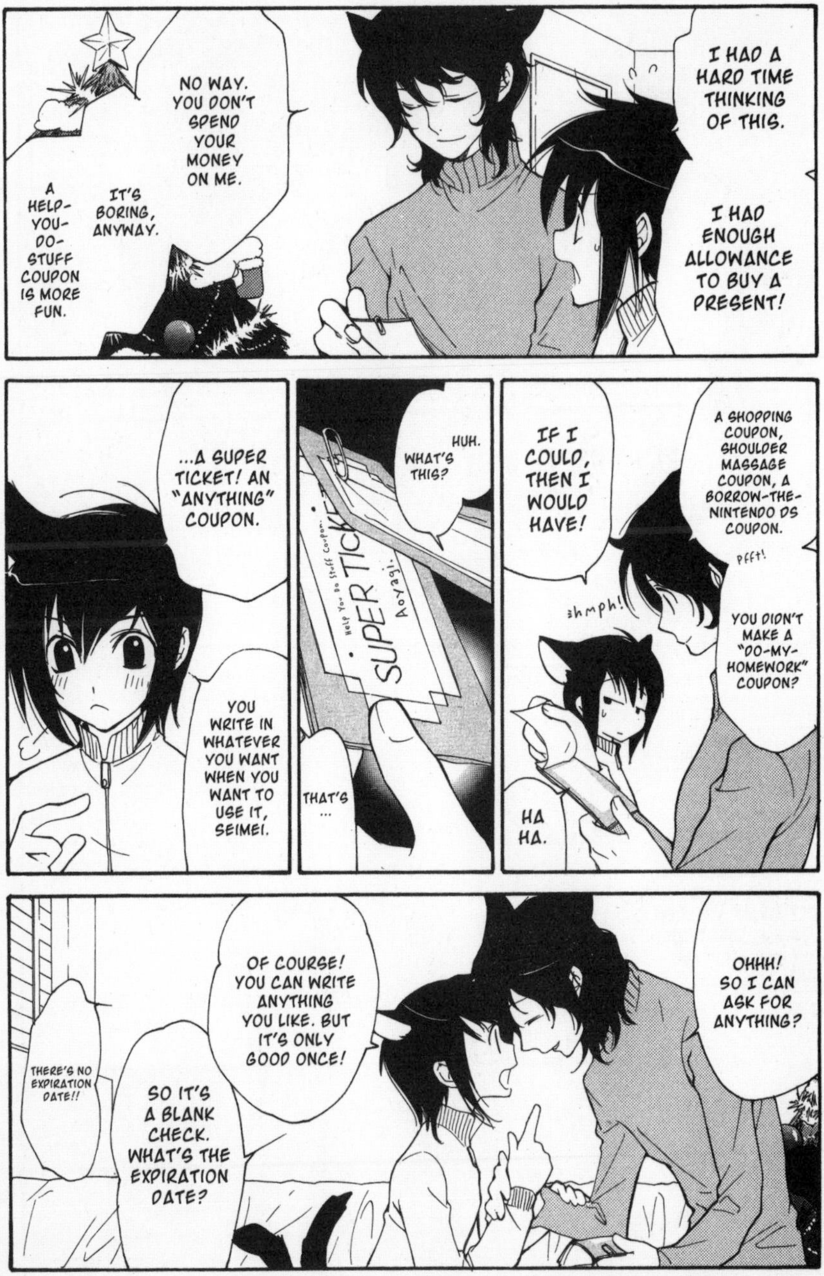
I HAD A HARD TIME THINKING OF THIS.
I HAD ENOUGH ALLOWANCE TO BUY A PRESENT!
NO WAY. YOU DON'T SPEND YOUR MONEY ON ME.
IT'S BORING, ANYWAY.
A HELP-YOU-DO-STUFF COUPON IS MORE FUN.
A SHOPPING COUPON, SHOULDER MASSAGE COUPON, A BORROW-THE-NINTENDO DS COUPON.
IF I COULD, THEN I WOULD HAVE!
PFFT!
YOU DIDN'T MAKE A "DO-MY-HOMEWORK" COUPON?
HMPH!
HA HA.
HUH. WHAT'S THIS?
Help You Do Stuff Coupon.
SUPER TIC
Aoyagi.
THAT'S ...
...A SUPER TICKET! AN "ANYTHING" COUPON.
YOU WRITE IN WHATEVER YOU WANT WHEN YOU WANT TO USE IT, SEIMEI.
OHHH! SO I CAN ASK FOR ANYTHING?
OF COURSE! YOU CAN WRITE ANYTHING YOU LIKE. BUT IT'S ONLY GOOD ONCE!
SO IT'S A BLANK CHECK. WHAT'S THE EXPIRATION DATE?
THERE'S NO EXPIRATION DATE!!

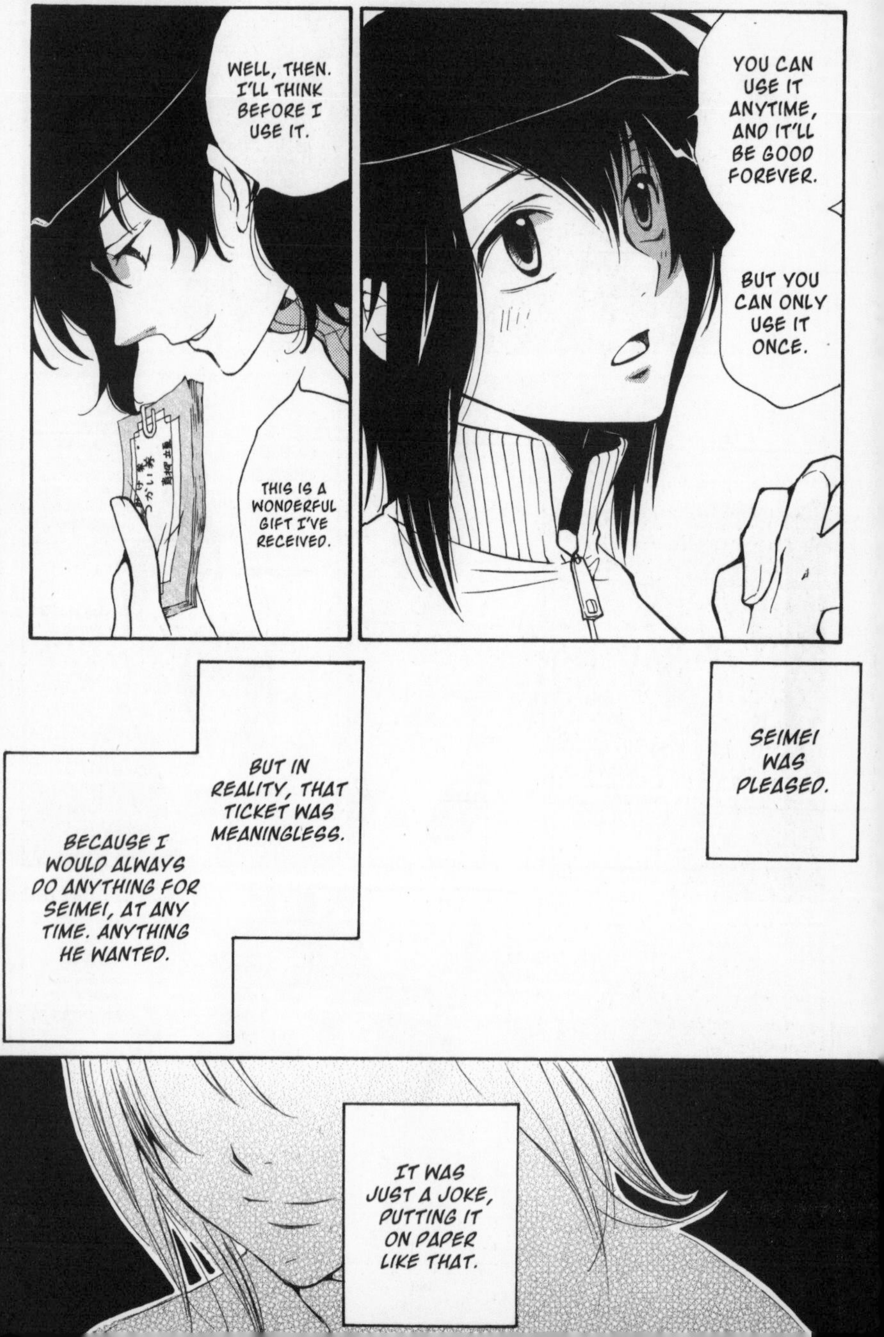
YOU CAN USE IT ANYTIME, AND IT'LL BE GOOD FOREVER.
BUT YOU CAN ONLY USE IT ONCE.
WELL, THEN. I'LL THINK BEFORE I USE IT.
THIS IS A WONDERFUL GIFT I'VE RECEIVED.
SEIMEI WAS PLEASED.
BUT IN REALITY, THAT TICKET WAS MEANINGLESS.
BECAUSE I WOULD ALWAYS DO ANYTHING FOR SEIMEI, AT ANY TIME. ANYTHING HE WANTED.
IT WAS JUST A JOKE, PUTTING IT ON PAPER LIKE THAT.

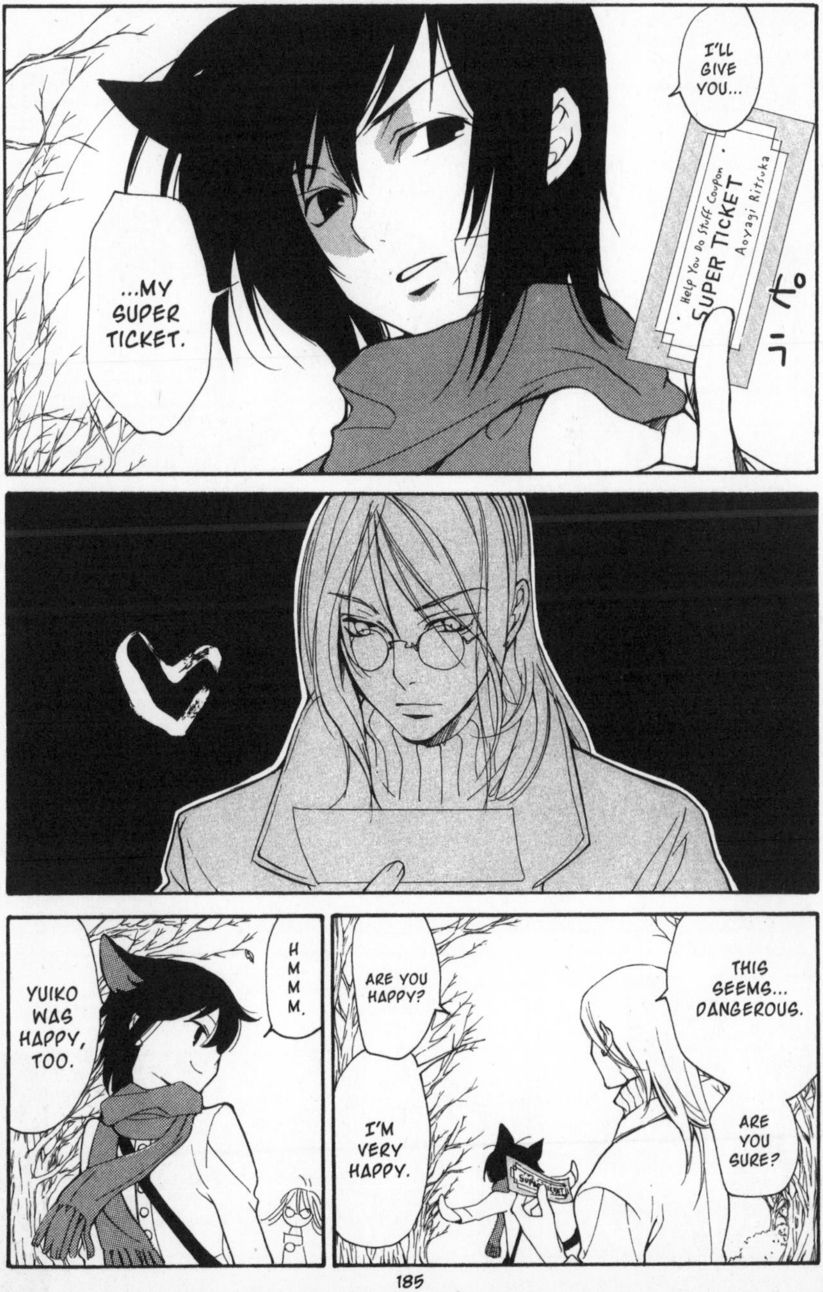
I'LL GIVE YOU...
Help You Do Stuff Coupon
SUPER TICKET
Aoyagi Ritsuka
...MY SUPER TICKET.
THIS SEEMS... DANGEROUS.
ARE YOU HAPPY?
ARE YOU SURE?
I'M VERY HAPPY.
HMMM.
YUIKO WAS HAPPY, TOO.

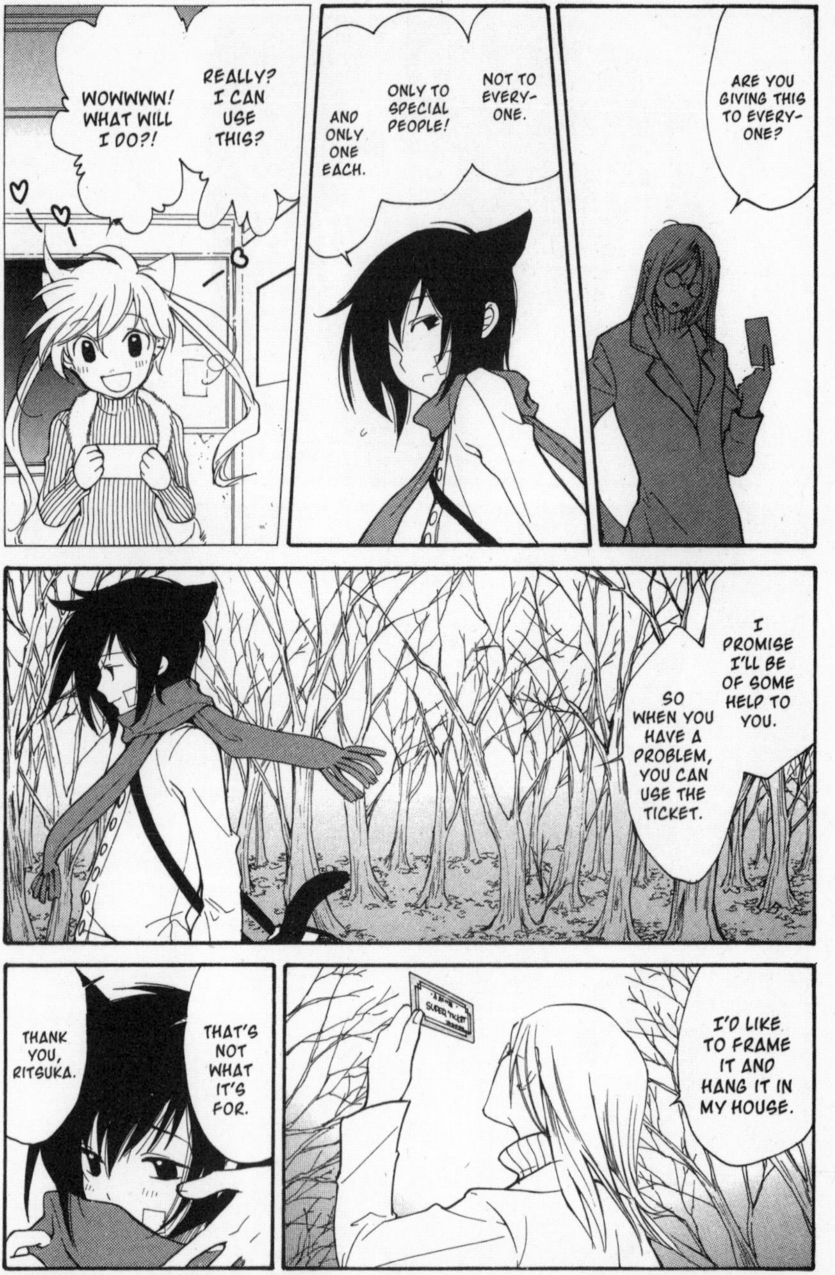
ARE YOU GIVING THIS TO EVERY-ONE?
NOT TO EVERY-ONE.
ONLY TO SPECIAL PEOPLE!
AND ONLY ONE EACH.
REALLY? I CAN USE THIS?
WOWWWW! WHAT WILL I DO?!
I PROMISE I'LL BE OF SOME HELP TO YOU.
SO WHEN YOU HAVE A PROBLEM, YOU CAN USE THE TICKET.
SUPER TICKET
I'D LIKE TO FRAME IT AND HANG IT IN MY HOUSE.
THAT'S NOT WHAT IT'S FOR.
THANK YOU, RITSUKA.

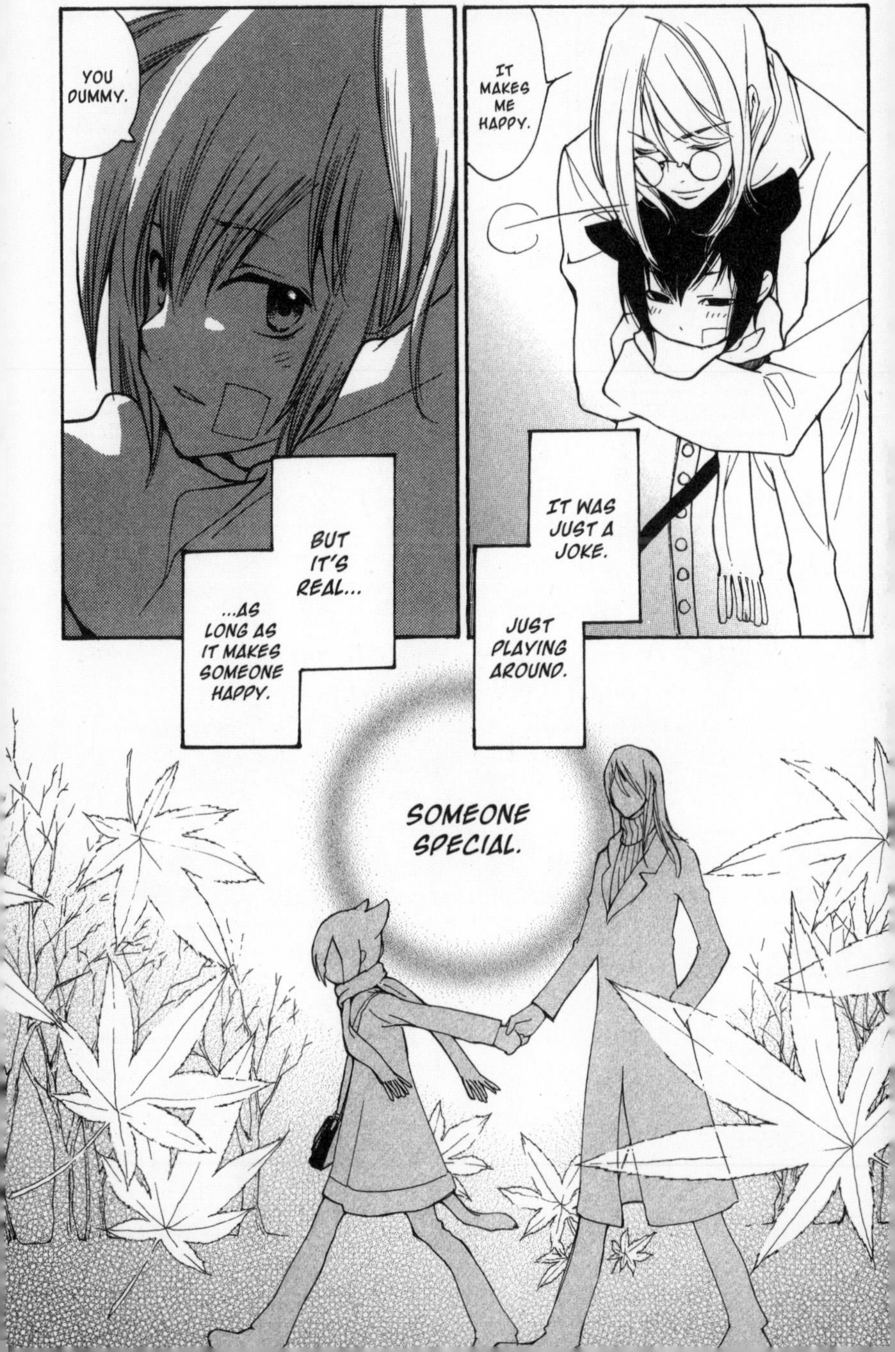
IT MAKES ME HAPPY.
IT WAS JUST A JOKE.
JUST PLAYING AROUND.
YOU DUMMY.
BUT IT'S REAL...
...AS LONG AS IT MAKES SOMEONE HAPPY.
SOMEONE SPECIAL.

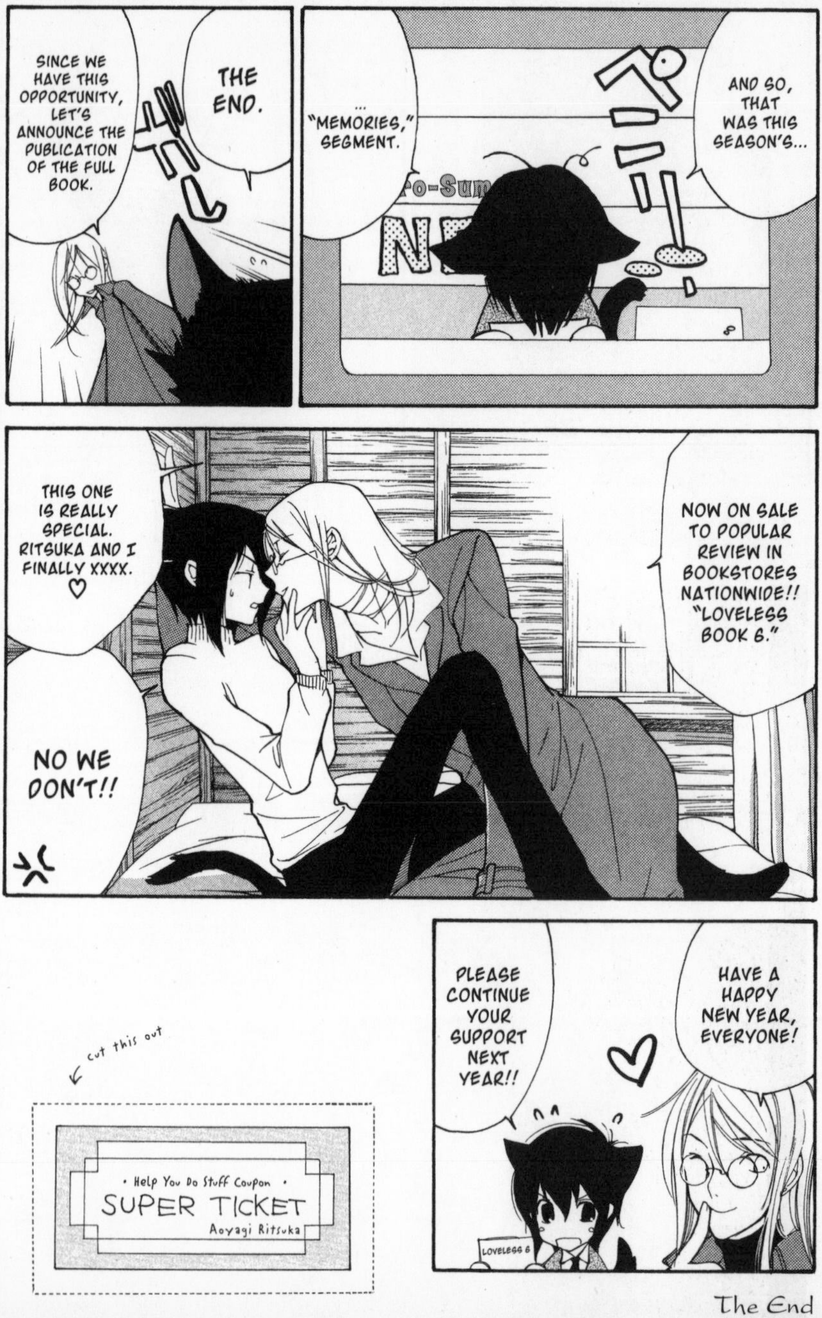
AND SO, THAT WAS THIS SEASON'S...
... "MEMORIES," SEGMENT.
THE END.
SINCE WE HAVE THIS OPPORTUNITY, LET'S ANNOUNCE THE PUBLICATION OF THE FULL BOOK.
NOW ON SALE TO POPULAR REVIEW IN BOOKSTORES NATIONWIDE!! "LOVELESS BOOK 6."
THIS ONE IS REALLY SPECIAL. RITSUKA AND I FINALLY XXXX. ♡
NO WE DON'T!!
HAVE A HAPPY NEW YEAR, EVERYONE!
PLEASE CONTINUE YOUR SUPPORT NEXT YEAR!!
LOVELESS 6
cut this out
• Help You Do Stuff Coupon •
SUPER TICKET
Aoyagi Ritsuka

The End

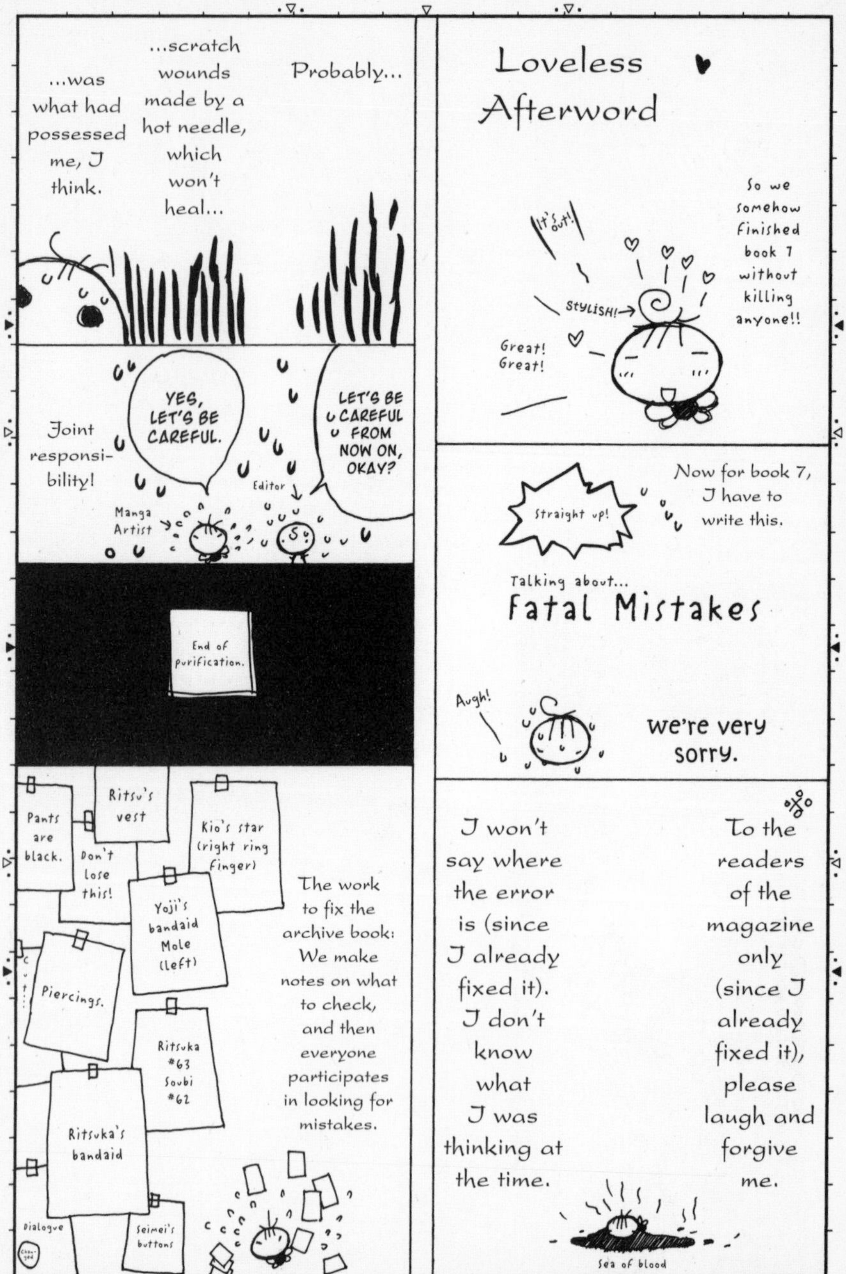
Loveless Afterword
So we somehow finished book 7 without killing anyone!!
It's out!
STYLISH!
Great! Great!
Now for book 7, I have to write this.
Straight up!
Talking about...
Fatal Mistakes
we're very sorry.
Augh!
To the readers of the magazine only (since I already fixed it), please laugh and forgive me.
I won't say where the error is (since I already fixed it). I don't know what I was thinking at the time.
Sea of blood
Probably...
...scratch wounds made by a hot needle, which won't heal...
...was what had possessed me, I think.
LET'S BE CAREFUL FROM NOW ON, OKAY?
Editor
YES, LET'S BE CAREFUL.
Manga Artist
Joint responsibility!
End of purification.
The work to fix the archive book: We make notes on what to check, and then everyone participates in looking for mistakes.
Kio's star (right ring finger)
Ritsu's vest
Pants are black.
Don't lose this!
Yoji's bandaid Mole (left)
Piercings.
Ritsuka #63 Soubi #62
Ritsuka's bandaid
Seimei's buttons
Dialogue

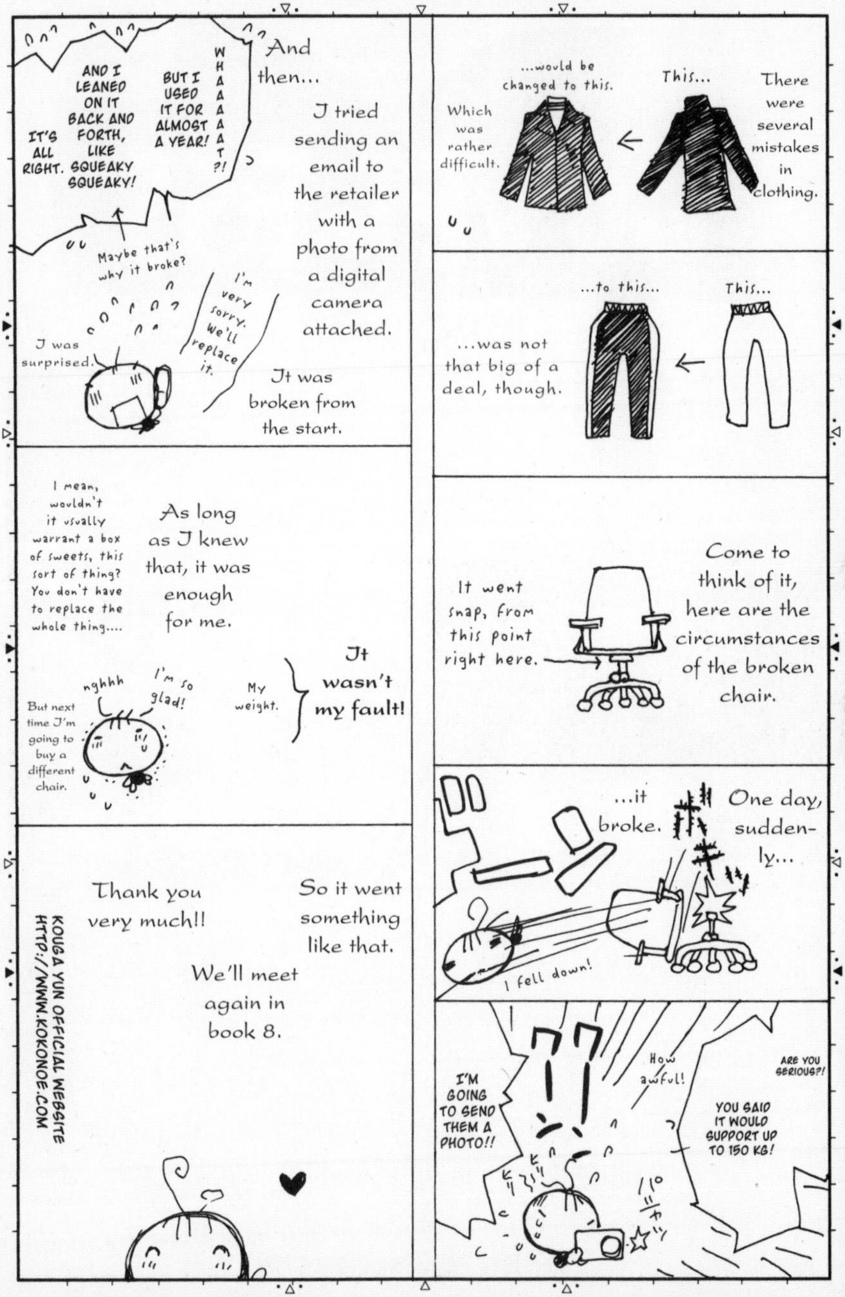

There were several mistakes in clothing.
This...
...would be changed to this.
Which was rather difficult.
This...
...to this...
...was not that big of a deal, though.
Come to think of it, here are the circumstances of the broken chair.
It went snap, from this point right here.
One day, suddenly...
...it broke.
I fell down!
ARE YOU SERIOUS?!
YOU SAID IT WOULD SUPPORT UP TO 150 KG!
How awful!
I'M GOING TO SEND THEM A PHOTO!!
And then...
WHAAAAAT?!
BUT I USED IT FOR ALMOST A YEAR!
AND I LEANED ON IT BACK AND FORTH, LIKE SQUEAKY SQUEAKY!
IT'S ALL RIGHT.
Maybe that's why it broke?
I tried sending an email to the retailer with a photo from a digital camera attached.
I'm very sorry. We'll replace it.
I was surprised.
It was broken from the start.
As long as I knew that, it was enough for me.
I mean, wouldn't it usually warrant a box of sweets, this sort of thing? You don't have to replace the whole thing....
It wasn't my fault!
My weight.
I'm so glad!
nghhh
But next time I'm going to buy a different chair.
So it went something like that.
Thank you very much!!
We'll meet again in book 8.
KOUGA YUN OFFICIAL WEBSITE
HTTP://WWW.KOKONOE.COM

In The Next Volume of

LOVELESS

The battle between Soubi and Nisei rages, but with Ritsuka by his side, Soubi may finally have just the edge he needs. But meanwhile, Soubi's own dark history begins to be revealed as Seimei and Ritsu face off as fellow Sacrifices...and what will happen if Seimei and Ritsuka finally meet?

Loveless Vol. 8 Available 2008

KNOW YOUR OPPONENT: STRATEGIES OF SPELLS AND SCISSORS IN *LOVELESS*

"Know your Opponent" is the advice generally attributed to Sun Tzu in his Art of War. After the emotional high drama of book seven, Yun Kouga uses Sun Tzu's lesson in a brisk story about a children's game, giving readers a key to the strategies of the spell battles in *Loveless*. Yuiko has the ability to read her adversary, to anticipate his next move and to know the spot of his greatest vulnerability; so, too, does Nisei, Seimei, Soubi and, finally, Ritsuka.

When Nisei and Soubi battle at the Academy of the Seven Voices, Nisei deftly wounds Ritsuka by revealing that his brother, Seimei, is alive, and that Seimei not only sees Ritsuka as a nuisance, but the only thing that would please Seimei is Ritsuka's death. Here Nisei pulls out Ritsuka's heartstrings and fiddles a violent tune: Nisei knows that Ritsuka would do anything for Seimei, and that the one thing Rituska fears most is his brother's rejection.

Soubi is impressed, observing that Nisei "really has to know his opponent to hurt him emotionally." Nisei shrugs it off, saying that Rituska's face is as easy to read "as a children's book." Soubi reverses the damage to Ritsuka by assuring him he'll always be by his side. Ritsuka rejects the idea of "always," since nothing is certain, but Soubi comforts him nonetheless. Later in the battle, Soubi asserts that he and Nisei are opposites, and therefore can never know each other. Is this assertion another of Soubi's spells of self-protection? For if Nisei, working on Seimei's information, can tear at Ritsuka's heart, surely he can break Soubi with even less effort.

The rock-paper-scissors tournament is as serious as a spell battle, but infused with greater humor. Like Nisei, Yuiko takes it for granted that she can read people, and approaches the games with the same brazen honesty she uses in her relationships. For her talent, she's feared and respected by her family and peers; she defies the laws of probability, and her puissance has taken on its own mythos: the class, a tabloid chorus, whisper that she's become a millionaire, dates celebrities and owns her own condo, all because of rock-paper-scissors success.

Because of his natural curiosity or his experience in spell battles, Ritsuka is the first to get over his awe and actually question how it is she's achieved such dominance. Yuiko, unlike Nisei in that she is confident without being cocky, explains exactly how she wins: she reads the slightest preliminary movements of her opponents' hands and bodies. Ritsuka is impressed with her sharp eyes, and knows his own limitations--he can't anticipate moves like she can. On the other hand, he knows his opponent, and when it comes down to the two of them, he's able to defeat Yuiko by using her shy nature and her personal feelings about him to his advantage. What Ritsuka doesn't realize is why Yuiko throws the game. If she wins, she could ask Ritsuka to obey one wish, no matter what it is. She loses on purpose, because she would have "asked for something impossible." Though she knows her opponent better than he knows himself, she loses the battle and her championship status when her heart gets the better of her. She can't ask Ritsuka to obey her, and ends up bowing to him in obeisance; by the rules of the game of *Loveless*, Yuiko would make an excellent fighter unit.
~Christine Boylan

ANIMA™

The fantasy-filled adventures continue!

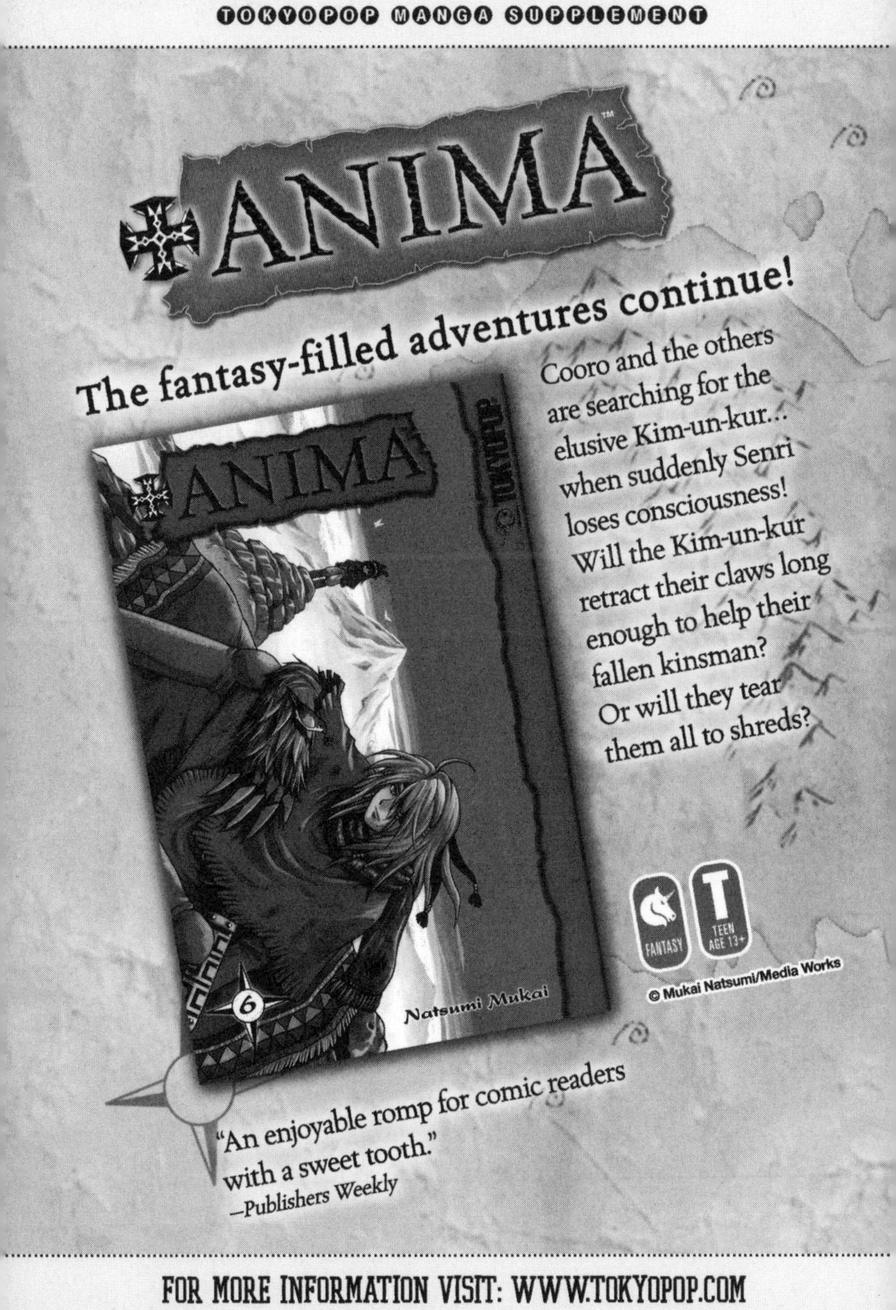
ANIMA
TOKYOPOP
6
Natsumi Mukai

Cooro and the others are searching for the elusive Kim-un-kur... when suddenly Senri loses consciousness! Will the Kim-un-kur retract their claws long enough to help their fallen kinsman? Or will they tear them all to shreds?

FANTASY

T TEEN AGE 13+

"An enjoyable romp for comic readers with a sweet tooth."
—Publishers Weekly

VOLUME 2: SILENT NOISE

TRINITY BLOOD ™
RAGE AGAINST THE MOONS

THE TRINITY BLOOD FRANCHISE RAGES ON!

Nothing is quite as it seems...

A mysterious weapon called Silent Noise destroys
Barcelona and threatens Rome... Abel Nightroad
battles personal demons... And the Duchess of Milan is in
more danger than she knows... The next volume of the
thrilling Pop Fiction series rages with sound and fury!

"INSTANTLY GRIPPING."
—*NEWTYPE USA*

POP
FICTION

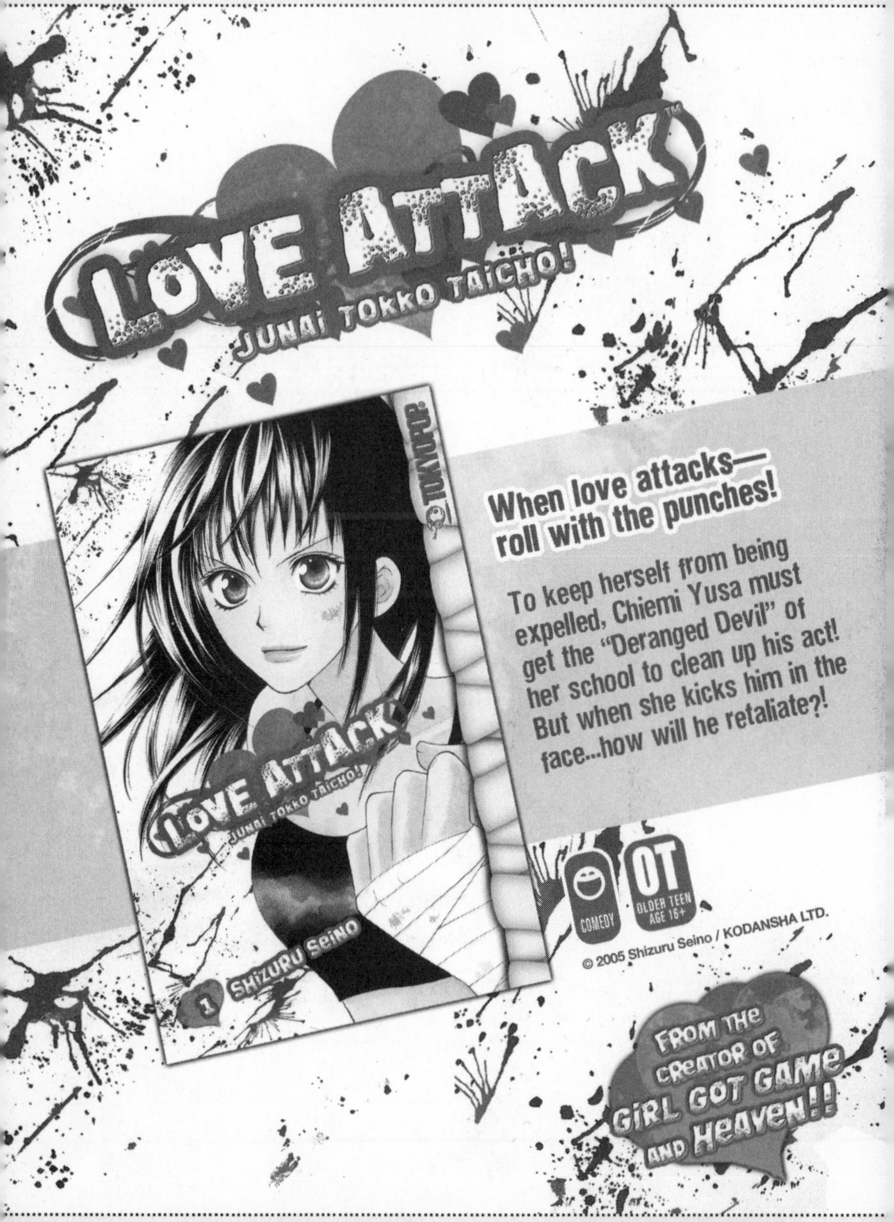
LOVE ATTACK™
JUNAI TOKKO TAICHO!
TOKYOPOP
LOVE ATTACK
JUNAI TOKKO TAICHO!
1 SHIZURU SEINO
When love attacks—
roll with the punches!
To keep herself from being expelled, Chiemi Yusa must get the "Deranged Devil" of her school to clean up his act! But when she kicks him in the face...how will he retaliate?!
COMEDY
OT OLDER TEEN AGE 16+
© 2005 Shizuru Seino / KODANSHA LTD.
FROM THE CREATOR OF GIRL GOT GAME AND HEAVEN!!

DEMON FLOWERS, BAKU AND THE DEMON ORORON: ULTIMATE EDITION
BY MIZUKI HAKASE

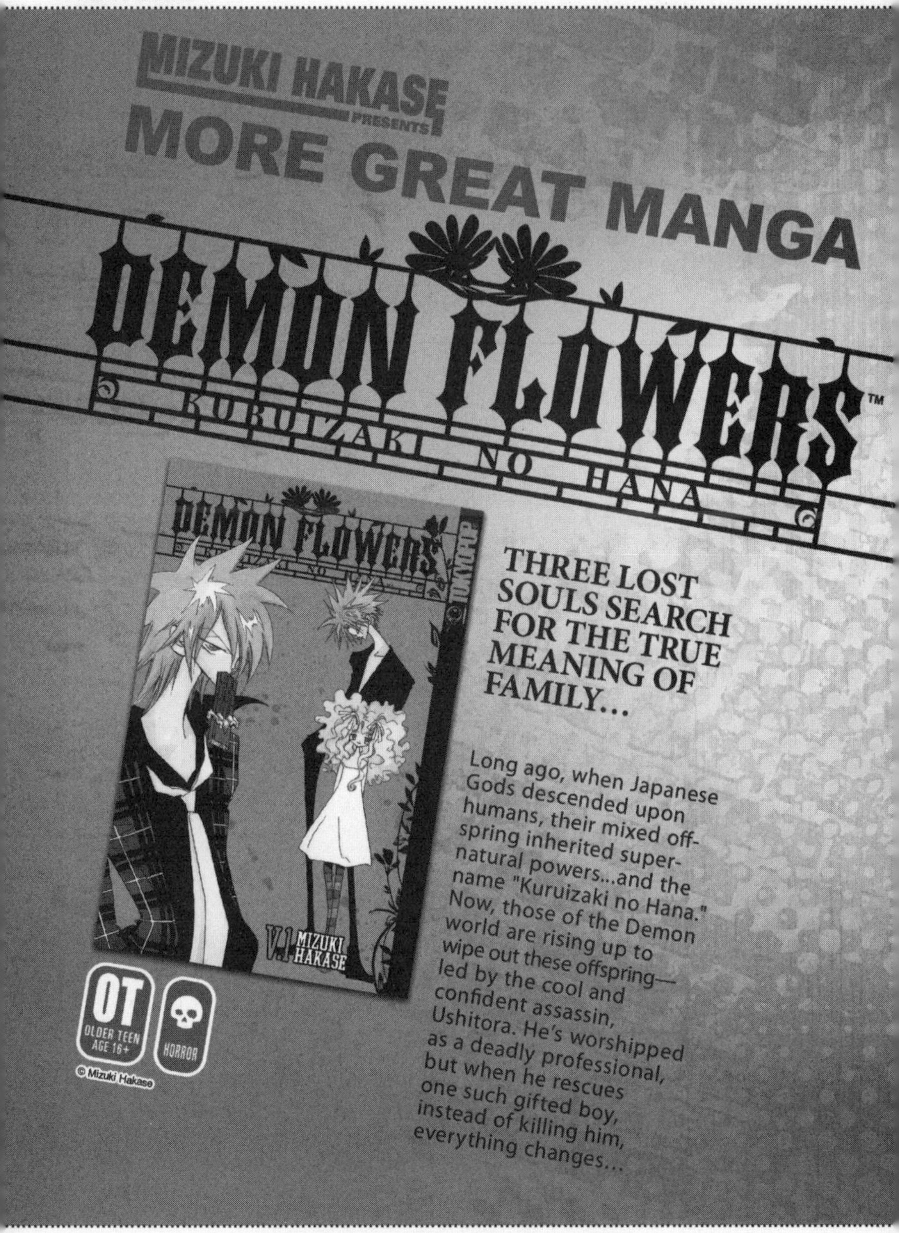
MIZUKI HAKASE
PRESENTS
MORE GREAT MANGA
DEMON FLOWERS™
KURUIZAKI NO HANA
DEMON FLOWERS
TOKYOPOP
V.1 MIZUKI HAKASE
THREE LOST SOULS SEARCH FOR THE TRUE MEANING OF FAMILY...
Long ago, when Japanese Gods descended upon humans, their mixed off-spring inherited super-natural powers...and the name "Kuruizaki no Hana." Now, those of the Demon world are rising up to wipe out these offspring—led by the cool and confident assassin, Ushitora. He's worshipped as a deadly professional, but when he rescues one such gifted boy, instead of killing him, everything changes...
OT
OLDER TEEN AGE 16+
HORROR
© Mizuki Hakase

FOR MORE INFORMATION VISIT:

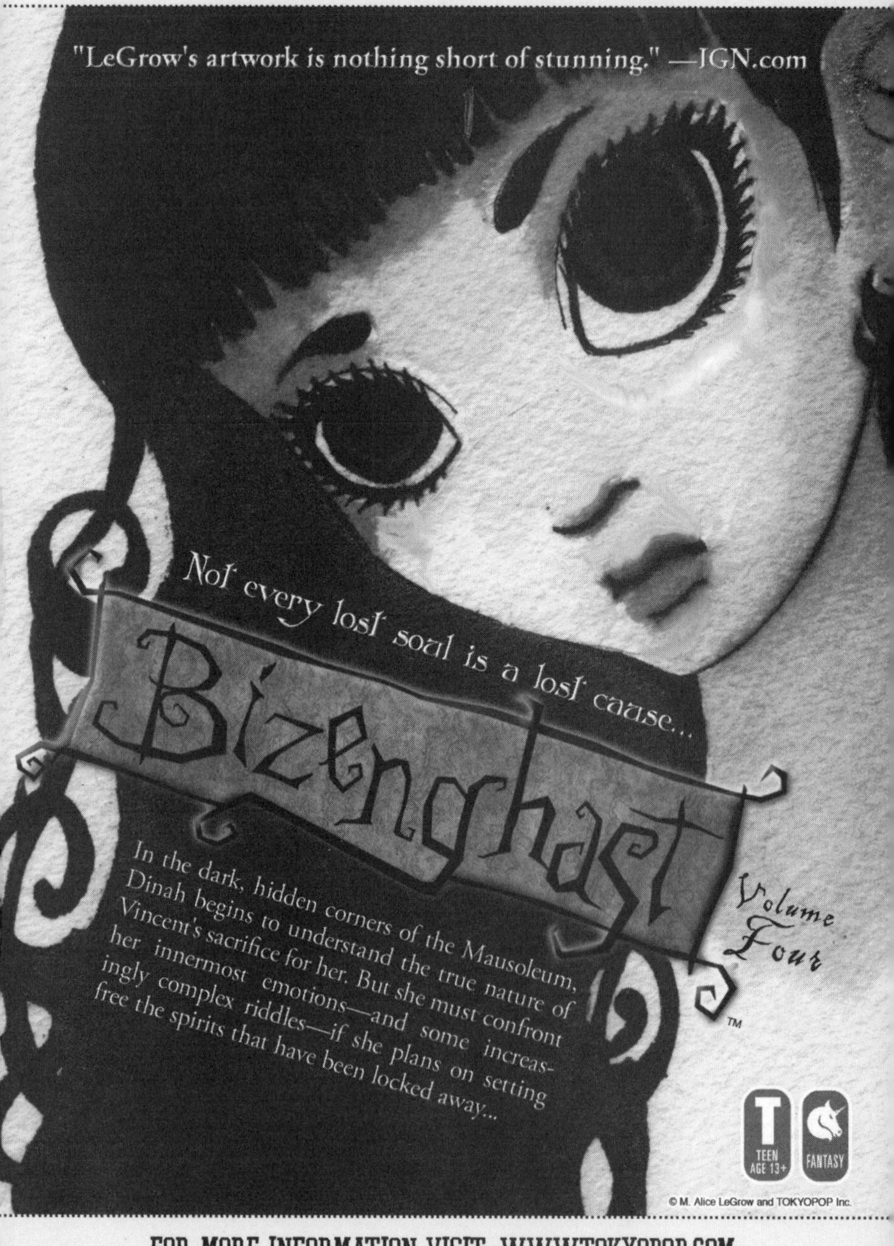
"LeGrow's artwork is nothing short of stunning." —IGN.com
Not every lost soul is a lost cause...
Bizenghast
Volume Four
TM
In the dark, hidden corners of the Mausoleum, Dinah begins to understand the true nature of Vincent's sacrifice for her. But she must confront her innermost emotions—and some increasingly complex riddles—if she plans on setting free the spirits that have been locked away...
T TEEN AGE 13+
FANTASY
© M. Alice LeGrow and TOKYOPOP Inc.

STOP!

This is the back of the book.
You wouldn't want to spoil a great ending!

This book is printed "manga-style," in the authentic Japanese right-to-left format. Since none of the artwork has been flipped or altered, readers get to experience the story just as the creator intended. You've been asking for it, so TOKYOPOP® delivered: authentic, hot-off-the-press, and far more fun!

DIRECTIONS

If this is your first time reading manga-style, here's a quick guide to help you understand how it works.

It's easy... just start in the top right panel and follow the numbers. Have fun, and look for more 100% authentic manga from TOKYOPOP®!